CITY ON FIRE

HONG KONG CINEMA

LISA ODHAM STOKES
AND **MICHAEL HOOVER**

VERSO
London • New York

For Tyler, whose interest in Chinese history, culture and people began this endeavor,
and for those who have made and are making Hong Kong movies

First published by Verso 1999

© Lisa Odham Stokes and Michael Hoover 1999

All rights reserved

The moral rights of the authors have been asserted.

Verso

UK: 6 Meard Street, London W1V 3HR

USA: 180 Varick Street, New York, NY 10014–4606

Verso is the imprint of New Left Books

ISBN 1–85984–716–1

ISBN 1–85984–203–8 (pbk)

British Library Cataloguing in Publication Data

A catalogue record for this book is available from the British Library

Library of Congress Cataloging-in-Publication Data

A catalog record for this book is available from the Library of Congress

Designed and typeset by Lucy Morton & Robin Gable, Grosmont

Printed and bound in Great Britain by Bath Press Ltd, Avon

CONTENTS

ACKNOWLEDGMENTS

Writing this book was a collaborative effort, much like the making of a movie. There are many people we would like to thank. Our dependence on scholarship, expertise provided by people in the industry, and the movies themselves means we need to recognize people who provided us with useful information and insights as well as those who helped us secure scarce Hong Kong publications, assisted us with contacts, and supplied us with hard-to-find movies. Through our work we have made distant new friends and discovered the warmth of the Hong Kong film community, both those who are a part of it and those who study it.

Our deepest gratitude goes to Terence Chang, whose knowledge and generosity is bountiful. His efforts on our behalf opened doors, and without him this book could not have been written. His encouragement means much to us. His assistant, Lori Tilkin, kindly and efficiently made things happen. André Morgan, of Ruddy Morgan Organization, also provided us with a wealth of information based on his work in Hong Kong and in the USA, and he considerately put us in touch with others now working here. Roberta Chin of Golden Harvest (USA) gave generous support with material, movies and contacts. We are grateful to them all.

We want especially to thank the moviemakers who responded to our queries and helped us think about many facets of Hong Kong movies and moviemaking. We love their movies, the contemporary stories told to make sense of the world that are there for all to share. We grew up watching movies and their films have brought back the thrill we experienced as children. So we appreciate their contributions and we thank them for giving of their time and first-hand experience of the industry. They helped make this study possible. They include: Jordan Chan, Peter Chan, Roy Cheung, Cheung Yuen-ting, Jasmine Chow, Chow Yun-fat, Chris Doyle, Ann Hui, Karen Huie, Amy Kwok, Lau Ching-wan, Alex Law, John Kit Lee, Tony Leung Ka-fai, Karen Morris, Nansun Shi, Misha Skoric, Johnnie To, Stanley Tong, Tsui Hark, Anthony Wong, Ruby Wong, John Woo, Simon Yam, Donnie Yen, Michelle Yeoh, Yim Ho, and Ronny Yu. Unless otherwise noted, all quotations from the above-mentioned are from personal correspondence and interviews. We would like in particular to acknowledge directors Peter Chan, Stanley Tong, and Ronny Yu for their patience with our extensive questions and long phone conversations, and Donnie Yen for his assiduous responses to our e-mail enquiries. We are also very grateful to Christina Lee, Head of Creative Development at Milkyway Image, who went a long way out of her way to help.

Of course, many people helped behind the scenes. Thanks are due to Mellissa Tong (for Stanley Tong), Diane Wai (for Peter Chan), Laurence Walsh (for John Woo), Janet Ma (for Tsui Hark), Thomas Leong, Yin-leung Yee and Tom Chan (for Leung Ka-fai), Kathy Jones (for Chris Doyle), Joyce Lee (for Jordan Chan), Florence Chan (for Leslie Cheung), Lolisa Chan (for Ringo Lam) and Maggie Ku (for Jackie Chan). And special thanks to Quentin Lee, director of *Shopping for Fangs*, who was helping out Peter Chan, to Doris Luey for aiding Anthony Wong, and to Christine Yen, Jean Lukitsh, and Bey Logan, for assisting Donnie Yen. We owe a debt of gratitude to Norman Wang of Wang & Gluck, New York, and Kathy Fung of the Hong Kong Directors' Guild, who assisted us with locating people in the industry. And proud parents Eleanor Morris and Klysler Yen kindly assisted us in contacting Karen Mok and Donnie Yen. We thank Eleanor for her warm correspondence.

We would like to thank the members of the Asian Cinema Studies Society who attended the 1997 biennial conference in Peterborough, Ontario and encouraged us to pursue this endeavor. We would also like to thank the friends and colleagues whose ideas and criticisms strengthened the writing of this book. John Lent, Andrew Ross, Betsy Sherman, and Tony Williams all looked at the work in its early stages. We have learned from John Lent's work on the Asian film industry and we are pleased he agreed to write the Foreword to the book. Thanks to Andrew for his moral and intellectual support, to Betsy for our interesting discussions and contacts, and to Tony for his work on John Woo's movies. We would like to thank John Hanhardt, Senior Director of Film and New Media at the Guggenheim Soho, for his thoughtful reading of the manuscript. Also, we want to acknowledge Tom Cheng, Mark Dery, Yoshie Furuhashi, Karen Huie, Karen Longtin, Bob Moore, Etsuko Nakano, Mee Kam Ng, Suzie Sau-fong Young, and John Snyder, all of whom read stages of the work.

Many other people were helpful in providing us with needed information, including David Chute, Clyde Gentry, Ken Hall, Juanita Huan Zhou, May Ng, Mee Kam Ng, Gere La Due and Bill Thompson. We want to thank journalists Betsy Sherman and Beth Accomando, who both generously opened their files to us. Special thanks are due to Roger Garcia, who provided materials for us, and to Ryan Law, whom we met through the Internet. Credit goes to Ryan for creating the Hong Kong Movie DataBase at http://www.hkmdb.com and we encourage his ongoing pursuit. and to Jerry Chan (Wolverine) at the Special Administrative Region (Hong Kong) Film Top Ten Box Office Homepage at http://www.geocities.com/Tokyo/Towers/2038. Also, the Hong Kong Cinema site at http://egret0.stanford.edu/hk/ was an invaluable tool when we first began watching Hong Kong movies. And we want to thank cameraman Tony Chiu for sharing his expertise.

We would like to acknowledge the work of our friends and former students Jo Jo Jo Ka-yi Wong and Shuang chi Wang, who worked as our translators for correspondence and also watched movies with us and answered questions. We offer them our hands. We are indebted and doubly grateful to the indefatigable Louise Tyler Odham, who proofread our manuscript and learned about Hong Kong movies. And we want to thank Colin Robinson, editor of Verso Books, for taking a chance and giving us this opportunity, and Robin Gable and Lucy Morton for their editorial production work.

Images from Hong Kong movies are difficult to acquire, and many people helped, including Jessica Rosner at Kino International; Winnie Lau, Gordon Cheung, and Ramy Choi at Golden Harvest; Chiu-yi Leung at Mandarin Films; Fran Hawkins at New Line Cinema; Terry Savage and Jessica Closson at Paramount. Bey Logan at Media Asia; Linda Lew at Tai Seng Video; editor Jeff Truesdell at the *Orlando Weekly*; Felix Lu, and private collectors Kazumi Fukumoto, Garo Nigoghossian, and Colin Geddes. We thank them. We acknowledge also Film Workshop/Toho Film HK Ltd and Circle Films for the use of images, and thank Peter Chan, Donnie Yen and Stanley Tong for allowing us to use their personal photographs.

Others facilitated our movie-watching, and we would like to thank Ange Huang at Asian Media Access in Minneapolis (amamedia@usa.net), Tom Cheng and Nancy Mak at Blue Laser (www.bluelaser.com), Linda Lew at Tai Seng (www.taiseng.com), and Debbie Quach at Florida Oriental in Orlando. Also, the librarians at our institution, Seminole Community College, assisted us in our research efforts, and we want to thank Norma Boehm, Vickie Arthur, Pat Tanzi, and most especially Kellie Gardino. And Wayne Ambrose and Peggy Pinder in our mailroom ensured a free flow of correspondence. We thank Mike Simpson for his electronic media expertise, Bill Edmister for his timely technical assistance, and Sheldon Gordon for printing services.

We have remained aware throughout this work that we write as Hong Kong outsiders. Under these circumstances we have tried to reflect as much of a Hong Kong perspective as possible based on enquiries and research. Since this book is primarily directed towards an English-speaking audience, we have for convenience used English names and titles when appropriate. Most currency figures are in US dollars. While introducing readers to the history of Hong Kong and its film industry, we focus on the period from 1984 to the present. Recent historical events, from the Sino–British Joint Declaration in 1984 to Tiananmen Square in 1989 and the subsequent handover/return of the colony in 1997, compounded Hong Kong's accelerated rate of economic growth; hence a 'city on fire' becomes its cinematic representations. We contextualize the movies and the industry in light of these occurrences and the increasing reach of global capital and cultural commodification. We also offer close readings of movies not widely screened outside Asia and North American Chinatowns but increasingly available on home formats. Our choices were based upon subject, genre, interests, and availability. We believe, considering the length of this study, that we have achieved a representative sampling of contemporary Hong Kong film output.

We hope this book can be used by both readers familiar with Hong Kong movies and those new to the experience. The authors take responsibility for the content and analyses of this book. Any errors are to be laid at our doorsteps, not those of the people who assisted us.

Lisa Odham Stokes and Michael Hoover
Orlando, April 1999

FOREWORD

Among the cultural winds that have come roaring out of Asia in the 1990s, few have been as explosive or cut as wide a swath as Hong Kong cinema. Whether with the swordfighting *wuxia*, kung fu, or heroic bloodshed genres that they created, Hong Kong filmmakers helped set the style for a cinema that fits the globalization age – full of action with high body counts and minimum dialogue, thus universally translatable.

The box-office potential for Hong Kong films was not lost on Hollywood, which joined Hong Kong studios in co-productions in the 1970s and 1980s, and absorbed its directors and stars in the mid to late 1990s. Except for Japanese *anime* and *manga*, no other Asian popular culture form has generated as large a fandom among non-diasporic audiences as Hong Kong cinema, popular in at least Japan, Korea, Macau, Malaysia, Philippines, Singapore, and Thailand in Asia, as well as in Australia, Canada, England, and the United States. Fan clubs (some specifically devoted to Jackie Chan) on four continents, fanzines such as *Cineraider*, *Fatal Visions*, *Hong Kong Film Connection*, *Asian Trash Cinema*, and *The Oriental Cinema*, Internet newsgroups and websites, retail and mail-order outlets, and a number of new books have sprouted in the 1990s to serve this growing market.

But Hong Kong has not just spawned action thrillers of the John Woo type, for, as Lisa Stokes and Michael Hoover point out in this book, other types of films have established the former crown colony's cinema internationally – 'Tsui Hark's wire-worked fantasies, Ann Hui's exile dramas, Stanley Kwan's limpid romances, and Wong Kar-wai's art films'; 'everything from 'gangster films and martial arts costumers to lightweight comedies and meditative dramas.'

These and other directors and genres have been written about in other works on Hong Kong cinema, such as Stephen Teo's *Hong Kong Cinema: The Extra Dimensions* and my own *The Asian Film Industry*, but the distinguishing marks of the Stokes and Hoover book are the socio-historical context in which the films are placed and the critical political economy approach of the analysis. Reading the first chapter, which maps the territory, one already expects that films will be perceived as commodities and actors and actresses as merchandise. From the beginning, Hong Kong was a place of commerce (for the opium trade), and today the state is the world's freest market economy and most service-oriented economy, with Asia's highest per capita income in terms of domestic buying power and the world's highest yield of billionaires and millionaires per capita.

Part of this wealth found its way into movie production, with Shaw Brothers and Cathay heavily involved in financing filmmaking at the end of World War II and Golden Harvest and others later. After the 1980s, the Hong Kong movie world, mirroring early and late capitalist cultural conditions, to use Stokes and Hoover's phrase, ranked first worldwide in per capita production, second to the United States in exports, and third in the world in actual films produced. To get to this elevated stage, however, film producers faced many political and other obstacles: balancing between what the Kuomintang Party in Taiwan wanted against left-wing films or gingerly coping with and embracing the territory's organized crime, the Triad.

Stokes and Hoover capture these industry trends and problems; at the same time they treat film as an art form, providing interesting snippets of plots, describing film characters, and explaining production techniques and directorial motives. They textually analyze all kinds of films, from Woo's martial arts with weapons, to Ringo Lam's self-named docudramas, Ann Hui's new-wave works, and the Triad Boyz-type gangster films of the mid-1990s.

The result is that *City on Fire: Hong Kong Cinema* beomes the new major source on Hong Kong film – thoroughly researched and documented, critically inter-preted, and interestingly written.

John A. Lent

'When you make a movie you can't really expect anything from the audience. People like it for different reasons, they see it at different levels.... I don't get frustrated when people interpret my movies because, when you've made a movie, your movie is not your movie anymore — it's theirs. They have their interpretation and you can't change it. You can't tell them "but that's not what I meant." You're not standing in front of the theater trying to explain it.... I get a lot of bonus things from reactions from people to my movies that I never even dreamed of, that I never even intended to put there. And those become things that actually educate me for my next movie.'

director Peter Chan

'the actor's relation to the public is that of an artist, but in relation to his employer he is a productive laborer.'

Karl Marx, *Theories of Surplus Value*

ONE

MAPPING THE TERRITORY

Emerging as a newly industrialized city-state, Hong Kong, a former Asian tiger, has become a leading finance-capital center of the world and functions as a commercial center for Southeast Asia and southern China. A postmodern city with an international airport, skyscrapers, traffic jams, and cellular phones, Hong Kong has been at the forefront of neo-liberal free-trade policies. The former British colony, now Special Administrative Region (SAR) of China, has the world's freest market economy, the world's most service-oriented economy, and Asia's highest per capita income in terms of domestic buying power. Hong Kong has the world's second most competitive economy and the world's seventh largest trading economy. It is the world's second largest per capita holding of foreign currency, the world's fourth largest source of direct foreign investment, and the world's ninth leading exporter of services.[1] Today successful businesspeople thrive in what has become one of the world's capitalist showcases. A mapping of Hong Kong reveals high-walled private homes, neon signs advertising designer goods from every continent, and blocks of luxury hotels and indoor malls. Another dimension of this landscape, however, is its sweatshops, storefronts, urban pollution, and shantytowns of unrelieved squalor, with too many people for too little land. Poor laborers, sole proprietors, and street people inhabit this terrain.

Hong Kong, with an approximate population of 6.5 million people, encompasses but 414 square miles on one principal island (Hong Kong), a peninsula (Kowloon) and former hinterlands (the New Territories) that extend to the

Shenzhen river, the territory's border with China.[2] Numerous islands, with the exceptions of Lamma and Lantau, remain mostly uninhabited. Hong Kong Island proper, heart of commerce and finance and home to almost 1.3 million residents, is only about thirty square miles. Kowloon, today a shopping hub, houses 2.1 million on just 16.5 square miles. Over 2.25 million inhabitants now reside in the 355 square mile New Territories, most of which were still farm and swamp land into the 1970s. The fact of limited land is exacerbated by that of restricted utility because much of the area is hilly and mountainous.

As might be expected, differences exist between colonizer and colonized opinion as to the state of Hong Kong before the 1841 British occupation, an armed intervention brought on by English traders' illegal opium importation into China. While the British claim that the territory was a fishing village and a shelter for pirates operating in the South China Sea, the Chinese maintain that it functioned as a trading port and was well developed in population density and local government control.[3] China ceded Hong Kong Island's commercial and territorial rights to Britain in 1842. The Treaty of Nanking brought an end to the first Opium War and satisfied British merchants on the China coast who sought both a trading station and unfettered access to the Mainland. Hong Kong, as it appears on a map today, took shape when Britain wrested Kowloon from China through the 1860 Treaty of Peking, following the military capture of that city during the Second Opium War, and then acquired the New Territories from the Mainland under terms of a 99-year lease in 1898. The latter region offered the colony tillable lands, but not before the Chinese population residing there was subjugated by force of arms.

From its beginnings, Hong Kong was a place of commerce. The British, in distributing land to private interests on the basis of their ability to pay and declaring the port free, initiated economic relations that dominate to this day. Speculation, fueled by the inherent scarcity of land, ran rampant. Expatriate merchants and colonial governors quarreled for years over the housing of the military on valuable 'downtown' property as well as over the local tax burden necessary to maintain an army garrison and a naval dockyard. The traders' early success in keeping tax levies to a minimum allowed lawlessness to abound as gamblers, gangs, pimps, and racketeers overwhelmed a small and incompetent police force.

Opium trading was important to Hong Kong's economy for decades after British annexation, accounting for as much as 45 per cent of the total value of China's imports in some years.[4] By the early twentieth century, amidst fluctuating periods of boom and bust, economic development took the form of an entrepôt port and made Hong Kong a warehousing hub for goods shipped to Southern China, Southeast Asia, and the West. Expanding shipping produced local industries: boat building and repair, dry docking, rope-making, and ship chandlering, among them. Business-sector service firms in banking and insurance emerged shortly thereafter. However, infrastructural development and provision of public services were hindered by limited tax revenues. Drainage and sewage disposal, hospital infectious disease wards, and a potable water supply all went lacking due to in-attention and insufficient funding.[5] Social class polarization was evidenced by the contrast between the more than five hundred people per acre living in the central district of Victoria at the turn of the century and a wealthy residential district (off-limits to affluent Chinese until the mid-twentieth century) that arose on Victoria Peak following the opening of a tramway in 1888 that provided quick transit to and from places of business.

Early-twentieth-century Hong Kong experienced nascent modernization: trams, automobiles, and electrification were introduced in the years prior to World War I. Handicraft industries making carvings, cabinets, furniture, jewelry, and tailored clothing emerged during the same period. While manufacturing was still insignificant in the territory, textiles expanded in the 1920s and 1930s. Non-profit-making public services, however, did not keep pace. Education developed haphazardly; public subsidies were minimal as the colony remained virtually tax-free. Some Chinese children attended crude primary schools for a few years before being tossed into the colony's competitive, low-skilled, low-wage labor market. The University of Hong Kong granted its first degrees in 1916, but there were only about five hundred regular students enrolled more than two decades later.[6] On the eve of World War II, outbreaks of beri-beri, cholera, and dysentery spoke volumes about the financially strapped colonial government's inability and un-willingess to address basic public health issues.

Governability was a problem from the moment that the British government officially declared Hong Kong to be a colony in 1843. The formal political state consisted of a British-appointed governor with broad-based policymaking authority, a detachment of the British Foreign Office charged with administrative responsibilities, and hand-picked executive and legislative councils with limited advisory powers. Parliament in London frowned upon proposals to grant Hong Kong some measure of home rule, while the acumen of colonial governors varied and their turnover was frequent. Thus did the civil service come actually to govern Hong Kong. As a free port, there were no customs duties to collect. An initial property tax caused such a firestorm among the expatriate merchant class that the governor was forced to reduce it to an insignifcant level. Government revenue was generated through the one-time sale of certain trading rights, including ostensibly illegal opium, through the leasing of public lands, and from license fees that shopkeepers paid to engage in business.

In 1869, almost three decades after colonization, the British foreign minister at Peking noted that Hong Kong was 'little more than an immense smuggling depot.'[7] Much like any frontier outpost, piracy and general lawlessness were met by impromptu governance and inadequate policing. The expatriate merchant class was unswerving in its opposition to every governor's attempt to levy taxes aimed at regularizing refuse collection, building hospital baths and infectious disease facilities, or alleviating overcrowded and filthy prison conditions. Meanwhile, poorly remunerated British civil servants found ways to augment their incomes in a society devoted to personal aggrandizement through networks of graft.

Exacerbating such potentially explosive circumstances was social segregation based on the tiny European population's sense of itself as racially and culturally superior. The British government's complicity in promoting the export of opium to the Mainland provoked anger in many of the twelve thousand or so Chinese living in Hong Kong at the time it was colonized. That anger became enmity when this largely laborer and proprietor population was required to register with the colonial government a few years later. The expatriate British ruling class, comprising the heads of government departments, directors of large business concerns, and military commanders, met the Chinese working class only as oppressors.[8] Chinese residents were subjected to unequal tax rates; they were tried in alien courts of law when charged with crimes; and, when convicted, they were sentenced under a separate penal code allowing for both branding and flogging.

A Chinese elite emerged in nineteenth-century Hong Kong despite the discriminatory and unjust conditions of life. Among the thousands of people who fled the Mainland during the Taiping Rebellion of the 1850s were individuals with the requisite knowledge and skills, regional connections, and financial means to do business. Economic growth offered opportunities for some to establish themselves as successful merchants and for others to serve as compradors for Western 'hongs' (firms) operating in the colony. By the 1880s, all but one of Hong Kong's eighteen largest property owners, according to government assessments, were Chinese.[9] A Chinese member was appointed to the Legislative Council in the decade as well; no Chinese would be seated on the Executive Council until the 1920s. Life for the Chinese majority living on below subsistence wages, however, often consisted of ramshackle housing and inadequate food. The mortality rate for Chinese infants was almost six times that of the children of Europeans. Charitable hospitals and schools, most of them endowed by a few wealthy Chinese residents, did little to ameliorate conditions wrought by colonial capitalism.

The fact of the matter was that Hong Kong capital, whether European or Chinese (the latter was increasingly visible by the early 1900s), needed cheap Chinese labor. Colonial overseers faced the persistent dilemma of governing the colony 'on the cheap' in the interests of competing merchants, generally united only in their desire for limited government, and guaranteeing that protests by the majority population of exploited wage laborers would be managed and contained. British and Chinese elites began to work towards a *rapprochement* on the basis of their class interests and their mutual dependence upon the colonial government. While workers established trade unions, their potential was undermined by a continual flow of surplus labor arriving from the Mainland. Despite the importance of Chinese capital, labor strikes and work stoppages often assumed a nationalist rather than a class character by taking aim at the British presence.[10] Neither a seamen's strike in 1922 nor a general strike and boycott of British goods in 1925–26 lifted wage rates in Hong Kong's perpetually overcrowded labor market.[11] In the years preceding Japan's 1941 invasion, the highest paid manual workers earned 80 cents a day.

Hong Kong has always been a place to which Mainland Chinese migrated. The colony was regarded primarily as a place of refuge before 1949, with people crossing the border when circumstances were bad in China, always expecting to return when they improved. While settlement of the colony was gradual, fortune-seeking, commercial progress, and increasing socio-political unrest on the Mainland produced a growing population: from 32,983 (31,463 Chinese) persons in 1851 to 878,947 (859,425 Chinese) in 1931.[12] The numbers swelled particularly after the Chinese Republic was established in 1912, and did so again (by about 750,000) during the Sino–Japan War in the late 1930s when Hong Kong's population increased to 1.6 million. The estimated one million residents who fled the Japanese occupation of the territory during World War II began to return in late 1945 at the rate of almost 100,000 per month. The impending success of the communist-led Chinese Revolution initiated a mass exodus (approximately 750,000) in 1948 from the Mainland to Hong Kong that continued unabated until the border was closed in 1951 to prohibit further undocumented travel. Later, an estimated 100,000 persons crossed the border in the midst of a 1962 famine associated with Mao Tse-tung's 'Great Leap Forward' policies and almost 500,000 legal and illegal immigrants streamed into Hong Kong between 1976 and 1981, the years immediately following Chairman Mao's death and the fall from power of the Gang of Four.

An adequate understanding of present-day Hong Kong's 'economic miracle' begins with the Chinese – mainly from Guandong province, Shanghai and other commercial centers – who began leaving the Mainland in 1948 with the Nationalist government facing defeat at the hands of the communists.[13] The colony was then still reeling from the economic collapse and outmigration of an estimated one million persons during the Japanese occupation of World War II. The economy experienced further disruption when first the United States, and then the United Nations, imposed trade sanctions against China, the territory's most important trading partner. Forced to develop internal industries, Hong Kong took advantage of a cheap labor pool, local and regional capital input, and government tax policies favorable to entrepreneurs. Constant influx of both people and capital from the Mainland led to the establishment of light manufacturing throughout the territory in the 1950s.

Britain's return to Hong Kong meant no serious institutional changes in pre-war colonial governance as the bureaucracy reclaimed control over an essentially administrative state. Denial of basic rights for the Chinese population assured continuance of the political status quo. Chinese residents recognized the worthlessness of a restricted franchise granted for elections to an advisory Urban Council in 1952. The government, meanwhile, saw a low turnout among the ten thousand or so eligible voters as an indication of political apathy. Some measure of substantive reform – including an expanded right to vote, a lower voting age, more directly elected members of the Legislative Council, and a diminution in the Executive Council's function – would have to wait forty years, until the eve of Britain's handover of the colony to the People's Republic of China (PRC).

The colonial government's economic role, however, changed dramatically in mid-century. Virtually tax-free, but faced with immediate shortages in basic needs (food, fuel, housing), reconstruction and revitalization tasks, and future growth and development concerns, Hong Kong began to assess both business profits and salaries and wages earned within the colony at an effective rate of 15 per cent. The government adopted more interventionist policies, ranging from emergency rationing of rice and temporary trade controls following British reoccupation to subsequent public housing projects, land reclamation, and education and health services in the decades that followed. Moreover, from the colony's inception, all land was owned by the Crown and leased to private interests through auction or tender. Thus those such as Milton Friedman who have routinely sung paeans to Hong Kong laissez faire ignore the political state's contribution to the area's succeess.

Hong Kong's tax policies began to attract foreign investment in the 1960s, fostering export-led economic growth. Textiles, electronics, toys, and many other low-priced goods stamped 'Made in Hong Kong' flowed from the territory in ever-increasing quantities. Today, Hong Kong is the world's largest exporter of clocks, toys, calculators, radios, electric hair and hand dryers, imitation jewelry, travel goods and handbags, umbrellas and sunshades, and artificial flowers. The territory is the world's second largest exporter of clothing, furs, watches, telephones, electric kitchen appliances, and shoes. And Hong Kong is the third largest exporter of textiles and fourth largest exporter of precious jewelry.[14]

The colony experienced social turmoil in 1967 when the Cultural Revolution created a flood of refugees that was to continue unabated into the early 1970s. Eyewitness accounts of vandalism and youthful malignity on the Mainland served further to alienate overseas Chinese from the People's Republic. However, local labor demonstrations and student confrontations with the Royal Hong Kong Police raised the specter of class struggle. As always in the colony, national and racial issues were prominent, due to the British expatriates' 'sahib' mentality. Disturbances went on for seven months, resulting in scores of deaths, material destruction, and random violence, while discrediting Maoism among the population. The Mainland government made no move to intervene despite the violent riots in the colony and the presence of Red Guards just across the border. While offering Hong Kong Communists verbal support, Beijing apparently did not wish to have the territory's trade disrupted for long.

By the mid-1970s, Hong Kong's economy was moving towards service-sector activities. Networks of wholesalers and retailers developed to cater to the consumption patterns of a growing middle class. Department stores, shopping malls, and fast-food restaurants underline the change from a production-oriented economy. Entrepôt (warehouse) trade, which all but ended in mid-century due to the UN trade embargo against China during the Korean War, re-emerged in the 1970s (facilitated by the PRC's neo-'Open Door' policy), paving the way for diversification into finance, insurance, and real estate (FIRE) markets. Hong Kong has Asia's highest concentration of fund managers and largest number of insurance companies. It is Asia's second largest venture capital center and second largest loan syndication center. Hong Kong has the world's fourth largest gold bullion market, fifth largest foreign exchange market, and seventh largest stock market. It is the world's fifth largest banking center for external financial transactions and seventh largest center for financial derivatives.[15]

Today, the banking industry has become Hong Kong's most important enterprise, with manufacturing more likely to occur across the border. Nevertheless, export–import activities remain vital to Hong Kong's wellbeing because the territory has few natural resources and is dependent upon international trade for virtually all its needs. The former colony is entirely dependent on imports for all its energy needs, purchasing electricity and coal from China and oil from several Southeast Asian countries. Staple food imports from the Mainland include 71 per cent of Hong Kong's vegetables, 78 per cent of its poultry, and 92 per cent of its pigs. Furthermore, 70 per cent of Hong Kong's water supply is imported from Guandong province in southern China.[16]

Hong Kong's struggle to provide itself with clean and plentiful water, dating almost from its origins as a British colony, is illuminating. Only artists' renderings remain of a waterfall at what is now home to thousands of boat people, the port of Aberdeen on Hong Kong Island. Early population growth led the colonial government to construct the first of many reservoirs, which is still in use. Hong Kong's governors were lamenting an inadequate water supply half a century after colonization. According to one, neither 'the proposed works, nor works many times larger, would satisfy the wants of the city.'[17] Rainfall shortages, leaving the territory with too little fresh water, contributed to the bubonic plague that wracked the colony for several years in the 1890s. The epidemic forced an otherwise reluctant government to commit public monies to construction of a new reservoir. The government built more reservoirs when the flood of Mainlanders in the aftermath of the 1911 revolution and the beginnings of industrialization in the 1920s again raised the issue of water. Hong Kong's growing dependence on the PRC for water, resulting, somewhat ironically, from the surging numbers of people who fled China following the 1949 revolution, began in the early 1960s. This arrangement reveals Hong Kong as a source of trade surplus for the Mainland and points to Hong Kong's role in financing China's modernization.

Hong Kong is a land of immigrants, 98 per cent of whom are Chinese. Having fled political instability and social unrest, much of the population is apolitical, trading activism for materialism. Minimal interference from the British state, along with Western commercial and cultural influences, have contributed to the development of a pervasive entrepreneurial spirit. And while upward mobility was historically circumscribed, a combination of hard work, luck, and education nevertheless made it possible for some non-British citizens. The generation of Hong Kongers fortunate to have grown up during economic boom times in the 1970s and 1980s numbers many who have moved up the social ladder through schooling. However, social advancement has not come for working-class people (including many newer immigrants from the Mainland), who labor long hours (ten-hour shifts, six or seven days a week) at low pay in 3-D jobs – dangerous, dirty, and dead-end. In contrast, the territory has more millionaires and billionaires per capita than anywhere else in the world. The distribution of income and wealth in Hong Kong is thus highly unequal.

Classified as a high-income economy, Hong Kong ranks thirteenth among 133 countries surveyed by the United Nations. According to 1996 government figures, the median income from main employment of the working population was US$9,500 per year and the median income of domestic households was US$17,500 per year.[18] A World Bank report from the same year indicated that the lowest 20 per cent of households received 5.4 per cent of the national income and the highest 20 per cent of households received 47 per cent of the aggregate.[19] Declining income inequality in the 1960s and 1970s, the result of higher labor force participation and a movement of workers into the manufacturing sector, was reversed in the 1980s by the influx of Chinese and Vietnamese refugees and the growth of the service sector. Meanwhile, the median annual salary for a British expatriate manager was US$185,000 in the early 1990s.[20] According to *Forbes* magazine, the colony had three of the planet's ten wealthiest people in 1997: real estate magnates Lee Shau Lee (US$14.7 thousand million) and the Kwok Brothers (US$12.3 thousand million) as well as Nina Wang, the world's second richest woman, whose net worth of US$7 thousand million came from running the Chinachem real-estate empire.[21]

Nowhere is social class polarity in Hong Kong more evident than in residential patterns. Much of the population lives on less than 5 per cent of the land in the crowded towns of Victoria and Kowloon. Despite government efforts to eradicate hovel dwellings, each wave of immigration in this century has resulted in refugees erecting squalid shantytowns on the hillsides for shelter. In the mid-1990s, over 200,000 people were cramped into squatter camps, more than 100,000 individuals were living in what the government calls 'temporary housing,' and another 80,000 'resided' on boats in the harbor. Overall, almost 450,000 Hong Kong households, comprising more than 1.2 million people, suffered from inadequate housing in 1994.[22] Hong Kong's population density, one of the world's highest, is most graphically revealed in the 150,000 thousand people per square kilometer living in the Mongkok district.

Hong Kong's government began building public housing units following a Christmas Day fire in 1953 that left 50,000 people on the streets. Yet the unprecedented numbers of people arriving in the colony between 1946 and 1951 had already created intolerable conditions. About one million persons were living in makeshift huts on the steep hillsides throughout Hong Kong. Once again, overcrowding meant filth and disease and the toll of human misery rose amidst expanding urban squalor. The fire, then, was a catalyst for action, much as previous social crises had been. By the early 1960s, the government had initiated the so-called 'new town movement,' a massive city planning project intended to link the alleviation of housing shortages to industrial development. Today, almost 50 per cent of the population lives in subsidized housing, much of it in dense, high-rise dwellings that sit alongside production sites and commercial facilities in the New Territories.

Apartment size is generally limited to one or two rooms, with running water, electricity, and private bath facilities. It is not unusual for a family of six to share a 10 ft by 12 ft space for eating, sleeping, socializing, and working. Long lists for existing as well as future units means that the wait may be years. Meanwhile the wealthy, far removed from the hurry and scurry of life in the crowded metropolis below, live in lavish homes along the road leading to Victoria Peak and in high-rise penthouses on the 'far side' of Hong Kong Island or along Clearwater Bay in the New Territories. Some of the super-rich 'even have pools, which in a land with no fresh water supply is a true extravanganza.'[23]

Life for most people in Hong Kong is organized around family structure; and for the upwardly mobile, pooled family resources may be the only source of start-up capital to open a business. The rising middle stratum exhibits characteristics of both lower and upper class. While labourers are subjected to tedious low-skilled work and the rich relentlessly pursue moneymaking, middle-stratum proprietors operate their stores seven days a week, sixteen hours a day. Child labor laws are circumvented by working and middle class alike as children help their families by doing 'cottage industry' labor or working without pay in their parents' businesses. The Hong Kong middle class expects its children to succeed in school because education offers opportunities for advancement, so competition for grades is fierce. Children often feel enormous parental pressure; an increase in school-age suicide is testimony to this condition.[24] Indicators of middle-class success include the emulation of elites, who hire domestic help to cook, garden, and chauffeur, and the sending of children to Canada, Europe, and the United States for higher education training in business management, finance, and engineering. Upon their return the young help family firms expand operations, upgrade technologies, and deal with the intricacies of international markets.

Unlike Western nations, contemporary Hong Kong has experienced features of early and late capital accumulation simultaneously, and its development has been rapid. In the early period, force separates capital from labor, exchange-value in the market from immediate social use-value, and owner from worker. The structure of the accumulation process in this era is based on proprietary organization, pre-industrial machinery, proletarianized labor, competition buffered by a pre-capitalist sector, and repressive discipline through market measures. The history of eighteenth- and nineteenth-century capitalism reveals patterns of ruthless competition that created unstable social relations; conquest, enslavement, robbery and murder, and gangsterism characterized this initial phase. As Karl Marx wrote, 'Capital comes [into the world] dripping from head to foot, from every pore, with blood and dirt.'[25] Hong Kong's early capitalist economy is akin to that described by Adam Smith. More than 98 per cent of the 280,000 registered firms doing business in 1996 were small enterprises, and the average number of employees in companies in manufacturing industries declined from twenty persons in 1980 to thirteen in 1993.[26] Large local concerns include banks, diversified conglomerates, real-estate holding and development companies, and public utilities. Yet storefronts, restaurants, and light assembly plants constitute the economic infrastructure for the majority of people. Once found everywhere, 'home factories,' where both parents and children work into the small hours assembling toys and clocks, artificial flowers and umbrellas, handbags and imitation jewelry are now less prevalent. At the bottom are street hawkers, who daily set up temporary stalls from which to sell their wares.

This environment of small firms and proprietorships remains inhospitable to union organizing. Coupled with an unfavorable legal framework, it produces few labor leaders but much political fragmentation in a labor movement that comprises less than 20 per cent of all workers.[27] Surplus labor pools, which once migrated to the colony from the Mainland, are now either selectively imported (often women from Indonesia and the Philippines) or are employed by Hong Kong manufacturing capital in the cheap labor havens of Guangdong Province in southern China.[28] There has never been a minimum wage; the government sets no official poverty line; full employment policies do not exist; and social 'safety net' policies are minimal. Their absence continues, in part, because many among the Chinese population still rely on family support rather than government assistance.

In Hong Kong, gangs known as Triads (their symbol is a triangle uniting man, earth, and heaven) established themselves and spread quickly through the Chinese community prior to mid-century. With origins in secret criminal societies founded on the Mainland in the eighteenth and nineteenth centuries, these groups soon controlled illicit activities such as drugs, gambling, and prostitution. Upon Britain's return after World War II, Triads turned their street connections into extortion and bribery of the colony's police force; both English and Chinese. Law-enforcement corruption settled into an accepted and comfortable pattern whereby officers – euphemistically called 'caterers' – organized their colleagues into syndicates that liaised with gang members for purposes of permitting criminal operations to flourish without fear of official interference.[29] In return, Triad bosses undertook to settle their own inevitable differences through gang fights, intimidation and physical assaults, and murder. Though illegal, at least fifty such organizations exist in Hong Kong today, with an estimated 100,000 members (the Sun Yee On Triad is believed to have 45,000 members alone on its home turf in Tsimshatsui). Recently, Triad activity has expanded into the black-market sale of imitation luxury goods, money laundering and computer card fraud, pirating of computer software, and smuggling of illegal immigrants.

The term 'late capitalism' refers to more recent social and economic conditions of globalization, with its accompanying commodification of almost everything. Even the production of cultural goods succumbs gradually to 'money-making as an organized business.'[30] The structure of the accumulation process is increasingly based upon finance capital, global markets, capital-intensive production, dual labor markets, and the integration of science, capital, and technology. As Robert Heilbroner notes, the label '"Made in Hong Kong" stamped on commodities that embody the most remarkable capabilities of scientific production becomes a symbol of the ability of capital to move wherever low labor costs or strategic sites for distribution offer competitive advantages.'[31] In this respect, Hong Kong's emergence as an economic player has occurred relatively late in the game. The city's highly competitive industries – land speculation, real estate construction, electronics, apparel and textile manufacture, finance, and tourism – maneuver between two worlds, a local proprietary sector and a transnational corporate one. Foreign direct investment has grown more rapidly than trade as the territory has expanded its role as a base from which more than two thousand transnational corporations (TNCs) conduct regional operations. Credit card issuers, life insurance companies, engineering and manufacturing consultancies, fast-food franchisers, and courier services are among the accumulated overseas concerns that invested US$99.7 thousand million in Hong's Kong's economy in 1995. The largest investor was Japan (25 per cent), followed by the UK (21 per cent), China (19 per cent), and the USA (12 per cent). Banks constituted the largest share of investment (47 per cent) in the non-manufacturing sector, while electronics drew the largest share (31 per cent) in the manufacturing sector.[32]

Schumpeter's 'creative destruction' is on display everywhere in Hong Kong as industrial factories give way to opulent hotels, which in turn give way to office towers in only a few years. The most massive dredging project ever undertaken anywhere (reclaiming land from the sea in Hong Kong dates from 1851) made possible the construction of a new US$20 thousand million airport, Chek Lap Kok, which is connected to the city's business district by the world's longest road and rail suspension bridge.[33] If, as Raymond Williams suggests, culture is essentially a 'way of life,' then Hong Kong's late capitalist milieu is quintessentially postmodern, as materialistic consumption runs rampant. Mobile phones and pagers are commonplace, used by business people, professionals, and teenagers alike. There are probably few places in the world that can boast of such a concentration of luxury automobiles in such small geographical confines. Hong Kongers are very style-conscious; evidence of this can be seen not only in the designer label attire that accords the wearer enhanced social status, but in the popularity of television programs on clothing and fashion.[34] Public advertising displays clothes, electronics, gourmet foods, and myriad other consumer items that residents and tourists can purchase at the many malls.

The population's apparent acceptance of its colonial status, as well as its much noted political apathy, belie the fact that the most important issues revolving around the 'Hong Kong question' have become increasingly political. The PRC, in rejecting a 'three-legged stool' relationship between China, Britain, and Hong Kong in the 1970s, held fast to the view that discussions about 1997 (the date of expiration of the New Territories lease) did not include residents of the colony. Bilateral negotiations, culminating in the 1984 Sino–British Joint Declaration, established a 'one country, two systems' arrangement under which the British would hand over the territory to the Mainland. Public opinion was mixed from the outset. One source of anger and anxiety was the fact that Hong Kong representatives were not a part of the diplomatic discussions. The estimated 50,000 people per year emigrating from the territory after 1984, many from the professional–managerial stratum, reflected an unease about the future.[35]

On the heels of the signing, six times as many political officials and representative organization leaders (business associations, mutual aid committees, trade unions, and voluntary organizations) believed that the agreement would facilitate continued economic growth as those who did not. The ratio of those believing that post-1997 Hong Kong would retain political autonomy to those who didn't was four to one. In contrast, these former individuals split down the middle on the likelihood of future representative government and on the issue of protecting civil liberties.[36] Surveys from the mid-1980s onwards registering growing political pessimism did not significantly modify a general sense of economic optimism about the future SAR. While 65 per cent of those polled in 1988 expected living standards to decline in the short term following the handover, 80 per cent believed that the socio-economic status of their children would be better than their own.[37] The 1989 Tiananmen tragedy magnified fears, encouraging 1.5 million people to participate in street demonstrations against the Beijing government's human rights violations. By July 1995, only 23 per cent and 18.5 per cent of the colony's general public expressed trust in the British and Chinese governments, respectively. And while confidence in local government fell from 76.4 per cent in 1986 to 47.8 per cent nine years later, 61 per cent remained upbeat about the future of Hong Kong's economy.[38]

While the looming 1997 handover was of greatest concern and received the most attention, other matters forced their way onto the political radar screen. The local population scapegoated thousands of Vietnamese 'boat people' who began fleeing their war-ravaged country for Hong Kong in the late 1970s. By 1982, the colonial government had established closed-camp detention centers for Vietnamese refugees, and it initiated a forcible repatriation policy soon afterwards.[39] On another front, women, who have long dominated Hong Kong's most poorly paid labor markets, complain of unsafe working conditions, inadequate childcare services, lack of employment protection, and a shortage of affordable housing. While the autonomous grassroots women's groups that emerged in the 1980s successfully pressed for sex discrimination legislation in 1995 and disabilities discrimination legislation in 1996, certain issues, ranging from increasing instances of violence against women to disenfranchised housewives, will continue to exist in the SAR. Moreover, discrimination against gays and lesbians is not illegal in Hong Kong, despite the fact that in 1991 the colony abolished a statute prohibiting homosexual acts. Although the social climate is still not liberal, gay culture made its presence known in the arts and nightlife prior to the handover, and members of the gay community now view themselves as part of a movement for human and political rights.

Politics, such as it existed in colonial Hong Kong, only rarely exhibited working-class features. But the transition to a service economy eliminated 400,000 manufacturing jobs in the 1980s and 1990s.[40] Other sectors of the working class risked being abandoned by footloose industries looking elsewhere for ever cheaper labor. As public housing construction slowed, numbers of low-income people found themselves in danger of being priced out of affordable housing by rent inflation following the elimination of rate controls for all old private buildings. One of the consequences of the 1992 'Patten Reform' (after the last British colonial governor, Chris Patten) providing for elected members to the Legislative Council was that pro-democracy, grassroots, and trade-union councillors held a majority of seats in the final session to convene under British colonial rule. Responding to widening income polarization and growing poverty among single-parent families and the working poor, the assembly increased welfare spending and passed legislation favoring labor, including the right to bargain collectively on wage and benefit issues and protection against job discrimination. So Hong Kong experienced a foretaste of working-class politics in the years leading up to the 1997 handover. Whether such developments signaled a new territorial mapping would remain to be seen.

TWO

REELING IN THE YEARS

With a history spanning eighty years, the Hong Kong film industry gained international attention in the early 1980s, coterminous with negotiations over the 1984 Sino–British Joint Declaration. Not coincidental to film output, the relative uncertainty of 1997 compounded an already accelerated rate of capital accumulation. From the gangster films and martial arts costumers, to the lightweight comedies and meditative dramas, the subtexts illustrate both variations on the means of early capitalist accumulation and a fear of losing ground gained during Hong Kong's three-decade drive into late capitalism. Along with its new status, Hong Kong has become the 'Hollywood of the East,' home to a film industry first in the world in per capita production, second only to the USA in film export, and third in the world in terms of the number of films produced per year.[1]

The origins of Hong Kong cinema, however, reveal a series of starts and stops that continued over the course of several decades. Whether the problems were limited investment capital and restrictive social conditions or perennial water shortages (limiting processing work) and labor unrest, the colony's film industry was unable to come into its own during the silent era. Shanghai, Hong Kong's Mainland competitor, emerged as the first Asian Hollywood, in part because of its reputation as an international city. The colony generally produced low-budget movies for Shanghai companies, a relationship bearing likeness to that between the United States and Canadian film industries in the 1930s, which produced so-called 'quota quickies.'[2] The core made short-term investments in the periphery and imported trained personnel to churn out films in rapid-fire fashion. Resulting output was considered of lesser quality, although knowledge of Hong Kong's early movie history remains scant because few prints, scripts, and magazines have survived.[3]

Hong Kong's first movie house opened its doors in 1910. The colony's first motion picture, *Stealing the Roasted Duck* (1909), had been produced a year earlier. Financed by United States businessman Benjamin Brodsky[4] through his Shanghai company Asia Film, the movie starred and was directed by stage veteran Liang Shaobo. Brodsky also played a role in establishing Hong Kong's first film studio, Chinese American Film, in 1913 with theater director Li Minwei. The studio's only production, *Zhuangzi Tests His Wife* (1913), was scripted by Li and featured him in the role of wife because of a ban on women actors until the 1920s. Upon completion, Brodsky returned to the USA with the only print; consequently, the film was never shown in the colony.

Li Minwei was later the driving force behind Hong Kong's first film company owned and controlled entirely by Chinese, China Sun, founded in 1923. However, the colonial government's refusal to grant Li a permit to build a set stage led him to move the company to Guangzhou, where *Rouge* (1924), considered Hong Kong's first feature film, was made. The Hong Kong general strike of 1925–26 shut down both Hong Kong's nascent movie production industry and the territory's movie theaters. Li relocated again, this time to Shanghai, where he spent several years producing fictional films and making documentaries for the Nationalist Party (Kuomingtang, KMT) of Sun Yat-sen and Chiang Kai-shek. In 1930, China Sun merged with several other companies to form United Photoplay Service (UPS). Originally headquartered in Hong Kong, UPS shifted its principal operations to Shanghai. While the company maintained a production studio for several years in the colony, its reputation was built on the strength of several Shanghai films about feudal love starring Ruan Lingyu.[5]

Hong Kong's film industry received a boost when Shao Zuiweng (eldest of the now-renowned Shaw Brothers) decided to move Tianyi Studios from Shanghai in 1934. Tianyi's success with the first Cantonese-dialect talking picture, the opera film *White Gold Dragon* (1933), coupled with the Chinese government's opposition to certain issues and topics, made the British colony attractive to Shao.[6] On the one hand, there were profits to be had in the markets of Cantonese-speakers throughout Southeast Asia and in US Chinatowns. On the other hand, the studio's staple of martial arts fantasy films were considered debaucheries, and their future production in Shanghai was threatened by government proscription. Several firms followed Tianyi's lead, most notably Grandview Film, a company headed by Chinese-Americans that made the second Cantonese talkie, *Singing Lovers* (1934), in the United States.

Hong Kong movie production increased rapidly following the introduction of sound: four hundred films were made between 1933 and 1941.[7] The majority of these movies were in Cantonese, the language of the vast majority of the colony's Chinese population. The industry exploited its new-found ability to vie with opera for audiences long in love with stage performers and performances. But soon after, the KMT government required all films produced on the Mainland to be in Mandarin dialect. The ban on Cantonese movies started a migration of filmmakers, which accelerated following the outbreak of the Sino–Japan War and subsequent Japanese military occupation of Shanghai.

The influx of Mainlanders to Hong Kong between 1937 and the end of 1941, when the colony fell to Japan, impacted on the film industry in several ways. First, émigrés spoke Mandarin and made Mandarin motion pictures. While Cantonese films continued to dominate the Hong Kong market during these years, Mandarin cinema gained an audience share that would alternately rise and fall for four decades. Second, border-crossers saw Hong Kong as a place from which to shoot anti-Japanese propaganda and patriotic national defense films. Third, the talent of the new arrivals raised the Hong Kong films to a hitherto unprecedented quality. In contrast to the escapism for which Hong Kong films were known, Shanghai film veterans fleeing to the colony brought social concerns to bear upon the movies they produced. Perhaps the most outstanding of these individuals was leftist Cai Chusheng, the first Chinese director to win an international film prize, for *Song of the Fisherman* (1934), a drama about the plight of fishing villagers eking out a meager existence in urban Shanghai.[8] Cai's Hong Kong films portrayed guerrilla resistance to oppression, encouraged vigilante justice for traitors, and criticized both the class tyranny and the vulgar materialism of capitalist society.

Hong Kong film production came to a halt with the Japanese occupation of World War II. Resuming operations amidst Britain's reoccupation of the colony following the war, the industry witnessed the development of parallel cinemas as both Cantonese- and Mandarin-dialect films proved to be successful with audiences.[9] In general, Cantonese filmmakers thrived by returning to the popular martial arts and opera genres of the 1930s. In common with the pre-war era, critics derided this fare for its lack of quality and inattention to important social issues. Meanwhile, Mandarin producers and directors offered moviegoers *wenyi* (meaning literature and art) ranging from musicals and dramas to comedies and operas. Generally more costly and with longer production schedules, the perfomative and technical value of such films was appealing even to Cantonese-speakers who could not understand the dialogue.

Post-war Cantonese-dialect movies became known as 'seven-day wonders' because they were often completed in a week and then scheduled for one-week runs in theaters.[10] Upwards of two hundred such films were released each year from the late 1940s through the mid-1960s. Opera films offer the best example from that era of Hong Kong film production on the cheap – little direction, minimal sets, and pre-recorded sound. Establishing patterns of work that continue to the present day, the few familiar stars, such as Chow Kwun-ling, or the duo of Yam Kim-fai and Pak Suet-sin, appeared in multiple features during the years their careers were at a peak. Chow, for example, appeared in seventy movies in 1952–53 alone, while Yam (whose screen career was built on her portrayal of male figures) and Pak starred together in over fifty films in the 1950s and 1960s, and appeared separately in hundreds of others.[11]

The resurgence of Mandarin cinema in Hong Kong following World War II owed itself to the stream of refugees from the Mainland that began in 1946 and continued until 1952. Initially, Shanghai filmmakers accused of collaborating with the Japanese during the war fled south. Thereafter followed sundry actors, directors, and producers wishing to escape Chiang Kai-shek's censorship policies as well as movie personnel apprehensive about China's future in light of the civil war. Most early arrivals in Hong Kong expected their exile to be temporary; in fact the colony was generally absent from late 1940s' Mandarin releases. For both financial backers and film artists, Hong Kong served as a production site for Shanghai-like films intended for Mainland audiences. A third wave of people began flowing into the colony following the establishment of the People's Republic in 1949, continuing until the border was closed several years later.

Artistic quality and dialect were not the only issues dividing Hong Kong's film industry. The Cantonese and Mandarin blocs were split ideologically as well, although the divisions were less pronounced early on.[12] Directors might make films revolving around themes of gender and class oppression for the Great China studio even as they were helming late-nineteenth-century period-piece narratives of preserving the past for the Yonghua company. Crossover of this kind became virtually impossible after 1949 as studios polarized along political lines, with both the PRC and the KMT (a government-in-exile in Taiwan) attempting to influence the Hong Kong film industry. Socialists and communists began returning to China on the heels of the communist victory; among those who did so voluntarily (some were deported by the colonial government in 1952 for strike activities) was Cai Chusheng, who assumed the reins of the PRC's film ministry. Nonetheless, left-wing companies such as Southern Film, Great Wall, Phoenix, and Longma had box-office success with 'message movies.' Their release of meaningful quality productions captured Hong Kong moviegoers' interest during a time of political flux. Didactic, though generally not to a fault, the social-realist left made films criticizing class oppression, lampooning finance capital, telling stories of class and feminist struggle, and expressing the emerging collective identity of slum dwellers. Purveyors of right-wing cinema, sometimes financed by United States capital through the Asia Film Company founded in 1953, responded to attempts to win the 'hearts and minds' of film audiences with tales of exile, longing, and tradition.[13]

Hong Kong's film left experienced a crisis in 1955 from which it never fully recovered. The KMT-affiliated Hong Kong and Kowloon Cinema and Theatrical Free Enterprise General Association called for a boycott of left-wing films in Taiwan. Soon after, the Nationalist regime in Taipei began taxing foreign-exchange earnings from imported Hong Kong Mandarin releases and barring the entry of movies associated with 'bandits' (a euphemism for communists).[14] These measures served to limit important investment and revenue sources from Taiwan. As production declined and profits fell, leftists generally moderated their politics in order to capture new markets; an exception being the Union Film Enterprises experiment in egalitarian collective filmmaking that sustained itself from 1952 until 1967. Of course, the decline of Hong Kong's post-war left-wing cinema may have been inevitable; as the economy recovered from stagnation brought on by a United Nations embargo prohibiting trade with China during the Korean War, the film industry's revitalization was largely financed by individuals such as Run Run Shaw (the youngest Shaw Brother) and Loke Wan-tho (Cathay), whose interests were inimical to socialism and communism.

Shaw Brothers and Cathay studios were rivals through the 1960s. Controlling production, distribution, and exhibition (each owned theaters throughout Southeast Asia), the two firms developed industrial modes of organization common to vertical monopolies. They maintained stable workforces through long-term contracting with actors, directors, stagehands, and technicians. Their crews worked with modern equipment and employed sophisticated production techniques. Shaw Brothers, the more powerful of the two competitors, built a 46-acre facility that housed multiple studios, permanent outdoor sets, dubbing and processing departments, and staff living quarters.[15] Cathay and Shaw Brothers turned the Hong Kong film industry on its head as Mandarin-dialect films became dominant in a culture of Cantonese speakers.

Production of Cantonese-dialect movies fell precipitously throughout the 1960s – from 211 in 1961 to 1 in 1971.[16] As the colony's economic 'take-off' shifted into high gear, moviegoers rejected Cantonese cinema, which looked old and tired, turning instead to fare directed by the likes of the Shaws' celebrated Li Hanxiang, whose melodramatic cross-dresser, *The Love Eterne* (1963), was the highest grossing Hong Kong film of the era. On the one hand, efforts by committed Cantonese filmmakers to improve quality paled beside the Shaw Brothers' epics and romances and Cathay's comedies and musicals, which dominated both local and export box offices. On the other hand, commercial studios fostered possessive individualist values associated with consumer capitalism while exploiting the Chinese diaspora's curiosity about its culture and history.

By the early 1970s, kung fu swordplay movies and imported Taiwanese romantic 'weepies' were all the rage, a gender divide having emerged with respect to interest and taste.[17] Shaw Brothers had vanquished Cathay, but faced a new challenge from its own former production chief, Raymond Chow, who opened Golden Harvest studio in 1970. In contrast to the Shaw organization, Chow decentralized the production aspects of his firm through semi-independent 'satellite companies' identified with well-known actors and directors.[18] Golden Harvest maintained control of distribution and presentation of product through acquisition of theaters and exhibition agreements with other companies. Meanwhile, Chow took some of the Shaws' talent with him, including acclaimed director King Hu whose martial arts actioner *Dragon Gate Inn* (1967) had been a box-office smash throughout Southeast Asia.

American André Morgan, who worked at Golden Harvest between 1972 and 1984 and who is today a Los Angeles film and television producer, describes the 1970s as a 'family situation.'[19] He says:

> We did have directors under exclusive contract, such as Ma Wei who did the Bruce Lee movies, and Fung Fung who did the early Angela Mao-ying and Samo Hung pictures. The directors under contract had teams that worked with them from picture to picture, a cameraman, a stunt squad, and a martial arts choreographer. At Golden Harvest, we had full-time prop and wardrobe departments and these crews bounced back and forth between different pictures. Virtually all films made between the early 1970s and the mid-1980s were done using the same three or four prop and wardrobe people.

Golden Harvest scored big early on with several releases starring martial-arts master Bruce Lee, including *Enter the Dragon* (1973), a first-ever co-production between Hollywood (Warner Bros) and Hong Kong (Golden Harvest). The film was the second highest US box-office draw for that year and set the stage for future co-ventures. While the number of projects has remained few, and the results uneven, Raymond Chow's foray into mainstream US and international markets produced the box-office hits *Cannonball Run* (1981) and *Teenage Mutant Ninja Turtles* (1990). His company's consistent performance in Asia, however, spawned a distribution network of over five hundred theaters, which generated 70 per cent of the top-earning films by the mid-1980s.[20]

Excepting art house patrons and a few critics fascinated by the superhuman stunts in director King Hu's martial arts swordplay movies and a youth subculture of white working-class males attracted to the kung fu genre, Bruce Lee was the cinematic beginning and end of Hong Kong film for Western audiences in the 1970s. The industry itself thrived locally and regionally on a steady diet of martial arts heroes during those years, ones that saw the colony overcome economic uncertainties associated with the political turmoil of the late 1960s. It was this situation from which the comedic talents and social satire of the likes of actor Michael Hui offered moviegoers relief. In films produced for and distributed by Golden Harvest, Hui and his brothers Sam and Ricky employed gambling to

parody Hong Kongers' obsession with 'getting rich quick,' ridiculed the population's 'money mania' as mental illness, and mocked profit-motivated, ratings-
driven television executives.[21] Moreover, the hundreds of copycat and knockoff
martial arts 'hero' productions apparently left Hong Kong film audiences hungering
for change late in the decade, evidenced by the emergence of hybrid 'kung fu
comedies.'

Chow's success with Golden Harvest in the 1970s was only one of a number
of significant changes and developments in the Hong Kong film industry during
the decade. First, despite the glaring inequalities present in the colony, movie
audiences continued to grow. A more prosperous, aspiring middle stratum, with
relatively few entertainment and leisure options, flocked to theaters. Second,
Mandarin productions disappeared by 1980 as Cantonese-dialect films made a
miraculous recovery – due, in great part, to the crossover of popular Canto-pop
singers into film roles and the new-found power of young stars such as Jackie
Chan.[22] Third, half of the Hong Kong movie companies operating in 1972 were
out of business by 1981, some of them supplanted by venture capitalists whose
entry into the industry reflected both the expansion of the Hong Kong's bour-
geoisie and the culture's 'get rich quick' mentality.[23] Fourth, the present-day image
of Hong Kong cinema as action cinema was forged during the economic boom
of the decade – a period of high growth rates (except for the recession years of
1974 and 1975) that also witnessed renewed income inequality associated with the
rise of the colony's financial and service sectors. Lastly, a 'new wave' of young
directors, many of whom had been raised in Hong Kong and later educated in
overseas film schools, graduated from television to film as the 1970s waned.
Technically proficient, socially conscious, and aesthetically polycultural, this group
– including Ann Hui and Tsui Hark – displayed an awareness of and sensitivity
to Hong Kong in their early work, foreshadowing the population's search for a
sense of place and self in the face of the colony's impending return to China in
1997.[24] While doubts exist about a cohesive movement given the diversity of
talents involved, this generation of filmmakers spawned the 'anything goes' attitude
that producer Terrence Chang calls the 'Hong Kong film sensibility' of the 1980s.[25]

Chang suggests that filmmakers in the 1980s 'could let their imagination run
wild. There were no restraints on their creativity, other than that of budget
concerns.' Yet anxiety about increasing costs led Shaw Brothers to halt film

production in favor of television late in the decade. Not even the success of the capital-rich Cinema City company, whose extraordinary market growth (its *Aces Go Places* series broke box-office records) recalled that of Golden Harvest ten years earlier, could change the fact that finances are one important way that the Hong Kong movie industry differs tremendously from that of Hollywood. Budgets are smaller, generally between US$100,000 and US$1 million, although rising costs in the early 1990s drove some upwards to US$4 million.[26]

A second dissimilarity between Hong Kong and Hollywood filmmaking is that production time for the former is shorter, roughly seven to eight weeks from contract to screen (exceptions to such constraints have included Jackie Chan, King Hu, and John Woo). Postproduction is often out of the question, and many films are completed days or even hours before their screenings. Typically films are edited as they are shot and, until recently, without synchronized sound – shooting without sound allowing for easier simultaneous release in Cantonese and Mandarin. Subtitles are often cheaply added and mistranslations inadvertently humorous. British law after 1963 required that all films be subtitled in Chinese and English, but it didn't 'require that the titles make sense.'[27] Breathtaking stunts are filmed using harnesses, wires, and sandbags; forget blue screens, second camera units, and computer technology. With some exceptions, such as Tsui Hark's breakthrough *Zu: Warriors from the Magic Mountain* (1983), which gave birth to the local special-effects industry, high-tech wizardry has not been the norm in Hong Kong cinema.

Hong Kong film credits, much like subtitles, are often unclear. Producers may involve themselves in direction, cinematographers and second unit directors can be charged with handling outside shoots, and several directors might work on the same project. Swordplay flick *Swordsman* (1990) offers an example of the confusion. While the movie was co-helmed by Ching Siu-tung, Tsui Hark, and Raymond Lee, both King Hu, who quit the project before filming began, and Ann Hui, whose work was minimal, receive co-direction credit. On the ground, production may reflect the work of a small number of individuals performing a variety of tasks. John Woo, recalling the difficulties of making movies in Hong Kong in the early 1970s, remarks that, 'When I started directing I had to be able to do everything. I would be painting a set one day and dressing it the next. I would choreograph the action, then show the camermen how to do the tracking shot I wanted.'[28] Similarly, Tsui says,

> In terms of a working system, there is no established system in the Hong Kong film industry. Sometimes, it's up to the individual director to come up with his or her working system. I used to wonder how the HK directors in the past worked when they all sat on a chair comfortably wearing an expensive suit. In our generation, directors are all sweaty and constantly running around everywhere.[29]

Stanley Tong's experience with his first film, *Stone Age Warriors* (1989), included work as production manager, screenwriter, choreographer, set builder, stunt double, special-effects coordinator, props person, and makeup artist. Says Tong, 'I started with a crew of twenty-nine. Four months later, there were only eleven people left – a camera operator, an assistant, a gaffer, five stuntmen, two actors, and myself – to finish the movie.'[30]

With a shortage of screenwriters in Hong Kong, many films are shot without scripts. With few scripts, many 'authors' intervene in the process of bringing a movie to the screen. Wong Kar-wai claims that he was credited for only ten of sixty screenplays he wrote before becoming a director.[31] Starring actor Tony Leung Ka-fai is co-credited with director Yim Ho as a screenwriter for *King of Chess* (1992) but the final cut has producer Tsui Hark's signature written all over it. Director Kirk Wong boasts that in some of his films 'not a single word is from the original script.'[32]

Working conditions, even for the handful of Hong Kong film stars, would be unacceptable to Hollywood actors. Commenting on the heady days of the 1980s, director Cheung Yuen-ting recalls a 'friend that hadn't slept for four days [who] had to rely on an oxygen mask to keep himself going' and 'an actress nicknamed "Cheng nine sets a day" because she was making nine movies at the same time!'[33] Cantopop king Andy Lau averaged a movie a month in 1991, at one time shooting four movies at once on four locations, and sleeping in his car. Roy Cheung says that 'It is common for us to work for two and three days and nights non-stop without a wink of sleep.'[34] Commenting on his work, Cheung notes that

> With *City on Fire*, we finished filming in less than thirty shooting days within six weeks. With *Prison on Fire*, the prison was a set and over a hundred people were cramped without air conditioning or proper ventilation. For the finale 'Water Battle,' our feet had to be soaked in the same pool of stinky water for three days and nights.

Superstar Chow Yun-fat, who appeared with Roy Cheung in Ringo Lam's *On Fire* series, completed most of his seventy films in ten years. He relates:

It is one kind of way to survive in the Hong Kong film industry. We don't have very large budgets for the production, so the studio won't pay a lot of money for hiring the star. So everybody wants to work hard for more money before 1997. Sometimes I'm so jealous that the stars here [USA] can take two, three years [between] movies. In Hong Kong, if you take three, four years [off], you die. You cannot survive like that. It's tough, but it is the way that we treat ourselves to be a star. Sometimes everyone is proud of themselves when they make twelve films in a year, but on the other hand, there is a sadness, I feel shame that we have been working like a dog.[35]

The actor goes on to describe the limited space for filming and illegal shooting common to the industry: 'in Hong Kong, our buildings, our rooms are narrow ... we're always breaking the law, shooting on the streets without a permit.' His words have a striking similarity to Marx's description of

the transformation of the laborer into a workhorse, [which] is a means of increasing capital, or speeding up the production of surplus-value. Such economy extends to over-crowding close and unsanitary premises with laborers, or, as capitalists put it, to space saving; to crowding dangerous machinery into close quarters without using safety devices; to neglecting safety rules in production processes pernicious to health.[36]

Ann Hui's *Ah Kam* (1996) provides a disturbing visual reminder of Marx's words. In the movie, a reluctant stunt woman (Michelle Yeoh) is pushed from an over-pass onto a moving truck by her director (Samo Hung); the scene outtake shown as the closing credits roll reveals that Yeoh was painfully injured doing the stunt.

Historically, the portrayal of women in front of the camera as well as the number of women behind the camera in Hong Kong cinema bear a striking similarity to the situation in Hollywood. Male dominance of the industry often left screen women the object of what Laura Mulvey calls a 'male gaze' and rarely offered women opportunities to make films themselves. Some change manifested itself in the 1980s; more women working in creative and decision-making capacities in the movie industry appeared coincident with growing numbers of women in the labor force generally and the visible presence of women in professional and managerial positions specifically.[37] Actors such as Maggie Cheung, Brigitte Lin, and Anita Mui began receiving weightier roles, particularly in the latter years of the decade. Evolving gender attitudes became evident in the work of certain male directors, including Stanley Kwan and Ching Siu-tung, whose consideration of women and sexuality not only deconstructed the ways that cinema 'naturalizes' socially constructed masculine fantasies and ideologies but also problematized the essentialism of a 'heterosexual division of the universe.'[38]

Tsui Hark, well known for the assertive female characters in his movies, sees gender as a signifier distinguishing Hong Kong and Hollyood film sensibilities; Hollywood women, he says, 'no matter how unique and strong their characters, usually end up falling into some kind of conservative, traditional romance. In Hong Kong, we are never "threatened" by the females in our films and there is no bias in choosing which gender is making the interesting things in the story.' Cheung Yuen-ting maintains that 'the depiction of women in Hong Kong movies has evolved from mere decoration for the set to characters with independent thinking.' Cheung, who attracted critical attention with her second directorial effort, *An Autumn's Tale* (1987), is part of a still small group of notable Hong Kong women filmmakers that includes the aforementioned Ann Hui and Clara Law.[39] Remarking that 'I was told by my mother that only women of dubious backgrounds entered the film business,' Cheung says, 'it had never crossed my mind that I would one day become a film director myself.' She recalls but one woman filmmaker from the days of her youth, an actress-turned-director, 'who always wore a wide-brimmed hat and smoked with a long cigarette holder. All others were "macho" men who smoked cigars and wore shades. Wherever on the set they went, they were followed by a "chair boy" who carried a director's chair with him and put it down wherever the director fancied to sit.' More recently, she insists, 'The bosses of film companies do not care whether you are a man or a woman. All they care about is whether your film makes money or not.'

To that end, name stars are crucial for the Hong Kong movie business. The late director King Hu remembered, 'I was trying to get film financing from the Taiwanese distributors. All they wanted to know was: "Is there a part in your film for Chow Yun-fat?" When I said there wasn't they asked: "Can you write in a role for Chow Yun-fat?"'[40] Companies will guarantee their success by lining up a big star or a combination of stars. They pre-sell the film based on the lineup to movie distributors around the Asian market. Getting the film onto as many screens as possible is important, since the release will be in a set number of theaters and run as long as the movie makes money. Without Asian presales, which are declining, movies usually play for three weeks locally and most don't turn a profit.

Since 1989, the apogee of Hong Kong moviegoing, when almost 45 million movie tickets were sold, and Hong Kongers were among the most frequent moviegoers worldwide, some big-name stars made flops, and the domestic industry began a downturn. Only 29 million tickets were sold in 1991 and 24 million in 1995. In the early 1990s, more than 200 movies a year were made, but only 154 in 1995 and 116 in 1996.[41] T.C. Wang, founder of Salon Films, sees this as simply a correction in the market as more Hollywood movies have gone to Asia and home entertainment becomes cheaper and more readily available. He believes that 'the movie business always cycles up and down … After it's settled down, it will go up again, just like the stock market.'[42]

Movie companies toe the bottom line – films that are delivered on time and cost-effective. The attitude of Karl Maka, of Golden Princess Studios, is common. He recalls John Woo and Tsui Hark bringing him the landmark *A Better Tomorrow*:

> I never want to hear the story! They started to tell me what happens in the film. I stop them. I ask: 'How many stars in the film?' They tell me there are three and one of them is Leslie Cheung, who was a very big singer at that time. I ask them: 'How much of the running time is action?' They tell me about a third. I ask them, 'How much will it cost?' They told me and I said 'Okay!'[43]

Similarly, Terence Chang, in recalling his relationship with Golden Princess during his time as general manager of Tsui's Film Workshop, notes that 'I submitted a one-page synopsis, a rough budget, and an income forecast. When they saw it made sense business-wise, they greenlit the project within the same day.'

Differences aside, Hong Kong's film industry, no less than Hollywood's, has witnessed the decline of a consolidated system in which movies often bore the mark of their studios more than that of any individuals. And, auteurism notwithstanding, the genesis and nuturing of a film, always a collaborative and complex process, has been made even more so as film personnel, no longer under contract to specific companies, seek investors with the capital to put their ideas and stories onto celluloid. Decentralized production revolves around the development of integrated networks of specialized services. Terence Chang, who worked in Hong Kong throughout the 1980s, including several years as manager of overseas distribution for now defunct D&B Films, and who is currently a producer and manager in the United States and Canada, explains his function:

I have to oversee every aspect of a film production, from its conception to its release. I also have to make sure not to infringe on the director's creativity, but at the same time to deliver to the studio a film that they set out to make. Sometimes there might be a conflict between the director and the studio, then I have to find a way to make sure that both sides' interests are protected.[44]

Filmmakers must understand that their films are commodities. Recalling his first directorial effort, Stanley Tong notes that 'everybody was shooting *Police Story and Chinese Ghost Story*, but I didn't have Jackie Chan or Leslie Cheung because I couldn't afford them. So I tried to do something different, something that no one had done before so that I might get a chance in the market.' Tong's 'something different' was *Stone Age Warriors*, shot in four locations, including New Guinea, and involving the use of a thousand tribespeople from seven separate tribes, human-eating komodo dragons, poisonous scorpions, and a trip over a waterfall.[45] Eddie Fong's experience with *Cherry Blossoms* (1987), based on the life of Chinese writer Yu Tat-fu, is also telling. Golden Harvest, which bought the film rights from Shaw Brothers after the latter shut down production, took the project away from Fong when he refused to make the film 'more commercial' by shooting more nude scenes.[46] Actors, too, are 'only a merchandise,' says Chow Yun-fat. He cautions,

> Don't be naive. Film making is absolutely not an art. Everyone is only doing a business. Chow Yun-fat, Jackie Chan.... Why would investors spend money to hire you to act? Actually the math has been done long ago, calculating how much you are worth. How many overseas markets? Money to be made? Very commercial. As for yourself, you would use acting in exchange for salary.[47]

Marx indicates that 'actors are productive workers … in so far as they increase their employer's wealth.'[48] And, in a trade where film costs average about US$1.4 million, hiring several stars at almost US$260,000 each greatly reduces the salaries of supporting players and crews.

The business of film in Hong Kong is the dark underbelly of the screen glamour and fanzine hoopla characteristic of pop culture. Networks of money and people that comprise the financial infrastructure are shrouded in mystery. Add the involvement of organized crime to the territory's movie industry and a pretty chilling picture comes into focus. As Marx noted, the methods of early capitalism

courtesy/permission of Stanley Tong

BRAVE NEW WORLD   Stanley Tong and extras filming *Stone Age Warriors* in New Guinea

were 'anything but idyllic.'[49] Reported Triad activities range from face-offs, intimidation, payoffs and extortion, to death threats, armed robbery, and contract killings.[50] Actor Andy Lau, who has, ironically, played numerous Triad figures, has been pressured to appear in Triad-financed productions. Popular comedian Stephen Chiau has ostensibly been denied Canadian citizenship for alleged Triad connections. The deaths of movie producers Jimmy Choi Chin-ming and Wong Long-wai were linked to their organized crime activities. Director Wong Jing had his teeth

bashed in by known Triad members, supposedly for saying the wrong thing publicly. Movie producer Chan Chi-ming has been connected to a foiled attempt to
destroy the negative print of Leslie Cheung's 1992 vehicle *All's Well Ends Well*,
when Mandarin Films refused to release him for Chan's next project (the wrong
print was stolen). A cat's head was allegedly thrown into Chow Yun-fat's courtyard
when he failed to respond to a Chan script. Cantopop star and actor Anita Mui
apparently underwent a self-imposed temporary exile due to an unsavory incident
in a karaoke bar with movie producer and 14K Triad member Wong Long-wai. He
publicly slapped Mui across the face; he was beaten by Andy Chan in retaliation.[51]

In spite of such incidents, André Morgan, whose experience includes stints in
both Hong Kong and Hollywood, states pointedly that 'where there is organized
crime, there is a tendency to be attracted to the glamour and glitter of the entertainment industry, whether it is the stars, the money, or the flashiness.' Therefore,
according to Morgan, 'When the producer of *The Godfather* got the approval for
the making of that film, he was dealing with organized crime in America. There
has been and there always will be a Triad influence in the Hong Kong film
industry. But the industry is not controlled by the Triads.' Actor Karen Mok
asserts that 'it is very wrong to equate the Triads with the film industry, but
unfortunately that is what a lot of people think,' in part, because local press
accounts of underworld control are commonplace. Mok rebukes the media for
being irresponsible and unprofessional in this regard, citing a newspaper story
that

> wrongfully stated that I was the sister of some guy caught in a fight outside a karaoke [in
> which she owned a small share], and who was allegedly involved with a Triad, because
> he happened to have the same surname as I do. But Mok isn't my real surname, it's
> actually Morris; Mok is only a Chinese adaptation that I use for work.[52]

Meanwhile, director Cheung Yuen-ting maintains that organized crime was a 'problem in the late 1980s and early 1990s because there was easy money to make.'
Since then, she says, 'the Triads have moved on to other businesses because the
film industry is not as profitable as before.'

Some in the industry attempted to set aside their concerns and abide Triad
infiltration because it meant increased film output for a time. This political
economy was even examined in Ann Hui's *Ah Kam* (1996) and Derek Yee's *Viva*

Erotica (1996), both of which explore the Triad connection. Location shoots are often negotiated beforehand with local Triad bosses; director Wong Kar-wai freely says that 'It's better to deal with a godfather than an accountant.'[53] Chow Yun-fat explains Triad activity in this way:

> If the Triads were a serious problem in Hong Kong movies, I don't think we [movie industry] would survive for long … We have a funny saying … if the film industry is totally controlled by the gangs, then there are no more gangs because they are all businessmen.[54]

Fittingly, in 1989 Jimmy and Charles Heung, sons of Sun Yee On Triad founder Heung Chin, established the Wins Entertainment Group, which rose to second in prominence behind Raymond Chow's Golden Harvest in Hong Kong's early 1990s' film market.

While Hong Kong movies cover a broad spectrum, the "on the fly" approach to filmmaking has, at its best, brought an exuberant energy and fresh inventiveness long absent from Hollywood; at its worst, it has led to unabashedly commercial gimmicks and uninspired cheap products. The Hong Kong film industry, a commodified image-making machine, has taken appropriation to a new level. Formulas of successful films are duplicated, like the *A Better Tomorrow*, *Chinese Ghost Story* and *Once Upon a Time in China* sequels and series. Films feed upon themselves, as when Wong Kar-wai's arty *Days of Being Wild* (1991) is remade as the parody *Days of Being Dumb* (1992). Copycats and knock-offs are common – such as the spate of gambling movies that followed the success of the comedy *God of Gamblers* (1989) starring Chow Yun-fat and Andy Lau. Director Wong Jing and Wins Entertainment, both of whom understand well the art of moneymaking, released in quick succession *God of Gamblers II* (1990) with Andy Lau and Stephen Chiau; *God of Gamblers III: Back to Shanghai* (1991) with Chiau, and *God of Gamblers Returns* (1994) which saw the reappearance of Chow Yun-fat. The ever-prolific Wong then threw in a spin-off, *Saint of Gamblers* (1995), and a prequel, *God of Gamblers III: The Early Stage* (1996), for good measure.

Moviemakers also appropriate plots and concepts from proven product, as with Hollywood commercial successes. *Dog Day Afternoon* re-emerged as *People's Hero* (1987); *Splash* metamorphosed into *Mermaid Got Married* (1994); and *Backdraft* was rekindled as *Lifeline* (1996). In *All's Well End's Well* (1992), Maggie Cheung's character plays out Madonna's concert movie *Truth or Dare*, *Ghost*, and *Pretty Woman*, while in *60 Million Dollar Man* (1995), Stephen Chiau parodies *Pulp Fiction* and *Terminator*.

Paul S.N. Lee describes four ways in which Hong Kong, a meeting place of East and West, interacts with foreign cultures: (1) adoption of form and content; (2) assimilation, maintaining content but changing form; (3) assimilation, maintaining form but changing content; and (4) indigenization, leaving foreign and local cultures indistinguishable.[55] Cultural difference and social experience mitigate against wholesale adoption; *Run* (1995), a scene-by-scene rip-off that clones the cult hit *El Mariachi*, features a vacationing musician in Mexico rather than the unemployed guitar-playing drifter of the original. Similarly, *Black Cat* (1991), springing from the French film *La Femme Nikita*, adds a surgically implanted computer chip to the head of its assassin. Even as faithful a version of the Hollywood film *Same Time Next Year* as *I Will Wait for You* (1994) incorporates an issue (emigration) into the story of a long-term, one-weekend-a-year affair that is far removed from the concerns of mainstream United States audiences.

Thus do many Hong Kong films either maintain the content and change the form, or vice versa. Switching genders, *Easy Money* (1987) has Michelle Yeoh playing Steve McQueen's bored millionaire turned bank robber from the *Thomas Crown Affair* and George Lam becoming Faye Dunaway's insurance investigator. An innocent eight-year-old boy who sees a murder in *Witness* is transformed into a four-year-old girl in *Wild Search* (1989), and then appears as a dock worker in a Hong Kong release entitled *Witness* (1993). Glenn Close's parallel Nancy Cheung has a jealous Triad hitman boyfriend in *Fatal Passion*'s (1990) makeover of *Fatal Attraction*, while *First Shot* (1993) replaces the *Untouchables*' 1920s' Prohibition-era bootlegging in the United States with 1970s' police corruption in the colony.

In raising questions about what constitutes a Hong Kong film, the sci-fi comedy *Laser Man* (1986) may approach indigenization. With a Hong Kong producer (Tsui Hark), Chinese American director/leading actor (Peter Wang), African-American cinematographer (Ernest Dickerson), Japanese composer/performer (Ryuichi Sakamoto), racially mixed international cast (including Americans Maryann Urbano and Joan Copeland, Japanese-American Marc Hayashi, and Hong Kongers Tony Leung Ka-fai and Sally Yeh), and New York City location, the film crossbreeds but does not cannibalize. As Homi Bhabha points out, 'cultures are never unitary in themselves, nor simply dualistic in relation of Self to Other.'[56] Moreover, in what Uma Magal calls the 'reverse angle' of global cinema, Hollywood movies have been appropriating from Hong Kong.[57] Directors show close-ups, made famous by the likes of John Woo and Ringo Lam, of speeding bullets, and stunt actors imitate the physical martial arts moves of Jackie Chan and Jet Li. Quentin Tarantino lifts the final segment of Lam's *City on Fire* (1987) for his own *Reservoir Dogs*, while Robert Rodriguez mimics the gunplay scenes of Woo's *The Killer* (1989) in *Desperado*.

The finest of the best-known Hong Kong cinema crafts evocative stories rooted in character and exploits nuts-and-bolts filmmaking through rapidly changing camera angles, collision editing for action sequences, and changing film speeds to visualize narratives. While the movies' frenetic pacing has been identified with an apocalyptic sense about 1997, their characteristic rhythms draw on Cantonese and Peking Opera's sense of timing and pause. Coupled with Western influences on directors like John Woo and Tsui Hark, Hong Kong filmmakers have interpreted film language in a unique way, much as the territory's spoken Cantonese is sprinkled with Mandarin, English, and sundry other sounds, producing and reflecting a hybrid that Ackbar Abbas calls 'postcoloniality that precedes decolonization.'[58] Woo points out that the design for the gun battles and action scenes in his seminal *A Better Tomorrow*, which reinvented the gangster genre, combined elements from Hollywood Westerns and Chinese swordplay movies – the former revolving around opposites continually confronting one another, and the latter involving the use of martial arts choreography.[59] Moreover, the use of low-key lighting to produce shadows and chiaroscuro in movies such as Woo's *The Killer* (1989) recalls film noir, where passions run high on dank, dirty 'mean streets.'

Meanwhile, Tsui Hark, frequently referred to as Hong Kong's Steven Spielberg because of his fondness for special effects, has mixed and matched almost every genre imaginable in creating an oeuvre of 'multiple artistic personalities and ir-reconcilable differences.'[60] His early feature films – *Butterfly Murders* (1979), a gothic period-piece murder mystery with killer insects; *We're Going to Eat You* (1980), a kung fu horror-comedy about cannibalism; and *Dangerous Encounter of the First Kind* (1980), an unrelentingly violent urban realist, anti-colonial rant, initially banned by Hong Kong censors – reveal both his eclectic interests and his wide-ranging talents.[61] Tsui's wire-worked, martial arts spectacle-fantasy *Zu* and his 1986 epic

Peking Opera Blues, weaving together ballet, pomp, satire, stunts, and tragedy, so-lidified his reputation as an adventurous and visionary filmmaker.

While spectacle and speed, in both camera and footwork, have become the cinema's trademark in the West, contemporary Hong Kong film runs the gamut; its 'action-faction' of gangster pictures and martial arts costumers comprises only a portion of the territory's movie industry. Lightweight comedies and meditative dramas are regularly served fare as well. Amidst the frequent complaints of theater audiences and film critics alike that too many Hong Kong films are poor-quality productions with lackluster storylines, cloying dialogues, and second-rate perform-ances, some releases rise above the swamp to address political and social concerns. Filmmakers often utilize dislocation and displacement, as well as irony and meta-phor, which allows deflection in light of the the Film Censorship Authority's willingness to axe movies that focus on 'social rebels with anarchist tendencies' or films that may 'damage good relations with other territories.'[62] Their films have considered the former colony's triadic past – the axis by which Hong Kong, China and Great Britain are linked – as a way to understand current circumstances. They have looked for an identifiable Hong Kong present in a contradictory manner that recalls what Michel Pêcheux calls 'identification' (accepting the sanctioned dis-course), 'counter-identification' (attempting to modify the sanctioned discourse), and 'disidentification' (resisting the sanctioned discourse).[63] And they have used yesterday and today to express concern for Hong Kong's future after 1997, the marker to which, first, the signing of the handover agreement and, second, the 1989 Tiananmen massacre pointed.

In various ways Hong Kong cinema is revealed to be 'crisis cinema,' one that finds itself in a historic conjuncture where new patterns of language, time and space, place and identity, and meaning itself, are emerging. *Days of Being Wild* expresses anxiety through its use of mirrors and clocks. *Sixty Million Dollar Man* alludes to Hong Kong film industry problems and Hollywood's growing popularity. *Mary from Beijing* (1992) grapples with the handover both directly and indirectly, interpolating economic development, international trade, gender role, social class, vernacular, East–West, and Hong Kong–China themes.

The Hong Kong movie industry reflects the crisis of Hong Kong itself: on the one hand, the 'on the fly' nuts-and-bolts approach indicates an early stage of capital, 'reproduced' by the territory's vast pirating operations of tapes, records, videos and films; on the other hand, the emphasis on film as commodity epito-mizes late capital and its cultural logic. Similarly, the movie worlds themselves mirror early and late capitalist cultural conditions as they assimilate and narratively maneuver between both worlds. They place viewers in 'ideologically-produced frames of meaning' which makes representations 'not only feasible but natural.'[64] The oft-noted penchant that both the Hong Kong movie business and Hong Kong movie fans have for escapism may, in some measure, affirm Horkheimer and Adorno's depiction of the culture industry as amusement, diversion, and distraction.[65] But the Hong Kong perspective is of a 'city on fire,' representing not only the illumination of images on a screen but also a world burning with anxiety and confusion, and best imagined as icon Chow Yun-fat burning a counterfeit $100 bill in *A Better Tomorrow*.

THREE

WHOSE BETTER TOMORROW?

What better contemporary vision to describe early capitalism than the imprimatur of John Woo's martial-arts-with-automatic-weapons movies, where competition rages among petty capitalists in the guise of Triads? From *A Better Tomorrow* (1986) to *Hard-Boiled* (1992), Woo has tackled ethical questions by pitting his hero against a corrupt world built on the value of a dollar, where 'necessity knows no law.' In these movies, gunplay abounds and high body counts result. In the history of capitalism, 'weapons were the means of expansion for commerce and conquest.'[1] From multi-round 9 mm pistols to pump-action double-barrel shotguns, Woo's films unleash the destructive power of an arsenal as internecine feuds erupt bewteen Triads over money and turf, and cops battle with the underworld.

Woo was born in 1946 in Guangzhou on the Mainland. He was five when his family emigrated to Hong Kong, where he grew up poor in the area of Shek Kip Mei, a shantytown of wooden huts. After a big fire in the early 1950s, the government built a resettlement area of two-story buildings on the site, soon replaced by seven-story buildings like those featured in *Bullet in the Head*.[2] Having seen people killed as a child, Woo witnessed Triad activities and street violence, remarking, 'because we were poor, I always thought we were living in hell.'[3] It is tempting to equate Woo's memories with his films' 'mean streets,' but his experiences more likely shaped his vision of a brutal world of all against all in which brotherly love is anachronistic. Movies served as an escape for the young Woo, providing him with the dream of a better world. He elaborates:

> My mother was a huge fan of American classics, so she often took me to the movies. They were free for kids. Because we lived in the slums I loved movies so much for helping me escape from that hell. There was so much beauty in movies.[4]

While Woo's films metaphorically and accurately describe the forces of early capitalist conditions at work, it is another *Mean Streets*, Martin Scorsese's, which colored Woo's universe: 'a hybrid of all the worlds of all the films I loved, an imaginary place … I'm a dreamer.'[5] Of what are Woo's dreams made? Woo states that,

> Movies are my major language. I like to share my experiences and feelings about love and the meaning of life with my friends and, really, everybody. Movies act as a bridge which draws together everybody's heart. Through movies we can learn about the beauty among us. I want to make movies to the end.

A man of strong convictions, Woo 'envisions a better place with no war, no violence, and everyone loving and caring for each other,' far afield from emergent capitalist societies.[6] Although he has depicted a Hong Kong drenched in X-rated violence, Woo is hardly the 'master of disaster' that cult moviegoers see him as. In fact, Woo explains, 'I do find my heaven in musicals. The people, the places, the feelings give me great joy because everything and everyone is so beautiful'; Woo's dramatic violence is best described in terms of dance: aesthetic, balletic, graceful; and stylized, sometimes cartoonish. The violence that explodes on-screen is tied to characters deeply entrenched in networks of social relationships; greed and betrayal are at the root of the violence. Consequences of actions are evident and motivations examined. Narratives unspool as contemporary urban morality plays, in which people confront a world rapidly changing for the worse; the choices they make and act upon test their faith and values and distinguish the good guys from the bad. Provided with assistance from the Lutheran Church in his youth, Woo is a devout Christian and draws on his belief in Agape – the love of a Christian for other persons, corresponding to the love of God for humanity – to express his message. 'I'm most influenced by the values of Jesus Christ,' explains Woo, 'Loving one's neighbor, forgiveness, patience, kindness, charity.'

Woo also appropriates from the past, drawing heavily upon the code of honor of Chinese legendary heroes to develop characters. He is influenced by previous appropriations of that past in the *wuxia-pian*, or Chinese historical-period action films, and in Japanese samurai movies, which operate similarly. He exploits the film language and techniques of gangster movie mavens, from Jean-Pierre Melville to Martin Scorsese, Akira Kurosawa's samurai epics and the yakuza movies of Takakura Ken, and western mavericks like Sergio Leone and Sam Peckinpah to develop his style and enhance his characterizations and themes. Woo further reveals,

> Secondly, I'm influenced by the ancient Chinese qualities of chivalry (meaning self-sacrifice), friendship, loyalty and honor. Melville dealt a great deal with themes of friendship and honor. The characters will give their lives for their friends. Kurosawa gets into great moral arguments in his films and forces each audience member to confront, 'What would I do?', 'What kind of person am I?'

Woo's lead actor, romantic hero, friend, and alter ego, Chow Yun-fat, in describing the director, said, 'He is a very traditional Chinese.'[7] In turn, Woo comments: 'Chow represents everything I value in a person: morality, friendship, honor, love. He is like an ancient Chinese hero who really cares about people.' Chinese scholar Sung Longji explains that in traditional Chinese culture, a person is defined by body (*shen*) and heart (*xin*). The physical body determines the health of a person, but it is the heart which determines the spiritual; and the heart, which generates emotive feelings (*qing*), also shapes social relationships which define the person. Activities of the heart should be expressed as concern for others and empathy, 'having heart.' Care for the body and its survival (*jing*), on the other hand, is associated with pragmatism and cleverness, getting ahead in this world.[8] Hong Kong director Stanley Tong elaborates on the social relationships deriving from *qing*:

> In Chinese there are four main things that we have to know: *Jung* is loyalty; *xiao* is being very good to your parents; and *ren* is being good to people, forgiving them even when they're trying to harm you. The last thing Woo always puts into his movies.... It's *yi*. *Yi* means when you are a friend, you can give up your life for a friend.[9]

Characterizations of Woo heroes draw upon these basic ideals. The characters guided by *jing* over *qing* are the villains of his movies.

The code of honor by which Woo's heroes live and die, and which dignifies them, is based on Confucian values of mutual dependence and non-acquisitiveness, Christian values of compassion and self-sacrifice, and chivalric swordsman values of courage and loyalty. Whether hitmen, Triad muscle, undercover cops, or

A GUN TO YOUR HEAD   Chow Yun-fat in *The Killer*

detectives, they serve as romanticized figures who lament the loss of these values, and consequently their own place, in the films. In *A Better Tomorrow*, Ho tells Mark 'This is not our world anymore.' In *A Better Tomorrow 2*, Lung says, 'In our time we had a code of behavior. You respect me and the respect is doubly returned.' In *The Killer*, John tells Sidney 'It never used to be like this.' In one respect these heroes are anachronisms in a world ruled by those who get ahead by rejecting the honorable code and living by the mottoes 'greed is good' and 'survival of the fittest.' The villains commit 'merciless vandalism, and ... [exhibit] passions the most infamous, the most sordid, the pettiest, the most meanly odious,' character- istic of early capitalist expropriation.[10] Heroes who honor the code include the criminals Ho and Mark and policeman Kit in *A Better Tomorrow*; Ho and Kit, Mark's twin brother Ken, and Boss Lung in *A Better Tomorrow 2*; hitman John, former hitman Sidney, and cops Li and Chang in *The Killer*; and the cop Tequila, undercover Alan, and Boss Hui in *Hard-Boiled*. Villains include Shing in *A Better Tomorrow*; Wong, Ko, and their henchmen in *A Better Tomorrow 2*; Johnny Weng and the nameless contract killer who demands $300,000 to kill John in *The Killer*; and Johnny Wong in *Hard-Boiled* – all of whom disregard *qing* in favor of *jing*, showing indifference for the lives of others. Chow Yun-fat says that Woo is a 'very roman- tic and sensual director who puts a lot of himself in his films: love, human dignity, but also anger about the loss of tradition in the cities.'[11]

Woo explains: 'I like old-fashioned, traditional moral standards. People don't seem to realize what honor and loyalty are. I am fond of Chinese history. There are a lot of famous stories about honor and loyalty.'[12] Lori Sue Tilkin notes that 'the brotherhood and loyalty among [Woo's] male characters is derived from the heroic chivalry of the knights-errant,' and traces the archetype back to the *Shiji* (Records of the Grand Historian), a comprehensive history of China covering a 2,500-year period from the reign of the Yellow Emperor (2697–2599 BCE) to the Emperor Wu Han (140–87 BCE), written by Sima Qian (*c.* 145–85 BCE).[13] Early in his career, Woo worked for Shaw Brothers and served as assistant director to martial arts chivalry (*wuxia-pian*) movie master Chang Cheh for several films, in- cluding *Blood Brothers* (1973), considered Chang's masterpiece, which stages a one- man war against an army of thousands, and, like his other films, develops the emotions of characters to explore the make-up of a hero. Chang, says Woo, 'changed the techniques and the level of skill in the Hong Kong action film.'[14] He describes his mentor as 'a pioneer of martial arts films ... the equivalent of Kurosawa to Japan.' Taught how to create the stylistic conventions of the genre, to choreograph action and violence according to its rhythm and tempo, and to enable characters to express feelings, Woo also became acquainted with the actors that Chang made stars, including Ti Lung, Wang Yu, David Chiang, and Danny Lee, two of whom he would later feature in his gangster movies. Woo relates: 'I learned a lot. I learned how to manage action scenes. I also supervised some of

[Chang's] postproduction work, the editing and sound dubbing. I got a chance to edit, and I learned more about movies from that than anything else.'[15]

Working for Golden Harvest, Woo put his knowledge to use with *Last Hurrah for Chivalry* (1978). The story concerns the relationship between two swordsmen, Chang (Wei Pai), a 'righteous swordsman,' and Tsing Yi (Damian Lau Chung-yan), a wine-drinking hired killer, and celebrates and mourns the passing of such men. The villain, Kao (Liu Chiang), is presented as a good guy, but his true nature is revealed when he betrays his father's memory and anyone who stands in the way of his obtaining the Moonshadow Sword, the possessor of which will have marvelous fighting powers. He chooses *jing* over *qing*. Tsing Yi's characterization is drawn from historical figure Jing Ke, who in 220 BCE attempted to assassinate the megalomaniacal Qin emperor, regarded as cruel, superstitious, and arbitrary in his decision-making. Qin was the westernmost of the Zhou states, more rural and considered less culturally advanced than the East. With the Qin rise to power in 221 BCE, the Emperor imposed uniformity, leading to the destruction of many local traditions and the loss of much Chinese heritage. Jin Ke, a legendary Chinese figure, is one of John Woo's heroes.

When Janus-faced Kao deceives the two swordsmen, they unite in the name of chivalrous virtue and obligation (*qing*) and are willing to die for their beliefs. As Tilkin notes,

> One group of people who decided to take justice into their own hands and live by their own rules were the knights-errant. These individuals roamed the countryside and responded whenever their services were needed. They lived by their own code of honor and made their own laws. They were skilled at fighting and often engaged in combat. Romantic descriptions in literature dramatize the knights-errant as men who did not seek wealth from their work and were quite poor. They took pride in their skills and their personal ideologies; they were altruistic and not afraid to die for their principles.[16]

While the action sequences play according to established genre standards, with long takes and fighting choreographed rhythmically, Woo emphasizes the male bonding of the heroes based on a shared code and creates characterizations with feeling. In addition to the acting, the musical score and theme song greatly contribute to this effect. The music mirrors the powerful male heroes, using a full orchestra featuring strong horns and strings. Its counterpoint lyricism suggests regret and nostalgia for the loss of chivalric values in a mercenary world. The lyrics of the theme-song emphasize the protagonists' heroism and noble friendship.[17]

Last Hurrah For Chivalry (literally *Chivalrous Knights*) foreshadows Woo's first gangster picture, *A Better Tomorrow*, in many of its elements. First, the three main characters, Chang, Tsing, and Kao, serve as models for Ho, Mark, and Shing. Shing betrays Ho and Mark for personal advantage as Kao does the swordsmen. Ti Lung plays Ho, who resembles the righteous swordsman Chang, a character similar to many the actor portrayed in other Chang Cheh movies. Tsing sacrifices himself to destroy Kao and save Chang, just as Mark does to defeat Shing and protect Ho; freeze-frames of their deaths emphasize the selfless acts (*qing*). Tsing, the killer for hire, is also depicted as a womanizer and drinker, a characterization of someone who enjoys life, not unlike Mark, who is seen enjoying food from a street vendor and flirting with women. Woo recognizes the general influences, stating, 'To me the gangster films are just like Chinese swordplay pictures. To me Chow Yun-fat holding a gun is just like Wang Yu [star of Chang Cheh's *Golden Swallow* (1968)] holding a sword.'[18] Woo's use of the musical score and theme song is also strikingly similar, emphasizing the noble plight of its heroes and their regret at the loss of noble ideals.

A Better Tomorrow, the sequel, and *The Killer* open by introducing two motifs, guns and money. In the first film, the seeming tyro Shing (Waise Lee) through force and conniving, manuevers his way into Triad leadership, betraying Ho and Mark. Weakened boss Yui submits to Shing's leadership so long as the company makes money. Similarly, in *A Better Tomorrow 2*, retired boss Lung is set up by his manager Ko. In *The Killer*, the hit put out on corrupt politician and underworld 'scum' Tony Weng is financed by his nephew, Johnny. Financial gain and expanded profit margins are all that matters to these villains; the way they get it is through brute force; human beings, including relatives and loyal employees, are expendable.

Woo's opening credits in *A Better Tomorrow* introduce the relationship of guns and money. After Ho dreams of his brother Kit (Leslie Cheung) being gunned down by unseen adversaries, his body dancing jerkily as it is riddled with bullets and bathed in an eerie blue light, he awakens to conduct business. He meets Mark (Chow Yun-fat), first framed on a Hong Kong street, shot from below, with looming reflective office skyscrapers behind, dwarfed by the faceless, monolithic

courtesy of Felix Lu; permission of John Woo

MONEY TO BURN   Chow Yun-fat in *A Better Tomorrow*

world of commerce. Following is a wonderful sequence which plays like a video game; the camera picks up heightened neon reds and greens set against the jarring absence of color via black-and-white surveillance cameras. The focus is on moving parts and shapes, with complicated machinery at work, the mode of production of counterfeiting. Ho and Mark exhibit an excited childlike wonder at the goings-on, in contrast to the Dracula smile of Shing, silently contemplating his next move to claim all that money. Shing will be the vampire-capitalist, who 'only lives by sucking living labour, and lives the more, the more labor it sucks.'[19] Ho and Mark represent loyal employees, the physical labor part of the operation, but also set apart from the other Triads.

Woo based his screenplay for *A Better Tomorrow* on Lung Kong's 1967 Cantonese movie *The Story of a Discharged Prisoner*, using the bare-bones plot to develop and explore the code of honor among his heroes by revising and enriching their characterizations and his message. He also added the influence of Alain Delon's character Jeff from Jean-Pierre Melville's *Le Samourai* (a telling title) in Mark's characterization, borrowing the trench coat and signature shades. Woo uses telling freeze-frames for Ho, Mark, and Kit, to emphasize their emotions, a technique he says he learned from Truffaut. After Shing betrays Ho, Mark attempts to avenge his bloodbrother and is crippled. Released from prison, Ho reunites with Mark and they plan their comeback overlooking the shimmering lights and skyscrapers of Hong Kong in the evening. Their conversation provides a meditative and dreamy moment in the midst of the action, exemplifying one of many ways the story deepened the 'original':

> Mark: 'I didn't notice the beauty of Hong Kong at night. But it doesn't last. Not worthwhile. Let's start all over again. After this time then leave Hong Kong.'
>
> Ho: 'Those are memories.'
>
> Mark: 'I'm still alive. I don't want to lose my whole life. I want to take back the thing I lost. Did you fight for a chance?'

On one level, both have been stripped of their dignity by Shing. And, according to their code of honor, they are obligated to take on Shing and his minions. At another level, these words have meaning for both Woo and Chow. In 1986, both had fallen on lean times – Woo exiled to Taiwan by Cinema City to make inane comedies; Chow, having achieved great popularity as a television actor, not as successful in movies.[20] Director and actor identified with the situation, and these words represent the risk they were taking with this movie. Also implicit in this description is Hong Kong's impermanence: from fishing village, settlement, port, smuggling depot, colony, territory, hybrid, 'the Pearl of the Orient,' to a city on fire, a city of transients, self-conscious about the 1997 handover, its current incarnation the 'Special Administrative Region.' As Woo himself notes, 'I knew that my movies were not only action, that I put a lot of ideas into them, but people just didn't notice.'[21] He believes that after *A Better Tomorrow* 'I became a real auteur. (I found my voice.)'

A similar respite, and perhaps the most deeply moving moment of the movie, occurs when Ho first encounters Mark following his prison release. The scene is set up with Ho watching from a distance, the camera showing what he sees. Mark is first glimpsed from behind, swinging his injured and braced leg, limping to the expensive Mercedes of Shing, and cleaning the windshield like a homeless person on the streets, doing his regular job. Enter Shing, dressed in the white cashmere coat of the Boss, flanked by his cronies. He tosses a few bills to the ground for Mark, telling him to get some lunch, and drives away. Cut to a parking garage, Mark seated in his makeshift home, eating takeaway from a styrofoam container. His clothing old and torn, his body dirty, food dripping from his mouth, he is revealed at his nadir. A close-up of Ho's face, seeing his friend in such a condition, speaks volumes about empathy and pain. Mark's shame, then his righteous anger and indignation, are apparent. He asks Ho, 'What are you still standing here for? I've waited for you for three years. Three years! Let's start all over again.' Here is another example of the emotion and intensity Woo puts into his movies.[22] First, the contrasts between Shing's world and Mark's show laborers as a force to be exploited and discarded when no longer useful. Shing has kept Mark to use him one last time to get Ho's old contacts as business clients. Ho's days will also be numbered, once Shing gets what he wants. Their 3-D jobs – dirty, dangerous, and dead-end – are contrasted with Shing's power, the power of money. As Shing tells Ho at the climax, 'I've money. Three days later, I'll be released. I've money. I can change black to white.'

Shing's reliance upon *jing* and disregard for the bond of brotherhood and *qing* respected by Ho and Kit is condemned in Woo's moral universe. Shing's values are apparent in the offhanded way he throws Mark money for food, meaning to shame him. Food, the most basic element of survival and integral to *jing*, also relates to *qing*, carrying associations with emotions and relationships, as in the expressions 'mother's milk,' and 'home cooking.' Yet for Shing, food and money relate only to the survival of the fittest. The cheap takeout Mark regularly eats, bought with Shing's money, 'eats away' at him, reminding Mark of the indignities suffered by him and Ho; he nurtures a plan that will lead to Shing's death. Unlike Shing, Mark and Ho realize the importance of striking a balance between *jing* and *qing*. Without *jing* there is no *qing*, but *jing* without *qing* means no righteousness. The Chinese title of *A Better Tomorrow* translates literally as *Heroic Characters*, *Essence of a Hero*, or *True Colors of a Hero*, underscoring the heroic nature of Mark and Ho. Murderers, sinners, though they may be, their selfless acts of love assure their redemption.

A Better Tomorrow 2 picks up where the first film leaves off, starting with another of Ho's dreams, this time depicted as a montage of scenes featuring Mark's character from the first movie and repeating the guns and money motif. The story grows from the earlier narrative, just as the Triad counterfeiting has expanded globally. Ho and Kit work undercover against the Triads, and a new character, Uncle Lung (Dean Shek), a retired Triad boss now legitimate businessman, is introduced. As the action progresses, Ken (Kenneth Tsang), the taxicab owner is reintroduced, and two new characters, the priest Sam (Peter Wang) and Ken (Chow Yun-fat), Mark's twin brother, appear. Woo imports the world of the first film into the second, and emphasizes the social interconnectedness of the ensemble as characters are reunited or remember the deceased who link them together. A shared past and an unfolding present emerge, underscored by using the same theme music. Remembering is part of who you are. The close-up facial expression of Ho, for example, released from prison and visiting Lung, creates a touching feeling of familiarity and shared experience, not unlike their second reunion later in the story when Ho also sees Ken for the first time, mistaking him for Mark. Similarly, Ken and Kit exchange curious glances at the cemetery, Kit also seeing Ken as the ghost of Mark, both recognizing their shared little brother status.

In contrast to the genuine warmth and mutual respect enjoyed by these characters in their relationships are the cold, calculated business practices of Ko (Kwan Shan). Ko's ruling passions are avarice and a desire to get rich, shared by every capitalist upstart. First Ko goes against his own boss, Lung, by turning his stock in the shipyard business over to a competitor. His power is most effective when unseen. His immediate goal is to gain control of the business in order to use it as a front to move counterfeit money around the world, his primary goal being to monopolize the counterfeiting market and enlarge his wealth. Lung's disappearance, but not death, is required to enable Ko to take over the company and blame Lung for the elimination of his competition. Likewise Ko requires

Lung's daughter Peggy to be killed, as she would have inherited her father's company. So Ko betrays his old boss several times over, even setting up Peggy and unflinchingly witnessing her murder; it is business as usual for him. Loved ones, even Peggy, who respectfully and affectionately calls him 'Uncle,' are expendable. Distrusting Ho, who is vouched for by some of the older Triad figures, Ko arranges for him to kill the entreprenurial 'Billie' (Kit's undercover identity), telling him that they suspect Billie is an agent. After Ho shoots his own brother, Ko offhandedly remarks, 'Actually, we haven't investigated this kid. We just wanted to test you. Welcome to the company.' Human life is dispensable for Ko, and the past, along with one's reputation, means nothing.

Loyalty, so crucial to the older Triad members, means nothing to Ko, and he readily sacrifices his own men when attacked by Lung, Ho, and the two Kens (who enter the property like Peckinpah's *Wild Bunch*) in the climax. 'Let those out there take care of it,' he instructs his sharpshooter. To Ko they are a 'disposable reserve army of labor … a mass of human material always ready for exploitation.'[23] And when Ko thinks his side is losing, he trusts in money, not men, to save him. '$100,000 if you kill one,' he shouts to his men as the invaders unleash their offensive. When one of Ko's partners, a Triad member who remembers Ho from the old days, says 'If there's money to be made, let's all make it together,' the words echo the lesson the partner has learned from Ko himself: money matters. In a closed meeting with prospective international business partners, Ko announces, 'If there's money to be made, open up the doors.' Ko is a 'bad man,' in Lung's words, because he too values *jing* over *qing*. Lung has the last word: 'You think a bad man always has a good end?', thereby echoing Shing's death at Ho's hands in the first movie.

Set against the unleashed avarice of Ko's world is another, fashioned in loving detail in two drawn-out scenes which firmly establish the values of the story, deepen the characterizations, and define relationships. Both scenes involve food. Again, food represents not only *jing*, survival and good health, but *qing*, the social relationships of empathy and concern, which in these heroes relates to their loyalty, friendship and honor, and defines them as heroes. In the first scene, which takes place in Ken's Four Seas Restaurant, a contrast is set up between the presence and absence of these values. The second scene, which involves Ken and Lung in Ken's apartment, is an intensely and deeply moving enactment of the meaning of *qing*.

Both scenes take place in New York, and they build the characterizations of Lung and Ken prior to their Hong Kong return.

Woo often establishes a setting in which to place his characters and develop their attributes, a technique that is employed to contextualize Ken in his restaurant. Ken's skill in the kitchen appears as second nature; he is helping his cook get a green card; he is looking out for the younger generation. The famous 'Eat my rice' scene involves a mafioso diner demanding extortion money and Ken's righteous response; it also serves as Woo's tribute to Scorsese's 'You talkin' to me?' *Taxi Driver* scene. One kind of family business intrudes upon another as the mafioso complains, 'This fucking fried rice stinks' and demands, 'You will pay me $1,000 a month … You don't pay me and I'll blow up your restaurant.' In an extraordinary performance, Chow Yun-fat delivers most of his lines in English, running the gamut of emotions from calm considerateness to playful taunting to sincere tenderness and indignant anger. First, he tries to accommodate the mobster, offering to feed him any time. Yet he refuses to compromise, offering only a quarter for protection money. 'You want to blow up my restaurant?,' Ken repeats, adding, tauntingly, 'You make me so nervous. I'm really scared about it. Mama mia!', earning a good laugh from his gathered friends and employees. As Ken instructs his waiter to bring more plates of rice, the waiter, puzzled, mutters in Cantonese, 'Damn those foreigners' and (under his breath) 'white devils.' When the mafioso throws the plate of rice in Ken's face, Ken gets up from his seat, a position equal to the gangster seated across the table, and goes down to the floor to scrape up the rice; he then returns to his seat. He laughs. The dialogue that follows provides a quiet and reflective moment before the explosive action to follow. Ken eats a handful of rice, and speaks: 'What's wrong with the food? It is beautiful for me.… For you, rice is nothing. But for us, rice is just like my father and my mother.' Then he warns, 'Don't fuck with my family.' Chameleonlike, he continues, over-emoting, covering his eyes as if crying: 'I am very hurt about it. I feel sorry with my rice.' Finally, banging on the table, he shouts, 'If you have any dignity, apologize to the rice right now!' As guns are drawn, Ken holds one to the mafioso's head, demanding, 'Open your fucking mouth and eat the rice. Eat it!' Even an intruding cop telling Ken to drop the gun can't stop the action that has been set in motion. De Niro-like, Ken asks, 'Are you talkin' to me? Wait a minute, let the asshole eat the rice first' – which, of course, he does, like a dog at his dish.

Ken and his Chinese restaurant family understand the importance of rice – for sustenance, of course, but also as representative of those emotive feelings associated with one's closest and most significant relationships: the family. The mafioso discerns none of this, seeing the rice only as a pretext for him in conducting his business. The emotional range of this scene changes so quickly and unexpectedly, despite the skirmish and gunshots between the involved parties, that feelings are laid bare, dominating the episode; these passions become more meaningful as the story continues.

The second New York scene comes on the heels of Ken's rescue of Lung from the mental hospital where he has spied *gweilo* ('white devil') attendants force-feeding oatmeal to him. In his home, Ken attempts to revive Lung, both by providing him with physical nourishment and by restoring his dignity. He does this with food. Carefully preparing a sumptuous meal for the old boss, Ken offers him sausage, eggs, a chicken leg – but all to no avail. The scene continues with Ken trying to pour a glass of milk down Lung's throat. As the camera pulls back, a large spread is revealed, numerous dishes lovingly provided to suit any palate. Lung remains almost catatonic as Ken pleads,

> It doesn't do you any good not to eat. You're not a baby. I won't make you eat, you eat yourself. Whether we are husband and wife or friends, brothers or sisters, the worst is that I can't help you. Do you think there is not a single good person left who can help you? Why don't you help yourself?

Clearly, Ken's understanding of what Lung needs is based upon his recognition of the interrelatedness of *jing* and *qing*; he fathoms not only the concern owed to a fellow human being but the obligation due to an 'uncle' of his brother, reinforced by Ho's earlier call from Hong Kong.

When Ken fails to bring Lung back from his dementia, he commits himself to a similar plight: 'If you want to be ill, I'll be ill with you. If you want to give up, I'll give up too. If you want to starve, I'll starve with you.' While Ken throws food and plates out of the window, empties his refrigerator contents onto the floor, and kicks oranges, Lung tremblingly and slowly raises a raw roast to his mouth and tries to bite it, then picks up a rolling orange. Ken, immediately on his knees before him, encourages him: 'Come on baby, come on.' Peeling the orange, he continues, 'Yeah, so nice. Let's eat,' gently putting an orange section into Lung's mouth. Cake follows. 'It's wonderful,' Ken encourages. The feelings conveyed in this extended scene measure the values of John Woo, reflecting his aspirations for a better world. Putting these feelings into words reduces them to homilies at best and clichés at worst – love for one's fellow man, helping others, and so on – a world in which good triumphs over evil, but at a cost. Yet it is the expressiveness of such a scene that communicates to an audience and provides an alternative to a world corrupted by capitalism.

This alternative is also represented by using the same theme music for both movies, but varying the lyrics of the theme song. In the first film, the song is most directly linked to the relationship between Ho and Mark, emphasizing their loyalty to each other under hard times and extreme circumstances; it is also linked to the restored relationship of Ho and his brother. In the second movie, the song most explicitly refers to Kit and his wife Jackie. Kit is mortally wounded while amassing evidence of the counterfeiting as Jackie gives birth to their child; unable to get to the hospital before dying, he calls her from a payphone, christening their child Sung Ho-yin – 'Spirit of Righteousness.' As Kit collapses, strains of the theme song, sung by Leslie Cheung, pervade the images, momentarily overshadowing them, as Kit dies and his blood-soaked body disappears. He is reborn (in his child, through his voice, and in the unnamed cop outside the hospital whom Ho mistakenly sees as his younger brother). The song concludes: 'No tears, not a word/ Blood pours out, but I don't want you to see/ You and I are heading towards a future/ I'll be with you to find a better tomorrow.' Woo puts great value on the innocence and purity of youth, be it the newborn infant in this movie or the close-up open faces of the choir children in the first film; they preserve the innocent in all ages through memory.[24]

The final scene of *A Better Tomorrow 2* includes an image of the wounded and bloody seated figures of Lung (in the center) and Ken and Ho (on each side). 'We're dying, can we leave?' Lung is asked, to which he replies, 'If you want to, go.' This is Godot-like turn if ever there was one: no one leaves. Ken the taxicab driver sees them thus, and the police find them this way, Lung telling the inspector, 'You better not retire yet, there's a lot more for you to do.' According to Tony Williams, the *mise-en-scène* of this image resembles portraits of the emperor, flanked by former mortal Kwan-tu, now the god Kwan-yu, deified because of his loyalty, and a friend, one on each side. 'There are no longer any friends around as those three' was earlier used in the film to describe Ho, Mark, and Kit. With this scene, however, the friendship of Lung, Ken, and Ho becomes just as meaningful.[25] However, the closing frames of the film show the younger generation back in New York, with the waitress's voice-over, from a letter to Ken, telling him about the success of the restaurant, asking him when he will return, and explaining that his soup recipe is the 'hottest item' on the menu. This is the same soup that Ken earlier offered the young men in his restaurant, after criticizing their imitation of Mark, because they wore the trademark duster and shades (not unlike young men in Hong Kong following the success of the first film). 'Got a cold? Eyes gone blind?' he queries. 'You look like circus clowns. Take it off and have some soup.' Freeze-framed as a group of kids in a sunny setting, the film ends on the note of 'a better tomorrow' where food is understood as *jing* and *qing* in the proper balance.

Woo's gangster heroes, with their working-class roots and little opportunity for advancement, are an illustration of Hong Kong's 3-D jobs, clearly visible in the predicament of John (a.k.a. Jeff) in *The Killer*.[26] This hitman with heart is generally referred to by characters in the movie according to his function, that of killer, and only his friend (Sidney) and girlfriend (Jenny) call him by a first name. A hit can go badly even though the killer has eliminated his target: if his face has been seen, his own life is in peril. 'Just kill him,' Johnny Weng (Shing Fui-on) orders his men. The younger, nameless killer who Weng hires for the job is John's 'replacement killer,' an interchangeable part, as Weng sees it, made even more anonymous and dehumanized by the shades he wears.

Similarly, Sidney (Chu Kong) represents another cog in the money-making machine of underworld business. A former hitman whose trigger hand is injured on the job, left with no employment compensation or insurance benefits, he has had to remake himself as a hitman manager, the agent who finds John work. A middleman between the big bosses and the muscle, his position is even more precarious than John's, because Sidney is responsible to both parties. He is loyal to John due to their friendship and shared job experience, but also responsible to the Triads for ensuring that the job is done properly. He is the company man who must satisfy the boss's demand (eliminate John) when the killer supposedly botches the job. Weng intentionally double-crosses both John and Sidney. Based upon Weng's own business practices – 'distrust everyone' – the double cross is in-evitable. And John and Sidney, as the laborers who have produced Weng's capital, have made themselves superfluous to him. The code of honor by which John and Sidney live affects them in their professional and personal lives. This code is essentially meaningless to Weng. 'Don't talk crap,' and 'cut the crap,' Weng berates Sidney. In contrast, obliged to make up for his betrayal of John, Sidney sacrifices himself for John's benefit; likewise John forgives Sidney for his betrayal – 'That's what friends are for, right?'

The intimacy between John and Sidney is reminiscent of the relationship between Mark and Ho in *A Better Tomorrow*; their friendship develops from the code they share and the trust they must have in one another to do their jobs and survive. The quiet night-time hillside exchange between Mark and Ho, in which they lament their own impermanence in *A Better Tomorrow*, is similar in tone and content to a scene in *The Killer*. John mourns, 'Our world is changing so fast. It never used to be like this. Perhaps we're too nostalgic.' And Sidney responds, 'Nostalgia is one of our saving graces.' These exchanges suggest the powerful bonds between the heroic characters, as well as the weakening of those ties in the movie world of contemporary Hong Kong.

It is John's mirror image, Inspector Li (Danny Lee), who best describes this world, the world of Johnny Weng, a world Woo scorns: 'Life is cheap. It only takes one bullet.' In this dog-eat-dog environment of greed, killing, and guns, however, the single bullet that ends Sidney's suffering is delivered with love and tenderness. Sidney, who has demeaned himself by begging Weng for John's money, secures the payment by force; his face beaten to an almost unrecognizable pulp, wounded and near death, he returns John's money at the church rendezvous. Knowing that John always saves the last bullet, he relies upon their friendship and shared code of honor, telling John he doesn't want to 'die like a dog.' With Sidney unable to fight and Weng's army on its way, and a bloodbath guaranteed, John saves Sidney from an ignoble death. 'Am I a dog?' Sidney asks John. 'No,' John replies, 'You're a great man.'

The strong bond between these two friends, based upon *qing*, runs parallel to that between the cop partners, Li and Chang (Kenneth Tsang). Just as Sidney is the older killer ('I've had my day'), Chang is the older cop, and both serve as father figures and brothers to their counterparts, John and Li. The third friendship, that between killer and cop, develops in a variety of ways throughout the film. First, both characters are presented as principled men: John may be a gun for hire, but he kills only bad guys who deserve to die; Li is a good cop determined to get the bad guys, and he has no interest in gaining recognition or promotion; both are expert marksmen and caring human beings. Both men make mistakes but accept the responsibility for their actions. John has accidentally blinded the singer Jenny (Sally Yeh) while protecting them both from an assailant, and Li has inadvertently caused a woman's death by heart attack when shooting a murderer. Dialogue throughout emphasizes the similar characteristics of the two; Li remarks, 'We have something in common.' Jenny even mistakes Li for John at Club Nine. The rapport between the two men is humorously established in the cartoonish 'face-off' in Jenny's apartment, in which the two men, out of consideration for Jenny, who cannot see what is happening, pretend to be old friends cajoling and teasing each other. As complications ensue, involving teacups and added characters, the scene plays out like a Roadrunner–Wylie Coyote cartoon; Woo says he was influenced by 'Spy vs. Spy' comic strips.[27] Most significantly, the actors are similarly shot, and camera angles and framing are duplicated for each character throughout the film; in the scene where Li assists the wounded John, Woo shoots the scene as if John is looking into a mirror – that is, they become mirror images.

The friendship is ensured by two actions performed by John and recognized and appreciated by Li. Li tells Chang, 'He won't let the little girl die,' when a child becomes the helpless victim of a stray bullet during a beach shootout. At the hospital, during the 'face-off' between Li and John, the cop sees the concern on the killer's face for the child, that he 'has heart,' and from that moment their friendship is born. Just as John has used his hand-wrapped scarf to staunch the child's bleeding, he has earlier used his neckscarf to protect the wound of the accidentally blinded singer until help arrives. When Li connects the two events with the same perpetrator, what he has previously imagined through the portraits of the sketch artist become a reality: 'There's something heroic about him.... He acts like he has a dream, eyes full of passion.... This man is not a cold-blooded murderer.' When he sees for himself Jenny's loyalty to John and the sincerity of John's love for Jenny and his conviction to restore her sight, Li crosses the line from cop-by-numbers, to abettor and accessory, in the name of friendship.

Fairness, Li determines, in this ruthless and corrupt world, is no longer tied to a legal system of cops and courts. He and John have meted out moral righteousness), but in different ways. In a brutal world where codes of honor are nearly obsolete, Li, like Kit at the end of *A Better Tomorrow*, opts for ethical rather than lawful justice. As Johnny Weng grovels to officers arriving on the scene, Li kills him for being evil incarnate and in obligation to his friend, knowing full well that he will now be regarded as a criminal.

It's a romanticized and sad story, all the stronger because of the hardness of the world it is up against. Woo sincerely emphasizes the raw emotionalism of loss and regret. While many Western critics applaud his ability to bring new life to worn-out and clichéd genres, they just as often misread his sensibility, which is playful but never campy or disingenuous.[28] He is hardly an Eastern Quentin Tarantino. The lyrics and melodies of the songs used in *The Killer* very directly relate the movie's messages and values.[29] Life for these outsiders is loneliness, anguish, and lack of acceptance. Obviously, tragedy will come, but their actions will be noble. Woo used popular singer Sally Yeh to play Jenny, and, besides her sultry singing voice, she brought to the part a fragility easily broken but a resilience that is flexible when confronted by a deeply depraved world. The singer's other featured song, from John's apartment, also suggests the pain and fatalism of this story, but, like the songs of the *Better Tomorrow* films, looks towards a brighter future.[30] Both John and Li are deeply moved and comforted by these songs; the music brings spiritual contentment and balance to their lives. Despite the ends they meet, the repetition of both songs at the film's conclusion reiterates the importance of their values and celebrates their friendship. Li's last words, uttered in close-up, are 'my friend,' and his memory of John runs on-screen. Then, a harmonica-playing John, redeemed and resurrected through the power of Christian love, is featured playing the theme song. He is framed in a window casement overlooking the church. The movie's close reinforces their world and what it represents, set against that of Johnny Weng's avarice, loutishness, and savagery.

Woo has taken offense at the criticism lodged against him that his movies have glorified gangsters and recruited for the Triads. After the record box office of *A Better Tomorrow*, Hong Kong males did take to the streets in the dusters and shades favored by Mark, despite the heat and humidity (and Alain Delon wrote Chow Yun-fat a personal note of thanks for boosting the sales of his signature sunglasses).[31] The effect was more a fashion statement, perhaps, because *The Killer*, although successful internationally, did not do well in Hong Kong. For *Hard-*

courtesy of Colin Geddes; permission of John Woo

SHOT OF TEQUILA   Chow Yun-fat in *Hard-Boiled*

Boiled, Woo put both protagonists on the right side of the law as role models, but this film also didn't pass muster in Hong Kong. Woo comments thus on what has been most important to him in his movies.

> Strong visuals, original action, sympathetic heroes and villains, and a story which forces these elements to the hilt combine to create emotionally powerful situations. This is what I look for and create. A film should bring out your emotions, whether it's happiness or pain. I hope my movies will fill people's lives and, through their expanded feelings, teach them love and honor.

The English title *Hard-Boiled* puts Woo's movie firmly in the film noir cop tradition. The literal translation of its Chinese title, *Hot-Handed God of Cops*, suggests the Chinese titles of Clint Eastwood's *Dirty Harry* movies. Woo also uses a Western jazz club, and his cop of the title is Tequila, a jazz clarinet player. 'Alan'/Tony (Tony Leung Chiu-wai), the deep-cover cop who bonds with Tequila, functions in a way reminiscent of the mirror relationship of John and Li in *The Killer*, but also draws upon the older cop/younger cop tradition of countless Hollywood films. The moral dilemma facing Alan, easily seen in his tear-filled eyes when he shoots Uncle Hui at point-blank range, as well as in Tequila's guilt at unknowingly killing a fellow cop, which he tries to assuage as the narrative develops, borrows not only from Hollywood movies but also from martial arts films in which young masters are indirectly responsible for the deaths of fathers, friends, or masters. The climactic hospital scene, in which the two cops join forces to battle with hundreds of bad guys with guns and explosives, comes straight out of *wuxia-pian* movies, where a lone warrior fights hordes of enemies. Tequila's name pays homage to William Holden's character Pike in *The Wild Bunch*, drinking tequila just before the climactic bloodfest. The name also provides a contemporary reference, coming from the popular tequila-and-soda slammer which Tequila drinks, popular in Hong Kong when Woo was making the movie. Woo further updates the story by cutting between Tequila's jazz set and a montage of Hong Kong newspaper headlines about illegal gunrunning and crime.

Tony (known as Alan to the Triads) and Tequila are presented as characters given few options; they serve to reflect the harsh social reality for the many stepped on or over in a capitalist society. Tony has lost his sense of identity immersed in the Triad world and acts the part, beating and murdering without hesitation. The numerous paper cranes he has made to signify each death show Alan's loyalty to the family; all Tony wants is a passport and money to leave Hong Kong and live elsewhere. At least he has a boat to call home; Tequila is looking for a place to live. 'What a drag this is,' he complains, searching the newpaper, 'I can't even afford a pigsty. There's no way I can. How can I get hitched without a decent place for the boss to live? Just because I'm single I can't even get government housing. I'll take to the streets.'

The relationship between the two cops is closely developed in the symbolic interior space of the hospital morgue, ironically a place of death, where their intense intimacy is born. Trying to figure out the situation, they talk seriously about their lives and dreams; they also joke, Tequila jesting, 'If we die they can just chuck us in here.' A big brother's concern for a little brother, as well as a little brother's respect for his elder, emerges – a reminder of Ho and Kit's relationship in the *A Better Tomorrow* movies. The blossoming of their friendship is all the more fragile set against the hell breaking loose inside and outside the hospital. When the violence breaks in on them, via Mad Dog, they fight for their lives by the code and great courage and professionalism they share. Tony grabs a live electrical wire and Tequila's marksmanship is breathtaking.

Set against the plight of the cops is the decadent lifestyle led by Johnny Wong (Anthony Wong), dressed in expensive clothes, chauffeured in luxury cars, and hanging out in smart clubs, always ringed by a group of bad characters to carry out his dirty work. As Johnny schemes to eliminate local competition and gain control of the international gun trade, he can hypocritically tell Alan that he admires his loyalty to Uncle Hui (Kwan Hoi-shan) while he has already devised a way to get Alan to betray his boss. Alan has just eliminated one of Johnny's partners; according to the code of criminals, Johnny should avenge his partner's death. Yet Johnny operates not by a code of loyalty but according to his own self-interest (*jing* over *qing*). Rather than kill Alan, he uses him; pretending to trust him, he also has his henchmen keep an eye on him, and doesn't trust Alan to finish off a snitch.

'Everyone knows you have the Midas touch,' Alan tells Johnny. Johnny bolsters the connection between guns and money: 'With your talents,' he advises Alan, 'you should be making big bucks. My arms business is real money. It's worldwide. Wherever there's war, there's Johnny. Most things go in and out of fashion – except war, my friend. When I say real money, I mean it.' So much for Woo's dream of pacifism. In a perverted twist, this Johnny never comes marching home. He functions as the greedy and power-hungry nemesis to be confronted by the cop buddies. Unlike some of Woo's other villains, he is present on-screen only long enough to set events in motion or to complicate the action. Like other villains, he disregards the value of human life. Johnny gives the order for his men to take innocent hospital patients hostage; rapidly firing his semi-automatic, he mows them down without a second thought, and he even kills his own loyal man, Mad Dog (Philip Kwok). 'I kill whoever's in my way,' he smirks. As Marx puts it, 'One capitalist always kills many.'[32]

If Johnny represents the new way of doing business, Uncle Hui embodies the older, traditional Triad way. Johnny complains that Hui 'doesn't want big bucks, but I sure as hell do. His prices are killing my market. I'm losing out. It's what you've got, not how you made it.' For Johnny, Hui is behind the times and in the way. 'Commercial wars … increase gigantically in the infancy of Modern Industry,' Marx reminds us, and 'the birth of the latter is heralded by a great slaughter of the innocents.'[33] When Johnny traps Hui and his boys at the warehouse, Hui asks that his men be spared and willingly sacrifices himself. _Qing_ remains important to him. Heartfelt, Alan wishes Hui to retire in Hawaii, and he genuinely cares for the old man. The special relationship Hui has with his boys is earlier foreshadowed in the scene where Alan visits him at his home. He arrives bearing a gift, beef jerky, which he knows Uncle Hui enjoys, and the elderly man's facial expression shows his delight and appreciation. Peeling pears and trying to get Alan and his boys to eat, one of them remarks: 'Mr. Hui treats us like kids, always at us to eat more.' The avuncular Hui responds, 'I'm an old timer. And I know that respect and face are vital. I'm old-fashioned.'

Also set apart from Johnny is his muscle, Mad Dog, whose firepower is matched only by his physical prowess. Throughout most of the story, Mad Dog follows his orders. When Tony's cover is blown, Mad Dog, having sized up Alan, tries to kill him, angrily telling him, 'You know who I hate? Two groups of people: fucking cops and creeps who betray their old bosses. You bastard.' Mad Dog is a part of the older established Triad code and faults Alan for betraying Hui, not Johnny. Even Mad Dog knows where to draw the line and also judges the bosses by the code. He not only questions his boss's decision to take the innocent patients hostage, but refuses to kill them as well. Tony and Mad Dog eventually stand off against each other. As a sign of respect, and living by a shared code, they recognize the expertise of the other, give face, and afford the other a fair chance. Mad Dog and Tony lower their guns, place them on the floor, and instruct the dozen patients huddled between them to leave. Abruptly Wong enters, Tony escapes, and the patients are gunned down by Wong. When Mad Dog tells his boss 'You didn't have to kill them,' Wong barks 'Don't question me! Bastard, go on!' Mad Dog, with hatred and disgust on his face, shoots at Wong twice. Out of bullets, he drops his gun, which falls, slow-mo, as he is gunned down by Wong; Woo cuts to a close-up of his prone body. Clearly, Woo suggests, Mad Dog's boss betrays him, and this number-two villain shares in the mutual respect for the heroic code.

The female cop Teresa, Tequila's estranged girlfriend, plays a similar (but more active) role to the women in *A Better Tomorrow* 1 and 2. Through her connection with babies, music, and beautiful flowers, she shares with other Woo female characters an association with innocence and virtue. Just as the cellist Jackie gives birth to 'the spirit of righteousness' and singer Jenny is characterized, despite her blindness, as optimistic and full of life, Woo gives Teresa a 'feminine' softness by linking her with babies. Several close-up shots of the newborns in the hospital nursery, being bathed, rocked, bottle-fed, are intercut with her yearning gaze upon them, suggesting her respect for life as well as her desire to marry Tequila and have children. (In the midst of the nursery evacuation Tequila asks her, 'You don't want this many kids, do you?' and she responds, 'Yeah. Sure, why not?') But, unlike Jackie and Jenny, as a cop she's a part of the 'man's world.' Although she is not permitted to carry a gun (by Hong Kong regulation), Teresa is entrusted to know about the super-secret vigilante force, Tequila trusts her to begin the police assault at the right time, and she is instrumental in devising strategy and carrying out the hospital rescue. She breaks the fire alarm glass when superintendent Chan is making no headway with the doctor in charge, and she notices the abandoned babies and assists in their deliverance. When a tough slaps her, she uses the gun she has lifted to shoot him. Teresa exhibits a matter-of-factness in her dealings, which suggests a no-nonsense approach to life; she is a survivor, not just a dreamer. Whether at the office returning Tequila's underwear to him after their breakup, or slapping Johnny's thug in the nursery ('I'd like you to shut up. You're scaring the babies to death.'), she's got the chutzpah to save the babies and teach Tequila to be her equal. When Tequila confides to Tony, 'Dreams are supposed to be attainable, like mine,' we expect that his dream will become a reality.

Woo says: 'The babies signify purity and hope. Even though the world is filled with ugliness, hatred, and crisis, I still think there's a hope for the future. We should cherish and protect these new lives.'[34] Teresa exemplifies this desire to cherish and protect (overprotecting and serving), and, as such, she is also linked to Tequila. Together they have stuffed the babies' ears with cottonwool to protect their hearing from the gunblasts, and, at Teresa's instructions, Tequila single-handedly saves the last baby to be evacuated, whose parents anxiously await their infant's return. During the rescue Tequila sings him a lullaby ('nursery rap'), describes the raging violence as 'X-rated action,' wipes away splattered blood from the infant's face ('Baby, excuse me'), coos to him reassuringly ('Give me a smile'), and kisses him twice. Woo gives us a kinder, gentler man to whom the beatific infant touchingly responds. Repeating Mark's offering of himself in place of the baby-faced Kit, Ken's rescue of the infantile Lung, and John's saving of the little girl on the beach, Chow Yun-fat reprises his role as a humanized character with great capacity for compassion, self-sacrifice and humor. 'As a Christian, I am strongly influenced by Christian beliefs about love, sin, redemption,' avows Woo.[35] While his 'hard-boiled' cop Tequila is on the right side of the law, there is blood on his hands. Tequila's concern for the baby, as well as his empathy, also stresses Agape and the proper human relations established by *qing*, and when the 'little pisser' puts out the cop's burning trouser leg by peeing on it, the baby naturally enacts the correct relationship, returning the consideration. 'You saved the day, there, you little pisspot. Thanks a lot,' Tequila responds, as they jump together from the burning building.

The enflamed building site suggests the intense passions which have erupted and points to a very human story. For the characters who survive a trial by fire, the hospital is a place of healing and rebirth, as symbolized by the babies, a place for birth. Similar to the church setting in *The Killer*, the space represents a respite from the harshness of a vulgar and violent world; both spaces are invaded, but arise from the ashes, phoenix-like – literally in *The Killer*, with the final shot of the church in the distance, and figuratively in the watery imagery as *Hard-Boiled* concludes. Tony sails away from Hong Kong under bright skies and calm seas to a better life.

Woo has described the hospital as a 'microcosm for Hong Kong, surrounded by darkness and chaos.'[36] The explosion of the hospital and the weapons arsenal epitomizes a 'city on fire,' a place of death, destruction, and uncertainty. Since these forces come inside, the hospital-under-siege scenes have led most commentators to describe *Hard-Boiled* as Woo's 'over-the-top' movie. Besides the heavy artillery, the stockpiled arsenal, and the flying corpses, this extended scene, with a running time of more than half an hour, includes numerous face-offs – Tequila against Mad Dog, Mad Dog against Tony, Tequila against Johnny, hundreds of baddies against the good guys, each first framed as a man with a gun facing a man with a gun. The redundancy of these face-offs goes beyond good versus evil, to reflect the open face-to-face encounter of Hong Kong and the Mainland. The 1997 handover looms large, present in Woo's signature face-offs interspersed through all his gangster movies, whether Li and John at Jenny's apartment in *The Killer*, Ho and Shing dockside in *A Better Tomorrow*, even Ken's pyrotechnics with the Mafioso in New York or with Ko's assassin in Hong Kong, in the sequel. Consider Woo's contradictory statement:

> I have no intention to talk about politics in my films. I'm not interested in politics and there's no political system that's perfect. People are always using politics to gain certain power for themselves. But subconsciously I can't help putting my own personal feelings towards some politics into the film. For instance, I do have very strong feelings towards 1997.[37]

Woo's gangster movies create a political and social subtext of early capitalism as a bloody battlefield. The return of Hong Kong to the Mainland, in light of the PRC's recent market-economic policies, as well as its guarantee of 'one country, two systems,' links the handover and its aftermath to capitalist expansion. Woo's rawest and most brutal film, the 1990 *Bullet in the Head* would draw upon the face-off motif but make it more horrifying, its title emphasizing the controlling metaphor – a gun to the head, time running out.

FOUR

SO MANY WAYS TO BE
COPS AND RASCALS

Woo's films began the genre known as 'heroic bloodshed,' a term first used, according to Logan, by Rick Baker and his staff as a film category in the British Hong Kong fanzine *Eastern Heroes*.[1] With *A Better Tomorrow* Woo reinvented the gangster film and was commercially successful. Others took the opportunity to explore the genre, like Ringo Lam with his 1987 *City on Fire*, released six months after *A Better Tomorrow*. Lam, after leaving Hong Kong disappointed with the television industry, studied film at Toronto's York University and took Canadian citizenship. He returned to Hong Kong in 1981 to make movies. He made four comedies, based on scripts written by others; all were successful at the box office. But Lam, who generally dislikes comedies, wasn't happy. When Karl Maka gave him the chance to make whatever he wanted, Lam wrote the script for and developed the first *On Fire* film. Lam selects the English titles for his movies, and chose 'On Fire,' he says, to give them 'a sense of energy, of action.'[2] Unlike Woo's romanticized protagonists and dream-like settings, Lam's 'On Fire' films, including *City on Fire* (1987), *Prison on Fire 1* and *2* (1987, 1991), and *School on Fire* (1988), present conflictive characters and hard-hitting urban realism. Lam provides a social critique of controversial issues that most would prefer to ignore: street violence and abuses of the police, prison and school systems. If Woo films his dreams, Lam shoots his nightmares.

Lam calls his films 'docudramas'; his social realism is gritty, intense and realistic – he makes 'dirty' movies. Growing out of actual events or institutionalized conditions, they reflect the social reality of 1980s' and 1990s' Hong Kong.[3] The director's technique is a 'you are there' approach to filmmaking, cinéma vérité style, with live shooting and tracking camera, which further extends the realism. Besides the actors, the visual settings are Lam's stars, like the literal teeming Hong Kong streets and neon of *City on Fire*. Lam moves his actors through a physical space with its own explosive character, and the camera eye grabs and pulls the viewer into the setting through its perspective. Lam's 'show and tell' is a Hong Kong accurately described as a 'city on fire,' a site of contestation, where anxieties and tensions ignite. It is a place of fervent passions and fears of the unknown, growing out of the uncertainties following the 1984 Joint Declaration and the escalation in violent crime. The prevailing attitude is 'grab as much money as possible and be prepared to get out,' observes Terence Chang.

Like Woo, Lam puts his personal feelings into his movies. 'Each film comes from inside of myself. I am a human being. I am a part of this world, and, what I feel, maybe people can feel too,' Lam relates.[4] When Woo says he puts himself into his movies, he does so by walking in his characters' shoes when he writes and when he directs his actors (especially Chow Yun-fat's roles); by naming good and evil characters ('John' and 'Johnny,' respectively) after himself; and, literally, by making cameo appearances (the Taiwanese cop who haunts Ti Lung in *A Better Tomorrow*, the bartender/retired cop and Tequila's friend in *Hard-Boiled*). Woo is close to his characters in a way that Lam is not. After an early acting stint, Lam decided to remain behind the camera; furthermore, he prefers editing to shooting a movie. These inclinations may point to a more distant relationship to his characters, but there exists, nevertheless, a closeness to human feelings and an understanding of them in context. 'I never have problems with making stories'; Lam remarks, 'I only have problems with getting exactly what I want, which is what I'm feeling about a present moment. And I bring this feeling into my film.'[5]

Lam's characters are often hardened and self-serving, sometimes ordinary, and frequently capable of extraordinary action under stress, even though the outcome seems ultimately meaningless. Their moral conflicts come from within and without; they are simultaneously introspective and action-oriented; their motivations are inchoate. They unleash violence, desperation, and pain on themselves and each other abruptly and unexpectedly, suggesting a war of all against all. The particular environment and detailed social setting, seen clearly through Lam's camera eye, is an integral and crucial factor in explaining a character's emotions – for instance, an ambitious cop interested in promotion, a harried teacher trying to help his students. Oppressive conditions and the characters' extreme emotional turmoil contribute to the drama – their feelings of powerlessness, guilt, fear, and cruelty fight it out with nobler sentiments. Lam's carefully chosen music and color tones represent the feel of his movies, like the cool blues and saxophone in *City on Fire*. In these ways, Lam establishes a visceral look and sense that is raw, rough, immediate and powerful.

At first look Lam's stories are bare-boned. An undercover cop is torn between his duty and his friendship with a criminal; there's no honor among thieves, and one of them takes revenge; a small child can testify against an underworld figure and the criminals try to eliminate her while the cops try to protect her. A second and deeper look, however, reveals the complexities of narratives built on strong character and compelling visuals to tell the story. As a film rolls, Lam twists and turns recognizable genre elements to circumvent narrative expectations. In his own words,

> What I like to do is make up the story according to a formula, then break it down again, try to mess it up out of control. You shift it around, and the audience will lose direction. They will find their emotions out of control. They will become more involved. I push the audience. That's the way I make stories.[6]

With his inventive *mise en scène*, Lam fits characters into an environment, or reveals how they don't fit; he positions actors within the frame based on their developing relationships. Camera angles are also intimately tied to characters' emotions and setting. Rhythmical editing builds tension and sets the range and degree of emotions. Film school taught Lam how to analyze a movie; experience gave him the confidence to create 'film threats' which agitate and disturb audiences.

The literally translated term in Lam's *On Fire* films is not 'On Fire' but 'Turbulence.' *Dragon Tiger Turbulence* (*City on Fire*) grew from Lam's thinking about a newspaper story detailing a jewelry store robbery. The cops were at the scene, but failed to apprehend any of the criminals. Lam began wondering: 'All the police surround them, but still the baddies can escape! I thought about it. Why? It's the inefficiency of the policemen. That was what drew my attention. That led to my thinking about the hero. Who is the hero?'[7] Lam interviewed cops and criminals

courtesy/permission of Media Asia; © Star Filmed Entertainment

EXPLOITED   Chow Yun-fat in Ringo Lam's *City on Fire*

while working on this story, and he noticed the poor appearance of the robbers as well as their lack of education. He cast Chow Yun-fat as an undercover cop, 'victimized by his own feelings,'[8] and Danny Lee, who had become known for his portrayals of cops, against type as one of the robbers.

Violent street crime in Hong Kong, including intentional homicide, assault, rape, robbery and theft, escalated between 1981 and 1986; the same period saw a 185 per cent increase in drug trafficking and possession.[9] The streets of Hong

Kong serve not simply as a backdrop but as the emotional terrain of the movie. Nathan Road and Cheung Lok and Nanking Streets, where high-rise buildings and shops alternate with makeshift stalls, are lined with cars and the sidewalks thronged with people on the move or doing business, with people often running in fear or confusion. Much of the story unfolds in the streets, in both daytime and night-time scenes. The film opens on a blue screen and the sound of a saxophone, with a slow pan down into a night-time city of neon lights and fluorescent blues as the camera introduces the city and drops its audience into the midst of the action. A desperate man navigates through Kowloon market stalls, pursued by a group of thugs. A hand-held camera tracks alongside the man, an exposed undercover cop, and it stops only to record his multiple stabbings and bloody death, all over so quickly that the audience is left reeling. A stall owner who witnessed the murder refuses to give evidence to the cops. Similarly, later in the film, Ko Chow (Chow Yun-fat) is chased by cops through traffic-heavy streets; the camera follows, photographing the blurred images of the city as Ko Chow experiences them, with a sense of urgency; when he jumps into an open truck, the camera tracks the streets unfurling behind. These two men-in-the-streets scenes graphically and vividly show a Hong Kong outside the tour books. The daytime jewelry store heist takes place on the second floor of a building, but much of the tension of the scene comes from the threat of invasion from outside – the invasion of the criminals to begin with, but extended by the other people, including a building manager, a delivery boy, customers, and the beat cops who come into the building and complicate the already tense situation. The 'outside' comes in and then the robbers take the action out into the streets: there is a shoot-out, two police cars crash and explode, and the street bursts into flames. While people flee in terror, fire trucks arrive and the streets are bathed in chemicals to prevent the fire spreading. Such is the characterization of the city in this movie: dangerous, tumultuous, intense.

The second robbery, in which Ko Chow takes part undercover, occurs in the evening at the height of Christmas shopping. As chimes ring out 'Joy to the World,' and brightly lit streets and decorated store windows welcome shoppers, the robbers move in on the Tai Kwong Gold Company, which directly opens onto the street with a large plate-glass window. Surveillance cops doze. Dozens of cuts and camera positions register the rapid-fire action as well as the ensuing confusion and out-of-control feeling when the heist goes wrong. As the cops spring into

ARMED AND DANGEROUS   Ringo Lam's *City on Fire*

action, long and medium shots give some semblance of understanding, while close-ups register emotions of shock, anger, and pain; the collision editing matches the violence and the authentic realism of a shoot-out. Cars crash, gunplay is fast and furious, and criminals retreat to a darkened warehouse to regroup. The cops count three dead, five hurt.

The protagonist, Ko Chow, characterized as a man whose choices are made for him, is forced to deal with the consequences. Already harboring guilt over betraying a former confidant and criminal, and haunted by nightmares of his death, he is reluctant to remain undercover and tries to resign. But his duty to the force and obligations to his family prevent him from doing so, despite the pressure put on him by his girlfriend to put her before his job. Likewise, the criminal Fu (Danny Lee) seems to have had little choice. 'My father was a thief, same as my grandpa. I hope my son will not be a thief,' he confides. His son having gone when his wife left him for another man, Fu can think only about spending the money from the robbery. Unable to read, he can't imagine using the money to start a small business, as Ko Chow suggests. Trapped in oppressive circumstances, both men suffer. Fu, the only survivor of the robbery, is handcuffed and incarcerated; Ko Chow dies like a dog, unable to explain to his girlfriend or his uncle. Their manhood toughened by circumstances, but also vulnerable, both men are characterized by the sax tracks which play throughout, driving and mournful. The saxophone also accompanies the theme song, sung by Filipina Maria Cordero, with her raw and harsh voice, belting out the song in a red-lit club scene like an inferno, appropriate for this 'city on fire.'[10]

Ko Chow and Fu come together numerous times, from their initial rendezvous in a public park, where Ko Chow waits, dancing and singing to himself, to their confrontation in a cemetery and their final moments under siege. Lam frames them equally on screen, their misery shared; when they are on camera with others, they always look to one another for a response. Fu even asks a photographer to snap a picture of them with their bar-girl companions, and Lam's camera reveals a brotherly Fu enjoying his friend's company; Ko Chow is deeply affected. When they are holed up before the robbery, the men share a smoke and, hearing music from a party across the way, hang out the window casement enjoying the night air. The camera is angled directly across from them, and the pair are framed by the window, trapped.

The helpless plight of both characters is not unrelated to the difficulties Ko Chow's uncle, Lau (Sun Yeuh), is having on the job. 'They don't give a shit about me … more than thirty years. My position was made with my life,' he laments. Replacing him is John Chan (Roy Cheung), an upstart 'kid,' interested only in cracking the jewelry ring case and claiming credit. The conflict between old-timer Lau and newcomer Chan is established early on, immediately following the first jewelry store robbery. Chan appears on-scene, face covered with a handkerchief, characterizing him as giving no 'face.' He refers to Lau as 'Uncle,' which suggests familiarity, and Lau corrects him. Their superior appoints Chan to head a special unit to crack the case. Chan is officious and full of self-importance. He can cite regulations chapter and verse to rationalize whatever he wants to do. Chan, who suspects Ko Chow of arms trading, has his men tail the undercover. When they lose him, Chan is furious and shouts, 'I don't care how you do it. I just want him, got to show that old guy something.' Chan condones police brutality and watches as Ko Chow is beaten for information, a harrowingly realistic scene. He also sets up the strategy for entrapping the gang for the 'big catch,' and almost botches the job through indolence. When the special-unit task force is removed from the job to save taxpayers' money, Chan's men sleep on the job. They are unaware of the robbery until it's almost over, and the officer fatalities are their fault. That only one of the criminals is taken alive is also Chan's responsibility. His dogged refusal to force a peaceful surrender results in the criminals' panic. He hurriedly explains to his superior, 'Chow, Sir, I didn't let you down. Our special unit has been set up for two months. And we broke a big case. I'll report to you soon.' Lau, having glimpsed the wasted Ko Chow, can stand it no longer, and hits Chan with a brick, knocking him to the ground. But this irresponsible cop – endemic to the force, Lam would have us believe – will have to wait until his next reincarnation, as the prison official in *Prison on Fire*, to receive the punishment he deserves, at the hands of the criminal character played by Chow Yun-fat.

Both *Prison on Fire* films were scripted by Nam Yin, with plot revisions by Lam. The stories are based on 'real life experience' of prison, from the unit leaders to the gang fights and hunger strikes.[11] In each, Lam takes on the prison system as a corrupt and inhumane institution. Surviving prison life is the theme, and Lam accentuates the brotherhood between men trying to survive. Again, the characterizations are firmly rooted in social relations within an oppressive, authoritarian environment. *Prison on Fire* was released nine months after *City on Fire*, Nam Yin's first draft script was written in seven days, and the film was shot in twenty days. Perhaps the speed of its creation influenced the tone of this story – it is hard hitting and genuine, neither glorifying the criminals nor sensationalizing the events that transpire. The prisoners' solidarity, which allows them to survive, is honestly portrayed. The everydayness of events, established routine and accepted practices of the inmates and their keepers thread the film's narrative.

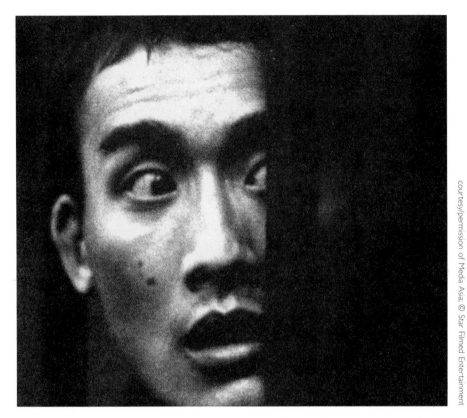

FEAR   Tony Leung Ka-fai in Ringo Lam's *Prison on Fire*

In *Discipline and Punish*, Foucault reminds us to judge a society by its prisons, and that is what Lam does in this film. The Hong Kong prison system remains overcrowded by one-third.[12] The system itself, Lam asserts, is inhumane and oppressive; the people within it incompetent and irresponsible at best, self-serving, abusive and perverse at worst. Critic Law Kar suggests that *Prison on Fire* works as an 'allegory of political confrontation between different groups in a Hong Kong going through the transition towards 1997.'[13] Clearly, the prison setting, with its fighting among inmates, the clashes between inmates and authorities, as well as the kill-or-be-killed competition among the Triads, mirrors the unrest of a pressure-cooker society. Marginalized working-class people call to mind the inmates. The prison-like features of the Vietnamese refugee detention centers are reminiscent of this movie's setting, as are the sweat-shop conditions of Hong Kong's most poorly paid laborers, its women.

Lam turns his gaze to the educational system in *School on Fire*. Using a solo bagpipe theme, he holds the British accountable for the ineffectuality and collapse of the schools.

> The bagpipes are very Scottish. When I was young, I used to hear your (British inter-viewer's) national anthem: (*sings*) Dah-dah-dah-dah dah-dah! (*laughs*). Hong Kong is a colony, and our education is stuck in this system. If the system is going wrong we have to go back to: Who made this?[14]

If the prison serves as a microcosm for Hong Kong in the *Prison* films, the school in this movie functions likewise; Lam lays the blame upon the British for Hong Kong's current state of uncertainty and upheaval. In counterpoint to the bagpipe instrumental, Lam intersperses a chorus of young voices, alternating male and female choirs, representing youthful hopes and fears.[15]

A simple story of Triads invading the schools, recruiting members to sell drugs and fight, the movie becomes much more as the parties involved – teachers, students, administrators, parents, cops, and Triads – come into sharp focus. Teachers, with one exception, are portrayed as uncaring and their curriculum as irrelevant to students' needs in preparing for life. One teacher's daily lesson is always 'self-study'; another punishes students – 'copy that sentence 1,000 times.' The principal is weak and hypocritically maintains order while striking deals with the Triads in the boys' toilet. The physical condition of the building is dilapidated, with paint peeling from the walls, and the overcrowded Kowloon facility is squeezed between tenements and Kai Tak Airport, competing with the constant noise of air traffic nearby. The working-class parents shown are too preoccupied trying to eke out a living to involve themselves in their children's education, much less their lives. Cops walking their beat at the school warn a Triad member to move his Mercedes, then comment to each other: 'You see, they've even got Benz. What's the use of being a police?' The Triads exploit young kids eager for some cash, a better life, and a way to belong, somewhere, anywhere; young girls prostitute themselves to support their boyfriends, who betray them. Such are the complications of this no-holds-barred look at Hong Kong's teenagers.

Besides being in the grip of raging hormones, the kids are enraged that nobody seems to care. A 'lost generation,' they show their disrespect for the teachers by throwing objects, using obscene language, disrupting classroom teaching, and engaging in physical violence. This 'school on fire' literally burns when one student locks herself in the school library and sets it ablaze. Lam's subject reflects a general concern with juvenile and youth crime, including shoplifting, miscellaneous thefts, wounding and serious assaults, as well as narcotics offenses, which are all illustrated in the film.[16] The director asks why the youth behave as they do; the answers, he shows, are deeply rooted in psychological needs, the product of a one-track materialistic society that neglects them.

Many have noticed that in the movies of Woo, Lam and Kirk Wong, the action emerges from characters' emotional conflicts and carries them forward towards the story's resolution. Kirk Wong's movies focus on the lives of the cops, who fight not only the criminals but also each other over who calls the shots with regard to the criminals. No wonder many of his cops are on the take when their 3-D jobs barely put food on their tables. Like Woo's heroic brothers, the good cops have codes of honor, while the others are only self-interested. From the action director's *Gunmen* (1988) through *Crime Story* (1993) and *Organized Crime and Triad Bureau* (1994), Wong's subtext is police corruption and abuse. Although the cops continue to battle outside criminal elements, the real fight is within.

One of the world's largest, in per capita terms, the Hong Kong Royal Police Force numbers 27,000 officers, representing a ratio of 1 officer to 210 citizens. Early on, the force was dominated by expatriates in number and rank, but currently 97 per cent of the force are ethnic Chinese, even though expatriates, particularly the British, have held the majority of senior ranks above superintendent.[17] The Independent Commission Against Corruption (ICAC) was established in 1974 to investigate rampant police corruption involving large-scale high-level police-organized 'syndicates' on the take, which used rank-and-file policemen to protect ongoing criminal activity. Between 1974 and 1977, ICAC vigorously prosecuted numerous offenders, leading to some high-profile convictions. In 1977, however, off-duty policemen took to the streets in demonstrations against the ICAC 'witchhunt' and old-guard officers became outspoken against the commission.

Some suspects were granted amnesty, and the ICAC was partially stripped of its powers. Certainly, the investigations reduced police corruption. By 1986, 251 cases of bribery and corruption were registered by ICAC, compared to 478 cases in 1981, a reduction of almost half. However, increased drug activity in the 1980s and 1990s, coupled with the declining number of arrests, prosecutions, and seizures over the same period, suggests that fewer cases are registered by ICAC because fewer members of the public report crimes to it.[18]

Wong is a master of gutsy action sequences as well as a reveller in the darker side of human character. His films start *in medias res*, with big-bang action set-pieces. Realistic and violent action is recorded by shots varying from aerial to medium and close-up, with fluid camera movement, tracking, hand-held, wiping, and swirling, and lots of cuts from inside the scene itself. Such an opening is a prelude to the other action segments that follow, leading to an explosive climactic scene. Putting the viewer in the midst of this, Wong also introduces and gets into the mind of a cop character whose will is crucial to the outcome of the story. Lighting and color are associated with the characters and used to establish mood. A signature blue-filtered light effect for enclosed spaces and night scenes makes Hong Kong appear like an underwater underworld. Frequent light-and-shadow effects suggest a murky atmosphere, into which Wong easily imports the language of film noir, with its blurred line between right and wrong, good and evil, black and white. Atmosphere is linked to the characters and their motivations, which helps determine our ultimate judgement of them.

Wong's *Organized Crime and Triad Bureau* (OCTB) (literally *Important Case True Record 'O' Department*) announces its focus in both English and Chinese titles. The story centers on the O Department (the Organized Crime Department, an actual division of the Hong Kong Police Department) and its Chief Inspector Lee (Danny Lee). Lee and his elite team of officers are employed to ensure that other cops do their job. This involves taking issue with superiors; circumventing the internal affairs division CAPO (Complaints Against the Police Office, also a real unit); and fighting renegade cops like Chiu (Roy Cheung), a Triad brother who has infiltrated the police, leaked information, and destroyed records, thereby hampering the work of the OCTB. The villain and fugitive Ho Kin-tung (Anthony Wong), OCTB's present target, is really secondary to the heart of the story, which involves police corruption and abuse.

Danny Lee has made a career out of playing cops, especially in movies produced by his own Magnum Films (like this one). In *Organized Crime and Triad Bureau* the character's inner and outer conflicts come into play. He is ostracized by other cops, except for his loyal team. At the local police bar hangout, uniformed cops refer to him as 'just a joke, so full of himself it's disgusting,' and when he approaches the bar where they've been drinking, everyone deserts him as if he has the plague. While Lee is a hot-shot cop, referred to as 'Rambo,' he is also determined and dedicated to getting the bad guys, no matter what. To do so, he is willing to abuse suspects' rights, force confessions, and tamper with evidence. Guided by the words 'What man shall bring justice? If not me, then who?', he's an admirable but flawed human being. He is most vulnerable with regard to his ex-wife Anna, whom the new kid on the block (Chiu) appears to be romancing. Totally disarmed by his feelings for her, Lee is set up by Chiu, who uses her to get to him; Lee's disbelief and then anger rapidly change into stunned pain, evident in his halted movement and expression, when Chiu also frames Anna. Danny Lee's nuanced performance is complicated and fascinating to watch, revealed in numerous close ups. Lee is a cop who can act quickly on a hunch, but he's also contemplative and calculating. Scanning the wall of photographs and documents concerning Ho's recent criminal activities, he figures all the angles with intense concentration. He is often shot in a dim light and emerges as a shadowy figure, a member of the in-between world, where the lines between good and evil are blurred. Yet he also registers the hint of a smile; he's a man who can appreciate the joke life plays on him and keep going.

The movie's opening is revealing. Lee's voice is heard in a one-way phone conversation before he is seen; the first visual image is his face, dominating the frame. He is arguing with his superior, complaining that OCTB has been on duty for over thirty hours and is exhausted, and also a target because they are holding an informant. Refused assistance from SDU (Special Duty Unit) and his superior, who is at home with his family, Lee reminds him that criminals don't work office hours. He turns to the men and single female officer who make up his team, and asks for them to back him up as he takes matters into his own hands. When the OCTB stages an assault on Ho and his gang before they can attack, Wong uses a blue filter to re-create the submerged world of the criminal life, and the gun battle is fast, uncertain, and gritty. In a breathtaking scene, Ho and his girlfriend

Cindy (Cecilia Yip) escape by jumping from an upper-story window into an Olympic-sized pool; Lee, holding a tossed grenade he's grabbed to prevent it from exploding, dives in after them, and they all swim for it. The chase doesn't end until they've all rolled down a grassy hillside, Lee still holding the grenade.

The OCTB just fails to capture the gang. When the 'Big Sir' of the department loses the photo opportunity, Lee's superintendent demands an explanation because he has been reprimanded by his superior. Chiu, meantime, is told that he is 'a capable young man' and will be promoted soon. Lee is criticized – 'Stop thinking you're Rambo' – and warned he'll 'end up in misery.' The Superintendent reminds him of previous suspects: 'This one was driven to jump to his death, this Triad kingpin you shot, saying his car accidentally ran into you…' Unfrazzled, Lee taps Ho's wife's phone and is able to figure out the fugitives' whereabouts, tracking them to Cheung Chau Island. A massive search and manhunt ensues, involving marine assistance, helicopter, dogs, and the elite force. But the OCTB brings in only two of Ho's gang. Wong's camera shows them working as a team, four of the men framed frontally as they don their flak jackets, similar in appearance and moving in unison, spreading themselves through the marketplace and trapping the suspects. Again, Lee is on the verge of catching the couple, but interference from his superiors halts the search. Islanders have complained, a local politician running for office has been giving the police bad press, and the administration folds under pressure. Lee is departing when, in a moment of comic respite, Ho is discovered in a coffin, attempting to escape the island. When the coffin lid is removed, the camera is placed directly above, so there is a funny shot of a surprised Ho, lying as in death. Peering inside, Lee asks 'You want to stay in there forever, or come out?'

The Hong Kong police have considerable discretion in regard to the use of force in the exercise of their duties. According to Criminal Ordinance Cap 221, S110IA, police may use 'such force as is reasonable in the circumstances.'[19] In *Organized Crime and Triad Bureau*, routine interrogation by the officers is brutal and inhumane. One suspect is bound to a chair while administered alcohol by tube through the nostrils, effecting a slow drowning. His screams and gurgles are heard by the other suspect, also tied, whose head is covered by a wet towel as his testicles are squeezed by the (literal) ball-busting female officer. Lee, meanwhile, coerces Ho into writing a confession by threatening harm to the criminal's wife and son. Ho has committed forty-two jewelry store robberies, and Lee shows him photographs of his previous victims, unseen by the camera, but horrendous nonetheless. 'This one,' Lee indicates, 'killed when his wife was giving birth,' another 'beaten,' 'this one's arms and legs cut off' and 'castrated,' another, 'after death, his wife committed suicide. You destroyed their entire family.' He then pulls out a photo of Ho with his family. When Ho questions why Lee would bother his family, the cop responds, 'Not me, but these poor families. You've done the same to them. These people have a contract on your wife and son.' Ho writes a confession.

OCTB's interrogations are interrupted by the CAPO officers, led by Lam (Yee Fan-wai), the over-earnest cop who, in carrying out his duty of protecting suspects' rights, doesn't use his common sense and abuses his powers. He orders his men to take Ho, a dangerous criminal, to the hospital for examination, despite the fact that they carry no weapons. Lam bursts into the OCTB offices like a gangbuster; like the administration, with legitimate cause or not, he is presented as interfering with the work of the elite unit. In fact, other than within the unit itself, there are few examples of co-operation between cops in this story. Lam storms into the offices with his men and ludicrously orders that the location be sealed and treated as a crime scene. Lee approaches from the opposite direction, and the scene is first shot from above, the literal contested terrain of a large floor space between the two. As they face off against each other, Lee challenges, 'Are you the cops or the robbers? Is there any justice?' and Lam attacks, 'Justice? Even suspects have human rights.' As they meet face-to-face in the center of the room, Lee counterattacks: 'Human rights? These scums shoot and kill. Why don't you talk to them nicely? Maybe they'll tell you the truth. You're nuts!'

As far as Lee is concerned, according to his code of justice, he is right. But there's another story told, in flashbacks and present time, that shows Ho as a sensitive human being, more than 'scum,' and obviously, even as a killer, entitled to the basic rights of an accused. A flashback reveals the trauma Cindy experiences when she's raped, brought about not only by her attacker, but also by her parents and teacher, who refuse to help her prosecute. Ho, who witnesses the aftermath, undertakes vigilante justice (not unlike Lee's) and rescues her, 'making her his woman.' Notwithstanding the occasional prostitute he engages, Ho has tender feelings for Cindy, as evidenced in a beautiful and lyrical moment when this Bonnie and Clyde are hiding in the countryside of Cheung Chau. On a moonlit night under blue-tinted light, they snack on dried jellyfish and drink water from the spread collectors, the drops splashing sensuously over their bodies on-screen. They sing a love song and share intimacies. On two occasions, Ho is willing to sacrifice himself for Cindy. Ho also loves his son, and in a tense hospital operating room, his empathy is apparent as he surrenders to Lee rather than further torment a mother begging for her son's life. He also does everything he can to save Chiu, his 'good brother,' who likewise puts himself on the line for Ho.

Some viewers have criticized the movie for the fact that the cops are not truly good guys, and the villains not truly bad guys – 'generally decent people, other than the occasional robbery and killing.'[20] Yet this film does much more than suggest that the good guys aren't always that good and the bad guys not that bad; growing out of the emotional terrain of one character's experience, it actually raises questions about the ineffectiveness of a system, its practices and abuses. The film's conclusion follows a daring escape by Ho, assisted by Chiu and Cindy, and a wild shoot-out takes place along Lockhardt, O'Brien, and Jaffee Roads. Trapped, Ho shoots himself in the mouth with a revolver, a last-ditch effort to save Cindy; the violence is sudden and graphic. Cindy becomes hysterical and even Lee's stomach turns. In the aftermath, Lam accuses Lee of murdering Ho, and, after being photographed by the press, Sir turns a blind eye as Lee's team beats Lam, the CAPO officer left as a figure of ridicule, screaming 'Don't hit me, I won't complain.' The final shot is of Lee, at a distance on a crowded Hong Kong street, walking directly towards the camera, throwing on his jacket, looking around, and caught in a freeze-frame.

By 1996, the gangster genre, reinvented as 'Triad Boyz' movies, was introduced by the team of producer Manfred Wong and cinematographer/director Andrew Lau Wai-keung.[21] The original film, called *Young and Dangerous* (literally *Wise Guys: Man of the World*), was adapted for the screen from a popular Hong Kong comic book. In three years, there were four sequels (*Young and Dangerous 2, 3, 4,* and *5,* in English, with different subtitles for the Chinese *Wise Guys'* versions) and a prequel (*Young and Dangerous: The Prequel*, or *New Wise Guys: Youth Battle Chapter*). The English title says it all: these are movies created for a younger movie-going audience that craves speed and novelty; the films feature a younger cast of stars, like pop singer Ekin Cheng, whose skin-tight fashion might have done for Versace what Chow Yun-fat did for Armani a generation earlier. Reusing their predecessors' plots of righteousness and betrayal, these movies are generally episode-crammed and frenetically paced; they escalate the violence quota by using lots of chopping and slashing over gunfire; and they are more sexually explicit. They recycle style and create spectacle by using hand-held camerawork, animation fades, a driving soundtrack, and synch sound. They choose on-the-street locations for in-your-face attitude.

Typically, younger dangerous rascals are set against other younger dangerous ones (rival gangs) or are at odds with the established Triad elders who send them out into the streets to do business. Generally fatherless, the rascals are orphans in search of fathers, and Triad bosses serve as temporary surrogates. But the traditional bonds of respect and loyalty of the older affiliations are loosened by the pervasive conditions of capitalism – people are valuable only as long as they can be used – so they are easily discarded. And this is played out on both sides generationally, as young punks take on bosses, or older Triad members waste young muscle in the ongoing war of the marketplace. In addition to the ruthlessness of the younger generation, their desperation is emphasized as they chart an uncertain future. An incestuous inbreeding occurs as filmmakers satisfy the market conditions by recycling plot elements and popular actors, who reappear as the same or a similar character, killed off in one of a series to star in a clone or to be introduced as another character in the next installment of a series, dizzyingly interacting with the same characters (and actors) from the previous installment. In-jokes often bring this repetition to the audience's attention, as characters remark about the similarity of a 'new' character to a 'deceased' brother. Herman Yau's *War of the Underworld* (1996), for example, includes an early scene in which Jordan Chan (Mountain Chicken in the *Young and Dangerous* films) tries to see *Young and Dangerous* at a theater and loses face (living up to his name 'Mountain Chicken') when another Triad member bullies him. Or consider the case of actor Jason Chu. His character Chow-pan is killed in a Macau rumble in *Young and Dangerous*, only to reappear in *Young and Dangerous 2* as a new recruit, Banana Skin. He survives through the fourth installment as the same character, son of the newspaper stand hawker Cheung. In *Young and Dangerous 5*, he reappears as Lok, a green recruit, and is killed once more.

Hong Kong moviegoing began to decline in 1990. In the later words of Ron

Murillo, 'There is a gang war in Hong Kong.… I mean a war for box-office receipts.'[22] Wong and Lau's Triad gang formula movies delivered a temporary solution, and the phenomenon is indicative of a shift in the way capitalism works. Together with new and more vigorous efforts to manipulate demand, including gala premieres, tie-in soundtracks featuring the movies' actors, and appearances and concerts, the team's efforts reflect the integration of a global network of flexible accumulation. The speed with which the *Young and Dangerous* series was generated – both *1* and *2* in production simultaneously, and *3* released within the same year – was itself overwhelming, combined with the rapidity with which imitations as well as parodies have exploited the new genre; current film production indicates an acceleration in the development of film-as-commodity, epitomizing late capital and its cultural logic.

The plotlines of the *Young and Dangerous* series simultaneously recycle an old story while emphasizing a Hong Kong obsession with the new. In each installment, protagonist Chan Ho-nam (Ekin Cheng), Hung Hing branch leader of Causeway Bay, is somehow framed, distrusted by the Triad, forced to prove himself, and ultimately redeemed. Ho-nam's story is often interrupted by that of his right-hand man, Mountain Chicken (Jordan Chan). So many subplots intervene that the intent appears to be to engage as many audience interests as possible. Furthermore, it doesn't matter if the storylines don't exactly gel because the intermittent throbbing pop music anthems, usually cued when there are street rumbles, create a rhythm for the audience to rock to, fully supported by the flashy camerawork. *Young and Dangerous* (*Wise Guys: Man of the World*) and *Young and Dangerous 2* (*Wise Guys 2: Mighty Dragon Crosses River*) cross over between live action and comic panel images through a series of fades to emphasize characters' dilemmas, albeit briefly, in the same way that Woo uses freeze-frames. This practice was abandoned thereafter, but not the dizzying hand-held camerawork, jump cuts, and swish pans. *Young and Dangerous 3* (*Wise Guys 3: Single Hand Covers Sky*) ups the ante on the chaos and violence quotient in terms of its novelty, revisiting numerous scenes of *Young and Dangerous 2* to remind viewers of the ongoing story (not only are several locations returned to in an attempt to assist a character to regain her memory; one episode is even re-enacted by the others as the hapless girl watches). *Young and Dangerous 4* (*97 Wise Guys: No War Cannot Be Won*) updates Ringo Lam's *School on Fire*, adds more inventive ways to kill, and employs numerous flashbacks using a blue-filtered lens. *Young and Dangerous 5 (98 Wise Guys: Dragon Contend With Tiger Fight)* lacks the strong presence of Jordan Chan, but imports an underused Danny Lee as the anti-Triad cop; lacking the slashing and gunfire of its predecessors, *Young and Dangerous 5* enacts three Thai boxing fights to provide most of the physical action. The latest film, *Young and Dangerous: The Prequel (New Wise Guys: Youth Battle Chapter)*, suggests that the original 'young and dangerous' movies are no longer so young or so dangerous as to intrigue an audience; for the most part children not even old enough to be admitted to the category-III-rated movies play the more youthful characterizations. The *modus operandi* of the series is to keep it new and fresh, no matter what.

Newness and a fear of being outdated are supported by numerous attitudes expressed by a variety of characters throughout the series. In *Young and Dangerous 1*, the younger and villainous Kwan (Francis Ng, referred to as 'Ugly Kwan' and 'Smart Kwan') is able to unseat Hung Hing Triad boss Chiang Tin-sung (Simon Yam) because they need a 'change.' In *Young and Dangerous 2*, reinstated Chiang remarks, 'the world is changing rapidly … We have to be updated.' By *Young and Dangerous 3*, the evil Tung Sing Triad member Crow (Roy Cheung) warns Hung Hing members that they had 'better be as modern as me,' and after murdering his boss Camel Lok (Michael Chan) comments, 'How did you teach us? Now you are outdated.' In *Young and Dangerous 4*, Dinosaur, a character who is shortly killed off, comments, 'My brother said I'd be outdated if I keep on staying in Tuen Mun. So he goes downtown with me to have a look at the outside world.' When the others visit Thailand, Dinosaur remains behind, and, in his death, lives up to his name.

The rootlessness of the characters in the series is emphasized by shooting many scenes in Hong Kong streets, with groups of youths, either the handful of featured Hung Hing boys or *en masse*, several hundreds together, always in motion, moving through and moving on. This instability is lamented in a way that evokes the nostalgia evident in Woo's movies. Characters search for roots through substitute fathers and families. The villains are the ones who reject traditional ties and values. For example, in *Young and Dangerous 1* Kwan is ironically named, for Kwan, the god worshipped by both cops and Triads, is close to both codes of righteousness and loyalty. The villainous Kwan believes in neither. Writing the Chinese character for 'righteousness' and then partially erasing it, revealing the character for 'stupid,' he tells Ho-nam, 'Do you know what is righteousness? Do you know the word behind righteousness? That's stupid.' Similarly, in *Young and Dangerous 2*, Tai-fei (Anthony Wong), the apparent enemy of Ho-nam, recalls the incident, asking 'Do you know how to spell righteousness?' And in the opening scene of *Young and Dangerous 3*, the sadistic Crow beats and slashes a Tung Sing Triad member who has stolen money from him, then smashes a Kwan statue underfoot, addressing the deity: 'These days no guys are righteous, you are outdated.' While ranking and respect are given lip service, the rascals are more interested in making money than giving face. In the same movie, Hung Hing members reminisce at the playground where their gang activities began; they are bewildered by the fierce younger kids who challenge them over so little, a soccer ball, forgetful that in *Young and Dangerous 1*, they were confronted by Kwan and defended by Brother Bee, whose fellow gang members they became.

Short attention spans and rapidly fading collective memories persist through the series as the basic story is retold differently each time. Similarly, Hung Hing boys take on and discard 'their girls' like the fashions and hairstyles they change in each installment. The turf battles that erupt between internecine Hung Hing branches and among the Hung Hing, Tung Sing, and San Luen Triads, serve as a contested terrain upon which characters struggle to find a sense of place and self. Expressed matter-of-factly in *Young and Dangerous 2* by Ho-nam – 'being a rascal, fightings and killings are nothing special' – unpredictability is commonplace and reflects the uncertainty of Hong Kong. This genre, in a more exaggerated way than any of its predecessors, locates itself in Hong Kong's streets and neighborhoods, filmed as they slip away in the movement of the human actors. An attempt to record a specific space and time in a medium which conflates space and time, the movies' desire and drive for permanence is unrelenting. In *Young and Dangerous 4*, just before the film's climax, Chicken, in a debate for leadership of Tuen Mun, tries to create a verbal sense of place, inscribing a Hong Kong of disappearances:

Do you know why this place is named Tuen Mun? Why this place isn't called Ha Mun or Kong Mun? Let me tell you. In Qing Dynasty, many soldiers were stationed at this place to guard the gate of the Pearl River. Tuen Mun was named since then. Do you know how many hospitals are found in Tuen Mun? Four. How many secondary schools? Thirty-four. How many police stations? Three. Do you know how many metalwork shops in Tuen Mun? Come on, how can you buy weapons there? Let me ask you, do you know how many people live in Tuen Mun? Over 600,000. Starting from the 1980s, the government started to develop this place. You know nothing. How can you take over this place?

Tuen Mun, otherwise known as Castle Peak, recently developed to Hong Kong's west through reclamation projects, incorporates dense clusters of high-rise housing. Its new town 'history' (approximately twenty years) encompasses numerous changes in housing requirements and expansions of the original plan. It encapsulates the impermanence of Hong Kong itself. According to the Tuen Mun New Town Development Office, 'New problems, opportunities and needs are regularly being identified in Tuen Mun and as a result, new town planning proposals have had to be applied in a reasonably flexible manner.'[23] Chicken's detailed description reinforces the many images of this story which come from the characters' walking Tuen Mun's streets, housing estates, malls, and parks. Confrontations erupt on its sidewalks. As in the other films featuring Causeway Bay and Mongkok, a fleeting vision of history emerges, a simulacrum of Hong Kong, translated as moments and images collaged together in hyperreality.

The *Young and Dangerous* series identifies two paradoxical worlds: the world where one character states, 'Sometimes I admire you Hong Kong rascals … your life isn't worth a penny' (*Young and Dangerous 2*), and another where a character asks, 'Why do you want to be a rascal? Fighting? No, for money. It's the age of money.' (*Young and Dangerous 3*). Circumscribing a society with an ever-increasing gap between the haves and have-nots, Triad members are routinely defined as showing the extremes of either having or not having, and the Triads – substitute business conglomerates – as growing by leaps and bounds into transnational global enterprises. *Young and Dangerous 1* introduces a Hung Hing endeavor to take over a Macau Triad's interest, which is later revived in *Young and Dangerous 2*; the second film focuses on the relation between Taiwanese Triads and politics as Liu Kung canvasses for Legislative Council. *Young and Dangerous 3* expands to international drug dealing with a Netherlands underworld business cartel. The fourth in the series involves a Chinese expatriate businessman in Thailand who returns to Hong Kong to helm Hung Hing, where he's assured that 'If Hong Kong will be unchanged for fifty years, prosperity will continue, of course.' By *Young and Dangerous 5*, Boss Chiang Chun-sing (Alex Man) advises Ho-nam that 'Hong Kong is prosperous, Hung Hing is prosperous. Hung Hing goes well, Hong Kong will go better.' Returning by boat, in the harbor his arm sweeps the Hong Kong skyline as the skyscrapers of power come into view. The Hung Hing leader tells Ho-nam about his father, the Triad founder, who worked as a 'coolie' and 'fought the world with his fists.' 'At that time,' Chiang continues,

> he used force, not wisdom. It's different now. We should use our brains now ... liaising with the officials ... Think big, but forget the street fights. In the past, jeans and t-shirts were OK. Now wear a suit, be neat and tidy. This is what we call improvement. It's wise to know more rich guys. About the Triad business, always be low-key. For making money, you'd be high-key.

The fifth installment concerns a crooked Malaysian businessman Chan Datuk, who plays two Triads off against each other, involving them in a housing development scam and a tourist cruise line. Eventually exposed in a media nightmare, Datuk is replaced by Triad interests in the prosperous cruise line business. The series and its progression, then, reflect a shift from early capitalist accumulation to the global networking of late capital accumulation, moving like so many blips on a computer screen by a simple keystroke.

Along with *Young and Dangerous* imitators, kinder, gentler Triad boyz appeared, like reluctant gang leader Long Ching (Roy Cheung) in Yip Wai-sun and Kwok Wai-chung's *Mongkok Story* (1996). The camera identifies with the viewpoint of an outsider, the waiter Leung-ping (Edmond Leung), who narrates in retrospect. He quits his dead-end job to hang with the gang, but is torn between his attraction and repulsion to gang life; he learns life is no easier for boss Ching, who favors discussion to resolve problems instead of automatic reflex violence. Tellingly, the two younger 'bosses,' Ching and Lui Lone (Anthony Wong), are unable to keep the peace when talks break down and a fight ensues between their rival gangs. Elders, who earlier bantered about spending time in Canada, flee a situation that they are unable to control. The bloody and violent battle scene, common to the genre, conveys the fact that 'great disturbances ... must constantly occur' in capitalist society, and reveals that the need for social regulation is inescapable.[24] The alternative, depicted in so many movies, is violence as a means of settling disputes. Thus contractual relations replace personal associations as the institutions of the marketplace come to dominate community life. Ching's family is destroyed, and after murdering Ching, Lone himself, isolated in a dark alley, is brutally attacked and killed by street punks who are after his ATM card and code.

Triad Boyz or rascal movies, following heroic bloodshed and social realism gangster movies, parallel the shift from early to late capitalism and its effect on society. As Marx reminds us, 'Hegel remarks somewhere that all facts and personages of great importance in world history occur, as it were, twice. He forgot to add: the first time as tragedy, the second time as farce.'[25] If Woo's films describe the history of early capitalism, the *Young and Dangerous* genre must be seen as their absurd counterpart. The mixed bag of devices used in these latter films deserved the parody that was forthcoming with films like Cha Cheun-yi's *Once Upon a Time in a Triad Society 1* and *2* (both 1996), and Wai Ka-fai's *Too Many Ways to Be No. 1* (1997). Featuring some of the same actors used in the 'original' films, including Francis Ng and Roy Cheung, in which the actors seem to enjoy creating campy reincarnations, these stories include direct references to their predecessors but outdo them in experimental camerawork and deconstructed narrative. The English titles beginning *Once Upon a Time...* draw upon Tsui Hark's well-known six-part series *Once Upon a Time in China*, a homage to Chinese history and identity featuring folk hero Wong Fei-hung. But Kwan (Francis Ng, reprising his role in *Young and Dangerous 1*), in *Once Upon a Time in a Triad Society 1*, is revealed to be a cruel liar; and Dagger (also Francis Ng), in *Once Upon a Time in a Triad Society 2*, is an avid mah-jongg player and pimp averse to fighting. So much for folk heroes. *Too Many Ways To Be No. 1* nods to Johnny Mak's *To Be Number One*, the first 'big timer' movie.[26]

Once Upon a Time in a Triad Society (literally *Mongkok Holding Control Person*) opens with a fiction: a live-action slashfest is revealed to be the episode Kwan is reading from a Hong Kong comic book (the basis of *Young and Dangerous*). Puncturing the heroism intended by the protagonist facing an army of opponents, Kwan is shown to be reading while seated on the toilet, and he uses a page of the comic for toilet paper. The jazzy brazen soundtrack is irreverent and insolent, perfectly in tune with the tone of the story. After Mongkok gang leader Kwan is shot and hospitalized in present film time, he takes over the narrative from his hospital gurney, commenting in a gravelly rasp, 'I am bad. I should be killed. I don't deserve to be saved,' along with 'No one is born nasty.' And, as 'my past' flashes across the screen, a somewhat sympathetic story, with Kwan's interjected commentary, manifests itself for more than half the film. Then, suddenly and unexpectedly, he admits, 'What I told you before was fake. Use your brain. Sorry I cheated before

I died. I wasted your time. This is the true story…' And, as 'my real face,' appears onscreen, the story is retold, purportedly 'truthfully' this time, and showing a contemptible and irredeemable member of the species. The combined versions, put together by the audience, reveal the film's intent: to expose the current portrayals of the Triads as glorified and false, and the films as inflated commodities. 'Is there righteousness in Triad Society?' Kwan asks, 'It's only a lie! A fairy tale that cheats innocent people.'

The sequel, literally *Go! Control Holder Army*, uses time as an organizing device, featuring large white numbers onscreen against a black background, registering second changes as an omnipresent tension of time running out while the action builds. Dagger (ironically named, considering his aversion to violence), a wannabe punk named Dinosaur (Roy Cheung), and an Anti-Triad Bureau cop (Cheung Tat-ming) feature as the primary players, all victimized by the Triads in various ways; while they never interact directly, the trio appear in the same place at the same time. Dinosaur is a wide-eyed thug from the New Territories, enthralled by the stories of a notorious Triad, God of Sword. He is not easily disuaded when he phones Triad brothers to offer the help of his green followers (he calls Blackie, Kei, and Wah, all from *Young and Dangerous*); he drives into Mongkok for the brawl between the followers of Sau-fau and Fai-hung, is brutally stabbed and dies slowly and painfully, for nothing. Dagger, meanwhile, despite his numerous attempts to avoid doing so, is forced by his Triad to avenge Fai-hung's death and ends up in prison. 'The Boss won't go,' he thinks to himself, 'That's why everyone wants to be the Boss.' The cop is eventually reunited with his wife, despite being blamed by his boss for the rumble, and a close call on his life. Much of the film takes place in the Mongkok street of Dung Wong, and numerous hand-held cameras record the activity which transpires as tensions mount into an explosive climactic scene. Shopkeepers and local patrons, weaving through the gathering throng, are caught unawares and attempt to evade the activity. Registering anticipation and fear, the sequences shift from color to black-and-white. As pressures grow, with numbers mounting and police arriving from all directions, adding more noise and increasing restlessness and taunts, the cameras become more hyperkinetic. Abrupt whiteouts in the midst of the action add to the confusion. There is a tangible helplessness here, far removed from the slickness of *Young and Dangerous*, a serious indictment of the glitz and glamour of the rascals.

Too Many Ways to Be No. 1 (literally *An Alphabet's Birth*) goes one better than *Once Upon a Time in a Triad Society*, with mesmerizing camerawork that intentionally calls attention to itself in order to distract from the story. The aggressive camerawork stands in as perpetrator of the crimes, and it follows the so-called gang relentlessly, creatively, and destructively. The criminal gang is a bunch of incompetents who somehow muddle through. Two of its members, separated from the others, are Matt (Francis Ng) and Wong Ah-kan (Lau Ching-wan). Matt convinces Wong to help him carry out a Taiwan hit (but Matt forgets the address). A distorted lens shows them isolated and helpless after they have drunk themselves into a stupor at the hangout of the Triad boss they are supposed to kill (unknown to them at the time). Wong finds himself in the position of being offered 'too many ways to be no. 1' when he's not keen on the enterprise at all. The 'coarse freedom, noisy jollity, and obscenest impudence [which] give attractions to the gang'[26] of the world of *Young and Dangerous* is totally lacking here. With the exception of the gang leader, dispatched in the opening minutes of the movie (when the fleeing gang unintentionally runs him over with a stolen car – at least in one version of the story), the gang members are unknown to each other. One fight scene, lasting several minutes, is shot upside down; several others occur in total darkness with numerous gunshots providing brief flashes of light, but never illuminating the scene. A table discussion is shot with the camera centered on the table and moving from one side to another, like a rolling ship at sea, to record the exchanges. Other shots are from the ceiling, showing the characters at sea in uncharted territory. A black comedy, the story moves from absurdly comic moments to extreme violence and back again.

A collage of many gangster/Triad gang set pieces, the film reiterates, through many characters, their reason for being: 'If we don't get rich and famous, we won't return to Hong Kong.' Wong's love interest, the comfort girl at the bath house, leaves Hong Kong like the others to seek her fortune in Taiwan, because of the 'poor economy.' Director and screenwriter Wai Ka-fai uses the characterizations and extreme situations to present alternatives for Hong Kongers on the eve of the handover. Wong's watch, eternally set at five minutes to four, appears at crucial moments of the film, signifying a different telling of the story as already told, thereby suggesting an anticipation of what is to come, as well as a way of altering the future.

FIVE

LAST HERO(ES) IN HONG KONG

Long before John Woo's 'heroic bloodshed' films attracted international attention and acclaim, Hong Kong cinema was filled with action. Martial arts movies date from the silent era of the 1920s. Tianyi Studios relocated to the colony from Shanghai in the mid-1930s in the face of Chiang Kai-shek's ban on motion pictures that combined martial arts and magic, which were the company's staple. Cantonese-dialect productions appeared in the late 1930s in the wake of filmmakers who emigrated to Hong Kong from the Mainland to escape the Japanese occupation. In 1949, the first of what would become more than a hundred movies was made about Wong Fei-hung, the Chinese folk hero and martial arts legend. Mandarin-dialect movies emerged dominant in the late 1960s and remained so for a decade, the period when 'chop socky' flicks found an audience in the West. Between the end of World War II and 1980, the Hong Kong industry produced about a thousand martial arts (swordplay and kung fu) films.[1]

Wuxia pian (literally 'martial chivalry film') has its lineage in Chinese literature, sources of which range from the political upheavals of the Warring States era (403–221 BC) to the late Qing dynasty (1644–1911). As Lori Tilkin writes of the early period, 'a group of men from a myriad of different social and professional backgrounds roamed the countryside taking justice into their own hands.'[2] The 'knight-errant' (*xiake*), bound by a code of honor to fight for truth and equity, bears ancestral resemblance to the individuals portrayed in late Qing novels who sought to right the wrongs inflicted upon common people. Some early martial arts films, however, were criticized, censored, and destroyed for contributing to juvenile delinquency. Yu Mo-wan notes that movies such as *The Burning of the Red Lotus Monastery* (1928), featuring animated palm-powered flying daggers that could pass through walls and weightless leaps accomplished using suspension wires, often 'portrayed rebellious youths deserting their families in search of *fantastique* martial arts powers.'[3] Their progenitor, Tang dynasty (618–907) *chuanqi* (strange tales), told of martial heroes with magical powers able to perform physical transformations. But government officials, offended by young people's desire to break with tradition, saw 'flights of freedom' in the fanciful special effects, much as supernatural drama had raised the suspicions of earlier authorities, who feared that such plays would have deleterious effects on social morality.

From the beginning, Hong Kong martial arts films were influenced by the tradition of the Peking Opera, an art form with origins dating from the Song dynasty (960–1280). Stories are derived from Chinese folklore, historical events, mythology, and popular novels. Performances are noted for their dazzling costumes, face painting, and modest staging. Performers, having spent years learning their craft, are multi-talented actors, dancers, gymnasts, and singers. 'The goal is to give the audience a resemblance of life.... In order to achieve this goal, there must be adherence to aesthetic standards. This means the acting, singing, dancing and acrobatics executed must be beautiful and seem effortless.'[4] Believed to have been introduced into Chinese cinema by director Ren Pengnian in his 1925 film *Li Feifei* (*The Heroine*), the Opera's emphasis on physical movement and conditioning contributed to both rigorous and stylized celluloid fighting scenes.[5] Peking Opera's declining popularity after World War II – due, in great part, to the availability of mass-produced 'talking pictures' – led many trained performers to seek employment in the motion-picture industry.

Director King Hu, who travelled to Hong Kong as a young left-wing supporter of the 1949 communist revolution and found himself unable to return when the borders between the colony and the Mainland were closed, made extensive use of Peking Opera movement and action effects in films such as *Dragon Gate Inn* (1967), a commercially successful critique of political corruption and espionage in the Ming dynasty (1368–1644). Significantly, Hu maintained that 'I've always taken the action part of my films as dancing rather than fighting.... A lot of people have misunderstood me, and have remarked that my action scenes are sometimes "authentic," sometimes not. In point of fact, they're always keyed to the notion of dance.[6] Thus a relationship is established between the cadence and pace of the action scenes and the music that overlays them. Hu's movies also reflect what Lin Nien-tung calls the 'secularization of the hero,'[7] a process replacing the magical feats of earlier fantasy pictures with more realistic portrayals of the virtuous retainer committed to fair play. As the filmmaker himself reveals in speaking about *Dragon Gate Inn* and his Cannes Film Festival award-winner *A Touch of Zen* (1971), 'At the time I made those films, the James Bond movies were very popular, and I thought it very wrong to make a hero of a secret service man.'[8]

Chang Cheh's *One Armed Swordsman* (1967) is generally acknowledged as the movie that launched the 1970s' martial arts phenomenon. While the film's title announces that this is a swordplay movie – nothing new in itself – the hero's disability (his *sifu*'s jealous daughter has chopped off his right arm) produces a different type of character. Forced to undergo a strict and tough rehabilitative training program, the protagonist (Jimmy Wang-yu) becomes a 'lean mean fighting machine' with a blade. Notably brutal for its time, Chang's picture ushered in an era of the self-reliant individualist that, according to Sek Kei, simultaneously destroyed the image of the weak Chinese male by featuring 'beefcake heroes in adventure and violence.'[9] Within a few years, 'flying fu' swordplay flicks gave way to 'kung fu' movies. The transfiguration of the martial 'hero' from a mythic character endowed with magical powers to a mortal fighter engaged in personal hand-to-hand combat was consonant with the post-World War II generation's economic materialism as well as with its growing suspicion of traditional values. Both more individualistic and competitive, the 1970s' variant expressed capitalist modernity, what Engels called

> a battle of life and death … fought not between the different classes of society only, but also between the individual members of these classes. Each is in the way of the other, and each seeks to crowd out all who are in his way, and to put himself in their place.[10]

Upstart film studio Golden Harvest, founded by former Shaw Brothers executive Raymond Chow, scored big in the early 1970s with several releases starring Jeet Kune Do (literally 'way of the intercepting fist') martial arts master Bruce Lee. Lee's films – *Big Boss* (1971), *Fists of Fury* (1972), and *Enter the Dragon* (1973) – would come to define the genre.[11] Released after his death, *Dragon* is the most widely recognized martial arts movie in the West. Lee, who played 'Kato' in a short-lived, mid-1960s' US television series, *Green Hornet*, and who was rejected (allegedly for being 'too Chinese') in favor of US actor David Carradine for the lead role in the American Broadcasting Company's (ABC) early 1970s' series *Kung-Fu*, displayed a fluidity and pragmatism of movement that distinguished him from the broken motions, flashy techniques, and posturing stances associated with movies that critics disparagingly called 'chop-socky' films. Andre Morgan, who worked with Bruce Lee at Golden Harvest prior to the latter's untimely death in 1973, says that he

> brought a new style of acting to the Chinese film industry which, prior to him, was slightly stylized and exaggerated. Bruce had a very unique combination – he was a martial artist and an actor equally, not a martial artist who decided to become an actor or an actor who decided to make martial arts movies.

Lee, whose reference to himself as a 'Chinese boxer' recalls the legendary early-twentieth-century boxers who fought the foreign occupation of China, customarily outfought white Westerners and castigated disloyal Chinese. These features have led observers such as Stephen Teo to suggest that the martial artist/actor's films produced a 'cultural nationalism' expressing the Chinese diaspora's desire to 'identify with China and things Chinese, even though they may not have been born there or speak its national language or dialects.'[12] In showing face rather than losing it, Bruce Lee was a positive, albeit politically abstract, phenomenon. And Morgan maintains that

> Bruce brought to the Hong Kong cinema in the early 1970s the sense of the modern hero, the young macho man, that was being explored in American film at the time by Steve McQueen and Clint Eastwood. He tried to combine much more realistic acting with his philosophy of the martial arts and what they have to do with the essence of life. In trying to give that voice in his films, he hoped that he would reach not just an Asian audience, but an international one.[13]

The 1970s were the martial arts genre's most prolific period, with literally hundreds of Hong Kong kung fu productions, many of them by Shaw Brothers, including attempts by the likes of Bruce Li (Ho Chung-tao) and Bruce Le (Hung Kin-lung) to capitalize on Bruce Lee's legacy following his death.[14] Near the end of the decade, one in which the colony's economy boomed, kung fu comedies became popular. Bey Logan states that the 'straight faced Master Po-faced kung fu films had held sway for so long … it was evident audiences were hungry for something different.'[15] Inaugurated, perhaps, by Karl Maka's *The Good, The Bad, The Loser* (1976), these pictures wove slapstick elements and sight gags, as well as self-deprecating humor and goofy stunts, into their well-choreographed fight scenes. 'Heroes' neither possessed magical powers nor were always hardbodies; in fact, they often resembled the 'country bumpkins' of Cantonese comedy who 'not properly tuned … create all sorts of absurdities.'[16] In Yuen Woo-ping's *Snake in the Eagle's Shadow* (1978), for example, the kung fu master (Yuen Siu-tin) is an aimless wanderer whose simpleton student (a not-yet-sucessful Jackie Chan) spends the first half of the movie as a 'human punching bag' and the butt of fellow students' jokes. While conveying an innate 'everyman' populism, the self-parody of this subgenre does not do justice to the plight of common persons struggling against the harsh realities of life. As Li Cheuk-to notes, just as 'chivalry and gallantry have no place in the commercial metropolis … traditional morality has no place in this cinematic world … mutual exploitation defines personal relationships. Instead of ideals, the characters are driven by cynicism and a sense of resignation.'[17]

The most enduring figure in the cinematic history of Hong Kong martial arts has been folk hero Wong Fei-hung, a Chinese nationalist defender of Confucian values. Wong (1847–1924) practiced traditional Chinese medicine and taught Hung Gar kung fu in Canton, learning the former from his father and the latter from his father's teacher. As a physician, he is said to have treated indigents who could not pay for his services, as well as revolutionaries attempting to overthrow the corrupt Qing dynasty. As a martial artist, he was associated with the 'tiger-crane' style and with a fighting technique known as the 'nine special fists.' And as a citizen-philosopher, he apparently placed himself on the side of truth, justice, and righteousness. The actor Kwan Tak-hing became synonymous with Wong Fei-hung for a generation of post-World War II Hong Kongers, playing the character in a series of ninety-nine films over the course of two decades.[18] Young Jackie Chan's comic deconstruction of Wong as a lazy and less than dutiful son sent by his father to study with a cantankerous old drunkard in the kung fu comedy *Drunken Master* (1978) established the actor as a superstar.

With Hong Kong's return to China on the horizon, Tsui Hark, who says his movies must 'reflect what we are thinking at this moment in our time,'[19] serialized

Wong Fei-hung in six pictures between 1990 and 1997. Entitled *Once Upon a Time in China*, an apparent nod to Sergio Leone's 1968 *Once Upon a Time in the West* and its theme of inexorable progress, these Eastern 'westerns' are 'equal parts anti-imperialist tract, gleeful exploration of melodramatic violence, comic folk tale, and wistful quest for spiritual unity.'[20] They revived Wong as a movie subject, revitalized the martial arts genre, and made five-times Chinese martial arts national champion Jet Li, who played Wong, a movie star throughout Asia. Li's folk hero not only celebrates Chinese cultural identity and humanistic ideals (defending the weak, championing justice, and redressing the wrongs of the oppressed); he also denounces imperialism and considers loaded issues of modernization, progress, and the future. Wong is depicted dialectically: on the one hand, he deplores the 'fact that Western technology has overtaken the usefulness of kung fu as a traditional art of defence'; on the other hand, he views Westernization as a 'necessary step to rejuvenate the nation so that it may deal with Western intruders and rise up to face the world in equal terms.'[21] Centuries-old themes of identity and subjection remain relevant in Hong Kong's contemporary context, one in which the British colony's return to the Mainland would not mean political independence. As Tsui, commenting on the film's English title, contends, '*Once Upon a Time in China* can be now, can be the future.'[22]

Once Upon a Time in China (1990) opens with an indictment of colonialism: British soldiers, contemptuous of and ignorant about Chinese culture, respond to popping firecrackers by firing upon a troupe of lion dancers (a traditional symbol of unity). The end of the nineteenth century is drawing near; European powers are carving up China, and Americans are deceptively recruiting Chinese labor with promises of a 'mountain of gold' in the United States. Meanwhile, Chinese officials are both corrupt and incompetent, Chinese Triads kidnap Chinese women to sell into prostitution, and Chinese fight Chinese. China's very survival appears to be at stake, a point made early in the film when the 'Shaho Gang' demands protection money from a bun merchant only to be confronted by Wong Fei-hung and the 'Black Flag Army,' a somewhat madcap local militia that includes Leung Foon (Yuen Biao), Buck Tooth So (Jackie Cheung), and Porky Lin (Kent Cheng), which the local government alleges is a vigilante group. Told to take the fight outside because 'we're doing business,' Wong attempts, to no avail, to play peacemaker, saying that 'foreigners draw boundaries and set up forbidden areas. If we fight each other rather than them, soon we'll lose the flour to make our rolls.'

Tsui, apparently playing fast and loose with historical accuracy, introduces the character Aunt Yee (Rosamund Kwan), said to be Wong Fei-hung's thirteenth aunt.[23] Yee draws scorn from other Chinese because she dresses in Western-style clothing and speaks fluent English. When asked by Wong about the importance of learning from the West, she points to the invention of the steam engine and cautions about China falling behind. Yee, who has a camera, asserts that, 'There will be railways and telegraph companies soon. Everything will change. China will change with the world.' Wong, in turn, laments the presence of Western guns, ships, and clothing. Expressing the anxiety of late-nineteenth-century Chinese nationalists and pre-handover Hong Kongers, he remarks that 'Everything is changing. What will we change into? No idea!' While Wong Fei-hung and Yee develop an affection for one another that grows through the series, the former is uncomfortable acknowledging his feelings, much less verbalizing them. If Kwan Tak-hing's Wong was partriarchal, Jet Li's naive character reminds one of the teenage boy too shy to ask the girl he secretly admires to the school dance. Desexualized martial arts masters are in fact common to the genre; as Cheng Yu notes, 'Traditional Chinese folk morality has regarded sex as detrimental to the body.... Not only must the ideal hero abstain from sexual indulgence, he has to be practically celibate.'[24]

Tsui's hyper-kinetic homage to Sergio Leone turns the 'spaghetti western,' where 'action slowed to a snail's pace,'[25] on its head, although some martial arts film enthusiasts criticize *Once Upon a Time in China* for having too much drama and yet not enough action.[26] Fights are brilliantly choreographed, none more so than the one that brings the movie to a close following the Shaho's kidnapping of Aunt Yee. Set in a granary, Wong Fei-hung battles rival master Yim (Yam Sai-kuen) who has allied himself with the Shaho, in an extended scene that has the two combatants balancing high above the ground on bamboo ladders. After a time, United States soldiers fire indiscriminately, killing Yim, and setting off a chain reaction in which Foon hangs an American and US warships mistakenly fire upon the British. Jackson, the American slave trader, shouts that he 'won't let any Chinese live, then I won't have to explain to any government.' Having violated his own warning about Chinese people fighting one another, Wong consoles Yim in his dying moments. The latter's last breath carries with it the comment that 'We can't fight guns with kung fu.' In turn, Wong Fei-hung flips a bullet with his fingers that strikes and splatters Jackson's forehead. While Tsui Hark makes it clear in *Once Upon a Time in China* that Westerners are *gweilos* ('foreign devils'), a good portion of the film focuses on Chinese who 'join with foreigners to sell out the country.' References to 'unequal treaties' point not only to Qing dynasty concessions to nineteenth-century European imperialists but also to the Sino–British Joint Declaration on Hong Kong. The movie ends on a note of nationalist triumphalism: martial artists train on a beach underneath an orange sky to the booming strains of 'A Man Should Support Himself,' the Cantonese song that has become Wong Fei-hung's theme.

Tsui introduces interesting subplots as the series pursues themes established in the first episode. Wong and Sun Yat-sen meet and befriend one another in *Once Upon a Time in China 2*, set in 1895, the year in which China ceded Taiwan to Japan and sixteen years before the Chinese republic was established. Hanging over the images of hyper-nationalist sects running amok in *Once Upon a Time in China 2* and *4* (the latter directed by Yuen Bin) are specters of the 1967 riots in Hong Kong and the Cultural Revolution's Red Guards on the mainland. Wong Fei-hung's call for reform in *Once Upon a Time in China 3*, following bloodshed wrought by a Lion Dance tournament, a scene involving a multitude of actors played out as a massacre, is Tsui's post-Tiananmen Square comment that only political change in the PRC can give assurance to Hong Kongers that 1997 will not be a calamity. Wong's conservative nationalism is more evident in episode three. But his heightened state of resentment of the West, which he calls 'the land of barbarians,' appears to be more related to a foreign suitor of Yee. Tsui pointedly says that Wong Fei-hung is a 'male chauvinist from a chauvinistic society [who is] being threatened by a very strong woman who knows lots of things about the world that he doesn't know.'[27]

The final episode appeared in 1997, only months before the handover. Samo Hung's direction of this Tsui Hark production returns Jet Li (absent from *Once Upon a Time in China 4* and *5*) to the role of Wong Fei-hung. Shot in Texas and entitled *Once Upon a Time in China and America*, the film finds Wong, Yee, and Seven in the American Wild West to visit Buck Tooth So and celebrate the first anniversary of the Po Chi Lam medical clinic. Early on, the three befriend a parched-mouthed, bleached blond surfer-type dude named Billy (the Kid). When Indians attack, Yee becomes a 'damsel in distress' inside a runaway stagecoach that runs off a cliff into rushing river waters below; Wong Fei-hung and Seven try to save her. Yee and Seven are washed ashore where they are found by Chinese from the town, but Wong Fei-hung is nowhere in sight. It seems that he has hit his head on a rock and is suffering from amnesia. Taken in by friendly Native Americans, Wong eventually dons tribal dress, wears double braids, and answers to the name 'Yellow.' He even takes up with a tribal woman, a situation that leads to a tantrum by Yee, who, unaware that he has no memory, is offended when she finds him and he responds to her with indifference.

Memory-loss serves as a plot device that permits characters to become someone else. Both Native Americans and Chinese immigrants have been oppressed in the United States. In *Once Upon a Time in China and America*, Wong Fei-hung is twice marginalized, first for his Chineseness and second for identifying with Native Americans. Unfortunately, the film fails to draw out the implications of the two peoples' marginalized histories. On one hand, we see Chinese discriminated against ('No beer for Chinamen in town saloon'), exploited (coolies engaged in hard labor for menial pay), and segregated ('tell them to go back to their alley'). Further, Wong Fei-hung's statement that 'I can't remember where I'm from' is a poignant comment on the struggle against forgetting the past faced by those living in the diaspora, and a direct challenge to Hong Kongers living in a city that never stands still. On the other hand, the genocidal treatment of Native Americans is reduced to the comment that 'we were forced off our land' and a Mel Brooks-type scene in which three are forced to 'dance' when bigoted whites fire bullets at their feet.

Once Upon a Time in China and America, called a 'noodle western' by critic David Chou, has the look and feel of the 'original *Kung Fu* series colliding head on with *Blazing Saddles* and *Dances with Wolves*.'[28] Cowboys and gunslingers are variously lampooned; they have bad makeup, recite lines poorly, and generally overact – a fitting commentary on the way that 'the glossiness, sensuality, and technical excellence of Hollywood movies' covers up 'the ideology of the superiority of the American white race.'[29] The film's lineage includes 1970s' satiric-revisionist takes on the Western genre (*Little Big Man, Buffalo Bill and the Indians*) that deconstruct 'good guys' and 'bad guys.' The racist mayor who cheats Chinese laborers of their wages and frames them for a bank robbery gets his comeuppance in the end, while Billy the outlaw, who fights the power alongside the Chinese, becomes his successor. Of course, parody runs the risk of becoming travesty in its ambiguity. Is the portrayal of cartoon-character Native Americans absurd, in a manner akin to what Alan Wilde describes as postmodern 'suspensive irony,'[30] which signifies heightened recognition of incoherence? Or is the dressing up of white people in buckskin and war paint with bad hair pieces simply insensitive irrespective of the humorous intentions?

Martial arts are the one thing that Wong doesn't forget after bumping his head. During his time as a Native American, he snatches arrows out of the air and defeats a rival tribe by himself. Upon recovering his memory, Wong Fei-hung takes on a Mexican *bandito* (perpetuating a stereotype of its own in the process), who has also been ripped off by the mayor; the two maneuver the landing of a water tower in the series' final high-wire balancing routine. Samo Hung's razor-sharp choreography puts Jet Li's many skills on display; in one lightening-quick sequence, the master moves from *wushu* to northern mantis to chen tai chi style. The director's fondness for kung fu comedy is evidenced here as well when cowboys suddenly become martial artists, kicking and vaulting through the last fight scene. The picture even panders to theater audiences by contrasting the pacing of its action scenes with long orations by Wong that bore his on-screen audience to tears and puts them to sleep. 'No more political speeches,' says one actor, an allusion, no doubt, to stereotypical Hong Kongers and Western kung fu movie buffs alike.

Once Upon a Time in China and America concludes on an ostensibly positive note with a celebration and official recognition of America's first Chinatown, an erasure of the fact that the US Congress passed racist legislation excluding Chinese from entering the country in 1882, kept such laws on the books until 1943, and prohibited Chinese from becoming eligible for naturalization until 1952. This populist finale also contributes to 'historical amnesia' by presenting a classless democracy, a mythic type corresponding to the 'free, unharnessed fiction' that Parker Tyler suggests is 'capable of many variations and distortions, even though it remains imaginative truth.'[31] We see Wong Fei-hung and Aunt Yee leaving town for their return to China in the closing shot, but what are they going home to? The country was moving towards a last blow against the Qing empire, the 1911 Revolution, and the unsteady years of the early Republic that followed, a period marked by attempts at constitutional government and economic dependence on foreign loans. Other issues arose after the turn of the twentieth century as well, from political rights for women to male-dominated family authority and from sexual morality to youth subcultures. In essence, the series bears out Teshome Gabriel's claim that 'the individual "hero" in the Third World does not make history, he/she only serves historical necessities.'[32] The fact that westernized Yee and traditionalist Wong have not been formally betrothed by the end of this final episode is indicative of what Rey Chow describes as a 'struggle between the dominant and subdominant within the "native" culture itself.'[33] Identity, like memory, is always selective; like the cinematic couple, Hong Kong and China are already related yet several times removed.

The structure of many other films juxtaposes worlds to present a complex vision subtextually describing Hong Kong's curious present identity and suggestive of its future direction. Supernatural-based tales on particular present protagonists situated between the physical world and an otherworld. Ann Hui's *The Spooky Bunch* (1980) and Samo Hung's *Encounter of the Spooky Kind* (1982) were cinematic suggestions that a specter was beginning to haunt Hong Kong, the specter of 1997. The city-state was becoming apparitional; it is probably not surprising that the phantasmic *Chinese Ghost Story* trilogy, as well as the preternatural *Swordsman* saga, became popular when they did, in the years following the 1984 Joint Declaration and the 1989 carnage in Tiananmen Square.[34] From their post-Han dynasty (202 BCE to 220 CE) origins, a period of political turmoil and foreign incursion, such stories expressed anxieties about China's social order, criticized its dominant power structures, and toyed with conventional mores of Chinese society.[35] Government authorities were suspicious of novels and plays written about the supernatural and were not above suppressing publications and performances. Writing on the development of drama during the Ming–Qing period, Tanaka Issei suggests that elites had reason to be concerned since 'most of the theaters in small market towns were dominated by people with close ties to secret societies.'[36] Supernatural themes were especially popular in these settings, where itinerant acting troupes presented dramas for audiences generally composed of common people. As Colin Mackerras notes, the 'theater was more than a place for enjoyment and relaxation; it was also a major social force, the influence of which extended deeply into the lives of the people.'[37] Much later, Mao's wife Jian Qing called for the suspension of 'ghost plays.'[38]

Ghost story subjects derive from the traditional Chinese view that the human soul consists of two parts. At death, one part enters heaven where it joins with spiritual beings (*shen*), some anthropomorphic and some not, while the other part descends into the earth. If the latter has been vexed for some reason – violent demise such as an accident or a murder, untimely or unjust passing away – it can reappear as an erratic, sometimes pernicious ghost (*kuei*). Ultimately, the parts will be indistinguishable, but for a time neither differs markedly from living human beings. According to Charles O. Hucker, it is believed that both 'can influence affairs in the physical world; demonic ghosts can even take possession of human beings and cause them to do things contrary to their normal wills and natures.'[39]

Ching Siu-tung's *Chinese Ghost Story* costume trilogy was adapted from a collection of celebrated short stories by P'u Sung-ling (1640–1715) entitled *Strange Stories from a Chinese Studio.*[40] Most deal with diligent young scholars who are drawn into peril, shame, and ruin by fox-fairies masquerading as beguiling maidens. The 1987 debut opens with bill collector Ning Tsai-shen (Leslie Cheung) seeking shelter from a rainstorm inside a run-down temple. The story revolves around the ghost Sian (Joey Wong), who has become enslaved to the tree demon Lao-lao, a shape-shifting androgyne with an enormously long thick tongue that would make Gene Simmons jealous. Having been murdered and had part of her soul agitated as a result, Sian was apparently damned to seducing men so that her overseer could suck the life-force out of them in order to prolong her own existence. Sian, who says that 'all the men I killed deserved it' because they were bad, is changed by her feelings for the inexperienced and unsuspecting Ning. Their principal love-making scene is marked by an absence – Sian does not ring a bell that is used to signal Lao's reanimation. Unfortunately, the would-be scholar hits the chime secured around her ankle and all hell breaks loose. A ghost-busting Taoist rapper, Swordsman Yen (Wu Ma), helps the naive Ning rescue Sian's soul from perdition.

Chinese Ghost Story continued a collaboration between Ching and Tsui Hark that began in 1980 when the former served as action director for the latter's *Dangerous Encounters.*[41] As Terence Chang recalls,

> Tsui was good with comical scenes and situations while Ching was very imaginative with action scenes. Tsui grew up watching and was fascinated by Shaw Brothers period action films, whereas Ching literally trained in that world. They complemented each other and were tied together by their shared romantic vision.

Tsui Hark had achieved success several years earlier with the swordplay and sorcery of *Zu: Warriors from the Magic Mountain*, a movie in which he imported special-effects veterans from the Steven Spielberg stable to work postproduction, something that was almost unheard of in the Hong Kong film industry at the time. *Chinese Ghost Story*, a creation, in part, of Tsui's Cinefex Workshop, the SFX subsidiary of Film Workshop that he founded with his wife Nansun Shi in 1984, set a new standard for optical effects quality in Hong Kong cinema.

Transgressing genre boundaries, *Chinese Ghost Story* displays a kind of Derridean extravagance, overrunning everything in its sight, much as Lao's grotesque slavering and devouring tongue does when it is extended and on the move. Noting the film's rapid pacing, quick-edit cutting, and sartorial splendor, Ching Siu-tung says the design is 'like watching a Chinese MTV,'[42] a point made more telling by the inclusion of three music videos amidst the concocted swordplay, high-flying aerialists, and visual pyrotechnics. At one point, the movie breaks into a song about Taoism for no apparent reason, in the manner of a Hollywood musical. At another, the picture's eerie ambience is captured in cantopop queen Sally Yeh's rendition of 'Let the Dawn Never Come,' which expresses the impossibility of either Sian, as a ghost, or her transdimensional romance with Ning ever seeing the light of day. The movie's 'kinesis-thesis' is underscored not by the numerous action scenes, but by a classic comedy bit. Ching follows Lao's sadistic whipping of the young ghost for allegedly harboring a male, with Sian holding Ning underwater to save him from the demon (played by a man in drag) who detects 'the smell of a living man.' All the while, the director is conjuring up terror; the creepy corpses of the men that the ghost has killed resemble the zombies in *Night of the Living Dead,* George Romero's metaphor for 'the crass, spiritless consumption of goods,'[43] which characterizes Hong Kong in the minds of many. The townspeople become frightened of Ning because 'he's lived among ghosts' and they eventually flee altogether because of the chaotic situation brought on by his and Sian's tryst, leaving behind them a 'ghost town' of the kind that Hong Kong might become post-1997. In the penultimate scene, Swordsman Yen, having defeated the ghouls and goblins, nevertheless sighs, 'I don't know if I'm a man or ghost,' thereby alluding to Hong Kongers' identity problem.

Chinese Ghost Story 2 (1990) opens with Cheung, reprising his role as Ning Tsaishen, being unjustly imprisoned in a case of mistaken identity. The still-bumbling debt collector's cellmate is Elder Chu (Ku Feng), an intellectual who has decided that he has fewer problems when he is in prison. An author-philosopher, Chu's list of 'crimes' range from writing travelogues and history books – for which he is accused of revealing state secrets and satirizing the present – to penning works on military strategy and stories about fairies, which bring allegations that he is planning a rebellion and promoting superstition. Innuendoes concerning the People's Republic are transparent; *Chinese Ghost Story* was released in the year after the events in Tiananmen Square and subsequent official denials, which Ching Siu-tung acknowledges influenced him. Commenting on the series generally, Ching says that the films 'are about conflict against the authories, about how governments are very corrupt and the people always suffer as a result.'[44]

Two more instances of mistaken identity occur after Chu helps Ning escape rather than face execution. First, Ning, upon meeting Windy (Joey Wong), thinks he is seeing Sian. Then Windy misidentifies him as Elder Chu, when he reads one of the sage's poems that she interprets to be about saving her father Lord Fu from the dissolute government officials who hold him. Ning, sporting a wispy beard and sounding like a deconstructionist, says, 'meaning doesn't matter, interpret it anyway you like.' To which Autumn (Jackie Cheung), a Taoist priest who can burrow underground and freeze people, adds 'we should have our own views.' Ning and Autumn join with Windy, her sister, and some swordsmen in their quest to free the father. Upon his rescue, Lord Fu remarks that the 'emperor is surrounded by sycophants,' and he seeks the assistance of Swordsman Hu (Waise Lee) in attempting to save the nation from its government as well as from dogma and idolatry; the demon is a demon that materializes as a high priest with a droning mantra. Hu, after agreeing to help, 'even though our political views are different,' sacrifices himself for the cause, thereby living up to Fu's observation that 'the way you look death calmly in the face proves that you are loyal to our country.'

Swordsman Yen's (Wu Ma) punditry becomes explicitly political in this movie. In response to Windy asking, 'why does the wind suddenly blow so violently?' and Ning commenting that 'it's hard to tell which direction is which,' Yen, as if looking ahead to 1997, says, 'evil spirits pervade this road, our lives hang by a single thread.' The priest later sneers at him for his non-belief: 'The masses love to worship their idols. Why set yourself against the people?' Yen's retort is sharp: 'It's their ignorance that has allowed you to succeed. You'll never deceive people again. Justice for all!' Whereupon he destroys the false god and issues a clarion call for solidarity: 'Don't separate into sects, we're all fighting the same enemy.' Yet, in expressing resignation at the end with the comment that 'good deeds fade like the wind, no matter what you've done, it's just forgotten,' Yen leaves us with the questions that Hong Kongers were asking themselves at the time. Is forgetting good or bad? Should we have faith? Is false hope better than none?

Chinese Ghost Story rejected the obligatory cinematic happy ending, the gullible Ning's maxim from early in the picture – 'love conquers the world' – notwithstanding. There is no boy meets ghost-maiden; boy loses ghost-maiden; boy gets ghost-maiden back; boy and ghost-maiden live happily ever after. Thus the film unmasked an ideology that substitutes 'a spurious unity for the reality of conflict,'[45] one that posits the immutability of heterosexual coupling, denies the likelihood of irreconcilable differences, and resolves social problems in personalized ways. The refusal of *Chinese Ghost Story* to 'make things right' was magnified by the physical attractiveness of both Leslie Cheung and Joey Wong, as well as by the chemistry that the two displayed when onscreen together. So when episode two introduced Wong as Windy, a human clone of the ghost Sian, it appeared to be reconsidering the previous movie's conclusion. Despite her apparent death at the hands of Tsai-shen when she is possessed by demon spirits and conceivably subject to Sian's lot in the first episode, Windy reappears in time to leave an arranged marriage for Ning at the film's close. The rebuff of reactionary tradition in favor of freedom of choice is, however, narrowly framed, suggesting that restoration of the order Janice Radway calls the 'ideal romance,' which 'represents real female needs within the story and then depicts their satisfaction by traditional heterosexual relations,'[46] may be possible after all. The liberal, therefore, becomes conservative as the film takes a step (or two) backwards.

Tsui Hark and Ching Siu-tung began moving on while the ghost theme was running its course, their multi-helmed period piece *Swordsman* appearing in 1990. Tracing its lineage to *fantastique* films, the movie was an effort to revitalize the magical swordplay epics of an earlier era. Both filmmakers had made a previous stab in this direction, Tsui with the successful *Zu* and Ching with *Duel to the Death* (1983), but 1980s' film audiences had 'abandoned swordplay for gunplay' and their preferences ran towards 'trigger happy Triads, gambling goons, and Daoist priests prancing.'[47] *Swordsman* would do for swordplay flicks what *Once Upon a Time in China* did for martial arts movies. Its success resulted in two sequels, although little in the first release gave much impression of what was to follow. The films move subversively away from the Louis Cha novel that spawned them, as Ching Siu-tung's 'lysergic Shakespearean'[48] vision meets Artaud's 'theatre of cruelty.' The trilogy becomes a fiendishly satirical commentary on the chaos wrought by permanent revolution, be it Maoist or Hong Kong capitalist; yet, in postmodern fashion, it offers no clues to something better.

Swordsman 2, directed by Ching, opens innocently enough: Ling (Jet Li) and Kiddo (Michelle Reis) are on their way to a meeting with the swordsmen of Hua Mountain to discuss their future. Taking time out to visit Ming Ming (Rosamund Kwan), they find an empty encampment and learn that General Fong, a one-time Sun Moon leader, has seized her father, the sect chieftain. Fong plans to form an alliance between the Miao people and a band of Japanese ninjas to overthrow the Ming Dynasty Court. Moreover, he has taken a sacred scroll and used its 'Sunflower Scriptures' to gain supernatural powers in his quest to control China and, ultimately, conquer the world. This means that Fong has had to castrate himself as the scriptures dictate one must do to master the scroll's puissant techniques.[49] Fong's self-castration, and his assuming the nom de guerre Invincible Asia (Brigitte Lin), turn out to be the first steps towards complete transformation from man to woman; as such they also initiate what can only be described as cinematic polymorphic perversity. Ching plays it over the top with Dionysian abandon, creating 'ecstatic cinema'[50] captured by multiple cameras dramatically careening at all angles and sundry color schemes of permeating blues, reds, and browns. The wire stunts come fast and furious; in one scene the screen is awash with swordsmen flying to and fro as they attack the super-powered Zu. 'Slice and dice' computer effects cut people, trees, and disturbingly, Kiddo's horse in half. By the film's end, Asia's sex change is complete, an act of Nietzschean self-creation in which Lin 'reinvents' herself as a woman by altering her physical gestures. According to the director, 'When she is a male her movements are more like a man, after sex change more feminine.'[51]

Stephen Teo, commenting on *Swordsman 2*, writes that it is a 'telling attack on the stereotype of the male hero,'[52] swordsman Ling serving as a second to the transgendered Invincible Asia. As such, the film turns the obedient and submissive female (yin) and the aggressive and dominant male (yang) upside down. But Sek Kei points out that,

> Although China has long regarded the female as inferior to the male (witness the cruel practice of foot-binding), it is also true to say that China possesses a tradition of the superior female … and Chinese folk legend possesses numerous tales of martial heroes with extraordinary powers.[53]

Han-era Hua Mulan is the classic example; disguising herself as a man and taking her father's place on the battlefield, she was an adept, bold, and courageous warrior. Moreover, Hong Kong's cinematic history records that one of the first martial arts films ever made, *The Heroine of Lone River* (1925), featured a fighting woman in a starring role.[54] What distinguishes Asia from her predecessors is that she does battle not to maintain the status quo, but to shake things up.

Disorder is the order! Chaotic and unstable conditions are expressed by Ling Wu-ching's remark that 'wherever there are people there is inevitable conflict' and depicted as the earth's terrain turning back upon itself. The transsexual Asia suggests that identities are multifarious and open to change. Taking this to heart, Hong Kong twenty-something Cary Kwok enthuses, 'I am Chinese and I'm more than Chinese and I'm not Chinese at the same time.'[55] The indeterminancy that characterizes the film, like that which beset Hong Kong in the early 1990s, is also anxiety-ridden, as when Invincible Asia falls for Ling Wu-ching, portrayed here by Jet Li as a boozer and fool. S/he is unable to consummate the relationship and arranges for the swordsman to spend an evening with a bottle of magic wine and a surrogate, her/his female lover, Snow. Later, with the sex change complete, Asia refuses to employ her full array of powers, including exploding 'palm power' and soaring kung fu needles, to fight Wu-ching. Instead, she leaps from a cliff to her apparent death with him pleading to know the truth – was it with her that he had made love? Like those in the colony swept up by the Tiananmen Square effect, a manic condition that had people looking for any exit, Asia's suicide symbolizes her desire to get out no matter what the price.[56]

Swordsman 3: The East is Red (1993), for which Ching Siu-tung and Raymond Lee receive co-directorial credits, opens twenty-three years after Invincible Asia's supposed demise. Ming emissary Koo (Yu Rong Kwong), warning that it is 'not wise for living people to be here,' has led Spaniards to Asia's grave site, which they summarily plunder in search of the secret scroll and its scriptures. Whereupon Koo is snatched by the 'deceased,' who discloses to him that she has been living an ascetic life in the intervening years. He informs her of various cults of personality that have developed in her name, remarking that there are 'many Asia Invincibles in the world,' including a man who has his followers worship him as a god, and an Asia impersonator who is actually her concubine Snow (now played by Joey Wong) from the second episode. The two renew their affair and deck themselves out in Japanese rather than Chinese attire, while Asia proceeds to exact revenge from the pretenders and regain her rightful position; after all, she complains, it is 'painful to be ordinary.' Ching's trademark action and effects propel the movie at warp speed; Asia dispenses with a Spanish galleon and a Japanese warship that converts into a submarine (a wooden one, no less), all the while slashing through the water riding a swordfish bareback. Levitating ships, vomiting samurai, and kite-gliding ninjas contribute to the film's general mayhem. *The East is Red,* taking its title from a Cultural Revolution 'model' opera written to create positive and 'heroic proletarian images,'[57] is the final episode of the *Swordsman* saga. Like the overexuberant Red Guards who disrupted the country and carried it to the brink of collapse, Ching Siu-tung and Tsui Hark (the trilogy's producer) tear almost everyone and everything apart in a nervous Foucauldian joyride of 'bodies and pleasure' on a collision course with 1997.

Important social changes accompanied Hong Kong's 'economic miracle.' Women's labor-force participation grew and formal education levels rose, while the average age of marriage increased and fertility rates declined. Average household size fell as well, from 4.5 persons in 1971 to 3.3 persons in 1996.[58] As the position of women improved, it was, perhaps, only a matter of time before the impact of this change would affect the colony's film industry. Director Cheung Yuen-ting maintains that 'I am lucky to be a female director in Hong Kong because I think in all of Asia, Hong Kong is the place which has the least prejudice against women. On the set the crew members are too busy even to remember whether you are a man, a woman or an ET.'

Michelle Yeoh, recalling her 1984 screen debut, says, 'In my first movie, *Owl versus Dumbo*, I played the generic hapless female, but I saw the men having all the fun doing the action scenes and I wanted to do that too. It was a revolutionary idea and I hope I opened the door for many other actresses to do action in Hong

Kong.'[59] Yeoh, who appeared as a cop in a number of late 1980s' contemporary action flicks, plays real-life s/hero Yim Wing-chun in Yuen Woo-ping's 1994 film *Wing Chun*. Having learned martial arts in order to escape a forced marriage, Yim is mistakenly identified as a man by some because of her male dress and is forced to endure sexist comments such as 'women who fight are no good even if they are beautiful' and 'since you've taken up kung fu, you've lost all your femininity.' Her final battle with Flying Chimpanzee is peppered with the latter's remarks about sex and power: 'You are really gorgeous, I must have you.' 'Not everyone can tame a wild horse.' 'I'll give you a ride.' Wing-chun's superior fighting skills, however, reduce her adversary to a pre-pubescent boy.

With their social roles changing (even as certain traditional aspects are retained), Hong Kong women have raised issues ranging from birth control and abortion to health and child care, questioning male authority and power in the process. One consequence is an uncertainty about the functions of the family; at the very least, men must assume greater responsibility for childrearing. More profound is the possibility that heterosexuality will cease to operate as a cultural norm, and will give way to 'a situation in which the sex of one's lover is a matter of social indifference.'[60] Signs of growing violence against women in Hong Kong, therefore, represent an ominous development. The period between 1984 and 1992 has seen a 33 per cent increase in reported rapes and a 45 per cent rise in reported indecent assaults.[61] While increases in reported violence may reflect a greater willingness on the part of women to come foward in such circumstances, battered women often indicate that police do not register their complaints, instead telling them to go home and not anger their husbands again. In the meantime, requests for space in Hong Kong's battered women's shelters exceeded the available number of beds every year, forcing women and children to be turned away.

In cinematic space, 'fant-asia' films such as the *Chinese Ghost Story* and *Swordsman* trilogies depict she-demons and power-hungry castrators, the 'monstrous-feminine' that Barbara Creed suggests signifies (as does the female hero) a blurring of gender boundaries and representations. Creed asserts that such movies simultaneously express 'perverse masculine desire' for the collapse of gendered borders and male fear of becoming woman – 'the ultimate scenario of powerlessness.'[62] This schizophrenia, in effect, produces an unease similar to that found in Hong Kong, a place wrestling with East–West and traditional–contemporary tensions.

As filmmaker Ronny Yu puts it, 'Nowhere else in the world were you told that by 1997 your way of life might end, that a new boss is going to come in and tell you how to live.' Yu's *The Bride With White Hair* (1993) is a unique addition to the roster of Hong Kong supernatural films, slower paced and more ethereal, moody rather than frenetic. This is not to say that the movie lacks fighting, swordplay, and wire stunts, but to suggest that the action is secondary to the conflict and turmoil that its main characters experience. Freely adapted from *Bride*, a 1950s' martial arts novel by Liang Yu-shing set in the Ming dynasty, the movie is a magical-realist *Romeo and Juliet* that cannot help but reflect upon Hong Kong's unusual situation.[63] Cho Yi-hang (Leslie Cheung) falls in love with Lian (Brigitte Lin). Unfortunately, there is a problem: he is a Wu Tang clan commander and she is an assassin for the Supreme Cult, an opposing sect led by hermaphroditic Siamese twins (Elaine Lui/Francis Ng).

Ronny Yu, who has the distinction of having directed Chow Yun-fat in his only martial arts film, *The Postman Strikes Back* (1982), recalls thinking that the 'heroine with sword' movie had 'been done to death' in the early 1990s. Moreover, *Bride* was a romance; in Yu's words,

> I'd never done that genre. I kept saying that I can't do it, I don't have it. My wife told me, you just don't want to face it, explore that area of your character because you are afraid. Do it the way that you want, don't worry about how other directors have done it.[64]

Yu's wife suggested that he go to Tokyo to hire renowned costumer designer Emi Wada, a decision for which 'the HK press really gave it to me.' The director says it was as if 'I was being sacreligious. "Ronny Yu went to Japan to hire a Japanese costume designer for a traditional costumer Chinese story." But my wife was right. I thought that Emi Wada's visual colors and texture would stimulate me to think differently.' Armed with a big budget by Hong Kong standards (about US$3 million), Yu persuaded Leslie Cheung, who protested that he had never done a martial arts film, to come on board by telling him that

> it doesn't matter, I can use doubles. I need your acting skills, I need your face. The character in the movie is almost like James Dean. I want a James Dean. If I go to a martial actor, he will want me to change the story or the ending.

In the movie, Cheung's character Cho is smitten 'at first sight,' a film convention, according to Mas'ud Zavarzadeh, that 'asserts its underlying ideology about woman: she is reduced to that which is openly visible; woman is surface.'[65] Of course, Brigitte Lin's Lian is not just a pretty face; raised by wolves and trained as a warrior, she is another of the stirring and formidable characters that has brought the actor much attention and many accolades. Howard Hampton refers to 'The Look' in which Lin suddenly returns 'the camera's memerized gaze with a blinding, eye for eye intensity.'[66] Moreover, Lin's presence in several of these roles speaks to desire that is sexually ambiguous and polymorphic, and therefore not limited to gaping heterosexual males. Nor is the slight Leslie Cheung an ideal martial arts hero, bringing as he does a somewhat effeminate quality to the screen, simultaneously offering audiences a 'he's so dreamy' movie-star, a coquetteish boy, and a Peter Pan-like androgynous figure. When Lian, rescued by Cho after being wounded in battle, returns the latter's love, the stage is set for an explosive coupling that sparks conflict between their respective clans. What follows is a tale of personal anguish, divided loyalties, and doomed relations.

Shot entirely indoors on a sound stage (and at night in deference to heavy costumes the actors wore in summertime), *Bride* is beautifully designed (Eddie Ma), enchantingly shot (Peter Pau) and, masterfully choreographed (Philip Kwok). Polycultural costumes and sets blend Chinese, Indian, Japanese, and Tibetan motifs. Reviewers Guido Heinkel and Lieu Pham enthuse,

> Using light to its fullest extent, the films whisks the viewer through beautiful images and capitvating settings. The atmospheric lighting, as well as the heavy blue and red tinges … are typical for Asian movies, yet are utilized completely differently in this film. Every image, every camera angle, and every word has a signature that is singular and as a whole weave it as a compelling movie experience.[67]

Conceived as a complete package, the film was the first made in Hong Kong to have postproduction sound done in North America, becoming the first 'Dolby digital' Hong Kong picture.

Some reviewers of *Bride* complained about the film's rhythm and pace, arguing that it skimped on action and comedy, and therefore fell flat as entertainment. Such criticism, however, misses the picture's dramatic focus, its enactment of Cho Yi-hang's personal torment alongside Lian's forlorn yet tender woman turned ruthless kung fu warrior. Yu relies upon numerous close-up shots of Leslie Cheung's and Brigitte Lin's eyes to convey their characters' emotional changes. During the course of the film, he contrasts the emotional and physical horror of war – in one instance a swordsman is sliced into eight pieces – with erotic and passionate romance. Most memorable is Lian and Cho making love beneath a waterfall – a scene, Ronny Yu remembers, that 'required them to be in the water for hours … but they were professionals and they knew they were doing something good.' Yu's earlier remark about using Leslie Cheung 'doubles' in action scenes is a reminder that motion picture fighting is not real martial arts, and that 'celluloid heroes' are just that – images on a reel of film. This one illuminates how the cinema masks production processes in creating what moviegoers see on the screen. And both reveal the means by which a film, 'while giving the illusion of a single perfomance, actually requires of the actor that his or her performance be broken up in time and space.'[68] As Walter Benjamin noted, cinematic wholeness is verisimilitude, an appearance realized through technology.[69]

Sounding like a Hong Konger attempting to alter a destiny decided by Britain and China, Cho Yi-hang's love for Lian (to whom he gives the name Ni-chang) leads him to propose, 'Let us find a place far away and leave all this chaos behind. This world does not belong to us. Let them fight it out.' Supreme Cult master/mistress Chi Wu-shuang, who found the orphaned Lian and 'spent so much time and effort on you,' does not take Lian's request to leave the group very well. Telling her that she will 'leave like a commoner,' Chi forces Lian to crawl across hot coals and be beaten with sticks, a scene the audience sees as a long narrow shot that accentuates the brutality and humiliation to which she is subjected. In the meantime, Cho, believed to be too kind-hearted and independent-minded despite years of grooming as the next leader of the Wu Tang, is told that 'the fall of Ming is imminent. You should be defending the empire, not sleeping with the enemy. You may leave, betray even those closest to you. The master raised you, go back, explain in person.' Doing so, he finds bloody beheaded corpses, the Supreme Cult having carried out a massacre ordered by the male twin who is enamored of Lian. Told that the 'wolf-girl' is responsible, Cho Yi-hang confronts Lian, who responds, 'Their deaths are none of my concern. Are you coming with me?' Despite his earlier assurance that he would never mistrust her, Cho spurns Lian, much as doubters believe China will do in defying the terms of the Joint

courtesy/permission of Mandarin Films

DOING SOMETHING GOOD Brigitte Lin and Leslie Cheung in Ronny Yu's *The Bride with White Hair*

Declaration. Feeling betrayed, she asks him 'why didn't you believe me?' Where-upon her hair turns white and becomes a weapon; shaking her head, Lian can strike snake-like, entangling her targets in the strands and piercing their skin with the ends. Too late does Cho Yi-hang realize that he has been lied to by his own, much as the British misled Hong Kongers about the negotiations over 1997. His repentant call of 'Ni-chang' is met by his spurned lover's cryptic 'she is dead.' Lian goes on a killing spree, slaughtering the Wu Tang clan. The mournful Cho goes into self-exile on snow-covered Mount Shin Fung, where it is said a flower blooms that can restore her hair to its original color and end the murderous spell.

The release of *Bride With White Hair* came at a mid-point between the events of Tiananmen Square and the handover. Hong Kongers' mad dash for foreign passports had slowed, the long lines outside foreign consulates had disappeared, and voices calling for abrogation of the 1984 Joint Declaration had quietened. Britain's belated (and cynical) move to 'democratize' its last colonial possession and China's certain opposition to the Patten reforms appeared another instance of Hong Kong's future resting in the hands of those outside its boundaries. More evenly paced than other films with which it has kinship, the picture is also more sobering, reflecting perhaps the coming of an inevitable 'through train,'[70] to 1997 and beyond, with or without Hong Kong people on board. The movie presents a stark choice between love and loyalty; in opting for either, Leslie Cheung's character chooses betrayal as well, quite possibly to his eternal regret. Of course, most Hong Kong people had no choice at all in the situation confronting them. Whether or not that circumstance would be a tragedy had yet to be answered, but evidence would be uncovered that Hong Kong's capitalists and the PRC's communists fashioned a Basic Law suited to their particular and mutual interests. *Bride*'s closing credits roll over a collage of scenes from the movie, overlaid by song lyrics (written, sung and performed by Leslie Cheung) relating that 'love and hate I cannot resolve … all at once I held in my hand the past and the future.'

The picture's success, not unexpectedly, produced a sequel. *Bride with White Hair 2* was released only three months after the first film appeared in local theaters. Yu, who abhors repeating previous work, 'didn't direct except for two scenes with Leslie and Brigitte.' The filmmaker says,

> the producers wanted to do another picture right away, but I was totally burned out and told them I couldn't help. And I've never been one to say if my last movie was action-packed and made lots of money, my next film will be action-packed so that I ride the wave and cash in.

He did receive a producer credit for *Bride with White Hair 2* (1993), although he indicates that his involvement consisted primarily of 'supporting my editor David Wu, who was directing his first movie.' *Bride 2*, costing less money and made in less time than its predecessor, picks up the story ten years later. Leslie Cheung's on-screen time as Cho Yi-hang is minimal, his participation limited by other contractual obligations (a comment, in itself, on both the art and business of cinema). While the picture focuses on Brigitte Lin's Lian Ni-chang, it follows the efforts of a group of youthful and ambitious Wu Tangers, led by Fung Chung-kit (Sunny Chan), attempting to save their clan from extinction at her hands (or hair).

Bride 2 revolves around Ni-chang's dictum, 'men: see one, kill one,' a theory and practice materializing from her double abandonment – by her father as a child and by Cho a decade earlier. Abducting Fung's bride, Lyre, on her wedding night, Lian asks 'why do you suffer for such a bastard?' Overhearing a male musician complain that men can be killed but they cannot be toyed with and insulted, she asks 'Do you mean that women can be?' Whereupon she orders him to play; unfortunately for the musician, he chooses to play the waterfall lovemaking melody from the previous movie and she disposes of him. Committed to wiping out the last of the Wu Tang clan, Lian has gathered a band of female kung fu guerrillas around her to help carry out the task. Her hardened persona is augmented by Yuen-yuen and Lin-wai – the former forsaken by her male lover and on the verge of committing suicide when saved by Lian; the latter victimized by a man's brutal beating and his vicious branding with a hot iron. Consoling the sobbing Lyre following her kidnapping, Yuen exhorts:

> the more affectionate the man, the more callous he becomes. His love for you will vanish overnight. I was hopeless and in despair but then I realized that without a man's love, I can still live. Don't shed any tears for men.

Later, Lin-wai, confronting her abuser, recounts his verbal and physical terror, repeating what he had screamed at her: 'I want you to remember you're an animal. You're a pig, a cow. You must obey my orders.' As chants of 'kill him' arise from the assembled women, Lin walks slowly yet assuredly towards her former tormenter and proceeds to stab him repeatedly with her sword. Lyre, under the spell of a magic potion and 'brainwashed' to believe that she was wed for the sole purpose of producing offspring for the Wu Tang, imagines killing her husband. Commenting on the experiences of those who have used women's shelters, Nancy Fraser writes that, 'Whereas most had originally blamed themselves as victims and defended their batterers, many came to reject that interpretation in favor of a politicized view that offered them new models of human agency ... they came to affiliate with other women.'[71]

Gender and handover issues are conflated in *Bride 2*, sometimes without consistency. Yuen-yuen, echoing what Cho said to Ni-chang in episode one, reflects the sentiment of émigré Hong Kongers: 'why don't we just leave here together and find a better place to live?' Ni-chang's refusal elicits a tirade from her lieutenant and would-be lover that casts her as China: 'you're jealous of Lyre and her husband. What she has with her husband, you never had with Cho Yi-hang. That's why you had to break them up.' Her followup comment restores her as a self-deluded Hong Kong lamenting the departure of the British: 'You're still thinking about him. Please don't forget he's the one who turned you into what you are today. Why don't you just forget about this heartless man? You don't think he has hurt you enough?' To which Ni-chang's Hong Kong laconically queries Yuen-yuen's China: 'So you'll think we'll be happy together?' As the film draws to an end, the compound is under attack from Fung Chung-kit and the Wu Tang martial arts militia. The women's compound is burning and crumbling around them, as is their solidarity. Yuen stabs Lian, yelling 'no one will have a happy ending with you.'

Cho returns with the magic flower, but, as in *Bride 1* when he belatedly realized that he had been deceived about his lover's role in his clan's massacre, it is too little, too late. He can no longer save Ni-chang; he can only destroy her, along with himself. Fung's observation that 'the important thing is that they're finally together' is of little comfort. For many, 1989 was Hong's Kong's fatal moment, while others trace the treachery to 1984. Some assert that Hong Kong's future was sealed by Britain's 1972 decision not to object to the removal of Hong Kong from a United Nations list of colonies to be decolonized, which effectively shut the door on the right to self-determination.[72] Yet Hong Kong's lot may have been decided a century earlier, in 1898, when China 'leased' the area that became known as the New Territories to Britain for ninety-nine years, an agreement that geographically transformed the territory and put questions of its later sovereignty aside at one and the same time. If Hong Kong always comprised borrowed people living on borrowed land and borrowed time, quite possibly its fate could not be other than tragic.

SIX

NEW DRAGONS FOREVER

Ask Western moviegoers to name a Hong Kong film actor and the likely answer would be either Bruce Lee or Jackie Chan, both known for martial arts and action. Lee's success opened up a path for Chan, although the film type and screen persona of each is distinct. Whereas Bruce Lee kicked high, Jackie Chan kicks low. Lee broke through walls with a single punch; Chan hurts his hand when he strikes a wall. The former was serious; the latter is a comic. Jackie Chan is, in effect, an anti-Bruce Lee, a conscious and calculated polar opposite.

Jackie Chan's story has been told countless times: how he was almost sold at birth by his parents, who could not afford the doctor's delivery fee; how he was sent to a demanding Peking Opera school at the age of seven, and how he was a member, alongside fellow future Hong Kong stars Samo Hung and Yuen Biao, of the Seven Little Fortunes group, which combined acting, acrobatics, singing and dancing, and various martial arts in their performances.[1] Upon leaving the academy at the age of seventeen, Chan worked as a stunt man, martial actor, and film extra for Shaw Brothers studio, including an appearance in Bruce Lee's *Fists of Fury*. Upon Lee's premature death, he was among the many groomed to become the next great Hong Kong kung fu star. Needless to say, things didn't work out for the Bruce Lee wannabes, including Jackie Chan, whose *New Fists of Fury* (1976) was the first of several flops. Part of the problem was that Chan looked thin and appeared to possess little of the authoritative character that marked his predecessor's screen presence. But the younger actor had his own thoughts on the matter: 'Bruce was the best at what he did. No one can ever do it better. So why should we try? People want to see living ideas not dead ones. Bruce was a success because he did things that no one else was doing.'[2] With this sentiment in mind, Jackie Chan proceeded to remake himself.

The performer that moviegoers would embrace first appeared on screen in 1978 in Yuen Woo-ping's *Snake in the Eagle's Shadow* as a provincial ne'er-do-well, which offered Chan both physical and verbal comic opportunities that he had previouly been denied. The butt of others' jokes and a target for their punches and kicks thoughout most of the film, his character eventually prevails, becoming the Jackie Chan prototype in the process. While the picture may not have invented kung fu comedy, this Ng See Yuen production 'revolutionized the martial arts marketplace' by embracing 'Operatic influences wholeheartedly, allowing its players to bounce and flip across the screen with an energy and exuberance that bore little relation to real martial arts fighting.'[3] Contrasting *Snake*'s looseness to the rigid action pattern of traditional kung fu flicks, Shu Kei suggests that 'kids really could identify with the rebellion aspects of Chan's character.'[4] The film's spirit was amplified by a villainous character (Hung Cheng-li) played to type, and its appeal was enhanced by a storyline revolving around a fatuous student and his wayward teacher (Yuen Siu-tin, the director's father) that resembled popular father–son stories. The Bruce Lee comparison that had been hanging over Jackie Chan like a sword of Damocles was about to disappear.

Chan's star status was assured with the release of *Drunken Master* (1978) and *Fearless Hyena* (1979), movies borrowing from *Snake*'s impetuous youngster growing under the tutelage of an elderly and eccentric teacher that traded in having 'fun with traditional values.'[5] *Drunken Master*, containing one of the most famous martial arts scenes in history, a fifteen-minute piece of choreographed fighting between Jackie Chan and Heung Cheng-li, caricatures Chinese folk hero Wong Fei-hung. *Fearless Hyena*, Jackie Chan's directorial debut, fully liberates Chan the performer. As zaniness begets egoistic excess, he employs an acting style 'best summed up as shameless mugging for the camera.'[6] Chan's improved action-director skills are on display here. According to Clyde Gentry,

> The problem with much of Chan's earlier choreography was the absence of rhythm. Much of the motion on the screen would start and stop with each individual movement, hinting at the fact that the action was choreographed like numbered dance steps.[7]

In contrast, *Fearless Hyena*'s physical comedy and action scenes (including a famed spear fight) are graceful, offering evidence of the performer's suppleness that has earned him comparisons to both Charlie Chaplin and Gene Kelly. Everyday objects make their first appearance in these movies as Jackie Chan uses chopsticks, a bench, and oversized fake breasts as weapons. According to Marx, commodities have both use-value and exchange-value. Chan's appropriation for use of bigger and more expensive things culminates in *Rumble in the Bronx* (1995): a sports car races a hydrofoil through crowded downtown streets as the actor tears holes in the latter's rubber bumpers – an act of consumption not as an active process in which meaning is constantly re-created, as Hebdige argues, but of the 'destructive creation' evident in the making of ever more costly and sensationalized films in late capitalism.

Playing the smiling underdog instead of the earnest martial arts champion, Jackie Chan absorbs punches, slips and falls, and contorts his face and body in myriad ways. As the actor himself remarked, 'Nobody can beat Bruce Lee; everybody can beat me.'[8] The performer laughs at himself and moviegoers follow suit. Audiences throughout Asia (except in Japan, his success there having to wait a few years) and in parts of North America responded to the acrobatic zeal, innocent persona, and optimistic enthusiasm that Jackie Chan brought to the screen. Writing about comics, Bernard F. Dick suggests that, in 'becoming scapegoats for our sake and suffering indignities on our behalf … [they] are really asking for our approval, our love. They humiliate themselves to win our applause.'[9] Kicked and knocked around for most of the on-screen time in his movies, Chan would manage to come out on top in the end, and thereby make things right in the world. His comedic goal, much like Buster Keaton's, whom he cites as an influence and to whom he has been compared, is restoring 'order in the face of society's errors and false judgments.'[10]

Chan parlayed his late 1970s' success, which contributed greatly to the reappearance of Cantonese-dialect pictures in Hong Kong, into a 1980 contract with Raymond Chow's Golden Harvest company that offered him opportunities to 'make it' in Hollywood. By 1985, he had left the United States, complaining that

> When I'm in Hong Kong, I make sure that every shot is perfect – that it follows the rhythm of the fight, that it properly captures the flow of the choreography. I plan the action. I supervise the editing. I hire the fighters and stuntmen. I can make sure that

what I see in my head comes out on the screen. In my Hollywood movies, I never had that kind of freedom or that kind of control.[11]

Chan's Hong Kong career, however, continued to flourish during this period, one in which he again remade himself, becoming the biggest film star in Asia. Leaving behind him the restrictions of Qing dynasty kung fu, Chan turned to early-twentieth-century colonial Hong Kong in *Project A* (1983), to a 1930s' urban gangster spoof in *Miracles: Mr. Canton and Lady Rose* (1989), to contemporary settings and themes, including several *Police Story* pictures, which began appearing mid-decade.

In 1983 Jackie Chan took a break from his travails in Hollywood and teamed up in Hong Kong with his Opera School friends Samo Hung and Yuen Biao, themselves highly regarded members of Hong Kong's martial arts cinema. Hung, the oldest of the Seven Little Fortunes performance group and possessor of a rotund yet agile body (hence his nickname, 'Fat Dragon'), has been an action director, actor, director, producer, scriptwriter, and stuntman in his long career. As an action director, his techniques are among those that have set the standard in fight choreography. As an actor, Hung's on-screen presence, combining strength and style, is refined, yet his depiction of frail and innocent characters makes them believable. As a director, his work ranges from classic martial arts (*Enter the Fat Dragon*, 1978) to kung fu comedy (*Knockabout*, 1977) and kung fu horror (*Close Encounters of the Spooky Kind*, 1981) to action/adventure (*Eastern Condors*, 1987).[12] Meanwhile, Yuen Biao, considered the best acrobat of his Hong Kong film generation and perhaps the most physically gifted martial arts performer of his time, is a veteran industry team player.[13] Chan, Hung, and Yuen (known collectively as The Three Brothers) would make several popular films during the 1980s, including *Project A*, a pirate movie that takes place almost exclusively on land; *Wheels on Meals* (1984, directed by Samo Hung), Jackie Chan's first contemporary-setting picture shot on location in Spain and featuring a famous fight scene with then US kickboxing champion Benny 'The Jet' Urquidez; and *Dragons Forever* (1987, also helmed by Hung), a title not without irony, given that it was the last movie that the three would make together.

Project A is a tale of police corruption and institutional rivalry. The film opens with a Royal Hong Kong Police commander complaining that coastguard attempts to rid Hong Kong harbor of pirates is a waste of money that leaves his own force underfunded and ill-equipped to fight criminals in the colony. A remark about no pay raises recalls early colonial days when the British were unwilling to pay for law enforcement, a situation that left the town 'unsafe after dark with deserting sailors, Triad gangs, and remittance men … undeterred by the occasional police patrol.'[14] Chan plays Dragon Ma, a dedicated marine patrol officer with a nationalist streak; beneath the hijinks, which include a bar-room fight pitting coastguard against cops lifted from the John Ford school of brawling slapstick, is a jab at colonialism. When the marine patrol is abolished following the tavern mayhem, Chan and other unemployed sailors are transferred to their hated adversaries, the police, and forced to endure a rigorous program under a comprador training officer (Yuen Biao). When pirates kidnap a British official and several elite expats, Dragon Ma discovers that a deal has been struck to secure their safe return; an agreement that represents the selling out of Hong Kong. Stealing some rifles (a significant statement in itself given the ban on Hong Kong Chinese possessing weapons) and taking matters into his own hands, Chan eventually joins forces with his police department rival Yuen and a conman (Samo Hung) to best the marauders, the three defending neither a British possession nor a surrogate China, but a place that is their own. Produced while the Sino–British Joint Declaration negotiations were taking place, *Project A* fashions a 'colonial legend'[15] with present-day ramifications that expresses Jackie Chan's allegiance to Hong Kong.

Reading Fredric Jameson against the grain and pointing to a scene from the film in which Dragon Ma bursts into an exclusive club in pursuit of a criminal, Ramie Tateishi argues that Chan's world of cinematic pastiche is alive. Tateishi notes that objects occupying the scene's visual space, 'from the furniture to the chandelier, are not empty props devoid of meaning, signifying exhaustion of form – instead they are transformed into part of the action, this unique pastiche of motion as Chan stumbles over chairs while people fight with coat racks.'[16] Moreover, the transgression by martial arts in this scene of the fashionable European club (a blow against empire akin to that of breaking into the weapons depot) contributes to an invigorated stylistic blend that runs counter to Jameson's elegy to the demise of innovation. Playfully calling this development 'a new visual tradition,' Tateishi suggests that Jackie Chan's 'use of pastiche serves the purpose of reinvention – not just of himself as a performer, but of the genres that he ties together.'[17]

Two scenes from *Project A*, both among Jackie Chan's most memorable and each expressing his trajectory from kung fu to modern action, offer fans the kind of filmmaking that they thrive on and expect to see. The first is a wild 'high-speed' bicycle chase that has Chan expertly navigating a series of constricted passageways and wielding the bike he is riding as a weapon. The second, introducing what the performer calls the 'really, really, really dangerous stunt,'[18] is a tribute to Harold Lloyd and his celebrated 1923 feat in *Safety Last*. Lloyd's successful scaling of a wall in the face of myriad obstacles, the most famous moment of which was his hanging from the minute hand of a clock, satirized 'upward mobility' in the boom years of the 1920s in the United States. But it also showed that diligence pays off; after all, he did make it to the top (getting the girl in the process). Meanwhile, Jackie Chan's stunt has him losing hold of the clock and plunging several stories through awnings before slamming to the ground – much as the value of Hong Kong's dollar fell following a run on the colony's currency in 1983. With handover talks serving as a backdrop, depreciated currency was evidence of residents' growing anxiety. The actor's fall from the clocktower suggested that he had run out of time, something that Hong Kong was on the verge of doing in 1997, which in the hands of another filmmaker might have been the point. In this instance, the film's final cut included three separate falls, made to appear as if they were one drop shot from three different angles, and it ran stunt outtakes under the closing credits – both devices that would become signature Jackie Chan. In other words, the sanguine Chan survives to fight the 'good fight' another day and we can only expect that he thinks Hong Kong will do the same.

Dragon Ma's return four years later in *Project A, Part 2* (1987) as a member of the colony's police force has him assigned the task of ferreting out high-level and widespread department corruption. Recalling 1970s' scandals which disclosed Triad payoffs to many law enforcement officals and personnel, Ma complains that prostitution, gambling, and opium exist because police officers with dangerous and poorly paid jobs 'don't want to do anything.' Recognizing the discrimination that prohibits Chinese officers from carrying weapons and that pays them less than their British counterparts, he nevertheless believes (referring to his job as a 'noble mission') that they should perform their duties responsibly. In contrast, Chan's nemesis Chun (David Lam), a crooked police superintendent with ties to pirates, says 'You're a good cop, I'm a bad cop. We will always clash.' To prove his point, Chun frames Ma on a robbery charge – the latter having been responsible for

Chun's dismissal from the police force during the anti-corruption campaign – and gets his job back for a time.

The sequel, set on the cusp of the 1911 fall of the Qing dynasty, introduces the theme of revolution through three women (Maggie Cheung, Rosamund Kwan, and Carina Lau) who sell flowers to raise money for weapons. As with the cops, the revolutionaries are revealed to be divided when one among their ranks turns paid informer, betraying his comrades. In ultimately protecting the rebels and letting them escape from agents sent to Hong Kong to shut down its use as a base for insurgent operations, Jackie Chan takes the politically correct anti-Qing position. Moreover, this subject provides him with an opportunity to make the most direct political statement of his career. Invited to join the revolution, he hears Kwan's character assert that 'For great things to succeed you must suffer loss. We're always ready to sacrifice ourselves for the revolution.' Chan's refusal and rebuttal is a lengthy speech:

> No matter how great my goals sound I would never go to such lengths to achieve them as to break the law. Actually, I admire you very much because you will do great deeds. I also understand that to overturn the Qing government people have to make sacrifices. But I don't dare ask people to do that because I don't know what we'll get in the end after we put our lives on the line. That's what I like about being a policeman. I think one life is as important as another. I must protect everyone. A country of four hundred million is made up of individuals; if they don't like their daily lives, how can they love their country?

Her follow-up is a snipe at Britain's 'decaying colonial system [that] does not permit the existence of a true, good policeman. They will keep trying to destroy you.' To which Chan replies, 'As long as such people exist, I feel it my duty to be here.' But what about when British colonialism ends? His preference seems to be for the British over the Chinese system; thus his loyalty to Hong Kong appears to be contextualized (Ma is, remember, part of the Royal police). As Jackie Chan himself has pointed out, his Australian passport ensured that he would 'have a safe place to run if things went bad in the year 1997.'[19]

More than one reviewer has noted the absence of Samo Hung and Yuen Biao in the second of Chan's two Republican-era comedies, usually to suggest that his silliness is best served when tempered by more tightly structured scenarios. Of course, Chan's fans love the excesses that he is more than willing to give them.

The action in *Part 2* is delirious, particularly the final twenty minutes consisting of a seemingly endless array of acrobatic stunts as Jackie Chan fights dishonest cops and Qing government thugs. Feeding audiences what they crave, he incorporates the usual array of 'ready mades' such as hot peppers and ladders into the film's kinetic art, displays great dexterity in running across elevated bamboo shafts, and gets tossed about like a sack of potatoes. Jackie Chan afficionados consider two scenes – one comedy and one action – from this movie to be among his best. The first, reminiscent of Marx Brothers' hide-and-seek, has Maggie Cheung trying to conceal film characters from one another in her apartment; these include ruffians, a revolutionary, Dragon Ma and the cop to which he is handcuffed, the police commissioner, and superintendent Chun. The second, a homage to Buster Keaton, involves the actor running down the wall of a collapsing building. In his 1928 film *Steamboat Bill Jr.*, Keaton stood as an actual frame wall fell around him, the stunt accomplished because he was standing in a spot coinciding with an open window. Chan's stunt, requiring him to reach the window space with the wall coming down, is a feat of precision and timing that embodies what the daredevil calls 'the thrill of high risk.'[20]

In contrasting Chan's cinematic motion to that of Steven Seagal, Aaron Anderson argues that the two martial action stars 'exist on opposite ends of … the "reality spectrum" of mimetic fights.'[21] While the characters in a Chan fight rarely suffer serious injuries (in fact, there is often an absence of any blood), the physical punishment in a Seagal picture is graphically depicted and death is not an uncommon result. The latter's 'reel' fights are staged and shot to look and feel like 'real' fights, generally incorporating only a few moves into the filmed sequences. Jackie Chan's fight scenes, on the other hand, may integrate between twenty and thirty individual motions into a scene. Where a Stephen Seagal screen altercation is over quickly, a Chan battle is long, with the length of the fight itself sometimes contributing to its legendary status among the performer's legion of fans.

With *Miracles: Mr. Canton and Lady Rose* (1989) – a remake of Frank Capra's 1961 *A Pocket Full of Miracles*, itself a remake of his own 1933 *Lady for a Day* – as an interlude, Jackie Chan went on to make a variety of modern-setting action-comedy pictures from the mid-1980s to early 1990s that confirmed his position, in director Stanley Tong's words, as 'the King of Action.' *Miracles* takes its place between Chan's 'Three Musketeers' schtick with Samo Hung and Yuen Biao in the

Hung-directed *Wheels on Meals*, and the Tsui Hark/Ringo Lam helmed *Twin Dragons* (1992) knock-off of Jean Claude Van Damme's *Double Impact*, in which Chan plays twins separated at birth. *Miracles* tells the story of an unemployed Chan who stumbles into heading a mob organization and running a nightclub after having the good fortune of crossing paths with a poor woman selling roses on the street. Chan is given the opportunity to repay her by offering the use of his club and resources to host her daughter's visit to Hong Kong. Tateishi, pointing out evidence of the filmmaker's increasingly complex hybridity, highlights a difference between the Capra film in which a rival gang shoots into Glenn Ford's nightclub after the singer has finished her song and Jackie Chan's version that incorporates the gunfire into a musical montage that includes Anita Mui's singing and shots of his club's growing clientele. Chan also uses the picture to make a statement about the wrongs of gambling, drugs, and prostitution.

As with *Miracles*, Jackie Chan directed himself in the majority of his films during this period; these included *Police Story 1* and *2* (1985, 1998), *Armour of God* (1986, the third highest grossing Hong Kong film of the decade), and *Armour of God 2: Operation Condor* (1991, the most expensive Hong Kong film in history to that point, costing some US$15 million).[22] With a string of successes and several mega-hits behind him, Chan's projects were increasingly unwieldy and cost overruns were becoming the norm. Consequently, the filmmaker again opted for a career change, deciding to hire others to direct his films. The first to be retained was Stanley Tong, a young director with only two movies to his credit when he took on *Supercop* (a.k.a. *Police Story 3*, 1992).

Tong believes that he got the *Supercop* job because of the production quality of his low-budget *Stone Age Warriors*, a story of two women's attempt to rescue a man who has disappeared in the jungles of New Guinea. He recalls that Golden Harvest's Leonard Ho

> brought me in and asked if I wanted to direct Jackie. I was kind of worried, he had been directing himself for so long and he has a huge entourage around him. I'd never worked with him but I knew he had eighteen people on his stunt crew. He can take over two years to make a movie.[23] It took me two weeks to decide because I didn't want to do it if I was going to be a director who wasn't in charge. My boss [Golden Harvest's Ho] confirmed that I could bring in my own martial arts team, choreographer, and production people. Jackie would only be an actor and, as director, I would get the final say on everything.

MAINLANDING   Stanley Tong and Jackie Chan filming *Supercop*

Upon agreeing to take the job, the filmmaker says that he looked at Jackie Chan's movies 'to find the best of Jackie. He'd done so many things and if I couldn't prove that I could do better or do something different I might hurt my career.'

Supercop became Jackie Chan's first Hong Kong direct sound movie. Stanley Tong relates that 'I had a hard time convincing Jackie to come in the studio, in fact, it was almost a deal breaker. I told him that I needed to do it in synch sound or I didn't want to do it.' Chan was accustomed to going on location without a script, doing the choreography on location, and doing multiple reshooting until he got what he wanted. In contrast, Tong, who says that low-budget directing 'forces you to be creative,' works by 'storyboarding all my action sequences because I could only afford to shoot the most important scenes over again.' He also performs the stunts that will appear in his movie beforehand to show the crew 'how I will shoot them, that I'm not putting their lives in danger, and that they will work.' A martial artist and stuntman with over two thousand filmed stunts to his credit, including going down a rushing New Guinea waterfall for his own *Stone Age Warriors*, Tong maintains that 'I have no respect for someone who comes up with an idea that is so unrealistic he is unwilling to attempt it himself.'

Two previous *Police Story* movies (1985 and 1988) relied upon the Jackie Chan formula of action and comedy – he gets knocked around through much of the film but eventually defeats the bad guys in an obligatory and protracted fight finale – while shifting the focus of his films to present day urban themes and settings. Together with the two *Armour of God* pictures, where he played an Indiana Jones-type adventure character, these films established Chan as a contemporary action star. *Police Story 1* found Chan as a nonconformist police detective battling a crime boss, attempting to protect a prosecutor's star witness, and trying to mollify his jealous girlfriend while simultaneously keeping his job. The movie includes two acclaimed Jackie Chan sequences, a high-speed fight scene that moves the action between the inside and the outside of a moving bus, and the actor's slide down a shopping mall light fixture amidst exploding light bulbs and electric sparks. Reprising his role in *Police Story 2*, Chan (demoted to beat cop due to the damage he wrought in the earlier film) takes on the same mobster (who has been released from prison because he has a terminal illness). The gangster seeks to exact revenge on the police officer by kidnapping his girlfriend. What follows is a roller-coaster ride of spills and thrills, the very thing that Jackie fans relish. Stanley Tong had some different ideas for *Supercop*. He remarks that

> People had seen *Police Story 1* and *2* and this was going to be the same story – some people coming from China to Hong Kong rob jewelery stores. I told Jackie 'there is nothing I can do to make it special. The story is still happening in Hong Kong, we have limitations in shooting, and the story doesn't feel fresh. Can we make it more international?'

Tong successfully pitched the notion of going to Malaysia, where, having worked there previously, he had good connections, 'I knew I could do a lot of things that I could never do in Hong Kong.' Tong also rewrote about 80 per cent of the script, turning the jewel heist into a heroin smuggling operation. His most significant contribution, however, was bringing in Michelle Yeoh as a no-nonsense Mainland police investigator to partner Chan in busting the drug-runners. Yeoh, who had starred in action films before her marriage and subsequent 'retirement' in the late 1980s, was set to make a comeback following a divorce. Stanley Tong had met the actor in 1986 when, as an assistant stunt coordinator, he doubled for her. Becoming friends, Tong trained Yeoh during the years of her marriage and the two made a promise that they would work together if she ever made movies again.

Tong, speaking as if he has Maggie Cheung's girlfriend role in *Police Story 1* and *2* in mind, says that 'all the females in Jackie's movies are just running around screaming and yelling. None of them really has a good part.' Yeoh's pre-marriage career, on the other hand, had included Corey Yuen's *Yes, Madam* (1986), a subgenre spawning action heroine flick that also launched the film career of American martial artist Cynthia Rothrock.[24] Tong's thought was that

> Michelle Yeoh is the best female action star. Jackie Chan is the best male action star. They had never worked together and I thought audiences would be very interested to see how Michelle matched up with Jackie. I had promised her that she wouldn't be just another character running around.

Of course, *Supercop* was still a Jackie Chan film and, politically, the director had to find the right balance, noting that 'I had to be careful not to overdo it when I choreographed Michelle's fighting.' For example, Tong says, 'In the negotiation scene she pulls out a gun and fights as all hell breaks loose but she only had four moves that I had to make clear, sharp, and memorable.' In fact, the single most striking moment in the film, a motorcycle-riding Michelle Yeoh jumping onto a moving train, was initially opposed by Jackie Chan who did not think that it would be convincing if a woman did the stunt. But Stanley Tong contends that 'if you see a man doing the jump, well, it's a stuntman, of course he can do it. Audiences will appreciate it more if a woman has the guts to do it.' Yeoh, who had never ridden a motorcycle before filming the movie, credits the 'Hong Kong stunt

HONG KONG HARBORING   Michelle Yeoh and Stanley Tong filming *Supercop*

coordinators and stuntmen [who] taught me my craft … they are some of the best in the world.' Although it was already planned as the story's ending, Chan admits that he felt that he had something to prove, after seeing her stunt, with his 'aerial tour of Kuala Lumpur,' in which he jumps from a building to the rope ladder of a hovering helicopter high above the streets of the city.[25]

Jackie Chan and Stanley Tong would work together on two more films, *Rumble in the Bronx* (1995) and *First Strike* (1996). While the former has been panned for inconsistencies such as mountains in the background (despite the title, the picture was shot in Vancouver), it completed its opening week in American theaters number one at the box office, thus becoming Chan's first United States hit. The film also finished the year as the highest grossing movie in Hong Kong (beating out *Thunderbolt*, another Chan vehicle and, at a reported US$25 million, the most expensive movie ever produced in Hong Kong). As with *Supercop*, *Rumble* features a scene that the star did not initially like, this time, according to Tong, because 'he wasn't doing anything. I asked him, "Can we not do fist fighting at the end like all your other movies?" I had to convince Jackie that it's not necessary to have the same pattern every time, him in a warehouse fighting for ten minutes.' So the film, which is about a vacationing Hong Kong cop who ends up fighting a biker gang and mobsters in New York, closes with a monster-like hovercraft speeding through Vancouver with Jackie Chan aboard.[26]

Between its opening, which finds Chan's character Keung helping his uncle (Bill Tung) sell his grocery to prepare for his wedding (Keung's face expresses culture shock when he learns that his uncle is to marry a black woman), and the finale, where he recovers some stolen diamonds, are Stanley Tong's highly choreographed fight scenes. Tong, who edits his own films, points out that

> When you do your choreography, you have to work with what you can see on the screen. The easiest things for the audience to see are what is in the middle and what is moving. If you want to bring up a kick in a hand-to-hand fight where the people are close, you need to change to a wider lens that can cover the kick. If the shot is tight, the audience will only see the kick coming in for a little bit. You have to see the punches and kicks travel to capture their powerful effect.... That depends on the point of view that you want to express. If a villain is fighting your hero, you want the hero to lose at first. The camera has to shoot from behind and back up with the hero. When I first began editing, I would look at something and think it should have been a wider shot, or a close-up, or a side profile. A lot of people who choreograph know how to fight, throw punches and kicks, but they don't know how to edit.

Rumble's first fight occurs when Keung intervenes to prevent the bikers from shoplifting from the food store, now owned and operated by Elaine (Anita Mui). In retaliation, they attack Keung unmercifully with flying beer bottles while laying Elaine's market – the kind of sole proprietorship that is under siege from chain supermarkets – to waste. A pool cue, a refrigerator, and a pinball machine are

IN-FLIGHT   Jackie Chan in Stanley Tong's *First Strike*

among the objects that become weapons in Jackie Chan's hands. In one sequence, a fight begins on a billiard table, proceeds over a couch and through the icebox, moves up to a roof from where Jackie Chan leaps to the fire escape of an adjacent building, and then descends to the floor where the pinball machine stands.

First Strike (a.k.a. *Police Story 4*), replacing *Rumble's* somewhat provincial story with one of international intrigue, finds Chan caught in the middle of a post-Cold War black market. On loan to the CIA from Hong Kong's police department, he tracks a rogue operative (Tsui) with plans to sell a nuclear device to a former Soviet KGB agent (Gregor) to Russia and Australia. The film's James Bond-like story includes high-speed snowboarding down a mountainside that recalls *The Spy Who Loved Me*'s snowmobile chase.[27] The scene concludes with Jackie Chan doing two stunts that neither Bond actors nor their stunt doubles would ever do: he jumps from his snowboard to a helicopter and then plunges into the icy waters of a lake below. Stanley Tong recalls that the frozen lake sequence involved a 'one hundred twenty foot drop with the wind blowing into a little hole in the ice. After five seconds the water hurt, like putting your hands on ice cubes.' The scene, requiring two eight-hour days of work, ends with a shivering Chan huddled on the ice; says Tong, 'he wasn't acting there.'

Chan later battles a baddie underwater in a sea aquarium tank as both live and mechanical sharks swim around. Little in the scene, however, conveys the seafish as metaphoric representations of fear. Rather, we feel like the oohing and aahing sea aquarium patrons who think Chan's antics are part of the theme park performance. Tong notes that 'Hong Kong director contracts provide little protection on foreign cuts,' a reminder of Marx's dictum that the product is the property of the capitalist. And he says, 'it's hard to argue when they say "we know the American market better than you."' Accordingly, the US edit of *First Strike* (done by New Line Cinema) 'tried to make it a hard-core action movie. To do that they had to cut the charm.' Hollywood cutting-room 'sharks' did keep intact two scenes conveying the 'move towards humor' that Stanley Tong was after; the first with the actor, without jacket, high in the Russian mountains, wearing a child's polar bear cap to keep his head warm; the second featuring a stilt-fighting Jackie Chan kicking a bad guy on a second-floor balcony from the street.

The film also has Chan making a rare on-screen political statement, albeit one that attempts to reconcile irreconcilables as liberalism is wont to do. Replying to Tsui's comment that 'Gregor is trading nuclear weapons for a Middle East oil franchise,' the actor expresses concern that the bomb could fall into the hands of a madman. To which the arms dealer, revealing his acumen, retorts: 'You're so naive. Do you know how many nuclear weapons were sold by these so-called superpowers to the rest of the world? The difference is that they sell in the name of country and I sell for myself. Do you think there will be world peace if I don't sell it?' Jackie Chan, acknowledging that there is truth in what his adversary has said, maintains that 'We can't change the world but we can't use that as an excuse. We humans have done enough harm to the earth and now we're still doing nuclear tests. Keep it that way and we're destroying ourselves.' Tsui's response that 'your heroic concept doesn't apply to me' corresponds to the 'realist' school of international power politics, which is itself derived from the Hobbesian conception of a 'war of all against all.' But the remark also comments on a Hong Kong cinema that draws the line between morality and immorality on uncomplicated grounds, that of *esprit de corps*. As Chiao Hsiung-ping writes, 'Whether it is drug smuggling, murder or even overthrowing other gang leaders, all you have to do is talk about brotherhood and you're still a definitive "hero".'[28] The scene closes with Chan discounting heroism, on the one hand, and offering no sense that the political economic realities of global capitalism can be changed, on the other. And his comment 'if we can't stop them, we can't encourage them' may well be his brief on the impending assumption of sovereignty over Hong Kong by the People's Republic as much as it is his final word on nuclear proliferation.

Meanwhile, Michelle Yeoh followed up her triumphant return to action cinema by pairing with director Stanley Tong again for *Project S* (a.k.a. *Once a Cop*, 1993), a story of good and bad Mainlanders. Continuing *Supercop*'s theme of co-operation between Hong Kong and the People's Republic, Yeoh's detective Hua is again sent to the colony, this time to help break a case against Chinese hoods suspected of a bank heist. Michelle Yeoh delivers more than a few swift and sharp kicks to the head; Jackie Chan, for his part, only appears in one of his recurring drag cameos.[29] During the course of the investigation Yeoh learns that the criminals are led by her former police trainer/boyfriend (Yu Rong Guang), who had quit the Beijing force to get rich in Hong Kong. With Yu posing as a legitimate businessman, the two temporarily rekindle what has become a star-crossed relationship. Legal and technological differences between Hong Kong and China are alluded to; Hua, for example, is astonished by the Royal Police Department's computer capabilities. The film's love story, unique for an action movie, reflects the influence of American pictures, which Tong says 'focus more on character development than Hong Kong movies do.' In the finale, Yeoh tries to save her malefactor boyfriend from a torrent of water that has broken loose inside an underground bank tunnel and then agonizes over his death despite the obvious barriers that had arisen between them.[30] Stanley Tong believes that 'people are not born bad, there must be a reason. I wished that he [Yu] could live even though he's done bad things. But I think it is a complete story, they both face each other at the end of the tunnel.' Moreover, the shot of Yeoh's Hong Kong partner sharing in her pain suggests that a bond has been established. While the lovers' reunion has proved fatal, a potentially stronger one has taken root between Hong Kong and the Mainland. Perhaps the future will be secure, after all, following the return.

Johnnie To's *Heroic Trio* (1993) teams Yeoh with Anita Mui and Maggie Cheung as wire-worked superheroes in a film that the director says was his hardest film to shoot because it was 'so imaginary, visionary, and unreal the environment was not easily captured.'[31] With Ching Siu-tung bringing his baroque sensibilities to the production as action director, To and company present moviegoers with a cinematic 'postmodern comic-book[32] revolving around a diabolical master's plot to kidnap babies whom he will prepare to become the emperor and court of a new imperial China. The picture is one about which Michelle Yeoh expresses special pride, claiming that it 'broke new ground … it was the first movie anchored by three actresses with actors in supporting roles.' For those who scoff at *Heroic Trio* as prancing divas with special effects, Yeoh reminds that 'wire work in Hong Kong is done with thinner wires than normal because there was never the capability of erasing them in postproduction.' In the film, Yeoh plays Invisible Girl, who is charged with stealing the newborns. While carrying out her assignment, she is confronted by Wonder Woman (Mui), a police officer's wife when not performing duties as a masked crime fighter, and Thief Catcher (Cheung), a punkish black-leather-wearing bounty hunter. Ching's taste for the macabre is visible throughout, whether it be a flying guillotine, indentured servants pissing in their pants as they are about to be slain, or the senseless murder of an abducted infant. One hellish *mise-en-scène*, painted in garish orange, is filled with emotionless killer kids, chained and fed human remains, programmed to destroy. A catastrophic scenario for millennial Hong Kong is foiled by the three women, who eventually come together to defeat the evil schemer and thwart his plans in the process.

Heroic Trio's color and lighting are subdued, befitting perhaps the movie's unspecified but ostensible near-future setting as well as providing a perpetual downside to the zest and energy that the actors bring to their parts. With *The Executioners* (1993), To and Ching (now credited as co-director) create an apocalyptic sequel in the form of a post-nuclear-war Hong Kong. Can one imagine a more pessimistic projection of life after 1997 than a dead earth? Commenting on the film, co-director Johnnie To says 'I wanted to put a lot of ideas into it.' The result, considered by some to be too depressing, touches on a number of topics relevant to Hong Kong people. Yeoh, Mui, and Cheung are back playing their same roles, but the unity they had forged at the end of the previous film was only temporary. Anita Mui's Wonder Woman has had a child and promised her police captain husband (Damian Lau) that her high-flying crime-fighting days are over. Michelle Yeoh's Invisible Girl sells her fighting skills to the highest bidder; in this case, she's a driver for the Clear Water Corporation, run by ambitious and dis-figured Mister Kim (Anthony Wong), who has captured monopoly control of Hong Kong's most valuable commodity, its fresh water supply. Moreover, Mui, seeing her daughter's wonder at a guppy in a fishbowl, alludes to increasing harbor pollution when she tells the young girl that 'once upon a time fish swam in the water.' In their critique of the Hong Kong government's continuing large-scale Victoria Harbour reclamation projects, Mee Kam Ng and Allison Cook note the possibility of this natural heritage turning 'into a river, if not a nullah.'[33] The authors cite the fears of environmental science that smaller volumes of flowing water will reduce the harbour's self-cleaning ability and they caution that dredging plans will dislodge heavy metals presently deposited in the seabed.

The greedy Kim, using the crisis of governability for his own ends (a news broadcast announces that price hikes are the result of the government's inability to protect deliveries), is in cahoots with a rogue general set on overthrowing the territory's president and establishing a dictatorship under his control. Hong Kongers would later witness the PRC's refusal to accept the legitimacy of a 1995 legislature – elected under liberalized procedures – that produced a more democratic result, and Chinese officials' subsequent decision to establish a 'second stove'[34] policy, creating a transitional government for the immediate post-handover period. Mean-while, Maggie Cheung's Thief Catcher (called 'Chat' here) is an outlaw libertarian doing battle with the monopoly capitalist and competing with other free marketeers to sell clean water. Having hijacked a water truck after the latest round of price gouging, she calls upon Wonder Woman offering some of her supply; upon dis-covering that Invisible Girl has also paid Mui a visit, the three women frolic in the tub, reviving the spirit that had originally brought them together. Engulfed by the picture's general bleakness, this bright moment is supplanted by the martyring assassination of Chong Hun (Takeshi Kaneshiro), leader of a protest against the government's water policy. The bedlam following this incident serves as pretext for the general's *coup d'état* and the decaration of martial law.

In the course of events, Wonder Woman's husband is killed, her daughter is kidnapped, and she is jailed. While in prison, a time so grim that at one point she squeezes blood from a rat for nourishment, Mui fashions a mask from a tin plate. Chat and Invisible Girl go into action; the former not only finds the abducted child but the source of a plentiful store of pure water, while the latter takes on the radioactive Mister Kim, who is brought down by an announcement about the available water supply. Unfortunately, this disclosure and the public's reaction come too late for Yeoh; she is viciously murdered by the depraved Wong when he rips off her arm and plunges his hand through her chest.

Filmmaker Cheung Yuen-ting notes that 'in the early 1990s … all film studios were putting out kung fu movies.' Yet, by the time Wong Fei-hung *Once Upon a Time in China*-style period pieces had begun to run their course in the mid-1990s martial arts star Jet Li was appearing in contemporary and sci-fi action flicks such as *Bodyguard from Beijing* (1994), *My Father is a Hero* (1995), and *Black Mask* (1996). Meanwhile, *Once Upon a Time in China* producer Tsui Hark, who directed four of the movies in the series, continued his eclectic ways with the contemporary ghost story *Love in the Time of Twilight* (1995), the first Hong Kong film to use real-time special effects digital compositing, a high-end postproduction computer graphics process. He followed up with *The Blade* (1995), a remake of Chang Cheh's legendary *One Armed Swordsman* by way of Wong Kar-wai's *Ashes of Time*. Two films, *Legend of the Wolf* and *Hero*, released a month prior to the handover of Hong Kong to China, may offer glimpses of future Hong Kong martial-action films.

One possibility, a return to unadorned kung fu, is represented by *Legend of the Wolf* (1997), the directorial debut of Donnie Yen, a favorite of genre purists for the no-nonsense martial arts skills he brought to such movies as *In the Line of Duty 4* (1989), *Tiger Cage 1* and *2* (1990), and *Iron Monkey* (1993). Yen's background is well known to kung fu movie enthusiasts. Originally from Canton, his family moved from Hong Kong to Boston, where his mother (well-known Tai Chi and Wu Shu master Bow Sim-mark) established a martial arts school. Yen, who received his basic martial arts training from his mother, recalls being a 'typical rebellious youth. My friends and I kind of ran wild in an area of Boston called The Combat

Zone.'[35] Whereupon his father sent him to Beijing for two years to study Wu Shu. In Hong Kong, Donnie Yen met renowned martial arts director Yuen Woo-ping, who cast him in *Drunken Tai Chi* (1984) at the age of nineteen.

Referred to as one of the 'new dragons'[36] of Hong Kong action filmmaking, Donnie Yen is critical of what he calls the 'old school' of martial arts filmmaking that spends a lot of time and money on choreographing movements. He maintains that most people in the audience are not concerned with the details because they are not martial artists. Thus Yen indicates that he no longer analyzes martial arts, saying: 'I agree with Bruce Lee; as human beings, we have two arms and two legs, so there can't really be many different "styles" of fighting. In making films, I've researched many different arts, so now I say I'm a master of them all and none, at the same time.' Influenced by his low-budget television production, experimental technique and working on the cheap appear to be the filmmaker's vision for reviving an uncertain genre and industry.

Legend of the Wolf, a period piece set mainly in exteriors and full of martial arts, employs two plot devices to relate its story. First, we experience the picture through flashbacks that serve to dramatize a past where explanations for the present ostensibly reside. Wolf (Donnie Yen) is an aged former hitman who tries to dissuade people from hiring killers by recounting a story to them. Second, the flashbacks reveal that the proverbial Wolf was a soldier who lost his memory after being shot at war. Wandering into a small village, he reunites with an old love (Carmen Lee), only to find that his past comes back to haunt him, the villagers, and the woman. Yen uses memory loss to disclose the contradictions of 'forgetfulness as the enabling condition of … self-knowing'[37] for people living in a 24-hour city. Much of the film is shot in low-key lighting, a high-contrast combination of key (primary source) and fill (auxiliary light of slightly less intensity, placed at eye level) light that produces penumbra effects and night-time ambience – images on a movie screen and ghosts of the past, electric light and shadows. Despite the painfulness of remembering, Wolf, like Coleridge's Ancient Mariner, is compelled to tell his story over and over. The movie's theme, remembrance of things wished forgotten, has been taken up by Hong Kong residents struggling against the 'historical amnesia' that observers maintain pervades their culture.

Donnie Yen considers himself 'completely apolitical … I'm interested in more human issues.' But the political is human and the human is political (to put a spin on the feminist adage), and *Legend*'s narrative runs towards primal passions ruling with absolute certainty. Including corporeal might as part of the story, Yen makes reference to what Sek Kei calls China's 'castration complex,'[38] a consequence of stressing the civil rather than the martial. Early on, the country established an examination system whereby one could earn merit and position by being a scholar. Bookish men would later be considered impotent and ineffectual in the face of the regular indignity of foreign invasion and subjugation endured by China. The film's depiction of male power recalls mythic kung fu movie history as well. As Sek suggests, 'the dominance of the male hero in Hong Kong cinema for the last twenty years is not ... without its unhealthy tendencies: witness the violence, the contemptuous sense of mischief-making, the misogyny running rampant in contemporary Hong Kong screens.'[39]

Humans possess great fear of wolves: as fable and literary material, lupines are generally ravenous, sly, and bloodthirsty animals. In fact, however, wolves by nature are protective, nurturing, and sociable. They mate for life and travel in packs.

> Wolves are probably the most misunderstood of the wild animals.... They are truly free spirits even though their packs are highly organized. They seem to go out of their way to avoid a fight. One is rarely necessary when a shift in posture, a growl, or a glance gets the point across quite readily.[40]

The wolf stereotype fits the character's younger days when he killed without compunction and when he was a hitman; the aged storyteller known as the 'Wolf' who advertises on the Internet as 'sender@wolf.net' more resembles the real species.

The movie is structured around the appearance of Ben (Edmond Leung), who, seeking out murder for hire, answers Wolf's ad. A conversation between Wolf and Ben about Hong Kong presents the latter's perspective of a forsaken world. Responding to his comment that the present is outdated, Wolf says: 'The airport is going to be moved. I remember I had nothing when I came here. People lived very happily. Now there is a new airport and new bridge. They gain everything they want. People do not live happily instead.' To which Ben replies: 'Things get old, then they will be replaced. If there is nothing new, how can they have progress?' Wolf points out that 'new things will get old soon.' A repeated motif in many films, this exchange brings together development, transformation, and

courtesy/permission of Bullet Film Productions Ltd and Donnie Yen

A SHEEP IN WOLF'S CLOTHING   Donnie Yen in his *Legend of the Wolf*

obsolescence, a way of mapping Hong Kong itself. Incongruities arise. As with Yen's memory and brute force, real and fabricated wolves, so with change and progress. As Althusser writes, 'A vast accumulation of "contradictions" comes into play in the same court, some of which are radically heterogeneous – of different origins, different sense, different levels and points of application – but which nevertheless "merge" into a ruptural unity.'[41]

Legend is part *Twilight Zone*, part gang tale, and all kung fu, the latter causing critic Po Kam-hung to gush: 'A single blade against the axe-gang, flying dagger between the legs, double crutches defeating the iron chain, bare fists against the "eagle's talons."'[42] Wolf, whom we see doing more than his share of fighting during his younger days, has adopted the motto 'Don't be a killer!' One wonders, however, whether his listeners (and the film's viewers) will heed his message (paradoxically an anti-violence theme in a violent movie with an aggressive sound-track). Wolf is no hero, but he has heart. The tear brought to his eye, as well as the repeated tellings of the story, suggest as much.

Notwithstanding the expectations of a martial arts audience, the picture feels like an elegy for a time when kung fu films reigned. The reasons include Donnie Yen's renowned martial arts skills and love of showing them on film; the movie's non-stop action, meaning high body counts, which re-creates the genre; and the nostalgic framing device, which 'remembers when.' Yen yearns for 'the human content, by which I mean, you feel that real people, rather than special effects, are responsible for the action.' But neither an ideology of kung fu as 'mythic narratives of individualist male triumph over large corporate systems of control and exploitation' nor a view that it is an 'experimental form which escapes from representation by offering a purely kinetic ballet of sights and sounds' can be sustained in the face of intensified economic conglomeration.[43] Thus, Yen's picture is not so different from the eponymous *Hero* after all. It is a stroll, or rather, a tear (a race) and a tear (drop), in this instance, down memory lane.

Former Little Fortune and acclaimed action choreographer Corey Yuen made *Hero* (1997), a type of nostalgia or 'retro' flick that Fredric Jameson suggests evokes a figurative past by re-creating the look and feel of a particular historical period. Produced in a post-hero era, Yuen's movie jumps off from a character's comment that 'Dangerous times make heroes of desperate men.' While everyone wants to believe so, does anyone really believe that? Set in Shanghai, *Hero* features teenage heart-throb Takeshi Kaneshiro as fighter Ma Wing-jing. Because of a drought, Ma and his brother head from their home town of Shantung to Shang-hai, where they are forced to work as coolies. Ma saves the life of crime boss Tam See (Yuen Biao, one of three Little Fortunes featured in the picture), and earns the enmity of Tam's rival, Yuang Shuang (Yuen Tak, also a Little Fortune). Ma takes control of a nightclub run by Tam See's girlfriend Yam Yeung-ting (Valerie Chow) and soon becomes a famous underworld figure (à la Jackie Chan's *Miracles*). In another irony, respected martial artist Yuen Wah (the third Little Fortune to appear), who has played villains throughout much of his career, portrays Wing-jing's likeable brother Ma Ta-cheung as a character serving comic relief with no fighting skills.[44] Wing-jing is either harrassing him or protecting him, and a free-for-all skirmish that breaks out in the nightclub plays up the contradiction to humorous effect.

Allegedly set in 1898, *Hero* includes club scenes with costumes and stage effects straight from 1930s'-era gangster stories and music from Latin mambos of the 1950s. Arsenals of machine guns range from World War I vintage to modern-day automatic weapons. The main women characters (played by Valerie Chow and Hsuan Jessica Hester) are 'flower vase' *femme fatales* whom Wing-jing can either pursue or extricate himself from; either way, fate calls. What Jameson writes of the retro-hero, 'the very style … is ambiguous,'[45] fits Takeshi Kaneshiro, who lacks the classic body type and requisite martial arts skills while offering a softer, gentler prototype for a post-handover era. Meanwhile, misty shades of blue dominate, giving the impression that night has settled on Hong Kong and that a fog has rolled in, which, for some, it was going to do following the handover. *Hero*'s decoupage construction and temporal discontinuities reflect the real situation close to handover time. The return is present by its absence; it is too late to change the course of events, and the actors 'play like it's 1997.'

The film opens with an extravagant martial arts action sequence, drawing from the look of the *Once Upon a Time in China* movies, the runaway stagecoach scene in the sixth of that series, and the moving train and motorcycle sequence in *Supercop*. When Wing Jing touches Tam See's horse, he is abused by Tam's men, but easily fights them off while Tam looks on. Curious, he asks for the young man's name, and, recognizing that they come from the same place, throws a dollar coin and offers him the job of washing his carriage. 'If you want to live well in Shanghai, don't argue with money. If you want money, pick it up,' he commands. When Ta-cheung encourages his brother, Wing-jing prepares to do so, but is hindered by Tam See, who next offers a challenge. 'If you want to get rich, you have to set a bigger goal,' he says. Attaching a pocketwatch to his horse's bridle, Tam See tells him to catch the more valuable timepiece, and sets his horse and carriage in motion. An extended battle between the two progresses, as they maneuver for balance upon the moving carriage and the racing horse, dodging encountered obstacles ahead. When they finally come to rest after crossing a bridge, Tam See explains, 'Don't kneel because of a dollar,' and suggests that if Wing-jing doesn't do so, he 'can reincarnate as a great hero.' It is a breathtaking scene, rewarding Corey Yuen afficionados in the opening minutes, as well as establishing the themes of the movie. Presented are two groups in conflict: Yang Shuang's group, supported by the police, and Tam See's, backed by the British. Survival is crucial, face is important, and time is running out.

'It's not easy to make a living in Shanghai,' Tam See tells Wing-jing, which is illustrated in the scenes to follow. 'Shanghai is so beautiful when looking from the top,' Wing-jing later says; Yam Yeung-ting tells him, 'You know why so many people want to climb up in Shanghai? In the past you couldn't see how beautiful it is from below. Now, when you go higher and higher, you will see a more beautiful Shanghai than it is now.' John Woo's *A Better Tomorrow* is reprised and so begins Wing-jing's social climbing. What are the costs? A horrific scene in which Tam See's horse is brutally slaughtered in the nighttime streets, its legs hacked away. A bridge scene in which the groups face-off, and Tam See's men are slaughtered. Yam Yeung-ting is raped and her face disfigured, Tam See is cast in prison and sentenced to death, and Wing Jing suffers from amnesia. They eventually join forces to defeat Yang Shuang. 'If we can start over again, I hope it would be started tonight,' Tam See confides to Yam Yeung-ting, shortly before his fight to the death. Finally, overlooking the Shanghai skyline and its river, Wing-jing remembers, as he leaves the city, 'The river is like a piece of gold brick. Many want to get it but they paid with their lives.' The movie ends with an image of Tam See, half turning and looking into the camera, in soft light, a bridge from the past to the present.

SEVEN

TO LIVE, LOVE, AND DIE
IN THE TIME OF TWILIGHT

Hong Kong's new-wave filmmakers, emerging on the scene in 1979, are characterized as being the first generation of directors to grow up in Hong Kong, thereby
loosening bonds to the Mainland. Having received their early education under the
British system, many studied film abroad and returned to Hong Kong in the early
1970s, working in television studios before making their first films. Yet the new-
wavers are an eclectic group. Let us consider some of their common interests and
differences. Ann Hui, Yim Ho, and Tsui Hark are all members of Hong Kong's
first new wave; Ann Hui spent her formative years in Macau and partly in Hong
Kong, Yim Ho grew up in Hong Kong, and Tsui Hark in Vietnam. All attended
film schools: Hui and Yim Ho in London, and Tsui in Texas. All trained in television studios before making movies. Each would bring a hybrid perspective and
a concern with politics, yet their intellectual, emotional, and aesthetic styles would
share little else. The new-wavers are so named because of their new vision and
experimentalism, as compared to the imported views and techniques of previous
Hong Kong films. A second new wave followed ten years later; this included
Stanley Kwan, the team of Cheung Yuen-ting and Alex Law, and the partners Clara
Law and Eddie Fong. Many second-wave directors, trained in television studios
rather than film schools abroad, learned moviemaking through experience. All can
be described as 'Hong Kong belongers.'[1] Home is, or has become, Hong Kong.
The phrase 'made in Hong Kong' implies a mixture of cultures and influences
because of the colony's history and its combined population of primarily Mainland

immigration and British presence. Not until the 1970s was Chinese declared the official language. In the 1970s, the advent of Hong Kong's economic miracle ensured that a cosmopolitan population was exposed to television and popular entertainment from the West. While family roots remain on the Mainland, Hong Kong belongers' feet are firmly planted on the ground.

Hong Kong has always been a place of shifting sands. In the spring of 1997, ten reclamation projects were under construction, including the Chep Lak Kok airport (opened in June 1998) and a new town for 200,000 people near the airport adjacent to Lantau Island.[2] Hong Kong maximizes its land use, with 28-story office towers and 20- to 34-story apartment buildings the norm. Coupled with its hyperdensity (on average 40,000 people per square mile, and much denser in districts like Mongkok and Shumshuipo)[3] is land speculation, which leads to constant demolition and reconstruction as perfectly useful buildings are destroyed to make way for the new. A local vernacular, including Chinese Qing dynasty influences and British colonial-style architecture, coexists alongside and is typically displaced by postmodern shrines to commerce as the skyline continually remakes itself. Ackbar Abbas refers to 'the changing cultural space of the city' and notes 'the cultural self-invention of the Hong Kong subject in a cultural space of disappearance.'[4] New-wave filmmakers produce movies that create a Hong Kong Chinese identity, simultaneously conscious of its paradoxical meanings. These Hong Kong belongers observe constant changes in landscape and record observations with 'love at last site,' a phrase used by David L. Eng, based upon Abbas's description of 'Hong Kong peoples' remaining years with their uniquely (post) colonial island.'[5]

Several events made these filmmakers more self-consciously aware of a crisis of identity and an uncertain future. The process began in 1982, when Margaret Thatcher's unsettling visits to Beijing and Hong Kong made people anxious. The 1984 signing of the Sino–British Joint Agreement increased the sense of foreboding and fatalism. The 1989 massacre at Tiananmen Square, witnessed globally on television, led to shock, horror, protest, and mistrust; 1992 saw Chris Patten's reforms and the breakdown of communication between the Chinese and British governments following seventeen rounds of talks over a seven-month negotiation period. During this time late capitalist features became increasingly visible in Hong Kong, with a growing financial sector, declining industrial base, and a burgeoning service economy. Economic and social changes exacerbated a collective concern for self and place, reflected in two decades of film production.

While Hong Kong filmmakers have always paid attention to entertainment and commercial interests, some directors are more willing to satisfy those aspects than others. Clara Law and Eddie Fong, for example, moved to Australia, finding it easier to make 'meaningful' and 'political' films there, free from commercial pressures and from censorship by the studios or the censor board. Tsui Hark delivers commercially successful products with political subtexts and gender playfulness. Stanley Kwan and his mentor Ann Hui avoid making commercial films, Hui favoring smaller dramas and Kwan art-house movies.

This group of filmmakers represent cultural alienation using a number of techniques. One means of expressing this estrangement is character displacement, in which a character questions his identity, or searches for a sense of self, usually by a journey that brings the character into contact with another culture or generation. Some leave the territory behind, in terms of location, though it looms large in their characters' concerns. A second way is to transpose time and place to disguise present-day Hong Kong metaphorically and comment upon its relations to the Mainland Chinese or the British or both. Many combine techniques to express Hong Kong's predicament.

Ann Hui's movies grow out of character and emotion, and most narrate a protagonist's story against a larger social backdrop. All address the past, which is a burden a character must carry and with which she or he must come to terms. The past is always linked to the formation of an identity politics: where do I come from, how does that relate to who I am, where am I going, who will I be? The individualized stories Hui tells connect to larger issues of a Hong Kong Chinese identity, in light of the diaspora that followed the 1949 communist revolution, and the repercussions from the throngs of Vietnamese 'boat people' who fled to Hong Kong and the USA following the fall of Saigon in 1975. Some criticize Hui for political naiveté, denigrating her 'liberal humanism of the middle class' and suggesting that her work lacks 'objective or logical analysis'; others describe her movies as 'products of social conscience' whereby 'political and social aspects … are not hidden in the entertainment … [but] stem from it.'[6] Careful storytelling, meticulous contextualizing of characters into the social fabric and specific locations, along with subtle emotions drawn from the actors – all contribute to pulling the audience into the story, told from the heart, ensuring that the politics are felt before they are intellectually understood.

Hui's films *Song of the Exile* (1990) and *Summer Snow* (1995) are told from a woman's point of view, a significant contestation of terrain in a largely patriarchal culture and industry in which male stories and perspectives dominate. Known for using women behind the camera, including scriptwriters and producers, the director constructs 'a picture of female experience, of duration, perception, events, relationships, and silences that feels immediately and unquestionably true.'[7] Hui's movies proceed slowly and quietly, building upon small gestures, fine moments, and nuanced contrasts.

Song of the Exile (literally *Guest Route Autumn Regret*) takes its English title from an old song in Southern China about a solitary and lonesome sojourner who sentimentally remembers his homeland. The autobiographical story concerns the relationship between a mother Aiko (Luk Siu-fan) and her daughter Cheung Hueyin (Maggie Cheung). The two have never got on, and when the 25-year-old returns from Britain to Hong Kong for her sister's wedding, the weight of their shared past is examined and leads both to new understanding. Hui, like Hueyin, was estranged from her mother and close to her paternal grandparents. As a teenager, she learned that her mother's distance was due to her being a 'stranger in a strange land.' Meeting her Chinese husband-to-be in Manchuria, Hueyin's conventional Japanese mother lived with her in-laws in Macau, not speaking Cantonese and unaware of traditional customs. The grandparents mistook their daughter-in-law's quietness for coldness, and, intentionally or not, turned child against mother. A largely absent unfilial son further complicated the situation. As Tolstoy writes in *Anna Karenina*, 'All happy families resemble one another, but each unhappy family is unhappy in its own way,' and Hui intimately dramatizes this one's unhappiness.

Important issues arise from this personal situation. First, mutual sentiments of distrust and intolerance on the part of the Chinese and the Japanese see daylight. Centuries of conquest and the Japanese occupation of Manchuria and Hong Kong during the Second World War are drawn upon. Second, communication, or its lack, is foregrounded. Aiko is unable to converse with her in-laws; mother and daughter talk at each other; when they visit Japan the tables are turned, as Hueyin cannot speak the language and misunderstands a friendly farmer. Miscommunication between peoples through ignorance and its possible dangers are apparent.

Third, social class is an element. The grandparents are cultured, well-to-do Chinese; 'origins' are important. Grandfather educates his granddaughter in the poetry of dynastic scholars. Grandparents snub their daughter-in-law, always making her aware of their superior wealth. Their son, out of necessity, works in Hong Kong away from his family. When he brings his nuclear family there, the living quarters became cramped and not according to their accustomed lifestyle. We later learn that the mother's Japanese family is in fact ancient and well-connected when Aiko and Hueyin visit the ancestors' tombs and the family home – a fact the daughter-in-law kept hidden.

Hui suggests cultural politics through this personal story. Hueyin's mother is not revealed to be Japanese until half an hour into the film. Audience acceptance of her as a dutiful and docile (although problematic) daughter-in-law in a Chinese family is turned inside out. This revelation raises questions about being Hong Kong Chinese – just what does it mean? If a Japanese woman passes as such, playing mah-jongg, wanting her daughter to wear a red dress for her sister's wedding, what is the ethnic make-up of the majority of Hong Kong Chinese? And what is to be made of a Japanese–Chinese daughter? Exile and the Chinese diaspora are also manifest. The grandparents are temporarily exiled in Macau. 'When our hometown is safe, I'll bring you back,' grandfather tells granddaughter; Hueyin joins her family in Hong Kong, but, isolated, she finds herself another 'stranger in a strange land,' and travels to boarding school in England. Similarly, when Aiko returns to Beppu, intending to resettle there, she finds herself out of tune with Japanese culture and returns to Hong Kong. Part of the Hong Kong Chinese psyche, according to Hui, is exile, always searching for a sense of place.

Is home where the heart is? 'Life is strange,' Aiko tells Hueyin during their sojourn; 'At every turn, life could have been different. Don't you think life is strange?' Hueyin learns life's strangeness through her Japanese experiences, walking in her mother's shoes, and observing her mother from a new angle – among her former friends, visiting her old lover, reacting to her warm and cold brothers. The flashback technique showing Hueyin's childhood is finely tuned; the same scenes, largely from Hueyin's perspective, are replayed, slightly differently, as daughter begins to understand mother. Likewise, mother shares intimacies with daughter concerning her relationship with father, and, more comically, admitting she prefers hot Cantonese to cold Japanese food. Daughter reconciles with mother, reflected in the way she describes her working method for the Hong Kong television station: 'I looked at their faces intently and listened to their voices.' This description serves as confession, when she 'forgot England and Canton' and began truly living as a Hong Konger.

If *Song of the Exile* is about the burden of remembering, *Summer Snow* is about forgetting and loss. Ostensibly concerning the plight of daughter-in-law May (Josephine Siao), who deals with her father-in-law (Roy Chiao) succumbing to Alzheimer's Disease, it's a heart-rending story that engenders emotions ranging from laughter to tears. The literal title suggests its perspective: *Woman, Forty*. May is first glimpsed at the market watching a slowly dying fish, foreshadowing the demise of the father-in-law, a scene that is revelatory of Hui's working style. Woman is seen managing the quotidian – marketing, cooking, hanging laundry, cleaning house, or working at her office desk, while man (her husband Bing, played by Law Kar-ying) is working, sleeping, or drinking with his companions, and the son is playing video games or involved with his girlfriend.

The larger story touches on social issues, first registered through the camera eye in numerous distance shots of Hong Kong high-rise public and private housing, which are subsequently interspersed throughout the film. The father gives money to his brother to purchase a private apartment, while his family lives in run-down close quarters, still waiting for public housing assistance. In addition to the lack of available housing, Hui zeroes in on the absence of basic and affordable care for the aged, ironic in a culture known for its respect for the elderly. The film opens with the activities of an old people's daycare center; it then follows the Sun family in their attempt to find daycare and a nursing home for the elder Sun. Hui's camera lovingly records goings-on in the center, herself playing a worker there – her character's relationship with a senile husband is touching.

Victims of Alzheimer's can often remember the distant past clearly and minutely, while consciousness of the present and memories of the recent past are haphazard or absent. The father-in-law often believes he is back in the war as a Chinese pilot fighting the Japanese enemy and mistakes his son and grandson for his foes. After his wife's sudden death, he remembers her as being away, helping to deliver a baby. In recent years the Japanese occupation has often been used by Hong Kong filmmakers as a stand-in for the Mainland's reclamation of Hong Kong, and here Hui uses the reference to good effect to allude to the return. Father-in-law asks daughter-in-law, 'Do you know what life is all about?' and tells her, 'Life is all about fun.' Without the immediate past and present, the anxiety of 1997, life is relieved of liability and urgency.

Relationships between Hong Kong and the Mainland are directly alluded to twice. On the first occasion, the father-in-law has wandered away from home; he stops in the middle of a busy street when a car approaches. An aerial shot shows him standing in the same posture as the lone student confronting a tank in Tiananmen Square on 4 June 1989. The car is positioned like the tank, and the driver blows his horn, yelling, 'Old fool, kill yourself somewhere else. Do you think you are a tank? Get out of the way. You want to die? Move, or I shall flatten you.' Later in the film, Hui alludes to the handover. The son's girlfriend asks, 'Will you leave me?' and he replies, 'No, never. I swear, if you don't leave me, I won't leave you.' He promises he will make her happy 'for fifty years,' the promise by the PRC to operate under 'one country, two systems' for the next fifty years.

Another version of what it means to be Hong Kong Chinese is addressed by Hui, seen in May's characterization, the daughter-in-law previously treated harshly by her father-in-law, but the one on whom he depends and eventually confides in when vulnerable. She negotiates his care and works with him by learning and speaking his language. She takes on the persona of his commander when he re-enacts his war battles; when he divulges his date with a fairy behind the mountain, she admits that she has a date the next mountain over. In a glorious interlude, the camera pans from below through a carpet of large, full trees, slowly moving downward to bring daughter-in-law and father-in-law into frame as they walk through a park. Large trees overhead drop white blossoms; the father-in-law, ecstatic, observes, 'It's snowing! Wonderful!' May, in wonder, replies, 'It's beautiful!' and the moment lingers. May is adaptable and a survivor.

'In one way or another we are all, or will be immigrants,' Guillermo Gómez-Peña announces in *New World Border*.[8] Peter Chan's *Comrades: Almost a Love Story* (1996, literally *Sweet Honey*, the title of a popular Teresa Tang song which figures in the story) sets two Mainlander opposite characters in Hong Kong on 1 March 1986 and follows them for ten years. Northern, male, and naive, Li Xiao-jun

(Leon Lai) is contrasted with Southern, female, and enterprising Li Chiao (Maggie Cheung); these border-crossers struggle to succeed in Hong Kong, despite the cultural barriers. Initially, differences are foregrounded: he has no experience of queuing up at McDonald's; she works there, is fluent in Cantonese, knows some English, and has learned to work the system. Interspersed repartee between them emphasizes difference and introduces their developing attraction. When Xiao-jun wonders 'How come you're so rich?', Chiao's quick comeback is, 'None of your business. How come you're so poor?'

Black-and-white 'arrival' scenes serve as bookends for a chronologically presented story, with dates occasionally appearing onscreen. Time is important to Hong Kong belongers; this was especially the case during the 1997 countdown. Voice-over narration of letters Xiao-jun writes home to his intended, Fong Xiaoting (Kristy Yeung), provides a structural device and indicates discrepancies between what is happening onscreen (and in his heart) and what the protagonist understands (particularly about himself) and tells her. Contradictions are comical, as when he relates that 'Hong Kong people don't have to work, sleep late, and dress up and go out for fun every night' (because he is living at a brothel); sometimes they are poignant, as when he writes to Xiao-ting 'it broke my heart too' when their dream unravels.

Chiao and Xiao-jun first meet, seemingly by chance, in McDonald's, a site emphasized by the illuminated sign with its familiar logo, unfocused then sharp and occupying two-thirds of the screen. For Xiao-jun, this is the Hong Kong version of the American dream. The protagonists have Mandarin in common, which Chiao speaks as fluently as Cantonese, and Leon Lai's expressions show that he is glad to hear a familiar voice. Chiao befriends him out of self-interest to earn another commission from the English school, which offers classes geared towards Mainlanders. Numerous 'chance' meetings later, their relationship progresses in a series of 'almosts,' reflected in the English subtitle.

Hong Kong identity and fitting-in is important to Chiao in a way that has no meaning for Xiao-jun. Asked if she is from the Mainland, she's affronted and retorts, 'Of course not! I speak fluent Cantonese! … People who speak good Mandarin may not be Mainlanders, but those who don't speak Cantonese are certainly Mainlanders.' The separation is a false barrier, of appropriated language and dress, cultural codes which signal Hong Kong 'belonger.' When she confesses

COMRADES-IN-ARMS   Maggie Cheung and Leon Lai in Peter Chan's *Comrades: Almost a Love Story*

to Xiao-jun that she comes from Guangzhou, he exclaims, 'I knew it! We are comrades.' Attempting to maintain the barrier between them by stressing Guangzhou's proximity to Hong Kong, she retorts: 'No way! We [from Guangzhou] speak Cantonese. We get Hong Kong TV. We are so much closer to Hong Kong.' Tongue in cheek, Li Xiao-jun replies: 'Right, your look, your gesture, your face, your hair are so Hong Kong.' He sees her in a way she does not see herself, and identifying her as 'comrade' suggests their similarities rather than differences. Both are immigrants, lonely and struggling to survive.

According to Sheila Rowbotham, 'The organization of production within capitalism creates a separate and segmented vision of life which continually restricts consciousness of alternatives.'[9] Chan emphasizes their great efforts to succeed in Hong Kong. Chiao's employment record reads like a laundry list: McDonald's cashier, English school recruiter, window washer, custodian, florist, masseuse, bridal shop operator, real estate investor, business entrepreneur, and stock market player. Likewise, Xiao-jun delivers for a butcher by bike and for Chiao when flowers need sending; taken on as a chef's assistant, he becomes a master chef. Together they are paid for holding a place in line for people waiting to get an apartment, one of the few times either sits and rests. Gruelling work hours and the labor involved are illustrated: both characters are shown exhausted, eating is related to providing energy to work, and time is of the essence, as they rush from one job to another. The Opportunity Furniture Store they walk past serves symbolically to galvanize them into earning more money. Chiao in particular acts out the Hong Kong dream: 'This is Hong Kong. If you work at it, anything is possible here.'

The protagonists share the loneliness of exile. When a cold and rainy Lunar New Year's Eve and financial loss in a business venture brings them closer, they consummate their relationship, a connection already defined by mutual dependence. Xiao-jun earlier realized he was being used but let it continue because he didn't want to lose his only friend in Hong Kong. Chiao, who boasted she could have many friends if she wanted, but would rather have time to make money, confesses, 'Through thick and thin you're always there for me. You are my best friend in Hong Kong.' In fact he is her only friend. They comfort each other and share their lives, learning *almost* too late that they belong together.

Chiao's big thinking, which earns enough money for her own apartment and a house for her mother in Guangzhou, leads to her *almost* missing the opportunity the furniture store represents. Likewise for Xiao-jun, whose smaller dream of bringing his intended to Hong Kong, *almost* denies him a chance at love. When Xiao-jun buys identical gold bracelets for the two women in his life, Chiao is reluctant to risk the dream that brought her to Hong Kong in the first place, and she tells Xiao-jun: 'My dream is very different. We are two different kinds of people. In fact, I don't know where I am going and I don't know what I am doing. I feel very insecure. I hate that feeling … What have I done? I don't know what will happen tomorrow. I am scared. I don't know what to do.' Feelings of fear and uncertainty reflect the Hong Kong psyche as it anticipates the return. Chan uses the predicament of the couple to register these emotions. They revisit room 527, the 'love motel' room of their intimacy, introducing impermanence as another Hong Kong factor – 'Nothing here was ours.'

'Fate is predestined,' the movie tells us, and Chiao's first spoken words to Xiao-jun prove providential: 'Can I help someone over here?' The Mainlander steps forward. The closing replay of the opening arrival scene shows something not seen in the beginning. Seated behind Xiao-jun on the train, and the person whose head his head is leaning against, is Chiao. They disembark, each going their separate way, the first *almost* of the story. Their coming together is meant to be, unlike their decision to be together, which they arrive at through pain and sacrifice only after overcoming numerous obstacles. Like the couple, the Mainland and Hong Kong are separated by their past, in this case nineteenth-century British–Sino relations, yet also to be reunited because of that history. Foregrounding the Chinese factor are numerous playings of the much-loved singer Teresa Tang, associated with sentimentality for the homeland and pride in being Chinese, especially among Mainlanders. Two featured songs in the movie are 'Sweet Honey' and 'The Moon is My Heart's Representative.' Both are love songs; the first serves as the couple's song, and Xiao-jun sings it to Chiao lying in bed and Leon Lai sings it again over closing credits. Several lines indicate its meaningfulness for China and Hong Kong and for the couple: 'Where did I meet you before?/ Your smile.../ It's you that I dream of/ Where, when did I meet you before?/ Your smile is so familiar/ I can't remember right away.' The two protagonists reunite in front of a New York Chinatown store window where television screens play Teresa Tang footage, which would have been running all over every Chinatown on the day she died, 8 May 1995.

Other filmmakers have transplanted their characters to locations other than Hong Kong or the Mainland to examine cultural identity and the effect of the diaspora. What does it mean to cross a border and relocate? Self-proclaimed 'border artist' Guillermo Gómez-Peña describes the border as 'a multiple metaphor of death, encounter, fortune, insanity, and transmutation.'[10] In two films set in New York City, Cheung Yuen-ting's *An Autumn's Tale* (1987) and Clara Law's *Farewell China* (1990), this description is dramatized, in different ways with opposite outcomes, for the Chinese emigrant.

An Autumn's Tale (literally *Autumn's Fairy Tale*), true to its English and Chinese titles, is a fairy-tale romance between distant cousins; its autumnal reference suggests the seasonal changes – colder weather, colorful and dying leaves, preparation for winter. Depicting difficulties faced by Chinese emigrants, the urban setting makes good use of local color, including Chinatown scenes, a Halloween parade, parks, a college campus, and airport and train terminals. Jennifer (Cherie Chung) goes to the Big Apple to study acting but also to pursue her two-timing boyfriend; Chow Yun-fat plays Figgy (Figurehead), the name given to the outlander cousin and former sailor there to help her.[11] Jennifer thinks he looks like 'a jerk,' but her mother insists he is a Chinatown community leader and 'lives like a king … he must be somebody.' Relying upon family connections, Jennifer embarks; she discovers Figurehead is beneath her class and that they have little besides family in common. Her accommodation is crude but adequate, and, after her initial shock, she begins, with Figgy's assistance, to make the place her home. She learns that, unlike her boyfriend, who is of the same class (it is he who is the real jerk), Figgy is there for her in every way that counts. As they eat egg sandwiches in a Chinese food shop, he tells her that 'a country is only as good as its people, and its people are only as good as their food,' and in believable scenes like this daily existence becomes real. Figgy provides Jennifer with shelter and protection, feeds her, assists her in finding jobs, rescues her from the unwanted attentions of male employers, and helps mend her broken heart.

Apparent differences between the two are accentuated in an early scene when Figurehead and his pals pick her up at the airport in Figgy's beat-up car and get into an altercation with a car of Latinos. Following the hurled insults, Jennifer remarks, 'They didn't understand a word you said,' and Figgy good-naturedly responds, 'They don't have to, as long as I'm happy.' Jennifer cares about appearances and propriety, while Figurehead doesn't 'give a fig.' Figgy's attitude towards life, which involves his remaining in a close-knit community of men like himself, reflects one way of dealing with the émigré predicament. Jennifer's horizons are wider, her problems more complex. She makes Anglo college 'friends' who show up for food and booze when she throws a party. When the ex-boyfriend arrives to reclaim her, Figgy goes on a binge and loses the woman he loves. While he has survived New York City, he cannot overcome the feelings he has for his cousin, despite his belief that 'women are chable [trouble].' Jenny, having seen through her boyfriend and set out on her own, knows the difference between substance and flashiness. Figgy brushes up on his English, gives up drinking and gambling, and opens his dream restaurant on the beach, named The Sampan. The name is reminiscent of his sea days, the crossing, and his search for love; it also represents his (now) Americanized identity – his name is 'Samuel Pang.' Class differences disappear as the couple reunite on the restaurant pier. 'Table for two?' the smartly dressed Samuel offers, and there is smooth sailing in America for this acclimated emigrant couple in the days ahead.

The hard-hitting *Farewell China* (literally *The Season of Love in Another Land*) dramatizes the coming apart of a relationship and the adversities faced by (and that destroy) emigrants. This movie makes the difficulties of *An Autumn's Tale* appear as surmountable complications and inconveniences. Here, lives weigh in the balance. First the wife Li-hung (Maggie Cheung) emigrates to New York City for the chance of a better livelihood, leaving her husband Nan-sun (Tony Leung Ka-fai) on the Mainland with their child. Director Clara Law and screenwriter Alex Fong carefully set up the difficulty of making the emigration possible, indicating the sacrifices the couple go through to create a better future. In small gestures, like the sharing of food, or the smoothing of a hair into place, the nurturing of their small child, love between them is expressed; it is also evident in the speechless nervous laughter and smiles and tears which spread across Maggie Cheung's face when she tells her husband that the visa has been granted. Subsequently, hearing little from his wife and having letters returned unopened, Nan-sun goes to New York to find her. Thus begins the bad dream from which he can't awaken: he discovers the hell his wife's life has become.

Nan-sun encounters Jane (or 'Jing' as he calls her), a fifteen-year-old Chinese-American runaway, whose characterization is second only to the leads. Enough of her background is filled in to suggest that she, too, is a victim of the diaspora and racism. Her response is to internalize the hatred of her tormentors, beginning with her Chineseness. Repeatedly she tells Nan-sun to 'speak English' but easily falls into Cantonese herself. She reveals her ugly childhood and bares her innermost feelings. 'I hated having Chinese parents. I hated being Chinese. I hated speaking Chinese. I even dyed my hair green and red and yellow so I wouldn't look like a Chinese.' Jane represents a distorted image of Chinese identity, a mirror reflecting what looks at it.

Jane gets by as a teenage prostitute, the same way Hung has survived, not unlike the scams Hung uses with older Chinese in the community to bilk them of their money. The sex depicted is rough and ugly, involving a rape, prostitution, and intercourse with a minor. Female characters become whores valued only for the exchange of their bodies and looks. Use or be used is the American way that both learn; beyond that the option is to get out or go crazy in an urban society based on force. As Gayle Rubin puts it, 'A woman is a woman. She only becomes a domestic, a wife, a chattel, a playboy bunny, a prostitute or a human dictaphone in certain relations.'[12]

Nan-sun's search for his wife provides structure, but Hung's story is inter- mittently revealed through flashbacks – characters remember her and convey to Nan-sun what they know. As he learns more about what has happened, flashbacks to their life together in China appear through his memories, including their finding a US sponsor for Hung and simple pleasures shared. His sweet remembrances sharply contrast with Hung's bitter experiences. In one scene a Taiwanese woman confronts him with questions he could never imagine, much less have within his power to articulate, although he is a loving and considerate husband. 'Do you understand what it's like to be a woman all by herself in New York? Do you understand the desperation when there is menstruation and no money for sanitary napkins? Do you understand what it feels like to be raped?' Hung had earlier written wanting to return home, desperately confessing 'I can't stand it any longer. I want to come back. Is that alright?' Nan-sun's response had been, 'Don't come back. For our son's future you must stay.' His words come back to haunt him as he and the audience discover the anguish and suffering that Hung has undergone. Nan-sun will come to understand her despair as he experiences life as a 'stranger in a strange land.'

When he is unable to find his wife and has nowhere else to go, Nan-sun returns to Jane, finding his level in the survival-of-the-fittest pool into which he has thrown. Next viewed on the streets in a medium shot, seen from behind, walking with a pseudo-streetwise swagger, Nan-sun has been 'Americanized' by Jane: he is a Chinese Elvis wannabe, wearing a baseball jacket and slicked hair, smoking a cigarette, and pimping for her. 'Chinese little girl, fifteen years old. Beautiful, clean and sexy. One hundred-fifty dollars,' he repeats like a mantra. On the verge of losing himself, he turns to Jane for comfort and the two have sex;

horrified at what he's done, he runs away, stumbling into a nighttime punk scene courtesy of Hieronymous Bosch, garish and surreal.

A mournful image follows. The camera pans the early-morning New York skyline, the cityscape of massive towers dwarfing the telephone booth to which the camera abruptly cuts. Overheard is Nan-sun phoning home, anxiously telling his parents, 'I want to come home immediately,' thereby repeating the words of Hung, adding 'immediately.' Their response echoes his to his wife earlier: 'Don't come back.' The camera creeps up on him in the booth, the bluish light setting the mood, editing and *mise-en-scène* underscoring the overwhelming feeling of abandonment and helplessness. Nan-sun wanted his wife to make a sacrifice for their son's future; his parents, old with nothing to lose, intimate that he has everything to gain. The camera gradually moves in on Nan-sun trapped in the booth, focusing on his pained face during the overheard conversation. He is all alone, alienated. As Marx describes: 'Alienation is apparent not only in the fact that my means of life belong to someone else, that my desires are the unattainable possession of someone else, but that everything is something different from itself, that my activity is something else, and finally … that an inhuman power rules over everything.'[13]

Hung has undergone a similar abandonment and alienation. She has not been as fortunate as her husband, who survives in the USA as a restaurant delivery person. First told by a consulate official that she was 'too pretty' for a visa to the USA, Hung became pregnant to diminish her good looks. After having a child and earning a visa, she still bears that burden in unforeseen ways. Alison M. Jaggar writes that 'Women are viewed relentlessly as sexual objects, whether or not they welcome sexual interest, and they are subject continually to sexual assaults and harrassment.'[14] Our first sight of Hung stateside is in a flashback related by emigrant artist Ah-mun: at his gallery opening, flashily dressed in red, she is uncharacteristically outspoken and edgy, speaking loudly and nonstop about the big deal she's working on. She leaves on the arm of an Anglo male. She is subsequently brutally raped by two men, but has no recourse to action. Looking like 'discarded dishwater,' she appears very different to the earlier image. Broken as a human being, unable to cope, she's lost her identity and her mind, and would probably be diagnosed as a paranoid schizophrenic. Nan-sun eventually finds her by chance while making a food delivery; she fearfully asks, 'Did anyone follow you? Anyone eavesdropping? … There are lots of their agents here and I am alone.' Slipping in and out of reality, she plays for him a tape which is her only solace, the song 'You Don't Understand My Heart.'

The film opens with another song, to which it returns at story's end. 'Thinking Of' is a popular tune, the theme of which is the leaving of one's homeland.[15] The song appears in fragments throughout the movie, and the lines parallel the action, resonating with characters' feelings and experiences. Snatches of song parallel characters' torn-apart lives. At story's end, Hung mortally stabs Nan-sun, believing a stranger is attacking her; he dies in a fetal position as she recognizes what she has done. She wanders off aimlessly. The scene cuts to a tracking shot from the train, repeating the image of their trip to the consulate. Other scenes, of trees arching over a road, the countryside, and a village, quickly pass as the song plays. The film concludes with their child toddling through a narrow alley, walking towards the camera before veering off into a side street. The images and final lines of the song cohere: 'Thinking of how each day passes and I sow/ For the sake of my children.../ Chinese people are born with patience unbounded.'

Yim Ho's *King of Chess* (1988) opens with a black screen and this statement: 'Past, present or future, China will always belong to the Chinese people.' 'My Beloved Comrade,' a Taiwanese pop song sung by Lo Da-yo, begins with electric guitars blaring.[16] The opening line 'I think of you every time I close my eyes' hardly signals a love song. 'You' is immediately associated with Mao, seen in multiple images onscreen while the song plays over Cultural Revolution footage. Crowds gather in Tiananmen Square; the sun shines, people are happy, dancing in the streets or waving red flags and books as benevolent Mao looks on; everyone is in motion in marches or parades. Collaged like an MTV video, the Cultural Revolution becomes a youth movement, with all the hope of the young looking forward to the promise of a bright future. As the song continues, the 'I' persona shifts to Mao and back again to the singer, so that all are one with Mao, 'hand in hand, an unchanging face.'

An abrupt jump cut shifts to present-day Tapei, where Ching (John Sham), a Hong Kong media executive, conducts business. Contrasted to rural Mainland settings and the People's Square in Beijing, Tapei teems with traffic, skyscrapers, neon, jumbotrons, and white noise. 'Now's your chance – wealth is at hand' is the constant refrain (courtesy of an insurance company commercial) that typifies this modern city. The adult Ching is out of place here, just as a child he was out of place on the Mainland, where his parents sent him to be educated during the Cultural Revolution. The story alternates between two time frames and places: 1967 in northern China and present-day Taiwan. The screenplay runs together two novels: *Chess King*, by contemporary Taiwanese author Zhang Xi-guo, and *King of Chess*, by Mainland author Zhung A-cheng (Ah Cheng) – a member of the 'search for roots' movement in the PRC. Although Yim Ho is credited as director and Tsui Hark as producer, 'when Tsui saw the Mainland part that Yim had shot, he was displeased and took over the film himself … Tsui had envisioned the entire film having a unified comedic tone,' according to Terence Chang, then running Film Workshop and the person instructed by Tsui to fire Yim. The resulting film has a curious double nature: two directors, time frames, places, tones, chess kings, chess sets, and identities. Mainland scenes are dramatic, Tapei scenes more comic.

'I met a Chess King once when I was in China. He gave me a lot of inspiration,' says Ching to Jade, a television personality and friend. He is trying to help her keep her job, despite resentment from Taiwanese industry people. The 'Chess King' to whom he refers is Wong Yat-sun (Tony Leung Ka-fai), a working-class chess genius he met in childhood. His memories are triggered by a present-day chess king, Wan Shing-fong, another working-class figure, referred to as 'the kid' or 'little money-bags,' and chosen to appear on Jade's 'Whiz Kids World,' the television show she hosts. Ching straddles both worlds, belonging to neither. In flashbacks, when he complains to his cousin Ngai that he is always criticizing him, Ngai warns Ching to behave or he will be severely criticized by Red Guards. His present-day Taiwanese friends grumble: 'Hong Kong people come to Taiwan to escape from the paranoia of 1997, they're so pathetic.' The filmmakers use this outsider's confrontation with past and present for the purpose of revelation. Ching reflects, 'I've struggled hard to package this city. In the process I've sold myself as a packaged product. I'm Chinese. I thought Taiwan was home. But I can't adjust.' Jade responds, 'Adjust? You have to face yourself.' Ching looks in the mirror and doesn't like what he sees, but complacency makes him unwilling or unable to change.

The filmmakers incorporate chess metaphors to discuss Hong Kong–Mainland relations and establish common ground for what it means to be Chinese. Chinese Chess, with elephants, soldiers, generals, and horses, is part of traditional Chinese culture, linked to intellectual/artistic pursuit and challenge, pleasure and enjoyment. Part of social activity, the game is shared among friends and comrades.

Good players achieve inner freedom, their endeavor linked to spiritual Taoist beliefs, being at one with the force of nature. Educated urban youth sent to the countryside to work on a collective farm include several chess players, among them Wong Yat-sun, Ngai (whose 'great family' dates back to the Yuan Dynasty), and Chung (played by Yim Ho), an art academy student who self-censors his art book. The labor camp where they live is run quasi-military style, serving as the site of their re-education. A critique of the Cultural Revolution, the scenes illustrate how abuses by team leaders and corruption of Party officials lead to the group suffering. Ngai's father has been denounced; because of his social status Ngai is victimized by a vindictive female Red Guard, as is the artist Chung. The intellectuals lack skill as laborers, as personified by the tall Ngai (nicknamed 'Lanky'), who, despite his inexperience and heart condition, is assigned to compete in basketball rather than use his talent at chess playing.

In the Tapei scenes, the whiz kid begins not by playing Chinese chess but instead the simple game of one-piece chess. Instructed by Ching's fellows, he learns on the computer after they discover his abilities. Testing the boy's prescience, they require him to visualize numbers they type onto a computer screen: tellingly, 00000001997. They use Wan to play the stock market and make money, and chess games he plays against the champion, Professor Lau, are pre-arranged to boost ratings. As the players' televised competition occurs, a projection board behind them simulates their moves, making play 'larger than life.' The media present a personalized, dramatized and fragmented world, television assuming a powerful and pervasive presence, making viewers less prospective participants than consumers, contributing to withdrawal from the public and community realm. Despite the Hong Konger being discomfited by the media-generated personalities, mass consumption culture, and greed and betrayal by the transnational suits on the edges of the scene, whose pervasive power is defined largely by their absence, Ching finds a place in this world by exploiting the child. His job in advertising is not unlike the business of the television executives. 'The "practice" of viewing television is part of the ideology of advertising,' notes Mark Poster.[17] Both agendas reflect capitalist relations, selling a Taiwan on the move, and the competition is fierce.

Chess appears metaphorically in this story to describe Chinese history and power relations and the position of individuals and classes within the power structure. Chung says, 'They [the Party members] play big chess, we play small chess.'

Ngai describes the game thus: 'Upheavals on a grand scale, territorial gains, emergence of a conqueror. The world is a chess game, unpredictable moves, heroes rise and fall.' When Wong takes on nine players simultaneously, playing blind, he relates, 'Ngai told me that if I win I can apply for transfer to a better place.' Chung and the others see him as the first with a chance, their inspiration. 'We're all waiting for a chance,' Chung replies.

Two chess sets symbolize class disparity in the Mainland scenes: one belonging to Wong and the other to Ngai. Wong's set is lovingly made and given to him by his now deceased prostitute mother, who collected toothbrushes to have the material made into a characterless set. It stands for her hardship and sacrifice, a representative of China's masses, as well as for his tender memories of her. Ngai's valuable ebony set, left to him by his father, is an antique and a family heirloom; it is just as meaningful to Ngai as Wong's is to him. Both men willingly give up their sets for the good of each other. In contrast, the expensive modern-design set with which Wan and Lau compete, and the backdrop board used on the television set, carry no value for either.

The camaraderie of the Mainland group is emphasized from their first encounter on the train ride to the countryside, through numerous scenes in which they gather to share food and stories. Ngai customarily regales them by telling stories about food: for example, a dramatized evening's tale about preparing and eating bird's nest and pigeon soup, a delicacy only Ngai has savored. When they catch, prepare and eat a snake, the huddled circle of men and the child Ching share the repast as a gourmet meal. 'I dread hunger,' Wong confides. From the overcooked rice and rancid meat of the train journey to the sparse meals available at camp, the conception of food under the Cultural Revolution, in contrast to the men's appreciation, is based upon basic survival rather than the heart, while the group values both (*jing* and *qing*). The attitude of the powerful during the Cultural Revolution recalls the words of Marx: 'Food is given to the labourer as to a mere means of production, as coal is supplied to the boiler, grease and oil to the machine.'[18]

In contrast, a Tapei beach scene featuring Ching's group emphasizes each member's self-interest: they have lost the whiz kid on it, and the conversation concerns their worry about themselves. One wonders about his stocks, another about exam questions he was going to sell, provided by the kid; Ching is concerned about losing his bet with Lau and leaving Taiwan. Only Jade thinks about the boy's interest, but her language is tainted by tele-speak, echoing commercial advertising: 'Let's look at the ocean of possibilities. Relax and decide that anything is possible. Take a deep breath and say, "Where there's a will, there's a way."' The characters appear in a natural environment (not unlike the countryside in the Mainland scenes), in contrast to the concrete, steel, and glass of downtown Taipei. Rather than gaining spiritual inspiration or insight, as Wong does from chess playing, they ignore life's simplicity and dignity.

The group's avarice and self-interest places them – especially Ching as a stand-in for Hong Kong – at odds with the cohesive Mainland group. The conclusion reinforces an indictment of late capitalist expansion through television and its promotion of consumerism. The neon sign for 'Everybody Insurance' comes tumbling down, and Wan is killed saving a little girl's life. The spirit of the Chess King (Wong) greets the spirit of the dead boy, observing the scene. 'Do you know why they're looking for you?' asks Wong. Wan replies, 'Yes. They want to know what their future holds.' Wong responds, 'Right, and only you know. That's why.' The collaged denouement brings together characters from both stories as a full-blown ballad version of 'My Beloved Comrade' plays. Wong holds out his large hand, taken by the small child. 'Let's go,' he says. Documentary footage of the Cultural Revolution and Taipei is intercut, as the song continues. Fear about the loss of Hong Kong's way of life, particularly its economic health, is foregrounded and critiqued simultaneously.

Second-wave filmmaker Stanley Kwan's mentor is Ann Hui. He served as her assistant director on *The Spooky Bunch* (1980), *The Story of Woo Viet* (1981), and *Boat People*; Kwan also worked with other new-wave filmmakers, including Patrick Tam, Ronny Yu, Yim Ho, and Leong Po-chih. Kwan's films are sumptuously lensed, with cinematographers Bill Wong and Christopher Doyle bringing great beauty to his images. Rich colors and lavish production design, with an eye for detail and patterning effects, contribute. Watching a Kwan film is like slowly opening a Chinese box. One admires the overall design and craftsmanship, then its intricacies and hidden relationships as each compartment reveals surprises and delights. Kwan's films draw from melodrama and the genre of 'women's films.' His sensitivity to women's issues and the way he avoids the male gaze is unusual. The director neither exploits nor objectifies women (in the sense of being reified by a masculine viewpoint), although the content depicts practices whereby women are exploited and objectified. He avoids presenting Chinese women as exotics, despite settings and time periods of stories being associated, from a Western perspective, with 'exoticism' – teahouses, brothels, Cantonese opera theaters, 1930s' Shanghai. Known for working closely in collaboration with actors, Kwan 'uses' women in the best possible sense of the word, responding to them and drawing from them qualities and performances rarely depicted onscreen. With Kwan's women comes loss and sadness; thus they are associated with a Hong Kong of disappearances, the movies becoming emotional meditations.

Rouge (1987) is told through the perspective of one-time courtesan Fleur (Anita Mui), a 53-year-old ghost (a nod at the PRC's promise of 'one country, two systems' for fifty years – the aftermath). Kwan avoids the usual accoutrements of ghostly spookiness and creates an even more displaced character and ethereal effect. Fleur is so pale and fragile she is 'barely there'; her fluid movements translate into masterful camerawork. One moment she is in frame, the next gone, and swish pans register the shocked reaction of characters discomfited by her disappearing act. Kwan also adds another dislocation strategy by comparing and contrasting past and present times, forcing the character to mediate between two worlds. In search of Chan Chen-pang (Leslie Cheung), also called Twelfth Master, the lover who survived their double suicide (in 1930s' Hong Kong), Fleur haunts the present (interacting with the middle-class 1980s' couple Ah Chu and Yuen). Abbas refers to the film's 'double temporal framework' as its structuring device.[19] The ghost's intensely passionate life is expressed through gorgeous deep reds: deep scarlet shadows, the brothel's elaborate wallpaper and window panes, the exquisite cheongsam materials and rouge Fleur wears. Richness intensifies through languid rhythms of gesture, slowly swirling camera movement, and editing of the past story – which begins the film and recurs through flashbacks.

At one level, Fleur's world is contrasted with the complacency and habitual existence of the quite ordinary modern couple (Alex Man and Emily Chu). Their relationship is one of convenience; their world is shown through bright neon lights of nighttime Hong Kong, glaring fluorescent tubes and harsh light of daytime, including the hustle and bustle of street activity. Bewildered by the changes in Shek Tong Tsui, where the Yi Hung Lau Brothel, the Gum-ling Eating House and the Tai-ping Theater were located, Fleur loses her way. While she is amused that the 'pleasure house' is now a nursery school (the restaurant is a shopping arcade and the theater a 7–11 store), she nonetheless cries at what is gone, complaining throughout the present scenes that 'the world is overpowering me … I'm getting weaker … I'm tired. I never thought it would end like this.'

The penultimate scene shows Fleur overwhelmed by a present-day Cantonese opera performance of *Shanbo on the Brink of Death*. Both joy and sadness fleetingly move across Anita Mui's face in medium close-up, cutting between her and the performer onstage. Fleur's emotion conflates past and present, remembering the pleasures of her opera going and the pain of watching Chen-pang, reduced to lowly status, working there. The song comments on Fleur's abandonment by her lover and ponders whether he has regrets: 'Fate has parted us. We have been crying ever since we said farewell on the terrace. Our tears fall like rain all through the night. Shanbo sits alone in a bare room lost in his infinite sorrow. Yingtail, Shanbo calls but you do not answer.' The roles are reversed here, the female nonresponsive. As Fleur wonders why Twelfth Master didn't die and hasn't come, the scene sets up the conclusion, where the lovers are briefly reunited and she then leaves him. Having squandered his fortune and abandoned his family, he is an old squatter waiting for work as a film actor, an empty shell, more of a ghost than Fleur. Relieving himself in a corner, he mumbles 'I had servants to help me piss. Now I get my shoes wet.'

At another level, contrasts between past and present are balanced by comparisons, and the dual context reveals that the more things change, the more they stay the same. The film's deep structure is overdetermined by repetitions of major elements. For example, all songs taken from *The Sorrows of the Autumn Traveller*, a Cantonese opera in which the scholar–traveller leaves his faithful concubine to return home, tellingly describe the relationship of Fleur and Chen-pang. In the film's opening song, performed by Fleur dressed as a male scholar, she sings in character: 'Today we are separated and unable to see one another. I am cold and alone.' When Chen-pang enters, mesmerized, she concludes, singing as herself, as she will become: 'Pity me pining after you in melancholy.' For his opera audition Chen-pang sings, 'Why don't you go home? Far, far, from home … so sad, so sad,' and later performs onstage as 'the master is tricked by a deceitful girl at the border.' Similarly, Yuen and Chen-pang are both 'soft-hearted' and buy presents for their lovers. Ah Chu is an independent woman, chiefly defined by her work; the same could be said of Fleur, who stands up to the Chan family when Chen-pang does not. The women exchange lip rouges, Ah Chu admitting, 'In your place I'd have done the same thing with a coward like him [Chen-pang].' Is the great passion which the modern-day couple lament as lacking in their relationship any worse than the one built on fear and distrust? Chen-pang loves Fleur but is too weak to commit, but Fleur has resolve and love for them both; cast as the femme fatale, distrustful, she adds poison to the wine he drinks to muster courage when they ingest the raw opium, because 'he was afraid.' The camerawork is generally more elliptical in the past scenes, and more dynamic in the present ones, but by the end styles merge, as is apparent in the bluish night scenes. Ah Chu returns to Yuen, the scene being shot as if it is the meeting of Fleur and Chen-pang. The climax contains the 'real' ghost (Fleur), an imposter (an actress on a movie set playing a ghost swordswoman), and a ghost of a man (Chen-pang). Instructed, 'You must be powerful like a warrior and scary like a ghost,' the imposter repeatedly flies through the bluish night air courtesy of wire-work, a suitable backdrop to Fleur's and Chen-pang's final encounter, observed by Ah Chor and Yuen.

Prostitute Fleur is socially oppressed not only for being a woman, but for being a 'peipa girl.' Opening moments include a series of three images of Fleur, soundless, divided by fades to black, where she gazes into the camera as into a mirror and applies rouge to her lips. The first is a dead-on medium close-up, the second a tight close-up as she slightly turns her head away from our gaze; and the third, a longer shot with Fleur dwarfed at lower right frame, moved from the viewer's left to right, as she begins to disappear. Tightly framed, she appears artificial, like the rouge concealed within her locket. But as she begins breaking frame, she moves ahead to her destiny at the film's end, a new incarnation, the embodiment of Hong Kong. Sold at the age of sixteen, she has measured life by the days, the first and fifteenth of every month, when she visits Manmo Temple, for readings from the fortune-teller. 'Now I have you instead and my life is worthwhile,' she tells Chen-pang. 'The prostitute is a fetish,' writes Rey Chow:

> In Marx's sense, she is a laborer whose work (performing sex) is appropriated from her while she is denounced by the same society that thrives by commodifying her services. The life of this prostitute is thus an emblem of the alienation of labor in a modern society, her form personifies the process of commodification that must conceal its origins.[20]

Alienation is apparent when Fleur visits her lover's mother for tea and is forced to model the material for her lover's future bride's wedding dress. 'I want to put my past behind me,' Fleur says, to which the mother replies, 'I must think about his future.' The proper Chinese woman is perfectly satisfied, however, with Fleur being her son's second wife. The wise woman knows her dutiful son well: 'If you let him go, he'll come back to you. But if you cling to him, he'll eventually come back to me.' The heir to a herbal medicine franchise, the well-stationed Chen-pang 'outclasses' Fleur in every regard, except constancy, despite the rouge locket he has given her as a sign of faithfulness. The wayward son who enjoys slumming is kept by a woman; Kwan includes a scene recording Fleur's skills with a stranger as she coyly bargains for more money. 'Are you saving for the future?' he asks. 'Maybe,' she replies. The transaction involves the customer touching various body parts for a price, and the camera consumes them, from ears to neck to calves to feet. 'One for each toe,' he offers. As Chow observes,

> Meanwhile, in the manner of Freud's theory, the prostitute's body functions as a fetish for the sexuality that a 'civilized' society represses. Before the camera eye, the different parts of her body, such as a smile, a leg, an arm, a coiffure, or a beautiful dress, serve as the loci of society's displaced desire.[21]

Displaced desire is the longing for Hong Kong's past, already gone and ever-disappearing, but seen in the moment recorded by the film's final image, as Fleur, walking away from Chen-pang, turns and gazes into the camera, an aching last look at Hong Kong fifty-three years later.

Character displacement, as used in the films discussed above, appears in many Hong Kong genres, raising questions about Hong Kong Chinese identity and the diaspora resulting from the impending return.[22] Even gangster and cop movies use the technique. Andrew Lau's *To Live and Die in Tsimshatsui* (1994), for example, features mirror-image characters. One is undercover cop Ah Lik (Jacky Cheung), who looks at his pained reflection in mirrors and thinks, 'Sometimes I don't know who I am.' His double (Tony Leung Ka-fai), a former undercover cop and small-time criminal, a 'failure,' knows too well who he is: 'I'm the one who can maintain Hong Kong for fifty years – horse will race, nightclub will open.' Both are alienated from their work, and reflect on

courtesy/permission of Milkyway Image (HK) Ltd.

THE 3-D JOB   Wu Chien-lien in Patrick Leung's *Beyond Hypothermia*

the contradiction between the individuality of each separate proletarian and labor. The condition of life forced upon him, becomes evident, for he is sacrificed from youth upwards and, within his own class, has no chance of arriving at conditions which would place him in the other class.[23]

Likewise, the Triad member played by Roy Cheung in Samson Chiu Leung-chun's *Rose* (1992) is incapable of leaving his violent past behind to start life anew with insurance agent Rose (Maggie Cheung), in a film that is an interesting mix of the bloody gangster flick and the sensitive woman's melodrama. In a self-reflex-ive scene the characters describe their relationship as what it would be like if the actors Roy Cheung and Maggie Cheung made a movie together – an impossibility, they agree.[24] The protagonist's circumstances in Patrick Leung's *Beyond Hypothermia* (1997) reflect alienation to an icy degree. Wu Chien-lien plays a hired killer, a hit woman so alienated from her work and desensitized by the violence it entails that she blows away a little girl without hesitation or remorse. She is 'beyond hypothermia,' aloof and unresponsive, contextualized briefly by the squalor from which she came, which suggests she had little choice, but defined mostly by the sterile apartment in which she lives – practically empty and seemingly uninhabited, a place to sleep between jobs. Her only connection to humanity is through the noodles she likes cooked by stallman and former Triad member Lau Ching-wan. For the most part, she is her job. 'In its blind unrestrainable passion, its werewolf hunger for surplus labour, capital oversteps not only the moral, but even the merely physical maximum bounds of the working day.'[25] Her work follows her as the associate of a Korean mob boss she has dispatched hunts her down. Her life, like her death, comes cheap as she is mercilessly wasted in a car; the scene happens abruptly, and lacks the well-choreographed and rhythmical gunplay seen earlier.

Displacement grows out of the predicaments faced by working-class characters. Johnnie To's *All About Ah Long* (1989), which Chow Yun-fat describes as a Hong Kong version of *The Champ*, is an upside-down Hong Kong version of *Kramer vs. Kramer*, yet this Chinese Kramer, called Ah-long (Chow), is far removed from Dustin Hoffman's yuppie dad. A construction worker and former motorcycle racer, he works harder and suffers more, both physically and emotionally, for the good of his son. Detailed attention to the everyday routine of their lives, the intimacies they share, and the adjustments they've made enrich the story. When his ex-wife reappears, as part of the professional–managerial stratum, she offers the boy social mobility and emigration to the USA with an upper-middle-class businessman stepfather. The son easily moves into his mother's world (she is an advertising executive, and the child is recruited for an ad campaign), while Ah-long is an outsider; no matter how hard he tries to belong, he is exiled, a displaced person. Numerous close-ups register Ah-long's pain and selfless love as he determines what is best for his son.[26] Ah-long's death, brought about through his attempt to race and provide financial stability for the boy, is to be expected. There are winners and losers.

Tony Au's *Roof With a View* (1993) is the female version of Ah-long's story. Hiu-tung (Veronica Yip) plays a working-class single mother, abandoned by her Triad member hubby, criticized by her family, taken advantage of by men, and raising her three-year-old son BB alone. Tony Leung Ka-fai plays Lau, an aloof

Hong Kong cop who has his own obstacles to overcome. A mixture of comedy and melodrama, the film overcomes the limitations of each genre by making believable the everyday difficulties of the woman's situation, and through strong acting. Both leads have a rapport with the child, and Tony Leung's scenes with the little boy are both joyful and intimate as they spend the day having facials, bike riding, playing on the beach, and visiting the grave of Lau's partner. Chemistry between the leads, and the child's presence, make this movie a touching family story and a romantic delight. A happy ending makes the film the up-side of the Ah-long story, but its opening shocks by graphically depicting the crude suicide of Lau's partner. Used as a foil to Yip's character, Lau is a man who bottles up his feelings, while Hiu-tung expresses herself too readily and freely, often to her own regret. The story's climax occurs when BB runs away and they search for him together; the resolution does not come until both express their feelings appropriately.

Hiu-tung's plight is grounded and duly dramatized. Following the suicide scene and Lau's introduction, a cut to her apartment and the family's morning routine bears striking similarity to the opening of *All About Ah-long*. While Ah-long's construction job leads nowhere and his motorcycle racing is literally dead-end, Hiu-tung, through her desire to better her circumstances and her willingness to work hard, eventually moves up the employment ladder, from shampooer in a beauty salon to car salesperson. Differences also emerge in the scenes where the respective parents push their children away. Ah-long berates and slaps his son as a pretext for sending him to his financially secure mother. Hiu-tung, exhausted from trying to be a 'modern woman,' caught between trying to be a 'good mother' and a 'good worker,' in desperation takes her frustrations out on her son, causing the child to run away. As such, she is displaced, 'at home' neither in her home nor at the office. Her complaints, spoken to a three-year-old, reinforce the visuals:

Will you be good and not make it any harder on Mommy? Mommy has had a hard life. Mommy has to take care of you. Mommy has to cook, do the laundry, and she has to go to work to make money. And everybody is giving her a hard time. Don't be like the others, don't make it hard on Mommy, okay? ... I don't really know how to take care of you. Leave, go with your father. Learn making a living with a knife from your father. You have Mommy to love you, but no one loves Mommy.

The character's self-pity recalls a description by Marx of the way the proletariat feels: 'annihilated in its self-alienation, it sees its own powerlessness and the reality of an inhuman existence.'[27]

Since the film is a romantic comedy, the female protagonist's contentment depends on her reuniting with her male counterpart. The movie closes with Hiu-tung, facing the camera, looking at Lau, with his back to the camera and his position in the foreground. Voice-over narration cements the *mise-en-scène*, as he commits to the mother and son, telling her he will carry BB on his back and Hiu-tung in his arms. The love of a willing man with a strong back, at least in the movie world, apparently provides comfort in a harsh world.

EIGHT

ONCE UPON A TIME
IN HONG KONG

Storytelling is celebrated in Hong Kong movies. Geoffrey O'Brien notes that the origins of the narrative tradition can be traced back to marketplace reciters in ancient China, classical novels like *The Romance of the Three Kingdoms*, *The Journey to the West*, and *The Water Margin*, and recyclable stock characters and situations in Peking Opera, all of 'which value the force of the episode and the flow of moment-to-moment continuity over large-scale plots and tidy resolutions.'[1] Movie stories are crafted and shaped through gradual addition and fine-tuning. O'Brien asserts that

> the uncannily lifelike quality of ancient Chinese fiction has a great deal to do with the way new characters and elements keep entering the situation and events move too fast to tie up all the loose ends. In a comparable fashion, the improvisatory messiness of Hong Kong movies – with their lurches of mood and their digressions that unaccountably become the main story line – gives them, despite their fantastic premises, a sense of underlying gritty reality.[2]

O'Brien accurately identifies significant cultural elements that have played a part in inventing Hong Kong film storytelling. Yet his description of the movies as 'improvisatory messiness' is more apropos of the filmmaking than the products onscreen. It is perhaps appropriate to consider the ways in which they are made.

The custom in the industry in the 1980s and 1990s was to set a budget and then allow filmmakers creative control over their projects. Because of the relatively low film costs and the presale of Hong Kong movies, investors have often put up money without even seeing a script, satisfied with a one-page synopsis. Terence Chang succinctly describes the attitude as 'anything goes.' In addition to having the freedom to experiment, filmmaker–storytellers share an openness towards the uncontrollable and the unknown on a film set: they 'go with the flow.' Through visual narration, filmmakers connect with their enterprise, directing their visions according to what is revealed as filmmaking progresses. This includes chance and the process of collaboration that filmmaking has become, with actors, cinematographers, designers, screenwriters, and so on, all contributing. A continual exchange of energies occurs as filmmakers draw from these resources, thereby stimulating their own skill of articulating the narrative. Storytelling is thus dynamic, a force producing motion, and 'moving pictures' is its most suitable medium. The production process involves phenomenal exchanges of energy, and Hong Kong moviemakers have unleashed cinematic powers long dormant, reinventing narrative Hong Kong style.

New-wave storytellers, as well as the autodidact auteur John Woo (who learned the basics from actually working in the film industry, and became, at twenty-six, Hong Kong's youngest filmmaker), have been able to develop personal narratives. Woo's movies reflect his own code of honor. He told film critic Betsy Sherman that he put himself in his signature Hong Kong movies to such a degree that his wife 'said I gave all the romance and love to the movie, and left the loneliness for her.'[3] Ann Hui's preoccupation with exile stems from her self-discovery of being part Japanese and separated early from family members. Tsui Hark, the creator of Film Workshop, realized his vision of making 'artistic, yet commercial pictures,' according to Terence Chang; the numerous films he has produced have a distinctive blend of comedy, politics, and gender-bending. Tsui explains: 'I am looking for ways to make my audience feel. If your audience doesn't have a strong feeling from your story, you fail as a storyteller.' Ronny Yu warmly remembers his father taking him to the cinema as a child, where he would see as many as four movies a day. Yu recalls one of his mentors, Michael Hui, telling him, 'Ronny, when you start a film, do you feel a fire inside? Are you dying to tell a story? If not, then don't do it.' Hui also reminded him, '"Ronny, don't forget, when we die, our movies don't die. Your grandson, your great-great grandson, will be watching that. Movies are immortal." … Every time I start a movie I remember this conversation he had with me.'[4] Wong Kar-wai, after authoring numerous scripts, turned to directing without scripts. By writing all his films while making them, Wong emphasizes process; this pursuit is richly visualized by cinematographer Christopher Doyle's paradoxical fluid and disjunctive camerawork. Their distinguished collaboration gives new meaning to the art-house movie.

Stories of dislocation have served these filmmakers well. Thematically, displaced characters are uprooted, which affects their sense of self and place; this is suggestive of Hong Kong's status leading up to 1997. These outsider-thinking-and-feeling narratives refute what Homi Bhabha calls the 'cultural binarism of relativism'; the films are good examples of

> the social process of enunciation, … a 'dialogic' process that attempts to track the processes of displacement and realignment that are already at work, constructing something different and hybrid from the encounter: a third space that does not simply revise or invert the dualities, but 'revalues' the ideological bases of division and difference.[5]

Used as a strategy, dislocation deconstructs film conventions, affecting plot, image, time, place, and character.

Dislocation was much on the mind of director Jacob Cheung when he made *Cageman* (literally *Cage People*) in 1992. The filmmaker relates: 'the editor-in-chief of a newspaper found me through a third party and asked me out to tea…. He said there's something that I should make a movie about; and if I didn't do it, no one else would. And that's *Cageman*.'[6] Cheung depicts a complex reality shared by 3,200 people (the government estimate; others cite up to 10,000) in Hong Kong. Cage-home dwellers are

> the most deprived group in slum areas … middle-aged and old singletons living in bedspace apartments in old private housing. Inside a bedspace apartment there are rows of bunk beds in double and triple tiers, with one lodger in each bed. Typically, the beds are surrounded by wire.[7]

Focusing on a handful of characters living in the forty-year-old Wa Ha Men's Hostel, Cheung constructs their concrete social existence as they interact within their community and outside it – with district councilors, the police, television crews – and are affected by powers beyond their scope – the Kui Fung Group that wants to take back the building for redevelopment. Koo Yiu-cho (Roy Chiao), former sailor and laundryman, has managed the hostel for twenty-four years and lives there with his simple-minded son Sam. Other residents include the 99-year-old called 7–11 and Sissy (Victor Wong), age sixty-nine, who cares for him; the dwarf Tong Sam (Teddy Robin Kwan), whose companion is a monkey; a Taoist philosopher who likes to drink wine; the tinker Luk Tung, with toolbox handy; and newcomer Mao (Wong Ka-ku), a recently paroled juvenile criminal and the son of police officer Lam, whose territory includes the hostel. The strong ensemble cast enhances the well-written characterizations and the characters have dignity, warmth, and a sense of humor. They discuss, argue, share, care, and make sure 'every day counts' – the wise words of the Taoist.

The director emphasizes the characters' closeness in an impromptu party that the cagemen hold during the Autumn Moon Festival because they feel happy. Singing and dancing to "Cherry Pink and Apple Blossom White,' they snake through the narrow corridors between stacked cages, merrily drinking wine and eating mooncakes. Their camaraderie stands in bleak contrast to the conditions of their existence, created in the name of progress and economic development. The situation of the 'cagemen' is not unlike that of the cellar-dwellers Marx described in the nineteenth century.[8] Established as an image in the opening shots of the film, the cages are barely large enough to hold a grown man comfortably. 7–11 uses a bedpan, the only running water being an outside faucet. The director remembers that, 'The moment I walked into a "cagehouse" I wanted to smoke a cigarette. The place just reeked of human. Human odor is fine, but when there's too much of it, it smells bad and makes you sick.'[9] 7–11, on several occasions singing English lyrics from Stephen Foster's African-American inspired 'Old Black Joe,' rightly connects their caged existence to slavery. Rather than dwell on present circumstances, however, his mind is set on heaven: 'Gone from the earth to a better land I know.'

As with the party scene, Cheung establishes the hostel courtyard as a communal gathering place, emphasizing the close-knit relations developed between those neglected by the government and its citizens. As the camera eye pans down from the uppermost level to the lowest, with people hung over balconies along with their laundry, the dismal living conditions are reinforced. Expanding on this image are aerial shots of seven-story tenement buildings packed together in the slums of Hong Kong. Writing of the English working class, Engels observed, 'Every great city has ... slums, where the working class is crowded together ... where removed from the sight of the happier classes, it may struggle along as it can.'[10]

Difficulties faced by the cagemen are an extreme case of the larger housing problem in Hong Kong. Confronted by the lawyer Ho, representing the Kui Fung conglomerate which will profit by razing the building, Koo is informed that the residents must vacate the hostel within eight weeks. Engels's comments on land- and real-estate speculation are reflected in the developmental activities of the Kui Fung Group particularly and Hong Kong generally:

> The growth of the big modern cities gives the land in certain areas, particularly in those which are centrally located, an artificial and colossally increasing value; the buildings erected on these areas depress this value, instead of increasing it, because they no longer correspond to the changed circumstances. They are pulled down and replaced by others. This takes place above all with workers' houses which are situated centrally and whose rents, even with the greatest overcrowding, can never, or only very slowly, increase above a certain maximum.[11]

The Taoist expresses the situation somewhat differently, explaining, 'People with different ideologies share different values in judging the meaning of their living dimensions. This is the origin of every dispute and quarrel.' Both statements identify the cagemen as voiceless and marginalized, their very living space contested by forces too powerful to be contained by the territory they fight over. Koo's venture downtown to present their case to district councilmen similarly shows their powerlessness. Koo and his son appear lost amidst Hong Kong belongers hurrying along the sidewalks, dwarfed by towering glass and steel skyscapers.[12]

In so grave a real-life situation, the cagemen use levity as a means of coping. Double-edged humor serves as an instrument for serious reflection. A courtyard voting scene and its aftermath, featuring the 'slumming' of the two councilors, illustrate this. The results of the vote by the inhabitants are mixed. A confused mêlée ensues, with Tong Sam observing that, 'Voting is fucking tricky,' and 7–11 complaining, 'Too many different voices out there.'

The motivations of the two councilors, Tsui and Chow, are linked to furthering their political aspirations and power; both use the cagemen as an opportunity for good publicity, each agreeing to live with them for three days. Their pretense of experiencing the cagemen's existence is only a game as they practice the art of one-upmanship, especially before the news cameras. The councilors' arrival is nothing more than a simulated media event, the result of their political double-speak. Splicing together interviews conducted by Chow in surveying the area, the director's cuts are abrupt, recording only Chow's responses. In all cases, he directs problems to offices other than his own. A background chorus chants 'another problem,' which grows louder and louder over the councilor's remarks, giving voice to the unheard tenants.

This carnivalesque atmosphere is suggestive of Russian theorist Mikhail Bakhtin's conception of carnival, adapted from the spirit of popular festivities carried out in folk communities for thousands of years.[13] Sanctioned by authority, these events provide release, even moments of exhilaration and freedom, for the masses. Carnival demystifies the powerful, using many elements of farce – sarcasm, irony, parody, innuendo, misquotation. Irreverence, humor, and contradiction operate as both critique and corrective. Such is the presentation of the voting fiasco and the councilors' appearance on scene. A 'utopian realm of community, freedom, equality, and abundance'[14] momentarily shows its face as the councilors share food, regaling the cagemen with song and stories. While the chance for social struggle and active contestation of the social and political realms exists, carnival more often functions as containment, as in the case of the cagemen. As Terry Eagleton observes, 'Any politics predicated on this [the carnivalesque moment alone] will be no more than compliant, containable liberalism.'[15] Cheung, for his part, describes the problem thus:

> From a sociological standpoint, people living in cages is a social problem that doesn't have an easy answer. There're poor people and there're rich people in society, but how much money should be spent on housing? That's a thorny issue because ultimately the decision rests entirely on each individual's sense of value.[16]

Notwithstanding these comments, at film's end stark images of cagemen being dragged and carried from the building using brute force are so disturbing that individualized humanistic values pale. Cheung frames the action as a media event. Police, firemen, and reporters outside the building are seen on television through the cage wire of Tong Sam's home. As the law agents break down the door, flashlights, axes, chainsaws, and a megaphone become tools of invasion and destruction. As the cagemen are carried out yelling, one can almost smell their fear. Luk Tung, wrestled to the ground, cries out: 'There are so many buildings in Hong Kong. Why do you have to tear down this one? Why?'

Cheung does not end the story on this note, however. He returns to the cage philosophy enunciated by the Taoist, who sees 'the beauty in the cage.' He has told Mao, 'You are not living inside the cage. Instead people outside are trapped by the cage.' These lines echo Cheung's own reaction to visiting real cagemen: 'I … remember myself looking at the cagemen, how suddenly I couldn't quite figure out if I was looking at them, or they looking at me. I felt like I was an alien or a monster.'[17] The aftermath of the vacating of the property shows Mao, Sissy, and Luk Tung reunited at the zoo, with Mao cleaning cages; the scene is filmed in such a way that it is difficult to tell whether the audience is caged looking out, or the characters are caged and the audience is looking in. Is this Cheung's comment on the marginalized cagemen, or a critique of citizens' and government's unwillingness to speak out on the issue and change it?

While *Cageman* won the Hong Kong Film Award for Best Picture, audiences stayed away. According to critic Sek Kei, unlike *Cageman*, 'few films from 1990–1996 portrayed Hong Kong society in all its reality.'[18] Other directors chose different means, using a metaphorical approach by developing subtexts which allowed their narratives to comment upon the real world. Director Ronny Yu sets *Phantom Lover* (literally *Midnight Song*) in Peking, shifting between 1926 and 1936, during a transitional period in China's modern history. Working within but stretching conventional genres, the film is both inspired ghost story and love story, intertwining *The Phantom of the Opera*, *Romeo and Juliet*, and a 1930s' film, shot on the Mainland, called *Midnight Charm*.[19] Washed in sepia tones, the look is aged, like period photographs. Reverting to color at key moments, expressive of the love and passion between male and female leads, rich reds and browns are set against darkened backgrounds, creating chiaroscuro effects; characters emerge from the shadows, giving the film a painterly style. Peter Pau's cinematography, combined with David Wu's rhythmical editing and Eddie Ma's architectural structures and detailed designs contribute to art-house production values.

An opening slow pan across *objets d'art* – including sheet music, a violin, a small carved music box, lit candles, and an ornate mirror, with an uncertain brief glimpse of 'the phantom' in its reflection – introduces the first appearance of color in striking reds. From young actor Wei Qing's viewpoint, a fleeting glimpse of a past moment appears as Da Yuyan (Wu Chien-lien), lover of maestro Song Danping (Leslie Cheung), runs through the frame dressed in red, against a background of rich velvet-textured red theater curtains. She runs from right to left, a ghost of the past trying to catch the past, playfully chasing after the unseen Danping. As Arjun Appadurai observes,

> The past is now not a land to return to in a simple politics of memory. It has become a synchronic warehouse of cultural scenarios, a kind of temporal central casting, to which recourse can be had as appropriate, depending on the movie to be made, the scene to be enacted, the hostages to be rescued.[20]

Yu's film confronts one past with another, engaged as a story for present and future. This encounter, like the rendezvous of Danping and Yuyan, delayed ten years, brings together old and new. Wei Qing (Wong Lui), only witness to the theater's 'ghosts,' links his story to theirs.[21]

High production values make atmosphere as much a character as the actors, and, as in Yu's other films, setting figures as a major element in the story. One of Yu's and his collaborators' greatest strengths lies in creating and sustaining aura and mood. In *Phantom Lover*, parameters are defined by the theater designed by Song and the ancestral hall of the Da family. Representative of the new and old, respectively, these sites serve to foreground characters struggling to find their place; as they contest the terrain, they develop a variety of responses to very confused times, assimilating old and new in a changing landscape, remaking themselves.

Uncle Ma, Danping's butler and caretaker of the abandoned theater property, relates: 'Mr. Song designed this theater himself. There was nothing like it. People even doubted it could be built. The elite ... flocked here.' Presented in a richly colored flashback, as Wu tells Wei Qing the story, the theater is a sight to behold. Cutting from the architectural plans to the angelic ornament atop the glass dome and slowly panning down into the interior space of the theater, the movement parallels filmmaking, from storyboard to image. Moving lovingly over the wrought-iron canopy frame grillework, interstices allow the interplay of daylight in the daytime scenes and a sky fretted with stars in the nighttime scenes. Other views

courtesy/permission of Mandarin Films

GRAND GUIGNOL Leslie Cheung and Wu Chien-lien in Ronny Yu's *Phantom Lover*

from the stage into the auditorium space, with rich red draperies and golden ornamentation, and the proscenium theater vastness, with box seats and balcony, is majestic and grand. Another perspective is from audience to stage; here, during Song's performances, liquid blue curtain effects swell and surge, suggesting tragic emotions. Visuals with sweeping camerawork are accompanied by full Western orchestration, touching upon the rise and fall of the emotional register. Romance, star-crossed lovers, and tragedy perform a visual duet with progress and new ideas brought from the West (including chocolate and French lingerie).

The architecture suggests a cross between Charles Garnier's Paris Opera House (1875), the setting for Gaston Leroux's *Phantom of the Opera*, and London's Crystal Palace (1851), the first in a series of Great Exhibitions to promote industry and showcase technological progress. When Song reveals himself to Wei Qing, many of his actions revolve around working the theater's hidden technological devices, putting in operation his plan to continue wooing the lost Yuyan. Song's innovations challenge tradition, the theater metonymically standing in for him.

Contrasted to the theater is the Da family ancestral hall, where Yuyan's parents and prospective father-in-law Zhao and his son discuss arrangements for Yuyan's marriage to the younger Zhao. Before Yuyan appears, to serve her father tea, a business deal is struck concerning Yuyan's industrialist-father's factory. Tradition weighs heavily, emphasized by towering columns embossed with Chinese characters and enormous ancestral portraits hanging on the walls, looking down on the scene. The expensive banquet held to announce the engagement uses the same setting. Both scenes use grandiose aerial pans over the room, as the camera moves down onto each scene. In the banquet, numerous red-clothed tables, richly laid out, suggest wealth and decorum; the camera moves in to track significant guests arriving and cuts to two shots of important figures seated at the family table. Likewise a Summer Palace scene represents male power and the burden of tradition. Similarly filmed, the younger Zhao forces an actress to eat buns in exchange for his assistance, and Landie, Wei Qing's intended, catches his eye; the camera shows him already devising her seduction – a scene suggestive of Marx's commentary on the bourgeois male: 'My own power is as great as the power of money.... I am ugly, but I can buy the most beautiful woman for myself.'[22]

Dialogue between old and new reflects the road to modernization taken by Chinese cities in the 1930s, as the urban middle class began wearing Western dress and European-styled buildings appeared on main thoroughfares. Song's acting style is 'bold and brilliant,' Ma relates, and his theater the place where the well-heeled of Tianjin, Shanghai, and Nanjing flock to see 'first-class theatre and bathe in Mr. Song's glory.' As Gramsci observed, 'For the bourgeois who has fed well and has three hours to kill between dinner and bedtime, a play is something in between a digestive and an aphrodisiac.'[23] Change brings difficulties. Ma continues: 'Girls sneaked away from home to come here. This made the elderly very angry.' Ma's voice-over occasionally interrupts the visual re-enactment of the story he is telling Wei Qing. This comment cited is synchronized with a theater scene showing Song's loyal audience swooning over him; the episode serves as a marker for Canto-pop star Leslie Cheung's following. Musical interludes, playing like Cheung's music videos, link spirit of place to onstage characters' emotions (*Romeo and Juliet*) and to the plot.[24]

Having purchased the theater to make their name, the acting troupe finds the structure in ruins. They work together to restore it to its former glory. The audience, however, deems the opening performance too modern. Rather than Shakespeare, they get nationalist theater, as advocated by the Communists and developed by the League of Left-wing Dramatists. People exit the theater throwing ticket stubs into the street. One remarks, 'He's not Song Danping.' The comment is prescient. Only when Song shows himself to Wei Qing and gives him the libretto is the troupe successful, as the next generation revives past glory.

Just as Song Danping and Da Yuyan are conflated with Romeo and Juliet, so Wei Qing and Landie fuse with Danping and Yuyan. History begins repeating itself. Song recognizes Wei Qing's similar talent, a desperate Yuyan sees Wei Qing as Danping, and Zhao sees Landie as another Yuyan. When Wei Qing delivers Danping's letter to Yuyan, he quickly improvises what she needs to hear: 'Ten years have passed. Thinking of you, of all that is past. After such long separation, I see you at last.' Yuyan snatches the letter and packs it into her suitcase. 'That's beautiful. I'll put it away,' she says, determined to hold it forever in her memory. When Yuyan appears in the streets, known as the 'madwoman,' the brutish Zhao spies her and grabs her. 'Cheap stuff,' he yells as he viciously assaults her, punching her in the stomach, whipping her back, and kicking her. 'Slut,' he spits out, 'I had you ten years ago, you stinking whore, feigning insanity.' Wei Qing rescues her as Danping would. Ironically, Yuyan's parents also reflect the curious fusion of past and present. Returned as 'damaged goods' because she is no longer a virgin, Yuyan's family abandons her in disgrace, fleeing the city, mother telling father, 'Don't look back.'

Danping literally loses face when acid is thrown on him by Zhao's lackeys; he hides himself away for ten years, in torment. Wei Qing sees his pain and vanity clearly, because he shares those feelings. He, too, wants to be famous, in order to marry Landie. 'Wake up to yourself,' Wei Qing tells Danping, 'You think this proves your love for her? You're fooling yourself and deceiving her.' This comment goes straight to Danping's heart; its truth and his wish to help the younger couple cause him to show his disfigured face in public. Singling out the Zhaos in a packed theater house, he appears. 'I never imagined you'd come between Wei Qing and Landie to create a new tragedy. I can be silent no longer.' He tells all.

The drama has a bittersweet ending: the Zhaos are punished and both couples reunited, but Danping is disfigured and Yuyan blind. After promising her that 'I'll never leave you again. Not for the rest of our lives. Our whole lives,' Danping sings into her ear the song he was writing for her when tragedy struck (it is also the film's theme song) accompanied by a close-up of her face and tears; another tightly framed close-up shows the pock marks and boils across one side of Danping's face. Curiously, the viewer's visceral response is associated with the pain the couple has had to bear. The final scene shows the carriage racing outside of the city, just as an opening scene showed the troupe's arrival by carriage. Rapidly moving through the dust-saturated trees, an active camera pans up to the sky and cuts into the carriage. Yuyan sleeps as Danping watches over her; he knows their time together will be brief. As light and shadows flicker across his face, he looks up and beyond the camera. Credit must be given to Leslie Cheung's natural beauty, the make-up artist, cinematographer, and lighting effects. Even with disfigurement, the character's beauty shines through, and in shadow the scars are hardly visible, even though he carries these signs of the past with him. As the song replays instrumentally, Danping looks into the unknown ahead. A wistful ending registers Hong Kong's perspective on its future.

Filmmakers have turned to recent historical events to examine the China factor. Vietnam has served as a source, for example. Ann Hui's first movie to use Vietnam references was *The Story of Woo Viet* (1981), which combines her concern for 'boat people' with the notion that post-liberation Vietnam is a place from which to flee. The film opens with a crowded boat of refugees approaching Hong Kong; a voice-over narration by the title character reads the letter he has written to his Hong Kong penpal, full of his aspirations for a better life. Woo-viet has befriended a boy whose family has died. While the child's presence might seem to suggest hope for a brighter future, the character's ordeals are in fact a descent into hell. In Hui's next film, *Boat People* (1982), she expanded the analogy with Vietnam, concentrating on the disappointment and horror a Japanese photojournalist experiences revisiting Saigon after the war's end and befriending two children – in his mind, victims of 'liberation.' Hui states that

> Vietnamese refugee stories are somehow connected with what people in Hong Kong feel as well. We too have no real sense of belonging to any country in particular. Different political forces pull at our lives, but we have to control our destiny. No one is going to ask us what we want to happen to Hong Kong. So, in a way, *Boat People* is a dramatization of that.[25]

Woo Viet also raises the specter of what it means to be a 'Hong Kong belonger.' Part of the film is set in one of the closed-camp detention centers; the chain-link fence and barbed-wire of the center reappears at film's end when the title character escapes by boat.

Tsui Hark, after producing *A Better Tomorrow 1* and *2*, directed *A Better Tomorrow III: Love and Death in Saigon* (literally *Heroic Character III*, 1989).[26] The prequel allowed Tsui, who spent his childhood and early youth in Vietnam, to make his own statement about the war and to create a vision of post-1997 Hong Kong. He displaces Hong Kong by re-creating the fall of Saigon, with its panic-stricken people and siege-mentality. Gender issues are significant for Tsui, and with *A Better Tomorrow III* the director added a strong female protagonist to teach the male lead just about everything he knows.

Opening with protagonist Mark's arrival (Chow Yun-fat) in the chaos and violence of Saigon in 1974, there to assist his cousin Cheung Chi-mun (Tony Leung Ka-fai) and his uncle (Shek Kin) in their return to Hong Kong, the film characterizes the city as a place of confusion and turmoil, where smiling young women conceal bombs, civilians are gunned down in the streets, and 'it's dangerous no matter what you do.' The black-market economy is everywhere evident, where 'accumulation of wealth at one pole is … at the same time the accumulation of misery, agony of toil, ignorance, brutality, mental degradation, at the opposite pole.'[27] Teeming with corrupt customs officers and complicit government officials, military loose cannons, and gangster entrepreneurs, the setting entangles its protagonists in situations beyond their control where they know too little to challenge their fate. Against the news blackout of the ongoing war an intimate love triangle develops (between Mun, Mark and Chow Kit-ying, played by Anita Mui) whereby each lover tries to spare the feelings of the others by not revealing true emotions. Cards are stacked, as Triad member Ho (Saburo Tokito) relates: 'Not many are willing to roll the dice in this world.' In addition to alluding to Hong Kong's state through manic disorienting and disconcerting camerawork, Tsui provides a topsy-turvy image of the colony seen from Mun's perspective when beaten and held upside down by Ho's gang members. 'Don't think just because you left Vietnam and came here that things will be peaceful. There's no difference,' Ho warns.

Tsui's introduction of a strong female protagonist in Kit reinforces the story's fatalism. While the director takes Woo to task for less than assertive female characterizations, Woo's storylines allows Tsui to play with the earlier films' characterizations. Kit here recalls Leslie Cheung's baby-faced Kit from the first two movies; Triad member Ho, Kit's former lover and teacher, is named after Ti Lung's Ho of the previous films. From the prequel the audience learns that Mark's trademarks, the distinctive shades and the duster, are Kit's invention; she not only shoots with two weapons (as Mark often does in *A Better Tomorrow 1* and *2*), but saves Mark at customs twice, Mark and Mun from the ire of local boss Tenth Uncle, and their family from corrupt officials, as well as holding her own in numerous shoot-outs. Of course, as a pre-scripted character tied to the previous two incarnations of the story yet appearing in neither, her death is guaranteed by picture's end. The Kit in this film, like Hong Kong, is destined to disappear.

Hong Kong's loss of its unique identity as a hybrid city conscious of its destined disappearance is visibly expressed in a medium two-shot of Mark and Mun as they walk across an airstrip upon their return to Saigon to rescue Kit. Through superimpositions of negatives of the same shot, Tsui creates ghost images of both men, gliding across the screen, both in shades and trench coats, in a noble attempt to prevent the inevitable. They illustrate the disappearing act that embodies Hong Kong itself. Tsui's most explicit Mainland–Hong Kong reference, however, is to

SHOOTING FRIENDSHIP   Jacky Cheung and Tony Leung Chiu-wai in John Woo's *Bullet in the Head*

4 June 1989 and an image that was seen around the world. In the explosive climax, first Mun and then Mark stands alone against an enormous tank driven by the vicious Bong, hellbent on their destruction. No one seeing the film in the fall of 1989 could escape the image of a lone student standing against a tank in Tiananmen Square.[28]

Woo admits that his brutal *Bullet in the Head* (literally *Bloodshed Street Corner*, 1990), in which three Hong Kong buddies undergo torture and unspeakable horrors during the Vietnam War, was influenced by the massacre in Tiananmen Square. He stated that, 'I also wanted to use Vietnam as a mirror for what's going to happen in Hong Kong in 1997'; Woo also explains that '*Bullet in the Head* is … the closest to an autobiography for me.'[29] Woo devised a fine allegory. Opening to an upbeat instrumental version of The Monkees' 'I'm a Believer,' the song links to one of the friends, Ben (Tony Leung Chiu-wai), whose ideals are destroyed by the brutalization that he, Frank (Jacky Cheung), and Paul (Waise Lee) undergo in 1967 Hong Kong and Vietnam. Befriended by Chinese–French former CIA operative Luke (Simon Yam) and torch singer Sally (Fennie Yuen), the friends' cohesiveness is decimated by historical events and betrayal by one of their own – Paul, whose determination not to end up like his father adds to the brutality and corruption he witnesses in Vietnam, blinding him to bonds of trust and loyalty. A former soldier, now a streetsweeper, Paul's father tells him, 'It's destiny. I'm a nobody. It's okay. But my son won't be sweeping streets. It's a cruel world, money talks. Without it, you're shit. Remember, if you get a break, hang on in there.' As Marx insists, 'Money is not just an object of the passion for enrichment, it is "the" object.'[30] When Paul intercepts a cache of gold leaf in a crate marked 'US Army,' his face reflects the gold sheen. He tells his friends, 'What you want? Today I saw some soldiers kill people. I learned something. In this world if you have guns, you have everything. Tell me how much is a human life!' Paul has learned well. He will shoot Frank in the head, choosing gold over his buddy's life. Frank's existence will become a nightmare, as the pain from his wound leads to heroin addiction, turning him into a hired killer to support his habit. Perhaps Ben suffers most because he experiences and witnesses others' pain and anguish; he is no longer the true believer. The film's cynicism is overpowering.

Tainted by greed, Paul's immorality is foregrounded by the question, 'Do you measure your friendship in gold?'[31] asserting Woo's traditional and personal code of honor. The intimate story of three young men draws from films like *West Side Story* and *The Deer Hunter* but is rawer and rougher. The extreme violence, including numerous street massacres, explosions, gunbattles among gangsters, and warfare, and of guns repeatedly being held to people's heads, operates to make the story simultaneously epic and intimate. Street scenes featuring lone young men standing against large tanks repeat as obvious references to Tiananmen. Ironically, producer and partner Terence Chang relates, 'John Woo attempted to put his personal feelings towards 1997 in *Bullet in the Head*, but unfortunately most Hong Kong people identified with the Waise Lee character and thought he was the real hero of the movie.' Woo adds, 'I think the movie was too painful for the audience, reminding them of the recent Tiananmen Square massacre and that is why it did badly.'[32]

Like Vietnamese sagas, Japanese occupation movies have provided rich material for filmmakers wanting to paint scenarios for Hong Kong's future while avoiding direct reference to politics, box-office poison in Hong Kong, and avoiding censure by the Censor Board.[33] One of the first was Leung Po-chih's award-winning *Hong Kong 1941*, a story of friendship, hope, and sacrifice. The film unfolds in retrospect, a female voice-over narrator, Nam (Cecilia Yip), retelling events and remembering two men in her life, her childhood sweetheart Huk-keung (Alex Man) and Fay Yip (Chow Yun-fat), the man who befriends them. Several scenes are difficult to watch. Nam's rape by a Chinese collaborator, for example, is not very explicit but extremely intimate, thereby enacting devastating psychological violence. Scenes of Japanese-style executions of Hong Kong Chinese are disturbing not for their graphic nature but for the parallel scenes of children at play imitating the beheadings. Overall, the story as personal recollection softens its impact.

Tsui Hark's *Shanghai Blues* (literally *Shanghai Nights*, 1984) appeared the same year. Unlike the serious tone of Tsui's later Vietnam saga, however, *Shanghai Blues* is a comedy with dramatic interludes. Briefly set in 1937 during a Japanese bombing raid and quickly jumping to 1947, the European-built city of Shanghai setting establishes an East–West dialectic with which Tsui plays. In a French concession nightclub, a bubbly-spirited songster sings the praises of 'French wines and English cigarettes, Chinese suits in this wonderful place.… An adventurer's paradise, a rich man's heaven, a lady's place of delight, a gentleman's den of iniquity,' reassuring her listeners 'it will go on forever and forever.' The Chinese/Western title suggests identity, place, and mood, being a reference to the song that figures significantly in the plot. 'Shanghai Blues,' written by protagonist Tung Kwok-man (called Do-Re-Mi, played by Kenny Bee), is in memory of the woman he met under the bridge during the 1937 bombing. Ten years later, unknown to both, she is Shu-shu (Sylvia Chang), his neighbor. The song's Western-style music features violin and accordion and traditional Chinese instruments; the lyrics emphasize the past, commitment and tender love, anxiety brought on by lack of time and loss of place, doubts, questions and hope for the future.[34] Presenting a nostalgic yearning for reunion, the song contrasts with the film's sharper comedic tone.

Also contrasted to the lyrical 1937 bridge scene are 1947 bridge scenes centered around a group of displaced soldiers who have returned home to live there communally and who take turns selling their blood to buy food. When Kwok-man shows up with his trombone, he is informed that his instrument doesn't go with an erhu (a traditional Chinese stringed instrument). One of the comrades (who are also musicians) complains, 'We're not playing Western music, tell him to leave.' Ironically, Western imprints appear all over this city's face. Much slapstick, coincidence, and many mistaken identities later, the hybridized Eastern–Western song reunites the separated couple as they depart for the colony. As the opening song announces, 'Have a laugh, sing a song, do a dance … this tiny place is our heaven.' Substitute Hong Kong for Shanghai and Tsui provides comic relief and ironic commentary on 1984's signing.

Filmmaker Wong Kar-wai stands apart from other directors: all his movies have been labelled independent art-house movies, in contrast to the more commercial Hong Kong product. Despite winning numerous Hong Kong Film Awards, his films have not been successful in the local market, yet he is recognized with an international audience and awards. Born in Shanghai in 1958, Wong came to Hong Kong with his parents at the age of five. Coming from the Mainland and speaking only Shanghainese, he had a difficult period of adjustment to Cantonese-speaking Hong Kong belongers, spending hours in movie theaters with his mother. Despite Wong's insistence that his films are not autobiographical, the stories he tells are about loss; his films have a meditative and evocative quality. Known for a distinctive style developed in collaboration with his cinematographer Christopher Doyle, and editor and art director William Chang, this visual poet of longing uses jump cuts, swish pans, step-printing, slow motion, and hand-held cameras to communicate raw emotions of regret, pain, and confusion. Doyle describes their relationship as 'complicitous' and calls them the 'Holy Trinity.' He says Chang 'comes up with wonderful things and pushes me towards a certain imagery.… We never talk about it, that's the beauty of it. I don't think it's because we make "successful films," I think it's because you know that what the other person gives is going to be so reciprocal to your own [work].… It's like good sex.… We share.'[35] Rather than realizing preconceived themes, the process is that of creating the content while shooting and editing the films. As Doyle says, 'the intention is to find the movie, and that's the journey.' In his six films to date, Wong has begun work without scripts, claiming that, 'From the place, I can tell what kind of person will be in that place and what they will do and what is their relationship, and the film takes shape.… Normally, I won't start from a story.'[36] Actors with whom he repeatedly collaborates contribute to the developing characters and emotional temperature.

Critics describe the metaphysical and existential nature of Wong's films, touching on Sartrean philosophy in which individuals are defined by their actions. Characters are simply there, without reason, whether 'there' is an unidentifiable desert or contemporary urban Hong Kong. Characterizations seem motivated by futile passions, lives constantly trying to escape from themselves, acts fated to be incomplete. Space and time are fundamentally subjective, gaining significance from that aspect alone; distance is experiential, psychic first, and secondarily measured. Characters look with expectation, surprise and question. They ponder.[37]

Critic Tony Rayns notes Wong's 'visual writing,' a description which hints at his aesthetic virtuosity.[38] Chinese storytelling privileges oral over written tales, and a visceral sensibility achieved through image and music, rather than speech or writing, sets stories apart. German director Wim Wenders' counsel is worth consideration. He writes, 'Images are fragile. Most of the time words don't translate them well, and when they have carried the image to the other side the emotion has all run out of it. Writing has to be careful with (E)motion Pictures.'[39] In his ongoing film series,[40] Wong deconstructs plot, image, time, place, and character to articulate 'emotion pictures,' the after-images that remain imprinted on the audience's consciousness. As Haile Gerima observes, 'In the innovative cinema, you find the introduction of vibrant aesthetics into the veins of film history in the way that content and form are organized, time, space and rhythm are structured.'[41] Wong's film output, through a combination of multiple talents, insight, circumstance, collaboration, chance, and the process itself, is innovative and visionary.

Ashes of Time (1994) is one of the most complex and self-reflexive narratives of contemporary Hong Kong cinema. Paying homage to the westerns of Sergio Leone and Sam Peckinpah, this eastern-western unravels the stories and lives of the swordsmen Malicious West and Evil East (called Ouyang Feng and Huang Yaoshi, played by Leslie Cheung and Tony Leung Ka-fai, respectively) and the people whose lives they touch, including Murong Yang/Yin (Brigitte Lin), the blind swordsman (Tony Leung Chiu-wai), the sister with a basket of eggs (Charlie Yeung), the shoeless swordsman Hong Qi (Jacky Cheung), the wife of the blind swordsman (Carina Lau) and the woman Ouyang Feng loves (Maggie Cheung). Wong's version of the martial arts actioner, the film features youthful versions of the middle-aged characters in Louis Cha's *The Eagle-Shooting Hero*. Juanita Huan Zhou conducted a close comparison of movie and novel; she concluded that the film is not so much a prequel of the whole novel as a focus upon one character, Ouyang Feng. She says that Wong chose to develop the character's story (only presaged in the novel) 'because he is such a tragic character.'[42] Ouyang Feng has more screen time, dialogue, and voice-over narration than the other characters. The literal translation of the film's title is *East Evil West Poison* (*Malicious*), which suggests the focus is on two characters, Huang Yaoshi and Ouyang Feng. What explains this discrepancy?

Wong's deconstructed narrative blurs character identities and merges character perspectives and voice-overs, questioning stable notions of identity. Ouyang Feng's problems stem from his inability to tell the woman he loves that he loves her; she marries his brother, who is never seen in the film, although the womanizer Huang Yaoshi substitutes for him. Ouyang Feng temporarily puts away his sword, while other swordsmen stand in for him. Ouyang Feng sees himself in the shoeless swordsman: 'Once, I could've been like Hong Qi…' As filmmaker Trinh Minh-ha observes, 'Any mutation in identity, in essence, in regularity, and even in physical place, poses a problem, if not a threat, in terms of classification and control.'[43]

Likewise peach blossom, symbol of life and immortality in traditional Chinese culture,[44] and here associated with the brother's wife, is linked to the blind swordsman's wife. The symbol floats between Ouyang Feng, who dreams of peach blossom; Huang Yaoshi, who likes it because of the woman he loves; and the blind swordsman, who wishes to see it once more (Peach Blossom is his wife's name). The permutations of character traits and resonances between characters describe fluid identities and selfhoods created by contingency, not distinctive individuals but a collective persona reflective of human beings coexisting over time. The final minutes, beginning with a long shot of a swordsman on horseback, reflect each character singly in a pool of water, one and the same; a collage follows, each image flowing into the next, as one, occurring simultaneously in time. The title *Ashes of Time*, therefore, appropriately suggests the philosophical bent of a story whose characters are residues and echoes of human presence in a seemingly timeless and eternal landscape.

The deconstructed narrative consists of numerous flashbacks, often indistinguishable from present film time, portraying repetitive actions and discrepancies between words and images. Ouyang Feng relies upon the Almanac to get his bearings; in his voice-overs, day six ('insects awaken') is followed by day four ('first day of spring … a fresh start'), and day fifteen represented twice, first as 'sunny and windy' and second as 'rainy.' Time is on the mind of the character, yet its curious representations are altogether meaningless as structuring elements of the story, with phrases mixed in like 'ever since that night,' 'a few years later,' and 'three years later.'

In contrast to the vicissitudes of human endeavor, the camera eye establishes the breathtaking landscape as a permanent feature imprinted on the film, grand and timeless. A long, slow pan of the mountains, desert, and sky shown in the early minutes is repeated near the film's end; reddish-tinted waves are the opening image and reappear throughout. A poetic moment of calm water appears, the soft ripple of waves as liquid color, reflecting the blue of the sky and the red-browns of the desert on water.[45] Exploding mountains and geyser-like spurts of water emphasize the power of nature, reinforced by a majestic soundtrack. Wind sounds echo throughout, and the atmosphere's intense heat is visible in glowing imagery. Earth, water, sky, and fire are represented, basic and simple elements ever present, but mostly unseen by the characters. Ouyang Feng, positioned on top of a mountain, silhouetted wearing a distinctive woven hat, waits. Like his way station, the landscape is a place where Ouyang Feng and others wait, some for death, others moving on.

The scenery in itself represents a void, a landscape of absence contextualized only by the human activity in it. Its visually stunning lyrical and lovely quietness is juxtaposed with jarringly frenetic and brutal human swordfighting. As such, the film metaphorically portrays contemporary Hong Kong as both dream fantasy and nightmare. Tied to a predestined future by the Joint Declaration, Hong Kong stands in for the unchanged landscape. Yet, like the landscape's changing climate, Hong Kong is in some ways able to determine its place in the world, by 'one country, two systems.' The way station is a 'borrowed place' stand-in for Hong Kong, what Curtis Tsui refers to as a 'middle ground' between the Chinese and British, lacking a cohesive or definitive sense of place.[46] As Marx writes,

> Men make their own history, but they do not make it just as they please; they do not make it under circumstances chosen by themselves, but under circumstances directly encountered, given and transmitted from the past. The tradition of all the dead generations weighs like a nightmare on the brain of the living.[47]

Unlike the blind swordsman, who seeks death, or Hong Qi, who desires fame, Ouyang Feng wants neither. And, unlike Huang Yaoshi, who forgets his own past and identity when he chooses to lose his memory by drinking magic wine, Ouyang chooses to remember his, though he is alienated by it. As others tell him their stories, the connections he makes between their experiences and his own slowly eat into him until he begins to reconcile his past and his present. The characterization of Ouyang Feng, tied to a past not of his own making, and waiting to make a future, personifies Hong Kong. Eventually he will choose to burn the way station and leave the desert behind, but first he must work through his current circumstances. Having turned his back on swordfighting, he is a deal-making middleman who bridges the gap between sole proprietor and transnational capitalist, leading 'the abstract existence of man as a mere working man, who, therefore every day falls from his filled nothingness into absolute nothingness, into social, and thus real, non-existence.'[48] While conducting business, he attempts to evade his personal problems, but the travellers who come his way provide him with the mirror to see himself.

In one scene, Ouyang Feng entertains a prospective client. He looks into the camera and speaks to the man offscreen:

> Buddy, you must be around forty. In forty years, you must have come to hate someone, someone who wronged you, someone you wanted to kill … murder can be very simple … I've this friend who's skilled in martial arts.… Pay a reasonable fee and he'll kill for you. Think about it. Be quick!

As he speaks, an out-of-focus white curtain sways. The scene introduces 'an important thematic and rhythmic element,' according to Doyle. 'Who is he,' this agent and former swordsman Ouyang Feng? It is 'dynamic,' Doyle says, with 'an unexplained element, concerned with light and giving energy.' Visually interesting, the moment communicates the uncertainties associated with the character.

Ouyang Feng's past is represented as the unnamed 'woman Huang Yaoshi loves' and the woman he took for granted in his past. Appearing only briefly compared to the other characters, her specter haunts the entire story as the woman waiting for Ouyang Feng across White Camel Mountain. In a significant scene, she is strikingly framed inside an open window casement, dressed in brightly colored reds and blues, looking out to sea, and at her frolicking son – and Ouyang's son. Both the framing and the presence of the child suggest hope and possibility for the future, but the woman's words add dimension:

> Nothing is important to me now … looking back, nothing matters because everything changes. I thought I was the winner until one day I looked in the mirror and saw the face of a loser. I failed to have the person I loved most to be with me in my best years. How wonderful if we could go back to the past.

She stares beyond the camera to the sea. The woman, like Ouyang, has been trapped by regret and by inflexibility in the face of change. She sends Ouyang the magic wine to forget her, but he prefers water.

Unlike Huang Yaoshi, Ouyang Feng wants to remember and thus cannot forget. Ouyang must, paradoxically, learn to remember and forget; that is, to recognize the past which has formed him but to bend it in the present to face his future – like Hong Kong. Combined, the other characters enable him to do so; Hong Qi and the woman with the basket of eggs in particular significantly affect him. Hong Qi, unlike Ouyang Feng, willingly fights for an egg, and after eating it tells him, 'This is me … I became another person since I've been around with you. I've lost my real self. No, I don't want to be like you.' Hong Qi's words invite self-reflection for Ouyang Feng, who remembers, 'I was like you. Thought my sweetheart would wait for me while I was making my name as a swordsman.' His attitude towards his surroundings changes also. Telling Hong Qi that across the mountain is only 'another mountain,' a landscape 'nothing special,' he begins to see the world differently. 'I sat at the door for two days,' he relates. 'Watching the changing clouds I suddenly realized that although I've been here for several years, I've never really looked.'

Similarly, the effect the young woman with the basket of eggs has on Ouyang Feng signals a change in characterization. Having initially crudely propositioned her, Ouyang Feng now re-examines the value of an egg. A carefully constructed scene shows the result of his contemplations. *Mise-en-scène* reveals the basket in the right foreground, bathed in a golden brown light, eggs and basket blending in with the sands. The side of a shaded brown figure comes from the left, and a hand gingerly, tenderly, reaches into the basket to pick up an egg. The figure turns slightly, gracefully, to reveal, miraculously, not the woman, not Hong Qi, but Ouyang Feng, who understands the price. Hence Ouyang Feng leaves the desert, burning his way station behind him. The Almanac reads: 'The fire forces the gold to move. Extremely favorable for going west.' Ouyang Feng will die in battle with the Northern Beggar, Hong Qi, but he will die living the present moment to its fullest, without regret. He meets death smiling beatifically, not as a doomed blind swordsman resigned to his fate. This battle is not the last appearance Wong gives his character. He is subsequently seen moving from left to right across the screen, slicing his way through a line of enemies; turning, at the right edge of the frame, he looks back at the past he accepts but is not resigned to, so that he can move ahead to face his future.

Wong illustrates waiting and longing, loss and memory, as represented by Ouyang Feng's voice-over recognition: 'The harder you try to forget something the more it will stick in your memory. I once heard someone say if you have to lose something, the best way to keep it is to keep it in your memory.' Wong, his cast, and crew did their fair share of waiting: the film took ten months over a two-year period to make, and cost HK$40 million (US$5 million). The rhythm of the film is slow, earning the label of 'philosopher's movie' by Lawrence Van Gelder, who described it as 'mythic, melancholy and mysterious.'[49] Long takes and repetitions of scenes abound, connected by the voice-over philosophic meditations.[50] Despite choreography by master Samo Hung and stop-motion photographic effects and swishing sword sound effects, martial-arts action audiences were largely disappointed, because they had to wait for brief action sequences in the extended metaphysical ponderings. Nonetheless, *Ashes of Time* is a haunting picture of reconciliation.

What, then, of longing and loss in Wong Kar-wai's oeuvre? Characters grapple with recurring regret and debilitating dismissal. Stories revolve around remembrance and separation, lack and chance. Nostalgia – the sentimental memory of, or yearning for, things past – apparently besets Wong. This disposition manifests itself in a cinematic image that Rey Chow maintains is an 'appropriate embodiment of nostalgia's ambivalence between dream and reality, of nostalgia's insistence on seeing "concrete" things in fantasy and memory.'[51] Much like Baudrillard's simulacra – copies for which there is no original – Wong's films share a romantic yen for a time and place that never was. Made possible by the advanced technique of film production itself, they incline towards longing and loss. The wistfulness that results, however aesthetic and emotional, is no less socially and politically enfeebling if the sentiments are understood as 'a nostalgia for lost origins [which] can be detrimental to the exploration of social realities within the critique.'[52] From this perspective, left to fate, people find little room for cognitive maneuver (even when they physically relocate) in either their private or their public life. However, as Michael Ryan reminds us,

> Film is fundamentally social because it draws on and reproduces social discourses and because it is a socially discursive act. Cinematic discourse is inherently social, for even the most formal dimension of film presupposes social codes of perception that allow it to be received and decoded by audiences.[53]

Ashes of Time's unspecified time and place likewise allow it the freedom of a free-floating signifier, which can be determined only by the viewer's sense of time and place, making it the more socially meaningful.

In a hiatus from working on *Ashes of Time*, Wong completed *Chungking Express* (literally *Chungking Forest*) over a period of several months. Featuring two of the actors from *Ashes of Time*, Brigitte Lin and Tony Leung Chiu-wai, the movie added pop stars Takeshi Kaneshiro and Faye Wong to its line-up, which incorporated the old and the new. In contrast to the expansive heaviness of the non-time-specific period piece (Wong says *Ashes* is set some time during or before the Song dynasty),[54] the light-hearted *Chungking Express* takes place in contemporary urban Hong Kong, replicating the brisk rhythms of the lives of end-of-the-century city dwellers. Seemingly a pastiche of surfaces created by the pop sensibility of Japanese author Haruki Murakami and MTV editing, filtered through the 'excitement and zest' of Godard's movies of thirty years ago,[55] the film addresses the same concerns as Wong's other movies, except that this version is much more hopeful, humorous, and fresh. With bemused puzzlement Wong examines alienation, assimilates longing and waiting, and, surprisingly, watches characters nonetheless connect with each other. *Chungking Express* presents two stories simultaneously, which fuse into an upbeat narrative about connections.

The film opens *in medias res*, with Brigitte Lin's unnamed drug-smuggling hired hand making her way through the streets of Kowloon, as plain-clothes cop 223 (Ho Chi-wu, played by Takeshi Kaneshiro) chases after a criminal. Rather than rely upon a much-used establishing shot of Hong Kong from Victoria's Peak, overlooking Central District, or an aerial shot from the harbor, showing the architectural skyline, Wong provides a little-seen version of Hong Kong. A briefly glimpsed, silent, blue-lit nighttime shot of swirling cloud-filled sky and silhouetted buildings with smokestacks superimposes an anomalous industrial city upon a postmodern, post-industrial landscape, defined by crowded, brightly lit market-places and transnational franchises. The anachronistic industrial landscape exposes what Abbas calls 'not seeing what *is* there.'[56] The shot deconstructs Kowloon, home to most of Hong Kong's tourist hotels and luxury indoor shopping malls, which also houses the overpopulated tenements of Chungking Mansions, where Lin's character finds Indian nationals to smuggle illicit drugs, a Hong Kong most tourists never see. Wong further emphasizes the unseen by showing the underbelly, what makes a postmodern city thrive: its mode of production and its disen-franchised labor force; the scene shows the way in which the drugs are secreted for transport – sewn into clothing, hammered into shoe heel compartments, hidden in stuffed animals.

The mostly hand-held camera follows Lin's character through the narrow alleys and hallways of this other Kowloon; it also shows the shimmering surfaces of Hong Kong by counterpointing the film's other primary location, upscale Central Hong Kong. This site consists of the colony's business district as well as large middle-class residental high-rise buildings and Victoria Peak's exclusive luxury skyscrapers, and restaurants and department stores catering to the middle class. Awash in the blues of the pre-dawn sky which hangs over both parts of the city are the blues and greens of artificial exterior illumination and the yellows of interior lighting; the colors bleed fluidly across the screen, unifying those within frame as well as various scenes at different locales. The characters traverse both districts, crossing from the peninsula of Kowloon to the island of Hong Kong, intimate camera following; Wong circumscribes Hong Kong and shows, as his camera eye sees, what is there.

When Cop 233 briefly bumps shoulders with the drug smuggler, his voice-over narration introduces elements of contingency and proximity that determine the story and its method of telling: 'At the closest point we're just 0.01 centimeters apart from each other. Fifty-seven hours later I fall in love with this woman.' Conventional film structuring would dictate past-tense narration and a flashback, yet here the voice-over uses the present tense ('I fall in love') and develops in present time. As the film unfolds, Cop 233 likewise jostles another woman, Faye, the counter girl of the fast-food stall Midnight Express; again in voice-over he remarks, 'At the high point of our intimacy we are just 0.01 centimeters away from each other. I know nothing about her. Six hours later, she fell in love with another man.' His use of the past tense here ('she fell in love') indicates that Faye's relation with the other man (uniformed beat Cop 663, played by Tony Leung Chiu-wai) occurs in tandem with the other couple. Wong uses countless jump cuts to map the similar arcs of the stories. Cinematographer Chris Doyle distinguishes between the different energies of a hand-held camera and a Steadicam, and notes the subjectivity and intimacy of the hand-held shot as well as 'the energy and speed with which a hand-held camera can move.'[57] The cameraman's closeness to the actors made possible the fortuitous happenstances of street shooting, which captures the already-disappearing spirit known as Hong Kong. The stop-motion photography and optical printing techniques, from the blurred action sequences to the mirrored reflections of Lin, Wong, and Leung, also imprint the elusive and contradictory image of Hong Kong onscreen.

Stuart Cohn writes that Wong 'portrays a city that ... is bursting with signs and messages selling an oppressive array of consumer products. There are logos everywhere in the film: McDonald's, the OK convenience store, Del Monte canned pineapple, Pocari Sweat [Japanese Gatorade], Coca Cola, Manolo Blahnik shoes.' Wong told him, 'Our world is going to be a chain store. You can have all these products in every city. McDonald's everywhere.'[58] Wong's characters maneuver through the consumer marketplace, extending the ideology of capitalism. Faye buys numerous goods to replace the old ones in Cop 663's apartment; Cop 223 buys cokes from Midnight Express when he's not ordering room-service chef salads; Cop 663 selects chef salads for his stewardess girlfriend; and the drug smuggler counts out lots of money as she arranges a drug deal. Lefebvre suggests that the privatization of consumption means a replacement of signs by signals and of symbols by images. This condition strips individuals of their ability to connect; people cannot 'totalize' their experiences. Commodified objects contribute to a condition in which alienation has become 'social practice,' creating what he calls 'the bureaucratic society of controlled consumption.'[59] All of the characters are as fragmented and individualized as the film is collaged; paradoxically, Wong uses the effects not to tell individualized, disparate stories but to bring characters together.

Marx suggests that 'The power to confuse and invert all human and natural qualities, to bring about fraternization of incompatibles, the divine power of money, resides in its character as the alienated and self-alienating species-life of man. It is the alienated power of humanity.'[60] When Lin's character, betrayed by her boss/lover who cuts a deal with the Indian courier, loses the drugs and the money, how does she manage to move from her room at Chungking House to a luxury hotel, much less make airline reservations for escape? Where does Faye find the resources to redecorate Cop 663's apartment from her Midnight Express salary as well as the wherewithal to get a stewardess job based on her job record? How does Cop 663 luck into purchasing Midnight Express? Although all the characters are alienated by 'the fraternization of incompatibles,' discrepancies between their dreams and desires and realities, they manage to surmount them. Their alienation, represented by all four talking to themselves or to objects, is regarded as a small step leading them to another person.

Faye, the 'fey' (enchanted) creature who wins the heart of Cop 663, is mistaken by Cop 223, who rejects outright the boss's offer to set him up with her. She embodies the 'persistent sense of dislocation between the unrealized female self and the projected female stereotypes'[61] envisioned by the male characters. She is not cop 223's unseen May, nor is she the curvy flight attendant for whom Cop 663 pines. In fact, because Cop 663 only has eyes for his missing girlfriend, he begins to see Faye only over time. She's a dreamer and a sleepwalker, characterized by two songs which repeat on the soundtrack, the Mamas and the Papas' 'California Dreamin',' and Faye Wong's own cover of the Cranberries' 'Dreams.' Commentators have seen her boyish haircut as a homage to Jean Seberg in *Au Bout de Souffle*. Her natural body movements in rhythm to the music, combined with her unaffected and spontaneous behavior, as well as her dreamy gazes, makes her a presence set against the forces of the marketplace, epitomized by the music she blares at the food counter.[62]

Sheila Rowbotham points out that 'Capitalism needs now people who can regulate themselves … on their own initiative at work, and spend and consume without repression during their leisure.'[63] Faye certainly doesn't fit the job description. Behind the counter she daydreams; dispatched to pay the electricity bill, she visits Cop 663's apartment, calls with excuses, and as a result the power is shut off. When she is sent to collect fresh vegetables, she lets Cop 663 do her work for her.

'This job is hard work,' he says, and she responds, 'All jobs are hard work.' Saving to visit California, with visions of warmth to shelter her from a cold, cruel world, she has worked numerous undervalued jobs, and probably been fired from most. The beat cop, dissatisfied with his work, will take his cue from Faye and slip into running Midnight Express as comfortably as he does the flannel shirt Faye leaves him in his closet.

Brigitte Lin's unnamed character, dressed in a raincoat and wearing a blonde wig and sunglasses, disguises her features and hides even from herself. Many have noted her resemblance to Gena Rowlands' Gloria, the no-nonsense mobster with heart in Cassavettes' film of the same title. Also commented upon is Faye Wong's general likeness to Brigitte Lin, and Wong Kar-wai has suggested that she is 'the same woman with ten years' of difference.'[64] Their paths cross when Faye is purchasing a huge Garfield stuffed animal and Lin's character is standing outside the large plate-glass window full of a smorgasbord of consumer goods. Like the unnamed woman, Faye later dons shades. The precarious nature of the middle-management drug dealer's work, one notch above courier, has all of the headaches and dangers and few of the rewards of drug dealing. A woman alone, she carries drugs, money, and a weapon, travels in high-crime areas, and arranges and super-vises all the details of the drug delivery. The work has taken its toll. In voice-over she confesses, confusedly, 'Sometime, somehow I became a cautious person. Every time I wear a raincoat I put on a pair of sunglasses. One never knows when it's going to rain, when it's going to shine.' The song associated with her character is Dennis Brown's 'Things in Life,' and the lyrics relate not only to her but to Hong Kong in light of its reunification with the Mainland: 'It's not everyday we're gonna be the same/ There must be a change somehow/ There are bad times and good times too.' The can of sardines, dated 1 May 1994, emphasizes that time is running out, and serves not only to reveal the desperate state of affairs she's in but also to connect her to Cop 223, fixated on that date prominently displayed on the cans of pineapples he buys and consumes. After coming together with Cop 223, Lin goes on to change the direction of her life by hunting down the Indian courier who has absconded with money and drugs, and killing him and her two-timing boyfriend/boss. Tossing aside the wig, she affords us a brief glimpse of her true face, with long, black hair whipping across the screen.

Cop 223, in contrast to the uniformed Cop 663, is less a creature of habit and more a denizen of the postmodern city. He is multilingual, speaking English, Japanese, Cantonese, and Mandarin; he relies on his pager and is perpetually on the phone; he is always mobile, moving between Central and Kowloon, chasing through crowds, jogging, or restless in a hotel room. Instead of a song being associated with his character, a clock is, and the constantly changing numbers on the clock face emphasize his awareness of time moving on/running out; these references, of course, relate to the handover.

Like Cop 663, Cop 223 has been dumped by his girlfriend, but unlike 663, he has given her a month to return to him. To ensure her return, he has collected cans of Del Monte pineapple, May's favorite fruit, to be consumed on the last day, prior to his birthday and the cans' expiry date, 1 May. Like Cop 663, cop 223 finds it easier to relate to objects than people. To the OK mini-mart clerk, he rants 'People like you always go for something fresh. You know how much effort is put into a can of pineapple – the farming, the cropping and the slicing? Throwing it out like that! Have you ever thought about the can's feelings?' Cop 223's outburst exemplifies Marx's observation that 'A commodity is … a mysterious thing, simply because in it the social character of men's labor appears to them as an objective character stamped upon the product of that labor.'[65] After he has consumed the thirty cans, as the camera pans over the discards, Cop 223's voice-over reveals, 'To May, I'm just a can of pineapple.' Counterpointed to May's consumption of him, only to cast him aside, is Cop 223's brief interaction with the unknown woman (Brigitte Lin), likewise connected to canned goods. 'A woman says happy birthday to me on 1 May 1994. Because of this, I remember this woman. If memory is canned, I hope this one will never expire. If a date must be added on to it, let it be ten thousand years.' The lines add hope and possibility as a new day dawns.

Cop 663 is distraught, not so much at losing his girlfriend, but the routine he had fallen into and taken for granted. Alone, he projects his feelings onto the inanimate objects in his apartment, his response replicating Marx's understanding of commodities as 'social things whose qualities are at the same time perceptible and imperceptible by the senses … a definite social relation between men that assumes, in their eyes, the fantastic form of a relation between things.'[66] To the soap, Cop 223 laments, 'You look so sad, having lost so much weight! What happened to the chubby chap? Why? Have confidence in yourself'; to the dripping dishcloth, he asks, 'So how long is this crying going to last? Can't just play dead lying there! Stop crying. Let me help you [wrings out cloth, hangs in window]. Feels a lot better now, right?' Holding a small stuffed animal, a mouse, he says, 'Don't just sit there. Don't blame her,' while to a large stuffed animal, a polar bear, he confides and pleads, 'Each of us has our moment of doubt. Give her a chance!' When Faye begins breaking into his apartment, invading his private space, much like the loud music she plays in the open public space of Midnight Express, she brings in bright, shiny yellow Loft bags full of new commodities, including tropical fish, a tablecloth, flip-flops, soap, a toothbrush and bathroom glass, a man's flannel shirt and red bikini underwear, a dish towel, sun and moon patterned sheets, and a huge stuffed Garfield. The diffidently winsome Faye reaches out to Cop 663 through the medium of commodities, and he responds in turn, surprised, 'I feel that things are changing.' He tells the soap, 'Take care of yourself. Two days and you're stuffing yourself to death. You still have a life without her. Don't indulge. Keep fit'; to the towel, he advises, 'Got to tell you this: you've changed. We need character. You can't give yourself up because of her. Reflect on this.'

Most significantly, to the Garfield, he says 'Do you think I've changed? Getting optimistic all of a sudden and things just turn beautiful. You look a lot cuter than before now. You were sort of neat and that was alright. But this goldfish look? With patches all over? Have you been fighting?' Marx notes that 'Commodities as such are indifferent to all religious, political, national and linguistic barriers.'[67] The border-crossing cartoon character Garfield, known for his limited, albeit acerbic, wit (he is, after all, a tabby cat), is reduced to a bloated-cheeked brawling goldfish. Most important, however, is Cop 663's realization that he has changed and the world is beautiful to him because of new-found love; he is hopeful. This change is likewise registered by his newly exercised discrimination. Returning the 'California Dreamin'' CD to Faye, in exchange for the one left behind by his ex-girlfriend, he tells Faye, 'This song [Dinah Washington's 'What a Difference a Day Makes'] doesn't suit you, stick to this one ['California Dreamin'].' Cop 663 and Faye begin relating to each other intimately and personally.

The film concludes with Faye returning to Midnight Express in her flight-attendant uniform precisely one year to the day following her unexpected departure. In a visual reversal, we now find Cop 663 behind the counter while Faye assumes his former place. Rather than suggesting the distance between them –

earlier visualized, as Tsui observes, through the use of a telephoto lens to keep the cop in focus and Faye at a greater distance[68] – the two are now intimately brought together, despite the counter barrier. They have essentially walked in each others' shoes. As Faye writes him a new boarding pass and asks 'Where do you want to go?', Cop 663 leans dreamily over the counter and, face to face, looking into the camera and her eyes, responds: 'Doesn't matter. Wherever you want to go.' The coming together of Faye and Cop 663, like that of Cop 223 and Lin's character, defines a new way of uniting that has meaning for the particular time and place – Hong Kong on the verge of its return to the Mainland, as well as the couples who make a conscious decision to be together in these uncertain postmodern times.

NINE

HE AIN'T HEAVY, HE'S MY FATHER, BROTHER, SISTER, MOTHER

Perhaps least widely known outside the Hong Kong and Asian markets are Hong Kong comedies, although these films have long been a staple among Hong Kong cinema genres. According to Hong Kong International Film Festival programmer Li Cheuk-to, 'comedy has become the mainstream of Hong Kong cinema' and has proved to be its 'most prolific genre.'[1] Between 1985 and 1997, comedies on average accounted for some 17 per cent of Hong Kong movie production.[2] Recent Hong Kong comedies can be traced to Cantonese comedies of the 1950s and 1960s; the comedies of the 1980s and 1990s appropriate and update their predecessors. Past and present comedies alike are rooted in Cantonese opera, folklore, and popular anecdote. The operas included lots of singing, movement, and stylization – elements easily converted to the big screen. Cantonese opera stars were the first Hong Kong movie stars; their equivalents today include Canto-pop stars who have crossed over into film, including Leslie Cheung, Jacky Cheung, Anita Mui, Alan Tam, Andy Lau, Karen Mok, Aaron Kwok, Leon Lai, and Ekin Cheng. Primarily directed at a working-class audience, the earlier movies emphasized physical comedy, with actors exaggerating gestures and facial expressions. Sight gags abounded. Comic dialogue, with nonsense verse and puns, was rampant, as the spoken Cantonese language 'has always been the liveliest of all Chinese dialects,' and the films drew from opera songs and contemporary slang.[3] Story played second fiddle to humor, so formulaic plots were easily recognized, characters were stereotyped according to class relations, and settings formed part of the everyday world of working-class people. Generally, plotting included the inhumane rich brought down a peg or two, while the ideal representatives of their class helped the poor; tenants lined up against greedy landlords; calculating in-laws got their comeuppance from dutiful and affectionate daughters and son-in-laws.

Cantonese melodramas never achieved the sophistication of their Mandarin competition; in the meantime, bigger-budget Mandarin-language films with Hollywood features appealed to a middle-class audience. The success of Shaw Brothers Studios into the 1970s with kung fu action movies, Raymond Chow's promotion of Bruce Lee at Golden Harvest, and the ongoing separation of the Mandarin and Cantonese cinemas, left plenty of elbow room for a few savvy movie people to bridge the gap between the languages and develop Hong Kong comedy. With the institution of Deng Xiaoping's open-door policy in the late 1970s, co-productions between Hong Kong and the Mainland and Hong Kong filming on the Mainland led to a general optimism, reflected by comedies. However, the politics leading up to the signing of the Joint Declaration in the early 1980s and its subsequent signing resulted in an underlying anxiety in the comedies.

Michael Hui was a schoolteacher turned HK-TVB variety comedy show host; after working for comedy director Lee Han-hsiang at Shaw Brothers, by the mid-1970s he had moved with his two siblings Sam and Ricky to Golden Harvest, where they set up Hui Brothers Company. Their early work was 'verbal and situational'[4] but in 1976, with *Private Eyes*, physical comedy became an essential part of their movies; their output was hugely successful in the East, particularly in Japan. The Japanese title for *Private Eyes* was *Mr. Boo*, and the subsequent series of movies featuring Hui's character became known as *Mr. Boo* movies; they included *Games Gamblers Play*, *The Contract*, *Security Unlimited*, and *Teppanyaki* (1974, 1978, 1981, and 1984), among others. Hui played working-class Hong Kong characters and introduced stereotypes familiar to Hong Kongers; his sense of place, coupled with everyman characterization, helped to establish new Hong Kong comedy.[5]

In *Private Eyes*, 'Mr. Boo,' a small-time private investigator (Michael Hui), and Rusty, his woebegone assistant (Ricky Hui), team up with an unemployed Vitasoy factory worker and martial arts expert (Sam Hui) to solve a big case. The PI fires Rusty and Ricky, who nab the criminals. While their former boss ends up in hospital, they get the reward and open the Mannix Detective Agency, subsequently inviting their former boss to join them. Hui incorporated two masterstrokes of physical comedy into the action. One involves a fight in a kitchen, in which 'Mr. Boo' employs a string of sausages like nunchucks while the enemy uses the jaws of a shark to 'eat' the sausages one by one. The other involves the preparation of a chicken. As Mr. Boo follows the recipe while listening to a chef on television, Rusty and Ricky change channels to an exercise show; unaware of this, Mr. Boo continues to operate on the chicken, lifting legs and stretching. This sequence became so well known that Stanley Tong used it in his first US release *Mr. Magoo* (1997), adding the additional switch to a home-improvement show whereupon Mr. Magoo sands the raw chicken. Hui continues to influence working comedians.

Meanwhile, Karl Maka, after a series of kung fu comedy hits with minimal plot but lots of action, founded Cinema City in 1981 with Dean Shek and Raymond Wong, and turned his attention to reinventing the martial arts comedy with bigger budgets and with 'the martial arts action integrated into the plot, rather than drawn-out fist'n'footfights of the kung fu movies.'[6] So began the *Aces Go Places* series of madcap zany comedies, featuring Michael Hui's brother Sam, Maka, and Sylvia Chang in a series of spy spoofs with numerous martial arts stunts and a fascination for mechanical gadgetry. In the first film, which revolves around the recovery of stolen diamonds, with allusions to *Pink Panther*, *Godfather* and James Bond movies, a thief joins forces with a Chinese-American cop and female Hong Kong detective to solve the case. The action and pacing is fast, furious, and funny, yet underlying it is a destructive and unfocused anger which is taken out on machines of all kinds, most strikingly automobiles. This transference suggests the uncertainty of Hong Kongers' way of life with 1997 looming large. As time went on, this undercurrent became stronger. Six films were made, the penultimate being *Aces Go Places 5: The Terra Cotta Hit*, with an all-star cast that includes Leslie Cheung. The terracotta warriors, symbolic of Chinese high culture and pride, are stolen, and a motley crew is assigned to recover them; in the final installment, Sam Hui and Karl Maka are tortured in a Mainland prison, giving the movie a more ominous tone. Maka's films used urban Hong Kong as their setting, incorporating fashion trends, as well as humorous and breathtaking stunt work. His kung fu action, no longer tied to period pieces, paved the way for Jackie Chan and others. Golden Harvest followed suit with its *Lucky Stars* series, featuring the kung fu comedy of Sammo Hung; along with martial arts comedian Jackie Chan; these action comedies reached an international audience. Maka's big-budget productions, coupled with Hui's Cantonese- and Mandarin-language films, filled the gap between the distinct movie traditions. Maka updated Shaw Brothers' martial arts, while Hui's Hong Kong Everyman, 'a mixture of materialism and humanity,' 'seemed to symbolize something of the Hong Kong lifestyle.'[7]

Mid 1980s' and 1990s' Hong Kong comedies don't fall into neat comic categories, although several themes are recognizable (often in the same movie); their unrepentant border-crossings have allowed them an uninhibited freedom and daring, the result of which is a cinematic dim sum distinctively Hong Kong in style. 'Hong Kong films … believe in a no-holds-barred approach to action, gags, and stirring up emotions, even to the point of loss of control and total overload.'[8] Family stories dominate the comedies, including many of the Lunar New Year movies. A number focus on relationships between fathers and sons or are prodigal son scenarios. Urban settings function almost as characters in the way they affect human relations and reaction to change. Consideration is given to the way characters cope with modern and postmodern cultural and economic conditions and maintain or abandon traditional values. Related to these contemporary tales are 'Ah Can' stories, a reference to the pejorative nickname used by Hong Kong Chinese to describe Mainlanders who come to Hong Kong. Mainlander country mice visit their city mice relatives and culture clashes are played for comic effect, with the bumpkin cousins often the butt of the humor. Money figures prominently in many scenarios; wealth is regarded as desirable and, with hard work and a little luck, obtainable, but it also threatens traditional values, the family, and an individual's basic humanity. Gender relations supply another common theme, and in contemporary Hong Kong settings character identities slip fluidly across shifting sands, with heterosexual romantic romps and alternative gender benders on the menu. Food appears as an important element, used to distinguish and type characters, to represent *jing* (survival) and *qing* (emotional empathy and relationships), and to promote trans-Chinese cultural pride. Recent trends have led to more character-driven plotting, on the one hand, and satire and parody, on the other. The latter runs the gamut from *mou lay tau* (nonsense, balderdash) vernacular to burlesque imitation of current fads and social critique. There is something for everybody in Hong Kong comedy.

Seemingly innocuous and entertaining, the comedy genre provides a rich subtext for understanding the Hong Kong dilemma. As Teo writes, 'The substance behind the reflective theory of Hong Kong cinema [is] that it mirrors the aspirations of Hong Kong people, and reflects their psychological mind-set and behavior.'[9] The movies construct a series of social realities and representations steeped in the everyday. As Henri Lefebvre notes, 'The everyday is ambiguous and contradictory. On the one hand, it provides satisfactions: it satisfies the very needs it produces. On the other hand, the everyday provokes a malaise, a profound dissatisfaction, an aspiration for something else.'[10] Contemporary Hong Kong comedies comfort their audiences even as they create cognitive dissonance. They emphasize progress, modernization and post-modernization, and material interests set against the traditional values of family, mutual dependence, and benevolence; they center on family life, contrast elite and common social classes, or feature a work ethic that leads to material success and personal satisfaction. The resulting internalized representation for the audience, then, is one of mixed messages – everyone can have red-bean buns and eat them too, regardless of the social or economic barriers. Of course, since these are lightweight and lighthearted features, the thrice-used title for several Lunar New Year's pictures sums them up – *All's Well Ends Well...*

Lunar New Year movies, screened during the celebration of Chinese New Year, a two-week period beginning with the first moon of the year, generally in late January or early February, have become an anticipated part of Hong Kong contemporary culture; they are equivalent to Christmas and summer blockbusters in the USA. Lunar New Year comedies are generally family-based. Families come in all shapes and sizes in real and reel life. Chinese families are particularly important because of the tradition of filial piety as well as regard for ancestors. Hong Kong is capitalism's major success story in recent history, with a higher per capita income than in the USA. But at what cost? Family unity serves as a bulwark against crass commercialism and a survival-of-the-fittest mentality, but family discord has become a sign of the times. Hong Kong families in Lunar New Year comedies are from the middle or elite class. Large extended families are represented, all the better for painting with a broad brush and exaggerating often outrageous complications, including unexpected plot devices, mistaken identities, confused characters, Hollywood borrowings, and earthy and crude jokes arising from bodily functions.

All these films portray characters unaware of who they are and what they need; for them, 'life's losing its meaning. Man loses the center, weight and connectedness of his own life, a fact life itself compels him to realize.'[11] Nonetheless, characters are enlightened and delivered by the story's end; all share happy endings and couples are united romantically; the characters then step out of frame to wish audiences love, luck, and money for the new year. While the cinema draws from Cantonese opera, the overdetermined unions of characters subtextually represent a wish-fulfillment psyche – may the reunification of Hong Kong with the PRC be as felicitous.

Raymond Wong produced and acted in the *All's Well Ends Well* series and another Lunar New Year comedy, *It's a Wonderful Life* (1994; literally *Big Rich Family*). The Chinese title plays upon the concept of richness. Presumably the family patriarch is affluent but emotionally poor because he has constantly criticized his four children their entire lives. His father, the grandfather (Kwan Tak-hing), not only parodies his Wong Fei-hung roles but ironically points out his son's shortcomings and reminds the family of the true meaning of richness. 'Rich family/Love is the core' is the calligraphy scroll he creates to celebrate the new year in traditional fashion. Of the four children, Kau-fu (Raymond Wong) is a preoccupied businessman whose wife leaves him, taking their daughter, because of his excessive drinking as a part of doing business; Kau-kwai (Tony Leung Ka-fai) is a struggling comic artist who stutters; Kau-ann (Teresa Mo) has fled to France to escape her father's criticism, only to come home as a liberated woman to the untoward romantic pursuit of her cousin Chun (Lau Ching-wan); and Kau-fee is the youngster who takes nothing seriously. When Kau-ann returns to celebrate New Year with her family, she brings an uninvited guest, the free-spirited Roberto (Leslie Cheung), who naturally solves everyone's problems, even his own, with a little advice from the relatives.

Secondary characters who eventually join the family include Kau-fee's spinster teacher (Carol Cheng) and her sister (Anita Yuen), with whom Kau-kwai falls madly in love. With parodies of current Hollywood features like *Jurassic Park* and *Mrs. Doubtfire* and references to the Japanese animation *Dragonball*, plus interspersed selections from the *Nutcracker Suite*, the story grows out of the mother's simple wish for her family to be together. The matriarch comes close to fulfillment of her desire when the wealthy Chun holds a traditional banquet to announce his impending nuptials; however, Kau-kwai's absence over a dispute with his father and Roberto's upstaging of Chun to proclaim that he has already proposed to Kau-ann (a fabrication) shatter her dream of happiness.

Michael Parenti observes that,

> At the very least, even if money does not guarantee happiness, it certainly makes life much easier; it makes it easier to deal with adversities or to escape altogether the many kinds of unhappiness caused by not having enough money for one's needs. Money creates the best possible life chances in a capitalistic society.[12]

Kau-fu has lost his wife and child, but has a comfortable nest to which he returns; Kau-kwai argues with his father and leaves home only to 'piss'; Kau-ann resents her father's criticism but accepts his financial support for her education. These children take money for granted. Roberto, however, along with the grandfather, serves as the film's conscience. A jack-of-all-trades, Roberto has studied engineering, fashion design, theater and stage make-up, and martial arts. Without expectation of recompense, he cheerfully helps the mother with her knitting and wardrobe, the father with his koi pond, and Kau-fu with his disguise to win back his wife.

While repairing the net on the family tennis court, Roberto is approached by Chun, who wants to beat him for taking Kau-ann from him. Roberto explains that Chun must suffer to win love, and punches and kicks him. He also reminds Chun that even though he is rich enough to buy what he wants, love depends on power. Chun, true to his limitations, equates love with sexual attraction, replying that women find him desirable. 'Some girls say I am "sex,"' he claims. Roberto counters, '"Sexy." It's not "sex" but "sexy," adjective. "Sexy." Follow me.' Chun proceeds to pronounce the word several times almost to himself, but adds, 'Don't say it too fast.' Roberto reiterates the pronunciation, slowly. The incident humorously underscores the movie's message: to have power through money without caring is to be emotionally bankrupt. In Cantonese slang, pronunciation of the English 'sexy' means 'eat shit.'

Johnnie To's *Eighth Happiness* (1988) and Clifton Ko's *Ninth Happiness* (1998) are true to the Lunar New Year pattern, presenting family stories with happy endings and a wish for the audience's good fortune; Raymond Wong was featured in and produced both.[13] *Eighth Happiness* is a contemporary story of three brothers;

Ninth Happiness is a period piece, also concerning three male siblings. Their quest for romance, happiness, and wealth structures the plots. Ten years apart, these movies suggest Hong Kong's ongoing and changing relations with the Mainland. *Eighth Happiness* is firmly rooted in urban Hong Kong. The catalyst for much of the comedy and misunderstanding is an elderly couple's automobile accident which scrambles telephone lines. Fang Chien-hui (Raymond Wong) is the elder brother and a women's cooking show host who falls in love with a Cantonese opera performer (Fung Bo-bo) guest-starring on the show. Fang Chien-lang (Chow Yun-fat) is the middle brother, a self-absorbed womanizer with conquests in nineteen districts who poses as gay to win their trust and affection, taking for granted his airline hostess girlfriend (Carol Cheng). The youngest brother is Fang Chien-sheng (Jacky Cheung), an innocent cartoonist who falls for Ying (Fennie Yuen) but lacks the self-confidence to win her. From cars to Rolexes to television cameras, characters interact with and are affected by machines associated with modernity; one repeated reaction they have is to destroy the machine. Indeed, much of the plot develops from the injury the opera star sustains when answering crank phone calls caused by the accident; her response is to damage the phone.

After many plot twists, it takes the old ways: a traditional Cantonese opera (with the men in costume), to reunite the couples and bring about the happy ending. Willemen describes cinema from areas with colonial histories as having a

> need to reinvent traditions, to conjure up an image of pre-colonial innocence and authenticity, since the national-cultural identity must by definition be founded on what has been suppressed or distorted. The result is mostly a nostalgia for a pre-colonial society which in fact never existed … perverted by imperialism or, in the most naive versions, perverted by technology.[14]

In its staging of Cantonese operas and critiquing of technology, *Eighth Happiness* sides with a mythical Chinese past and paves the way for its elaboration in *Ninth Happiness.*

When *Ninth Happiness* revived the three brothers' story, Chinese opera took center-stage: the movie is structured as an opera, with song and dance, combat and stylization, and interspersed dialogue and action. Traditional instrumentation and opera-like songs are included. Leslie Cheung does a hilarious send-up of his then-in-the-charts song 'Red,' dressed in a red period costume and mistaken as a 'fairy' by the village beauty Chi Wan (Wu Chien-lien). The music is a medley of 'Jingle Bells' and 'Dashing through the Snow' and Raymond Wong's version of 'Tea for Two' as a corrupt officer engaging with honest village folk. Set on the Mainland in Choi Hung village, an ideal communal setting with a benevolent village elder, 'Mrs. Minister,' it is a place without greed or hypocrisy where everyone shares its bounty. Lust seems to be the only problem the men have, but they confess and duly douse themselves with cold water; when a woman takes more than her share of buns and is caught 'bun-handed,' she admits her error and is forgiven in parody of Maoist self-criticism.

Enter three brothers, the elder Ma Lun-tai (Raymond Wong); his strong man brother, Ma Lun-kui (Michael Chow); and the young adventurer Ma Lun-cheung (Leslie Cheung), who, until the climax, goes by the nickname 'Tok Choi,' because 'my whole name sounds like foul language.' All their names, in fact, contain sexual references. Literally, 'Ma Lun-tai' means 'with a penis as big as a horse's'; 'Ma Lun-kui' means 'with an erect penis' ('kui' meaning 'up'); and 'Ma Lun-cheung' means 'with a penis as long as a horse's.' Hence Lun-cheung uses another name, 'Tok Choi,' that of a famous Japanese artist, an attempt to give himself respectability. The two older brothers are dishonest officers intent on exploiting the untainted villagers for their own gain; their avarice is set against the genuine good-naturedness of Tok Choi, who sets out to restore the village they corrupt. Many plot twists later, the resolution depends upon court proceedings and the interpretation of a contract described as a 'joint declaration' – a reunification state of mind. The two usurpers are upbraided and tamed by women, and all three Ma brothers are duly wed, along with the kind village shoemender Dup (Kenny Bee) and the resourceful Heung (Gigi Lai). Greedy Hong Kongers, it seems, can improve themselves with help from their country cousins. A comparison of *Eighth* and *Ninth Happiness* teaches that middle and elite classes thrive at the expense of the unseen suffering of the invisible poor. 'Since bourgeois society is ... a contradictory form of development, it contains relations of earlier societies often merely in very stunted form or even in the form of travesties.'[15]

Jacob Cheung's *Always on My Mind* (1993) is not a Lunar New Year comedy but focuses on a middle-class family in urban Hong Kong. The literal Chinese title, *Money Grabbing Husband and Wife*, is perhaps a bit hard on its protagonists Chang Yau-wai (Michael Hui) and his wife Yin (Josephine Siao). Far from greedy, the couple struggle to live with some security and raise their three children, including a daughter in need of a dowry, a lovesick son with plans to attend university in Canada, and a small daughter just starting school who requires some TLC. Chang Yau-wai is a news anchor diagnosed with intestinal cancer, and the housewife Yin wants to work outside the home but has a heart condition.

Unlike the formula Lunar New Year comedies, this film is built on strong characterization and has a satiric target – the Hong Kong news media. 'The postmodern person is a restless voyeur, a person who sits and gazes (often mesmerized and bored) at the movie or TV screen,' according to Norman Denzin.[16] When the television boys exploit Chang's illness to increase their ratings (including a televised spectacle party with a 'cake of death'), he willingly partici-pates to increase his salary until he realizes the havoc it wreaks on his family, and, by extension, society at large. He grows to understand Poster's recognition that 'the tv viewer participates in a communication, is part of a new language system … that is enough to constitute a social formation'[17] and takes responsibility for the content onscreen. He rejects the media's willingness to exploit human misery at any cost, to fabricate and exaggerate its stories, and he resigns, satisfied to have less. At his sign-off, he muses: 'Whatever TV shows us, whatever we read, what-ever the idols wear … The world is filled with "whatever you say," therefore I can't be sure about things either … I only do the reporting.' Hui reprises his everyman character, toning down the physical slapstick but heightening the comedy of situation (in moviegoers' minds was the awareness of Hui as a successful television personality). The relationships between husband and wife and between parents and children are touching, believable, and humorous, and the importance of family is emphasized. The English title, *Always on My Mind*, after the song used in the film, points to the strength and endurance of family bonding.

Other family comedies stress father–son relationships. John Woo's 1991 action-comedy caper *Once a Thief* (literally *Vertical and Horizontal World*) tells the story of good and bad fathers and their sons. 'Vertical and horizontal world' refers not only to gangsters and cops but also to the poor-excuse-for-a-father Chow (Kenneth Tsang) and the good substitute father Chu (Chu Kong). Joe (Chow Yun-fat), Jim (Leslie Cheung), and Cherie (Cherie Chung) play the adult characters of the three unrelated orphans exploited by Chow, who teaches them to be expert thieves for his benefit. Chu, enacting a code that embraces the values of *qing* and *jing*, feeds and clothes them and is a reassuring and generous presence in their lives. When Joe is injured during a heist gone wrong, and presumably loses the use of his legs, Chu takes his 'son' into his home and helps in his rehabilitation, while Chow pushes Joe in his wheelchair down a flight of stairs and has his cronies beat him. Chow as the greedy capitalist entrepreneur, albeit an underworld figure, has no use for a worker from whom he can no longer derive surplus value. As Marx points out, 'Capital is reckless of the health or length of the life of the laborer, unless under compulsion from society.'[18]

The movie includes a memorable scene of the graceful Chow Yun-fat in a wheelchair dancing with Cherie Chung, who partners Leslie Cheung as well; this scene and others reinforce the trio as essentially creating their own family. While much of the film was shot on the French Riviera and in Hong Kong, the story concludes with the three having emigrated to the USA, where Joe is called upon to care for the couple's infant. Dressed in an apron, he dusts while watching a football game; and in his excitement, he dusts and throws the baby aside. In the meantime, Cherie and Jim attend to their toddler playing in a baby pool, with Cherie in curlers as the typical 'housewife.'

In a society where sons are still privileged, prodigal son stories abound. In most, the first son has gone astray, usually by putting business and money before the family. In Peter Chan's *Back to the Future*-styled *He Ain't Heavy, He's My Father* (1993), a disrespectful son undervalues human relationships. The adult son's voice-over narration opens the film as we glimpse him admiring a train set in a shop window:

> The saying 'the child is the father of the man' is so true. According to the latest issue of *Fortune*, eight of the ten richest men had made it since they were kids. That's because they all had wealthy fathers to start nice. The other two were schemers and dreamers when they were young. That makes me a helpless case because my dad has always been poor and unimaginative.

He says he wanted to be a doctor but ended up a real-estate agent; he blames his father for always lending money and never buying him the train set. He represents

> the man of the fetishized world, who can cure his disgust with the world only in intoxication, [the man] who seeks, like the morphine addict, to find a way out by heightening the intensity of the intoxicant rather than a way of life that has no need of intoxication.[19]

courtesy of Kazumi Fukumoto; permission of Peter Chan

FATHER AND SON   Tony Leung Ka-fai and Tony Leung Chiu-wai in Peter Chan's *He Ain't Heavy, He's My Father*

For the son, Chor Yuen, the intoxication is women, whom he fetishizes and objectifies. Tony Leung Chiu-wai plays Yuen, the shameless womanizer, who is on the make even in the hospital where his father lies in a coma after sustaining a head injury. This comedy is set during the Mid-Autumn Festival, when anything can and does happen. Yuen time-travels to his father's youth and awakens in Memory Lane in the 1950s. He is readily accepted by his father and his father's extended family and friends – 'we're brothers from the same country … the neighborhood is a big family … we care for each other,' his father, Chor Feng (Tony Leung Ka-fai) tells Yuen; 'all for one and one for all' is the principle by which he lives. First Yuen must overcome the shock of encountering his father at his own age. Touched by his father's generosity and humanitarianism, he is also deeply impressed by the communal efforts of the group to share good and bad times together and by the rich social life in which they participate.

'If Lee Ka-shing had a father like you, he'd still be a factory worker now. You're out of date, that's why you're penniless. You're seventy, yet haven't lived a life. You're a loser.' The hurtful words spoken by Yuen to his father return to haunt him as he witnesses the fellow feeling among the group, which is held together by his father's efforts. Yet there is comedy as well when the young Lee Ka-shing (in real life a famous Hong Kong billionaire, here played by Waise Lee) is introduced as a part of the group living in Memory Lane. Driven home to the audience and Yuen is that he 'is not aware that the loss of communal life, the degradation and dehumanization of collective work as a result of the capitalist division of labor, and the severance of human relations from social activity have stupified him.'[20] Yuen returns to the present having gained an understanding of why his father behaves as he does. He sees the love between his parents as if for the first time. He is a changed man, affectionate and respectful towards his father and now ready to commit to a serious relationship with his girlfriend Yee (Anita Yuen).

Regardless of their differences, this son discovers that he is more like his father than he had ever imagined, therby reinforcing both his opening line and the Chinese movie title, which translates literally as *New Two of a Kind*. Chan closes the story with characters from the past magically intermingling with those in the present, the young Feng having followed Yuen back to present time, ready to pick up where they left off. The nostalgia for wholeness, of past and present, Hong Kong and the Mainland, is also reflected in the repetition of his parents' special song, 'Tell Laura I Love Her,' which brings the elderly father back to consciousness. Furthermore, appearing onscreen at the film's end is the dedication, 'A tribute to those who left behind a treasure of wisdom and memories,' stirring reminders of ties to the Mainland.

Chan's formation of United Filmmakers' Organization (UFO) in 1992 (partners have included Eric Tsang, Claudie Chung, Chi Lee, Jacob Cheung and James

courtesy of Kazumi Fukumoto, permission of Peter Chan

SECOND CHANCES   Anita Yuen and Tony Leung Chiu-wai in Peter Chan's *He Ain't Heavy, He's My Father*

Yuen) led to the output of distinctive comedies rooted in characterization; the films generally examine the relationships between members of a younger genera-tion, Hong Kong born and bred, who struggle in the contemporary urban setting, facing 'a mass-cultural onslaught that respects nothing, weighing everything from soap to revolution as merely items of marketable merchandise.'[21] In buddy flick *Tom, Dick and Hairy* (1994, co-directed with Chi Li, and co-written with James

Yuen and Gordon Chan), three male room-mates and bachelors, played by Tony Leung Chiu-wai, Tony Leung Ka-fai, and Lawrence Cheng, share a small apartment and therefore each others' lives. Lots of over-the-top comedic moments are equally balanced by an intense and subtle emotional range. Chan's movies are about relationships, pure and simple, and the misconnections, miscommunications, and missed opportunities that accompany them; they are also 'city-themed' and, as 'cultural barriers become less and less' in global cities like Hong Kong, more and more relevant to an urban audience.[22]

The film opens with an aerial view of the Tsimshatsui district and Tom's voice-over narration: "Tsimshatsui is a spot in Hong Kong filled with glamour and vivacity. A population of 200,000 people produces 200,000 different stories.' As the camera zooms in on Dick, running through the teeming streets, the voice-over continues, 'One of those is this guy. He's making haste for a wedding ceremony. Don't mistake him for the groom.' Next, there is a cut to a forlorn-looking Tom seated inside a church. 'He is the groom. The groom is me.' The visuals and voice-over immediately contextualize and contrast two of the title characters. The third, 'Hairy' of the English title, is so called because of his Chinese name, 'Ah Mo' (bushy-haired, like the character), and is soon introduced. He takes the name Giorgio, as in 'Giorgio Armani,' suggesting the brand names, logos, and designer appellations which communicate world-wide and cross cultural and linguistic boundaries – like Hairy himself, a Mainland cousin come to Hong Kong.

The plot follows the three male protagonists in their pursuit of relationships. Hairy's most fulfilling friendship is with Michelle (Michael Chow), whom he meets through a dating service after numerous mismatchings; ironically, 'Michelle' turns out to be a man, not a woman. The characters are contrasted by their varying successes, and in Hong Kong, as elsewhere, two out of three's not bad. Tom almost marries the wrong woman but is saved by Dick, who himself misses his chance for love but is instrumental in making Tom's happiness. Dick's reluctance to commit to Fong (Anita Yuen) at the right moment results in him being left alone, wondering 'who'll care about me?'; his failure and Fong's confession, 'I have never given up on love,' makes him all the more determined that his friend Tom should not meet his fate. Hairy, meantime, is bent on self-betterment, which includes 'chasing foreign girls'; for him this self-improvement program begins with foreign language lessons. Thinking that he is learning English, he instead becomes fluent in French; this wins him the attentions of Francis, a Vivian Chow-lookalike (played, naturally, by Vivian Chow).

The intimacy as well as the comedic interactions of the film grow out of the situations played out in the apartment. Everything, from Dick's promiscuity to Hairy's incense-burning to Tom's visiting sister's flirtations with Dick and Tom's brotherly consternation, stems from their close quarters. Dick's numerous jobs, taken to pay the rent, include that of guide to Japanese tourists, hiring out his paying tourists as extras on movie sets, and selling shoes. Tom, for his part, works as a host in a bank. Chan and Lee root the comedy and emotion in people's everyday working lives.

Gordon Chan's *Long and Winding Road* (1994, literally *Bright Future*) similarly opens with a long shot of Hong Kong beginning its day – people on their way to work – crowded subways, traffic jams, bodies in motion. Again, the city has taken on the labor market characteristics of the 'global city,' a marked trend towards a service economy with two different groups of people – a small, affluent business and managerial stratum and a large service population, much of which caters to the demands of the former.[23] The camera zooms in on out-of-work and broke womanizer Lam Chiu-wing (Leslie Cheung), who loses his current girlfriend, a restaurant hostess, to her customer, an older, established, and successful businessman who can buy her things. In response, Wing connives his way up the corporate ladder; his new boss, Bosco Chow (Kenneth Tsang), explains business to him: 'You bring me luck and money, what a smart boy. I want to employ you as my staff for I love you being nasty. You can make money only if you're nasty.' When Wing asks him what business he runs, Chow answers, 'Anything about making money,' which in this case means real estate.

Comparative characterizations are drawn of Chow and Wing's emulation of him, and of the working-class friends whom Chow leaves behind. 'The propertied class and the class of the proletariat present the same human-alienation,' Marx asserts; the film shows this shared state. Marx continues:

> The former class finds in this self-alienation its confirmation and its good, its own power; it has in it a semblance of human existence. The class of the proletariat feels annihilated in its self-alienation, it sees its own powerlessness and the reality of an inhuman existence.[24]

Set against Chow's character and Wing's climb is James, a frustrated musician (Tony Leung Ka-fai) who plods along overseeing a run-down home for the elderly who have nowhere else to go. Wing must confront himself and what he has become (less than human) when his boss and mentor doesn't think twice about making a real-estate deal that will not only displace the elderly, but will force Wing to betray his best friend. Whether it is having followed the 'long and winding road' of the English title or the consequence of seeking the 'bright future' of the literal Chinese title, the narrative concludes with Wing using his business acumen to outsmart his boss and help his friend.

Ronny Yu's *Shogun and Little Kitchen* (1992) likewise favors friendship, family and community over business success. Yet in cinematic representation lucky characters can have both, and this serves as one of the stories of the city. With nods to the rise of housing estates in Hong Kong in the 1970s and to the current housing problem, the movie is set around the market and apartment house at Tai Ping Fong, a poor Hong Kong community. Ng Man-tat plays Bo ('Little Kitchen'), the owner of the property and the local chef; Yuen Biao plays Ta Chi ('Shogun'), his Mainland uncle, an expert chef and martial artist; set against the working class is Lin Feng (Leon Lai), a rich kid who flees in disgust from his father's avarice and preoccupation with business. Feng's right-hand man Raymond hires a middleman attorney to negotiate the purchase of Bo's building; the lawyer hires gangsters to threaten Bo and his tenants. As Harvey notes,

> Capitalist development has … to negotiate a knife-edge path between preserving the exchange values of past capital investments in the built environment and destroying these investments in order to open up fresh room for accumulation. Under capitalism, there is … a perpetual struggle in which capital builds a physical landscape appropriate to its own condition at a particular moment in time, only to have to destroy it … at a subsequent point in time.[25]

The elder Feng plans to raze the building along with others to construct more modern high-rises. This smaller, modern version reflects the larger process ongoing throughout Hong Kong.

Meanwhile, Feng is subsequently adopted by the villagers of Tai Ping Fong; as Bo tells him, 'we're just like a big family.' Between Bo's well-intentioned cooking and apartment management, Bo's daughter Ai's attempt to 'develop better prospects' as a designer, Ta Chi's amazing martial-arts-with-food demonstrations, and exploitation by a business conglomerate, Feng's efforts to hide his wealth in order to win Ai's affection, and Feng's father's push to expand his business, the scene is set for a confrontation between wealthy business interests and the working poor. Ai adequately explains their situation when she describes the park in Wu City where the attendant brings the python its food, a live chicken. The chicken is afraid it will die and fights, jumping toward the python, pecking, until the snake is injured and the chicken is let go. 'We are like the chicken in this society. You'll be sacrificed if you don't persist,' she concludes. Through communal effort, represented by Bo, Ta Chi, and Feng, the villagers are saved from the fire started by the gangsters; furthermore, the relatives open a successful joint-venture restaurant, Feng is reunited with his father, and the offspring of Feng and Ai guarantee the continuation of both family lines.

Money matters and the making of money, as depicted in Hong Kong films, is a combination of hard work, ingenuity, and luck. The pattern was set with the rise of the Broker La character in 1950s' Cantonese cinema, and has been updated since. According to film critic Sek Kei, the broker is 'an economic animal making a living in a laissez-faire urban jungle ... symbolic of Hong Kong's total immersion in the capitalistic free-market system ... the classic archetypal figure, embodying the "Hong Kong mentality."'[26] Focusing on the gap between rich and poor, filmmakers not only brought to life the extremes but created entrepreneurial middlemen characters to maneuver between them, reflecting an easily adaptable attitude to the vicissitudes of a hyperactive urban and economic landscape. With the colony's modernization in the 1960s, and subsequent economic miracle, which led to prosperity and success into the 1980s, Hong Kongers' perceptions of the wealthy changed. So long as the rich retain their humanity, they can be accommodated and are generally depicted positively in comedies: the men as benevolent patriarchs, the women as soft-hearted and compassionate. Those who are greedy lose their human characteristics; more often than not, these characters are real-estate developers and lawyers, who are featured negatively, often as foolish, and are punished. However, those who see the light and willingly change are redeemed.

Gambling movies suggest risk-taking and an easy-come, easy-go mentality; although rooted in the sweepstakes movies of earlier Cantonese cinema, these movies lack the moralism of the earlier stories. Instead of portraying the crooked rich, or the poor transformed by wealth into nouveaux riches, the gambling movies of the late 1980s and 1990s communicate the desire for wealth and the fantasy that everyone, with a little luck, has the opportunity to become rich. The films mirror Hong Kong's transformation; they also reflect Hong Kongers' anxieties over the Tiananmen Square massacre on the heels of the Joint Declaration. Many middle- and upper-middle-class Hong Kongers emigrated; the psyche of those remaining needed stories to reassure them, including those that would calm their anxiety or serve as escapism.

Thus, the ultimate success of the good and the condoning of big risk-taking are values evident in *God of Gamblers* (1989) and its sequel *God of Gamblers' Return* (1994), the many spin-offs, and the parody *All for the Winner* (1990). In *God of Gamblers*, Chow Yun-fat plays Gambling King Ko-chun, suave, sophisticated and worldly. A bop on the head leads to him losing his memory, and he aligns with the working-class Knife (Andy Lau) to make his comeback. The story has it both ways: Ko Chun can be admired for his success (signified by his trademark clothing, hairstyle, the twisting of his jade ring, and eating of chocolates) and also be an average person (reduced to childlike innocence, trusting and charming). The sequel ups the ante with a great deal of gratuitous violence; this includes a child witnessing his family killed, the murder of Ko-chun's pregnant wife and placing of her unborn fetus in a jar for the hero to view. However, the anonymous Hong Kong gambling king comes out of retirement and joins forces with a Mainland small-timer (Tony Leung Ka-fai) and his sister (Wu Chien-lien) to beat the odds. Both extremes play out – disturbing violence and co-operation – for Hong Kong and the PRC.

Gambling, whether card playing, betting, or lottery and sweepstakes, remains a thread in many films. For example, in Joe Cheung's *Pom Pom and Hot Hot* (1992), 'Miracle Hands' Hong Kong cop Jacky Cheung is showing his Mainland country cousin (Bonnie Fu Yuk-jing) the sights. As the camera pans the Hong Kong skyline he says, 'There are six million people in Hong Kong. There are Hong Kong, Kowloon, and New Territories. Besides the nineteen District Boards there are sixty-five horse races and one hundred and four Mark Sixes annually.' 'Curry Chicken,' his partner (Stephen Tung Wai), replies, 'You are bullshit.' The exchange suggests that Hong Kong is defined by its legal determinations and gambling, on the one hand, but, on the other, that this mix of culture and commerce is meaningless. Furthermore, the 'sixty-five horse races' call to mind Deng Xiaoping's promise that after 1997, 'horses will keep racing and dancers will keep dancing,' a guarantee that Hong Kong will remain the same for fifty years, tied to the 1984 legal document; Curry Chicken's directness points to the difference between spoken and written agreements. The film also – like many gambling comedies – picks up on the wagering thread of luck, money and opportunity, a metaphor for 'casino capitalism,' where, regardless of the hour, investments move ceaselessly between currencies in response to political and economic events and expectations worldwide.[27]

It is also the case that numerous films depict the struggle of the little guy trying to eke out a living. In these films, hard work, coupled with co-operation, in which everyone pulls together for the good of all, leads to success. Wong Chung-chow's *Fractured Follies* (1988) explores the contested terrain between a mom-and-pop grocer and the corporate competition across the street; even worse, the competition is a relative – an entrepreneur who has sold his old business to his naive brother in order to go corporate. The story depicts the hard work of all those employed in the mom-and-pop operation, showing numerous scenes of their labor; their work is fun when they work together, as evidenced by various scenes in the family store – father, daughter, grandmother, and hired employees dance with each other and with mops as they clean the floors, play with the merchandise as they stack items, and Joe (Chow Yun-fat) bowls in the supermarket lanes with plastic Coke bottles and a can. Work can also be dangerous, as is apparent when the competition lets loose a poisonous snake in the store. The film culminates in a face-off street battle of sing-song between Chow Yun-fat (dressed as a pineapple) and the opposition. The duelling singers allude not only to the 'cutthroat' rivalry they have exhibited to lure customers, but to the essential manhood of the combatants, affirming the aggressive one-upmanship of competitive capitalism.

Tsui Hark's *Working Class* (1985) tells another story of working-class people and co-operation. Set primarily in a place of production, a noodle factory, the film initially displays the factionalism of working-class characters Sunny, Hing, and Yam (Tsui Hark, Teddy Robin, and Sam Hui, respectively). The men are at odds in a soccer game and then in a series of automobile mishaps; however, in the factory they join together against the manager (played by Ng Man-tat) and his relatives. The film harshly lampoons middle management, which is characterized as greedy, dishonest, and inhumane. The owner of the factory is generally invisible, having temporarily left for Canada, putting the business in the hands of his managers, along with his well-intentioned daughter (Joey Wong). Even when middle management pits worker against worker in a factory competition, the workers remain loyal to each other and ultimately save the company. They are empowered, running the factory themselves; yet the film compromises, because in the end they defer to the owner-capitalist who shows his compassion by giving them shares in the company. 'Power creates its very constraints, for the powerful is also necessarily defined by the powerless';[28] in this instance, the powerful prevail. So much for organized labor: in the celluloid world, as in Hong Kong, no powerful industry-wide unions exist; work proceeds with little interruption, and benevolent capitalists make even more money.

Johnnie To's *The Fun, the Luck, and the Tycoon* shows another admirable and wealthy character, 'the richest man in Hong Kong,' in a 1990 Lunar New Year comedy whose literal title, *Lucky Star Join Hands Shine*, suggests its story. The film has a tripartite structure: Lam Bo-sun, the tycoon, is a 'lucky star,' blessed with inherited wealth; unhappy, he gives it up and 'joins hands' with the working world when he works incognito in a fast-food restaurant; he 'shines' when he chooses happiness with the woman he loves (Sylvia Chang) over inherited wealth. Chow Yun-fat plays the character, who wears a bemused grin throughout; his good nature, which sets him apart from the greedy or idle rich, is evident from the start. When Bo's mother and aunt propose that he buy a $3 million necklace as an engagement gift for his cousin, he turns to the jewelry clerk and enquires, 'How much is your monthly salary? Six thousand? That means you've to work forty years for it.... Forty years for a necklace. What's the worth? No meaning at all.' Bo is not only considerate of those less fortunate than himself; he is genuinely interested in people. He converses with people of all classes, but seems more comfortable with working people – traffic cops, doormen, secretaries, busboys, and so on. He also belittles the idle rich, mimicking the pretentiousness of his cousin Cindy (Nina Li) and the miserliness of the wealthy.

Cindy, however, gives the tycoon something to think about: 'You'd be a nobody without money.' Thus begins Bo's soul-searching. He asks his manservant Fatso, 'What would happen if I had no money?' and Fatso runs down the list: 'That would be tragic: no house, no yacht, no cars, no servants beside you. No one to play fencing with, no gorgeous clothes, no fancy food, no Italian shoes, no expensive watches. Tycoon, you'd have nothing.' So begins the character's adventures in the working world, in which hard work and persistence 'can make our dreams into reality.' The simple life satisfies Bo. The cabdriver Stink (also played by Chow Yun-fat) has modest dreams as well: to own his cab once he has paid off the installments; to drive one shift and hire the cab out the rest of the time. His goal is sidetracked, however, when he is chosen and adopted by Bo's relatives as the new heir; his upward mobility suggests you can have wealth, happiness, and humanity too. On the other hand, Lawrence Cheng plays the cheap, rude, arrogant, and devious lawyer who connives for the wealth as well as for the tycoon's gold-digging intended. After the couple are hurled into a garbage truck full of trash, the lawyer's reward/punishment is to lose a fortune and gain a very fertile wife under investigation by the fertility clinics.[29]

Like other genres, the comedies abound with references to images of how Hong Kong sees itself and its relation to the Mainland. With a large influx of Mainland refugees in 1949 and 1967, Cantonese comedies had featured Mainlanders as outsiders who had trouble communicating and understanding Hong Kong social practices; by each film's end, however, locals and refugees were united by their Chineseness. Despite the assimilation, looming large in the Hong Kong psyche was the eventual return of Hong Kong to the PRC. As director Ronny Yu relates, 'Hong Kong is the only place in the world where you were told as a kid, by 1997 your lifestyle might end. A new force could come in and tell you how to live.' Mainland characters have not always been positively portrayed. Those who come to Hong Kong are often the butt of humor; in 1979, a television series called *The Good, the Bad, and the Ugly* introduced a Mainlander clown character called Ah Can, and film readily appropriated the image for the wide screen.[30] Ah Cans are often characterized as buffoons lacking taste and style without the knowledge to know better, or else they are easily duped; when they try to adapt to the Hong Kong style, they are even more ludicrous. As 'alienated life elements … these products of self-abasement, self-rejection, and self-estrangement … have been endowed with independent being and a life of their own.'[31]

Some 1980s' and 1990s' comedies portrayed them as naive but ultimately positive characters. Two films of Alfred Cheung will serve as illustration. In his *Pom Pom and Hot Hot* Mainlanders are an easy target. In a wonderfully comic mah-jongg game, the Hong Kongers get the better of their Mainlander male cousin (Alfred Cheung). The Mainlander wins early on; however, the others then decide to play 'Taiwanese' mah-jongg, changing the rules and making them up as they go along, at the expense of the Mainlander. When he insists on playing 'Mainland' mah-jongg and begins to win again, they protest, exclaiming they have made a 'joint declaration,' that he is 'changing our agreement,' and 'it's not yet 1997.'

In contrast, Cheung's earlier *Her Fatal Ways* (1990), which spawned several sequels, portrays Mainlanders more positively. Hong Kong inspector Wu Wei-kuo (Tony Leung Ka-fai) must co-operate with Mainland security officers Cheng Shih-nam (Carol Cheng) and Hsiao-sheng (Alfred Cheung); Wu is told by his boss that the 'sister' is escorting the prisoner from the Mainland to Hong Kong, that the extradition will be 'easy, a simple handover.' When the prisoner escapes, Wu must work with the Mainlanders to recapture him and find his boss, a businessman-cum-drug-smuggler. The dialogue is full of *double entendres* and allusions to the handover. 'Hong Kong comrades and we are one. What concerns us concerns Hong Kong,' volunteers Shih-nam; to which Wei-kuo replies, 'Thank you, leave Hong Kong matters alone.' When the Hong Kong cop complains, 'Isn't it troublesome having to explain everything to the people [Mainlanders],' his Mainland counterpart retorts, 'You'll get used to it,' an obvious reference to the impending return. This film directly addresses the strained relations between the Mainland and Taiwan, through the person of Wu's father, former commander of the 391st Brigade, 131st Division of the Nationalist Army. His loyalty is to the Taiwanese government, in contrast to that of the Mainlanders to the PRC. In a failed attempt to get the better of the Mainlanders, Wu and his buddies hold singing and drinking contests. In the end, old-timer Nationalists rescue the Mainlanders and Hong Kongers and assist them in capturing the criminals. Hong Kong's capitalistic enterprise is also at issue through the simultaneous attraction and repulsion of Westernized corruption for Shih-nam, in the form of fashion and makeup. While the Mainlanders may not understand the going lingo in Hong Kong, they do speak a common language and know how to get the job done. It's a 'successful co-operation.' The film concludes on a positive note: 'Perhaps we will co-operate again after 1997.'

Many of these films are Hong Kong versions, with new spins, of the country mouse and city mouse children's tale. Country cousins come to the city and cultural conflicts and comedy ensue. Alex Law's *Now You See Love, Now You Don't* (1992) is a variation on this theme. Chow Yun-fat plays Wu Shan-shui, headman of an indigenous fishing village on a New Territories island, and Carol Cheng plays Firefly Kwok, his girlfriend just returned from London and transformed by

Western culture; the film reflects the conflicts and compromises between the village and the city.[32] Terence Chang relates that he 'concocted a story of a country boy from Lama Island (Yun-fat's birthplace) who went to the city to find love and happiness. Alex turned it into a statement about love.' A romantic Lunar New Year comedy, the movie also features Anthony Wong as Dunno, Shan-shui's friend and village lackey; Teresa Mo as Dotty, Firefly's friend and a 'liberated woman'; Carina Lau as Susan, a gung-ho Christian and Shan-shui's new-found city girl-friend; and Chan Fai-hung, a popular Hong Kong DJ playing the bookworm Lam and Firefly's city boyfriend. Much of the comedy and warmth grows out of the chemistry between actors and the sheer pleasure they seem to be having onscreen. Alex Law credits Chow Yun-fat as giving 'a tremendously powerful performance … funny, witty, and touching.'[33]

The film opens with Chow's character in voice-over remembering a childhood ride on the merry-go-round, during which he cries and his mother scolds him for the money she's wasted. 'I always remember about that thirty dollars, so when I grow up I understand about life. You pay to ride the horsey, so you might as well enjoy the ride. That's the old saying, "Laugh while you ride."' Such is the homegrown wisdom and philosophy of Wu Shan-shui, and it serves him well in the impending action. Next shown is the tradition of which Shan-shui is a part and which he later discovers weighs heavily upon him; the camera pans the wall of ancestral portraits in his home, all large (and quite comically) with the face of Chow Yun-fat. Shown in his role as village headman, he visits the local market, school and temple, congratulating the new father No Teeth for spreading his seed and producing a male child. Such are the practices of this unnamed indigenous village, which could be one of many in the New Territories, according to the film's director.

Most of the dialogue is spoken in the Hakka dialect, what Alex Law calls 'native Hong Kongese.' He thinks that *Now You See Love, Now You Don't* is 'probably the only Hong Kong film that uses it.'[34] Its prominence is a good indication of the richness of local detail and the practices that receive attention; according to Chang 'the film had almost thirty sets, mostly constructed on location.' The dialogue is peppered with colloquial expressions, like 'Why don't you watch your mother peel onions?' Men drink alcohol measured by the foot – the more they drink, the more manly they are; women have babies and smile.

When Wu Shan-shui moves to the city, he changes his name from the Hakka to the Cantonese version, Ng Shan-shui. The change, and rivalry between city and village, is represented by the two women in his life, Susan and Firefly. When Susan says 'Oo nai,' offering him food, Firefly corrects her, saying 'In our dialect we say "oo nai" when somebody died or has bad luck or throws up some blood.' Firefly herself confesses that she doesn't want to be thought of as a 'bumpkin,' but the English she has picked up abroad is mostly slang or vulgar, including 'Hello love,' 'Catch you later,' 'Bugger off, wankers,' and 'bloody hell.' Try as she might to adapt to city life, Firefly adheres to the adage 'you can take the girl out of the country, but you can't take the country out of the girl.' By the story's end, Shan-shui has given up being village headman and settled into family life with this 'new woman.'

In one comical scene, the village men discuss women as their fish dry in the sun. The dialogue grows out of local wisdom. Dunno muses, 'Some people say, "Women are like grapevines. They go here, they go there. They go after money. And when it runs out, they go away."' Then No Teeth adds, 'It's said that women are made of water. Because they cry. But they're really acid. That's why they can burn you.' Law depicts 'a very typical village … where men enjoy all kinds of crazy but true privileges over women,' and the overt sexism of the village is reflected in Shan-shui's and Dunno's characterizations and various conversations. When Firefly returns, with a punk hairdo, wearing colorful patterned clothing with brassiere worn outside, torn cut-off jeans, and boots, she embarasses Shan-shui; her outspokenness is as loud as her dress and he loses face in the village.

Shuan-shui's response sets one of the extremes the movie explores, and Firefly the other. To Firefly, he exclaims, 'Good grief! You've changed. You used to be so nice. You were gentle and charming. You used to smile all the time.' Firefly counters, 'All women get mad sometimes. Smile all the time! Stop dreaming.' Confused, Shan-shui muses, 'But Uncle Ming's daughter, No Teeth's wife, Dunno's grandmother, they smile all the time.' Firefly quickly asserts her new-found identity with 'I'm not anybody's grandmother or daughter, I'm Firefly Kwok. That's who I am. Bloody hell, you!', to which Shan-shui responds 'Don't sneer at me. I should never have let you go to England. You sound like Maggie Thatcher.'

Shan-shui's chauvinism and Firefly's temper, and the fact that she has tasted another lifestyle, take her to urban Hong Kong, where her struggle to succeed at work and in her relationships leads to quite comical situations as she adjusts to city living and tries to find a boyfriend. When Shan-shui follows her to town to convince her to return home, her reaction is swift and harsh. Losing face in the fancy restaurant where she is working, she retorts, 'All men are alike. They want a car with a spoiler. They want a spayed cat to catch mice. They want a woman to cook and wash clothes. And to sleep on top of. I tell you, I don't want any of it, you son of a bitch.' In this battle of the sexes, the divide between Shan-shiu and Firefly, and men and women, is visualized by the characters divided from each other by the village river, as the women march off to the city and the men strut in tandem, taunting them across the water. Similarly, later in the film, a city women's consciousness-raising group is juxtaposed to the men's group that is shown subsequently.

Despite their different ways of understanding the world and their place in it, the love between Shan-shui and Firefly is symbolized by the tree found on the headman's property. Shan-shui is about to sell the property, described as 'beautiful land,' because change has come to the village too. Even the Londonized Firefly is shocked. 'Are you really going to sell the land?' she asks. "Well, it's already 1992. 1997 is just around the corner,' Shan-shui answers. Disappointed, Firefly protests, 'But you said we'd build our house here'; to which the practical village headman says, 'Yes, but then this was only $200 a square foot. Now it's worth $4,000 a square foot, dummy.' Their names are carved in hearts on the tree, the significance of which is carried over into the city scenes in which a tree is grown into the wall where Firefly lives, giving it 'good feng shui.' When the country boy moves to the city to win back his intended, he opens a store directly across the street from the residence; this enables him to look up to Firefly's window and she to look down into his store.

In a comic twist on the Ah Can structure, Shan-shui and Dunno decide to be 'trendsetters' and establish themselves in the city. Their conversation represents the dreams of many Chinese immigrants, incorporating the myth of self-made men as well as idealizing many well-known Hong Kong business corporations.

Shan-shui: 'Dunno, the world has changed … we can't hang around the village forever. It's a dead end. I think we should move downtown. Learn English, wear suits. We got to improve ourselves … Look at Lee Ka-shing.'
Dunno: 'Who?'

Shan-shui: 'Lee used to make plastic flowers. You know what Run Run Shaw used to do?'

Dunno: 'I dunno.'

Shan-shui: 'He used to be a foot messenger, running errands. Then the Queen knighted him. Now everybody calls him "Sir Run Run." You know what Rockefeller originally did?'

Dunno: 'Busted rocks.'

Shan-shui: 'No, that was your mother. He was the fellow who carried the rocks. Was any one of them village headman? ... I'm already way ahead of them ... I'm moving to Central to open a business. I guarantee you in three years I'll be mayor ... I'll take over Hong Kong Bank ... Chairman of the Board of Swires ... General Manager of Kowloon Motor Bus ... I'll run Hong Kong Land ... Take over Jardine Mattheson ... I'll be on top of the whole damned colony!'

With much wheeling and dealing and hard work, Shan-shui remakes himself, a miracle of upward mobility, and becomes a financial and social success, at least equally matched with Firefly, who has been tamed by the city. According to Alex Law, 'the film tries to reveal the two extremes of Hong Kong: the old and the new, the country and the urban, the east and the west ... in a comical way.'

The film concludes with the union of three properly matched couples. Shan-shui and Firefly are rescued from a precarious situation and embrace. Dunno and Susan pick guavas and see ducks at the duck pond, her preference for 'strong men, real men, macho men' satisfied. 'I like to see men sweat when they work. Wow!' she exclaims. Meanwhile, Lam rides Dotty on a bicycle through the coutryside. 'It's man's responsibility to drive and women's responsibility to ride,' the former feminist happily explains. Six months later, the couples get married. Shan-shui becomes 'a first-class family man,' which entails him wearing an apron while his kids throw food at him as he holds the baby. 'Little devils,' he calls them. 'Look at me, you little shit! Stop it!' Firefly admonishes them, 'Goldy, Silver, stop bothering your dad,' while sticking the baby in the fridge. Our last look is at the ancestral portraits still hanging on the wall, observing the scene.

TEN

WHOSE CHINESE FEAST?

Hong Kong comedies examine the life of the average person in detail, revealing patterns of behavior, thoughts and feelings, and living conditions. Gender relations have served as the subject matter for some Hong Kong comedies, either reflecting traditional male–female relations or challenging them. These comedies draw upon the 1950s' and 1960s' Cantonese opera movies, in many of which the female Yam Kim-fai and Pak Suet-sin together played male and female roles, respectively; these movies generally borrow from traditional Cantonese operas, in which men played women's roles. Other movies privilege heterosexual relationships, like Lunar New Year comedies, which pair off heterosexual couples in connubial bliss. As Gayle Rubin observes, 'at the most general level, the social organization of sex rests upon gender, obligatory heterosexuality, and the constraint of female sexuality.'[1]

One of the 1980s' romantic comedies that reaffirms gender norms is Chor Yuen's *Diary of a Big Man* (1988). The 33-year-old protagonist Chow Ting-fat (Chow Yun-fat) recalls writing a student essay in which he wished for 'six Benzes, several flats, and a beautiful wife.' A successful stockbroker working in the Lippo Building along with his pal Chi-hung (Waise Lee), Ting-fat meets Joey (Joey Wong) and Sally (Sally Yip), falling in love with both while Chi-hung courts fellow office worker Linda. The literal translation of the Chinese title, *Big Husband's Diary*, indicates the structure. Chow Yun-fat, dressed in tuxedo and wearing glasses, speaks directly into the camera, recording his diary entries and commenting on the dramatic action. 'What will my destiny be? Only one wedding ring. Who shall

I give it to? Wait and see.' Many compare Chow's performance in this comedy of errors to that of Cary Grant in screwball comedies like *I Was a Male War Bride* and *Bringing Up Baby*. Through a series of events Ting-fat marries both women, Joey in New York and Sally in Paris; with the assistance of Chi-hung, each remains unaware of the other's existence. Complications arise when the air hostess Sally decides to clip her wings to remain home with her husband. It is only a matter of time before the ruse is uncovered.

Women here are portrayed as objects, like the honeymoon souvenirs on Ting-fat's desk of the Statue of Liberty (Joey) and the Eiffel Tower (Sally), and as commodities. 'We handle stocks and shares,' Ting-fat tells Chi-hung; 'you have to keep the market going.' He arranges his schedule like that of the commodities company, 'buying' and 'active' in both the American (Joey) and European (Sally) markets. Eventually, the 'global market' is on to him, and Chi-hung and Linda are drawn into the intrigues, as are a nosy cop (Kent Chang) and the 'object' of his desire, a female cop. The solution to the problem is that Ting-fat becomes a 'big man,' a practicing Muslim with two happy wives. Dressed in Arab garb in a harem setting, served by Joey and Sally, he tells the camera, 'I'm a polygamist now. I can have unlimited wives, but I'm too kind. And so I'll be nice to my two wives.' Chi-hung appears to have outdone him with four wives, one of whom is the pouting and dissatisfied Linda. 'Very nice!' Ting-fat proclaims, reminding the audience of the theme song that underscores the movie's zany comedy. Far from politically correct, this movie is representative of the era in tone and theme. Just as important as the films' gender inequality is the normative value of the heterosexual relationships portrayed, something that has carried on through the 1990s.

Romantic comedies serve as a prime vehicle for examining gender relations. Hong Kong began the process of remapping itself with Margaret Thatcher's 1982 visit to Beijing; in the wake of the events in Tiananmen Square and on the advent of the handover, old and new cartographies coexisted. In times of flux, numerous contested terrains became apparent; these included, in the movies, alternative depictions of males and females. A ground-breaking mainstream gender-bending movie, Peter Chan's 1994 *He's a Woman, She's a Man*, challenged a conservative society. A crowd pleaser, the film was the eighth highest grossing film released in Hong Kong that year; two years later, its sequel, *Who's the Woman, Who's the Man?* fared less successfully.[2]

Peter Chan's movies possess an ordinary brilliance, mining the lives of average people and revealing gems. In *He's a Woman, She's a Man*, Wing (Anita Yuen) is young, idealistic and working-class, living in crowded and cluttered conditions near the airport. The movie's opening scene shows the debris that is a part of her life – crushed Coke cans, peanut shells, and food wrappers, all seen close-up from the viewpoint of a spunky cockroach she is trying to eliminate – before we see Wing. She is called 'an ordinary person'; she's a fan who lives vicariously through two pop stars – producer and songwriter Sam (Leslie Cheung), and his protégée, singer Rose (Carina Lau).

Disguising herself as a man to get near the famous couple, Wing succeeds in her ruse as a man (Wing), but falls in love with a man (Sam) as a woman pretending to be a man (Lam Lee Wing/Wing), while a woman (Rose) falls in love with her as a man (Wing), and a man (Sam) falls in love with her as a man (Wing). The complications that ensue provide a wry comment on the power of pop culture machinery, showing the business from both insider and outsider perspectives. In a city where the *Oriental Daily*, Hong Kong's largest circulation Chinese newspaper, devotes four pages daily to the entertainment industry and its stars, and *Next* magazine (the equivalent of *People*) is filled with the latest gossip and stars' pictures at staged spectacle events, the film makes evident the alienation of 'ordinary' people by their work and from themselves. The entertainment and media industries go hand-in-hand with late capital cultures, where identities and entertainment must be purchased and people rarely create their own. Both the music and film industries are targeted.

Rose is Wing's idol, and the story of Rose and Sam her idea of perfect love. The reality shows something else. When Rose appears at annual music awards, Sam is off jamming with his deceased father's musician friends, belting out a pretty mean 'Twist and Shout.' He and Rose have separate living quarters, so Sam can have some space; significantly, Sam is allergic to roses. The couple have an arrangement to see other people, as long as discretion rules. Neglected by her former lover, Rose takes up with Wing; on discovering that 'he' is gay, she accepts 'him' as a 'sister' and pours her heart out about Sam's silence and moodiness.

Wing discovers that the couple's lives are as fraught with problems as hers; she learns to value herself, in opposition to the lifestyles and commodity consumption – both of the couple and herself – sold to her by the media. She starts under-

FEAR OF KISSING   Leslie Cheung and
Anita Yuen in Peter Chan's *He's a Woman,
She's a Man*

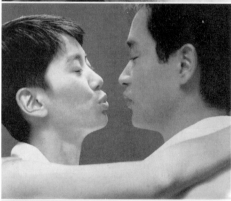

KISS ONE   Leslie Cheung and Anita Yuen
in Peter Chan's *He's a Woman, She's a Man*

KISS TWO   Anita Yuen and Anita Mui
in Peter Chan's *Who's the Woman,
Who's the Man?*

courtesy of Kazumi Fukumoto; permission of Peter Chan

standing who she is. Wing's identity crisis, however, is just the tip of the iceberg. Sam's is the more pronounced and ambiguous. Peter Chan says that he is drawing upon 'a formula that has always worked,' from ancient Chinese stories, where genders are confused by characters in disguise, whether Mulan-style where a woman appears to be a man, or the style appropriated by Tsui Hark in the third-century Eastern Jin dynasty period-piece *The Lovers* (1994), where a man falls in love with the person he thought was his best friend and male (who is later revealed to be female). Chan relates:

> The guy fell in love with a guy because he didn't really know the guy was a girl … I was just trying to add a contemporary touch, the music industry, and also dealing with one thing these age old stories never deal with – a sexual identity crisis.[3]

Sam's sexual identity crisis builds through the film in a series of comical scenes. First, he mistakenly concludes that Wing is gay; this conclusion is based on eavesdropping and innuendo, techniques similarly practiced by the media. Second, Eric Tsang plays the over-the-top gay character Auntie, Sam's associate and confidante, serving as an expression of Sam's inner voice. In a hilarious scene between the two, set in a buffet-style restaurant, Auntie picks numerous selections from the vast display of sweets. 'I'll have this, this, this, and this,' Auntie says, lastly pointing at the smiling gay waiter's penis. While fondling a large carrot he passes on to Sam, Auntie explains to him,

> See, there are some things you cannot face. I don't understand why you are so scared of Wing…. You just don't understand our way of thinking…. If I see something I like, I'll feel it, touch it to see whether there's any response. If it's good, I'll go for it, just do it. If not, don't waste our time.

As they finish their meal, Auntie lays it on the line: 'The question is not whether Wing is gay, but whether or not you are. So are you gay?' Fast, jerky movement ensues as the camera zooms in close-up on Sam while a taunting and jittery sax plays a riff.

The question 'Who is Sam?' serves as the plotting line of the story. He has been so preoccupied making others, including Rose and now Wing, he's not sure. As his attraction for Wing grows, he proves himself in bed with Rose, not out of love but out of doubt of his manhood. A series of kissing (or near-kissing) scenes serves to up the ante and increase Sam's worries. As Sam and Wing collaborate at the piano on the beautiful and inspiring song 'Jui' ('Chase'), they almost kiss, but Wing pulls back. Later, the Bert and Ernie puppets Wing talks to (which likewise 'speak' her inner thoughts and fears) are used by Sam and Wing to talk honestly to each other about their feelings; here, the puppets kiss for them. Next, again at the piano, Sam takes the initiative and passionately kisses Wing; as she begins to respond, he pulls back, horrified at what he's done, and flees. Of course, the audience watching the film accepts the relationship throughout, knowing that Wing is really a young woman. At the film's end, Wing appears as her true self, in a white dress; a final, romantic kiss between the two in an elevator restores the place of heterosexuality.

Nevertheless, Sam's phobia concerns himself and reflects many straight men's fear of gays, stemming from an anxiety within. Several times an updated version of Michelangelo's 'Creation of Adam' from the Sistine Chapel ceiling appears, featuring Adam with a microphone in his hand, and used as an advertisement for the male singer contest for which Wing auditions. At one point Sam stares at the image. Prominent, of course, is the athletic and perfect nude body of Adam, with male anatomy visible. Michelangelo's image raises the issue of origins; 'where do I come from and who am I?' are questions that preoccupy Sam. Whereas the first film was mostly played for laughs, the gender ambiguities it raised are explored more seriously in the sequel. Also capitalized on in the second film are Sam's selfishness and fears. The first story's message, 'love conquers all,' is supplanted in the second by 'love is messy,' or, in Chan's words, 'a relationship is a relationship; that's reality, that's life.' If the first film plays strictly for laughs, the second has many comedic moments, but rides between comedy and a more serious theme about relationships. Says Chan, 'If the first one is a fantasy, the second one is an anti-statement of the first.' He relates that he was thinking of one of his favorite films, Stanley Donen's *Two for the Road*, with a nod to the Rosebud motif in Orson Welles's *Citizen Kane*. What happens after 'and they lived happily ever after'?

The story of *Who's the Woman, Who's the Man?* picks up where the previous film left off, in the elevator, with Sam and Wing making a promise and a deal. His first spoken line – also the film's opening line – is, 'I don't care if you're a man or a woman. All I know is that I love you.' 'What next?' she asks, and he replies, 'Move in with me.' When she does, she brings her childhood friend Yu Lo, now called Fish (Jordan Chan), along with an entire menagerie of furnishings. The legendary singer Fan Fan (Anita Mui) moves in downstairs, along with her lesbian assistant O (Theresa Lee), and Fan Fan becomes Wing's idol. Both Wing and Sam make adjustments to their new living arrangements. As Sam's girlfriend, Wing takes on a position similar to Rose in the first film, even though Rose reappears briefly. Wing also maintains her public image as an androgynous male pop star, while Sam suffers from writer's block. Although Wing serves as the cornerstone for the average person, the film's point of view still centers on Sam, and the various disruptions and changes produced by the comings and goings of others lead him to re-evaluate his life, overcoming fears and selfishness, and grow up.

Changes and similarities between the past story and the present one occur. This time, Wing as the star is accepting a music award, and Sam attends. Riding in the limo with them is Fish, who assumes Wing's working-class viewpoint as hundreds of fans jam around the car. With a broad grin and a royal wave of the hand to the fans pressed against the glass, Fish comments inside the enclosed car, 'Thank you, thank you. I like you too. Am I pretty? Wing, your money! Your big mansion and fancy cars … I pity your parents. You're too fat to be a fan. You look like a pig.' As Fish runs interference so Wing can get into the auditorium, Sam is accosted by an overzealous fan. Grabbing him by the shirt collar, the fan threatens, 'You have to be good to Wing or I'll kill you.' Breaking away, Sam is confronted by the media with questions like, 'Has Wing bought you a house?', 'Do critics say you are "the new comrades of the era"?', and 'Does your new piece "Gay Man Forties" say you're out?' 'Comrades' is a slang term for gays in Hong Kong; 'Gay Man Forties' is an in-joke reference to Leslie Cheung's age and well-known 1996 World Tour Concert, in which he performed in red-sequined women's pumps. Throughout the scene, Sam's version of 'Twist and Shout' plays in the background. Poor Sam is just beginning to recover when, during the acceptance speech for Best Male Vocalist of 1996, Wing, like Rose before him/her, thanks Sam and says, 'I love you, Sam.' This time Sam sinks down in his seat. So begin gender identity problems for Sam.

Sam is uncomfortable with Wing underfoot; her return to work, however, leaves him dissatisfied. As she renews her career and takes up with Fan Fan, he plays the role of jealous partner and housebound husband. The public man/

private woman gender identification theorized by Jean Bethke Elshtain is inverted here.[4] Wing tells Sam, who is still in bed, 'I'm going to work, you stay home and compose. If you're bored, go shopping with Auntie. Or go see a movie. I'll come back right after work, okay?' The stunned Sam replies, 'Your eyeglasses,' which Wing is about to forget. Scenes of Sam before a magnifying mirror in the bathroom emphasize his identity crisis, as do the maskings and misrepresentations of the major characters at the costume party Auntie throws for Wing. Initially mistaking Fan Fan for Wing, because both wear Whoopi Goldberg masks, Sam engages her in conversation because of their common interest in African music, but when Fan Fan, not knowing the Woody Allen-masked man is Sam, mentions that Sam Koo is gay, Sam feels his manhood threatened and proves himself (only to himself) by having sex with her. As Bertell Ollman notes,

> What ocurs in the real world is reflected in people's minds: essential elements of what it means to be a man are grasped as independent and, in some cases, all powerful entities, whose links with him appear other than what they really are.... The whole has been broken up into numerous parts whose interrelation in whole can no longer be ascertained.[5]

Director Peter Chan expressed his bewilderment that 'most audiences, especially women audiences, did not hate him [Sam] at all, even in the beginning.... They had no problem with guys like that: this is what guys are, I've known guys like that, and that's life, you know. I think it's weird.'

Rather than be honest with Wing, Sam smoothes over his absence with flowers, a custom he fell into with Rose. He keeps his thoughts to himself; when Wing brings up the trip to Africa that he has wanted to make for a long time for musical inspiration, he orders her never to mention Africa again – a guilty reaction to his sleeping with Fan Fan. As Wing tries to please Sam, their relationship falters as Sam treats her more and more like Rose. When problems arise, he is never around, but always returns with flowers. He withdraws into himself selfishly. It is all about him. Thus, Wing turns to Fan Fan for solace and finds someone who cares. Fan Fan indirectly points to Sam's selfishness when, in the intimacy of her bedroom, she tells Wing 'When men like someone, they would make themselves happy. When women like someone, they would make their partner happy. And then, they will naturally feel happy.' Fan Fan massages her foot; Wing comments how good it feels, not knowing before now because with Sam she always gave the massage.

When Wing and Fan Fan are cast together in a cross-dressing film, Fan Fan's Rhett to Wing's Scarlett, Sam witnesses a kissing scene between them, following Fan Fan's announcement to him that she thinks Wing is happier with her than with Sam and that anything is possible, to which Sam retorts, 'He is not my boyfriend. She is my girlfriend.' The tension mounts, and the scene is reshot twelve times. On the thirteenth take, the women kiss passionately and Sam freaks out, as usual escaping. He returns home with flowers, only to find the two women in bed together. Chan insists, 'It's really not about homosexuality, the movie's not about that. The movie's about two people connecting at a very platonic level.' The shared intimacy between the women is significant, as is Sam's reaction. Sam runs away.

Just as Wing has confided in her, Fan Fan has opened her heart to Wing. She confesses that she has been robbed of her childhood.

> When you were skipping jump rope, I was learning how to dance. When you were learning, studying, I was backstage learning lines. When everyone was talking about love, first love, I've already played the bride eighteen times in the movies, sung scores of lovesongs. If I could have my innocence, my first love, that would be great.

Wing asks, 'What kind of first love would you choose?' Fan Fan answers, 'A rabbit. Kind. Simple. Innocent.' Her words underscore what we've learned about Fan Fan, who has been given a lifetime achievement award for her music, having begun in the business at the age of five. She has spent the last ten years searching for her rabbit. She was 'spotted at carnival in Rio in 1987 dancing the samba with four pineapples on her head, windsurfing near an unknown island in the South Pacific in 1989, and in the war zone in Mozambique in 1992 feeding the war-torn orphans.' For this world-weary traveller, a little comfort and renewed belief are not too much to ask. Wing, in Fan Fan's eyes, is the rabbit she has been searching for, and, ironically, just as Fan Fan discovers her innocence, Wing undergoes the process of losing hers.

Having been abandoned by Sam once again, Wing leaves and boards a plane to Africa because 'Fish said it was the furthest place away from Hong Kong.' Hurt by Sam and the discovery that the promise she and Sam made has become a lie, and confused by her own feelings, she doesn't know what else to do. The older Sam, however, finally does; he stands before the African landscape mural in his study, just completed, a surprise from Wing. The animals miraculously come to life and tears come to Sam's eyes. He runs through the streets just as Wing did in the first movie, and scenes are intercut between the two endings. He arrives just in time to sit next to Wing. 'Let's go home,' Sam tells her. 'Can we still go back?' asks Wing, uncertain. Sam answers, 'Why not? No matter what happened, there were ups and downs, it's still our home.' But Wing prods deeper. 'If after a few years, it doesn't work and we part again, then what?' Sam insists, 'It won't happen.' But Wing won't let it go. 'What if it does? In case it does?' Sam continues, 'If you don't give us a chance today, how do you know what will happen tomorrow? Promise me.' 'Promise you what?' asks Wing. 'Promise me,' Sam says, 'take the challenge, marry me.' Shot in a close-up two-shot throughout their conversation, the camera moves closer as they kiss passionately, a grown-up story about the reality of relationships.

This ending, and Rose's last appearance in the first film, have in common the situation on the mind of many Hong Kongers in the 1990s, their future in relation to the return. The crisis of identity, and Hong Kong's unique situation, can be represented in numerous ways. Accepting another music award, the 'Samless' Rose thanks him for

> helping an ordinary woman blossom into a rose.... And because of you, I can stand alone in the future. Whether I succeed or fail, I will face the unknown challenges of the future with confidence. Sam, I won't let you down. I promise I will be standing here again next year.

Then she announces her planned concert on the Mainland.

Food features prominently in many Hong Kong movies, including comedies. If there is a single phenomenon that is common to all the movies, it's eating, perhaps the most vital necessity of living. Director Stanley Tong suggests that food's prominence in Hong Kong cinema is due to the colony's status as a gourmand's paradise as well as to people's desire in the film industry for a good meal.[6] He says,

> Hong Kong is known to be the best food center in the world. For Chinese food, Hong Kong is the best place. People in the industry, because they work so hard, they always go for good food and are willing to spend a lot of money on food. It's become a major thing for everybody, especially in the industry. Hong Kong is called 'the heaven of food' center. You can have any kind of food from anywhere in the world – Greek, Indian, American, French, Italian, German, Dutch, Swiss, Taiwanese, Indonesian, whatever.

Others suggest that, 'Apart from patronizing cinemas, Hong Kongers are keen on eating out. Restaurants often provide an alternative venue for socializing, given that most homes are not spacious enough to entertain large numbers of guests.'[7] As described earlier, the two ways that food functions in Hong Kong films relate to *jing* (survival) and *qing* (emotive feelings).

A large part of food stories is about bringing people, especially families, together, and this theme, along with others, appears in Tsui Hark's *Chinese Feast* (1995). The movie begins with a gastronomic feast for the eyes and stomach. With the opening credits, a sumptuous display of traditional Chinese dishes is viewed, as the camera slowly pans in one long take over the carefully laid out courses on a richly brocaded table, the hundreds of dishes creating a detailed and broad patterning effect.

While part of the story is about reuniting former master chef Lui Kit with his lover, and a rebellious daughter with her father, Tsui Hark uses food as a symbol of Chinese pride, achievement, and identity. The scene cuts to a photograph of the Forbidden City at sunset, and then to the present-day Daioyutai Hotel in Beijing, where a food competition is being held between Lui Kit of Guangzhou (Kenny Bee) and Lung Kwun-bo of Hong Kong (Zhao Wen Zhou). The event's seriousness is emphasized through the announcements, judgements and ritual categories of the food prepared – rice, food sculpture, and fish. Cut and contrast, five years later, to Hong Kong and the Hotel Mandarin of Canada, which is recruiting Chinese chefs to emigrate, where successful Triad member Sun (Leslie Cheung) has entered the competition and turns it into a shambles. Sun is a wannabe chef who wishes to emigrate because his girlfriend already lives in Canada and because he no longer wants to do the 'bad things' his Triad member brother requires of him. When Kwan-bo overhears Sun's conversation, he sends him to a competing restaurant, Qing Han, owned by Au Siu-fung (Law Kar-ying), as a joke, and the comedy begins.

Enter the heavy Wong Wing (Hung Yan-yan), a wealthy, power-hungry and conniving Mainlander intent on controlling the Hong Kong food business. He is the director of the Supergroup. Riding in his limo, twisting his gold jewelry, he hatches his plan: 'The food industry is the kingdom of Chinese. I'll conquer it step by step. I'll control the food industry of Hong Kong soon. Qing Han is the oldest restaurant in the district. So it is my first target.' Showing up at the

courtesy/permission of Mandarin Films

GUNG HEI FAT CHOY   The cast of Tsui Hark's *Chinese Feast*

restaurant, he challenges Siu-fung to a Qing Han Imperial Feast competition for ownership of the restaurant or $50 million. Both demonstrate their expertise in the kitchen, whetting the audience's appetite with an amazing demonstration of cooking skills, a martial-arts-with-food extravaganza, with accompanying sound effects identical to those used for swordplay; the process is described with a master's eye for detail and the results wondrous – mouth-watering crispy noodle with beef, and sweet and sour pork.

Wong Wing has bribed Siu-fung's employees, all of whom abandon the chef; the shock and a heart condition lead to a heart attack and hospitalization, and Siu-fung's punk daughter and the Triad join forces to save the restaurant. Kwan-bo comes to their aid, and they find Liu Kit, a chef who knows how to prepare Qing Han Feast. A mini re-enactment of a period-piece set in the Forbidden City is intercut into the story with splendid setting and lavish costumes, as Kwan-bo's voice-over narration describes the history of the event.[8] The antagonism between the Manchurian Qing and Han Chinese, resolved with the intervention of food, and the later conflict between factions, including the Niu (Wong Wing) and the Chiu (Siu-fung), serves as an allegory for relations between Mainlanders and Hong Kongers today.

Food as representative of *jing* (emotion) is obvious in the punkish Ka-wai's transformation from a daughter uninterested in the family business to one eager to be a chef and play her filial role. Her failures at cooking reveal her struggle and underscore her eventual success at the story's end. A touching scene between Liu Kit and his former lover is reinforced by food and tender music. She tells him, 'I want you to cook good things for me to restore my feeling for food. You have to make Qing Han for me.' Apparent in the Qing Han preparation is the communal effort made on the part of Liu Kit, Kwan-bo, Ka-wai, her father, and Sun, reinforced by the theme song, about working together, no matter how difficult the times.[9] Sung by a chorus with a rousing beat, it also plays at the close while the cast of this Lunar New Year comedy toasts its audience.

The competition progresses over three days with three main courses prepared, each stage described in loving detail, an esoteric exposition on the fine subtleties of great cooking, from 'Snowy Palm' (bear claw with sturgeon) to 'Put up the Mountain' (elephant trunk braised and stewed with wild birds). Tension builds with a tie, the audience getting an insider's look at the tribulations of the Qing Han restaurant family. On the third day, they succeed with 'Golden Eyes and Burning Brain' (bean curd simmered in chicken, duck, and cuckoo brains) over Wong's 'Monkey King and Shark' (goat brain); Wong, dressed in Manchu Emperor garb, loses face and is left disputing the 'agreement' signed with Fung.

All appear in the communal kitchen at the film's end, crowded with the entire cast and crew, and the camera pulls back in the dining room to reveal the hanging microphone as Leslie Cheung raises his glass with 'Cheers' and the others, including Hung Yan-yan, toast. Offered are two imagined wish-fulfillment futures for Hong Kong and the Mainland; it is left to the audience to decide which is best. The film highlights the industry and commitment of the smaller Qing Han group, their hard work validated as ensuring success (substitute Hong Kong, its size and its economic miracle in contrast to the Mainland, its size and its untapped markets). Closing with the real Chinese feast, the celebration of cast, crew, and director in a toast to their camaraderie at the end of their production, the Hong Kong film industry and its ability to capture an international audience is acclaimed.

Marx asserted that history occurs twice, 'the first time as tragedy; the second time as farce.' Comparing Woo's 'heroic bloodshed' films to 'Triad boyz' movies and the parodies which followed them, this statement rings true in the celluloid world. Elements of farce, parody, and satire abound in recent Hong Kong comedies; nowhere is this more apparent than in the movies of Stephen Chiau, currently Hong Kong's number one box-office draw. Chiau's 1996 *God of Cookery* (literally *Eating God*, co-directed with Lee Lik-chi) parodies established Hong Kong movie trends: it is a food movie fused with gambling and Triad movies. The resulting cinematic hotpot indicates the self-reflexive and insular nature of recent Hong Kong comedies, as 'local' style makes a last-ditch effort to assert its unique identity.

Like *Chinese Feast* and others, *God of Cookery* features close-up sequences of food preparation which cause viewers to salivate, in addition to elaborate cooking contests where competitors' dishes are expertly described. Chiau's movie adds contrasts between the restaurateurs' dishes (King's Fried Rice, Multifish, Secret Roast Goose, and Buddha Jumping Wall) and the simpler fare of the working class (Assorted Noodle and Barbecued Pork, Fried Egg and Rice). The 28th Competition for the 'God of Cookery' takes place aboard one of the well-known Jumbo Floating Seafood Restaurants in the harbor, where Chiau's character, 'Stephen Chiau,' announces, 'There's no God of Cookery. Maybe everyone is God of Cookery, even parents, brothers, sisters and lovers. As long as they have heart, everyone can become God of Cookery.'

Kwan Yin (Karen Mok) descends from the heavens with two Bodhisattvas, to commend him: 'You finally know the truth of food.' Of course, this truth is discovered only through the hard journey he makes via food preparation. This includes the 'Deep First Love Gold Silver Lovers' Set Meal,' a pricey HK$99.90

at his branch restaurant, a rip-off of the Assorted Noodle dish he steals from a Temple Street Stall;[10] and finally, the 'Sorrowful Rice,' made from the heart, with love, in memory of the 'most tasty thing' he has ever eaten, prepared by a woman in love with him.

The plotline follows Stephen Chiau's fall from grace as the reigning 'God of Cookery'; Chiau plays his typical obnoxious, mean, and egotistical characterization, yet somehow redeems himself before the film's end. In this story he has sold out his cooking skills for money; he has become a greedy business entrepreneur and scam artist, arranging numerous spectacles and gimmicks to preserve his reputation, while delivering an inferior product (without heart) at his fifty restaurants. A big boss Triad/businessman (Ng Man-tat) proposes a new product: instant cup noodles featuring the God of Cookery's image on every package. Double-crossed by the big-timer and his protégé Bill Tung (Vincent Kuk), Chiau loses everything; forced to start over, this time he finds love and financial success.

Chiau's character as a 'god' of cookery, of course, alludes to the blockbuster 'God of Gamblers' characterization Chow Yun-fat made famous in 1989 and reprised in 1994 in *God of Gamblers' Return*. Chiau, however, adds the mischievousness and heartlessness of his usual characterizations. *God of Cookery*'s opening title duplicates that of the second film, and while the gambler disappears for a year before a big competition, Chiau does so for a month. Similarly, in the first gambling film, the character is bopped on the head and loses his memory; in the cooking movie, Chiau is thrown from a truck, hit on the head and seems to lose his sense of who he is. Using the gambling, food and cooking references, Chiau's movie emphasizes them as business enterprises, allowing his character, united with Temple Street muscle, to 'become public companies and collect capital. We can sell shares and do real estate business, nuts. We can make a subdivision in the stock market. With the dividends, we needn't work at all.' Lampooning the money, luck, and hard work formula of the 'little people' who make up the backbone of Hong Kong's economy, Chiau suggests that the ultimate goal is not to work at all. With the success of 'pissing beef balls,' quality-controlled, canned and on the shelves of 2,800 supermarkets and convenience stores, his character concludes, 'I find it like a dream. It also proves Hong Kong is a place for miracles. If you work hard, all dreams may come true,' thereby reiterating the wish-fulfillment projection of Hong Kong in so many movies.

Triad movies are parodied in this story, where the big-timer's idea that 'doing whatever you like proves your power' is reduced to a food title and restaurant conglomerate. What better industry than food, however, to illustrate basic survival of the fittest, where your next meal may be your last? The small-time Temple Street Triads fight over rights to food dishes, and even their leader, Sister Turkey (Karen Mok), is named after food. They join forces with Stephen Chiau against the big-timers, and there's a face-off between the groups. 'I don't mean to show others I'm capable,' Chiau confesses, 'I just want to tell others that I can get back what I have lost,' a direct reference to the characterizations of Chow Yun-fat and Ti Lung in *A Better Tomorrow*. Furthermore, Sister Turkey's song, which Chiau mutters like an epiphany during the competition, doubles as Triad-style code and cook's kitchen motto.[11] Karen Mok's Sister Turkey upstages Chiau, as she grounds the movie in a recognizable type (hard on the outside, soft inside) but humanizes the character as well, moving beyond the others' stereotyping. With a disfigured face and mouth, she is almost unrecognizable until the story's end when she appears, first as Kwan Yin, a heavenly vision, and then as an earthly one, as the 'pretty woman' who wins Chiau's heart, thereby reinforcing the notion of Hong Kong as the place where miracles happen.

Another late 1996 release, *Viva Erotica* (literally *Sex Man Woman*), took on the film industry as its subject. Co-directed by Derek Yee and Law Chi-leung, the movie, full of insider jokes, serves as a humorous disputation on the state of Hong Kong film. An unemployed art filmmaker named Sing (Leslie Cheung) is persuaded by Chung (Law Kar-ying), his producer, to direct a Category III film financed by a Triad boss named Wong (Paul Chun). Witness to the way in which the Triad deals with his problems, the apprehensive Sing comes undone as his art film is rewritten before his eyes. He is forced to use Mango, the Triad boss's untalented young girlfriend (Shu Qi), as the lead. Her Triad 'Sugar Daddy' suggests plot elements and titles. '*Double Seven, Dork and Dorkier*.... Add in some eroticism and violence.... It'll be better to have her do more scenes in the nude, right? ... It will profit for sure, especially in the overseas market,' he insists. When difficulties arise on set, the producer tries to usurp the director's role; once the director resolves this struggle, he faces another in his personal life as his relationship deteriorates with his neglected girlfriend May (Karen Mok).

With the last shot in the can, an electrical fire burns down the set and the filmstock of the climactic scene. Unwilling to listen to Chung's reasonable request for 'just a little more money to complete the film in order to profit,' the Triad boss refuses to invest more, intent instead on editing and selling the movie as it is to the European underground market. Not just his profit, but power, is the bottom line. 'I'm a businessman, not an artist,' he retorts, fed up with the movie business. An argument breaks out into a fight along a narrow hallway, a melee ensuing as Wong's Triad muscle and cast and crew go at each other. All the stories that anyone has ever heard about Triads in the movie industry are brought to mind. 'The worst producer, director and crew. You're lucky to have a job. Without me, you eat shit,' Wong tells them. Even Mango's cajoling is met with a cold and cruel, 'Shut up, woman. What a big mouth.' Chung decides to make amends; one of the stunned crew remarks, 'You broke the boss's nose. We're in trouble. He's going to kill us.' Triad investment in the industry thus depicted exemplifies Haile Gerima's point that 'the power structure finances all cultural activities on the basis of its own notions and its own criteria of aesthetics.'[12]

One interesting question posed in this movie is, what do audiences want? The film opens with the first of many fantasy sequences in the director's mind, a fairly intense sex scene between Sing and May, all legs, thrusts, and Leslie Cheung's naked bottom. Close-up into the camera, May, a woman on top, commands her lover, 'Fuck me, come on, fuck me,' biting him on the neck. The scene lasts for five minutes before being exposed as a fantasy woven in with the couple's love-making. Set to throbbing guitar and sax, red-tinted, with pelting raindrops to suggest the passion, the payoff begins when the camera pulls back to reveal the couple on a set, and the crew behind the scenes, with producer Chung yelling 'Cut!' as Sing cries out as well. The film cuts to Sing's impassioned face, written upon it his worst nightmare, being directed instead of directing. 'No way, I can't stop now,' he yells. Later, a puzzled May asks 'Why did you yell "Cough"? I wasn't coughing,' mistaking 'cut' for 'cough.' After this scene, and notwithstanding several 'sex scenes,' the movie settles into being a film about filmmaking, not the erotic film its Category III designation suggests. The nudity and simulated sex scenes play more like adult MTV videos than a soft-core porn movie. One sex fantasy uses speeded-up, at-a-distance, cartoon-like action, set to the 'William Tell Overture.'

Many scenes focus upon the camaraderie of unemployed filmmakers who gather together to commiserate with each other over their beers, discuss rumors, and

SHOOTING MOVIES Leslie Cheung in Derek Yee's *Viva Erotica*

evaluate fellow directors. These scenes ring true, as do the doubts which pursue Sing, like 'other than making movies, what can you do?,' and 'I just want to get my message across.' His relations with his producer, girlfriend, and mother also reflect the complexities involved in inhabiting both the world of illusion and reality, and being the director who tries to maneuver between them. 'No one's interested in your biography,' Chung tells him, 'There's no point in making an art movie. Nonsensical movies are good too,' while his girlfriend tells his mother, 'He cares only for his work. It's hard on me.' Sing's mother advises her, 'Leave him, then. My husband was a director too. He was always living in his fantasy world. He didn't know how to care for his family or himself. Just like a little kid. Some of them will never grow up.... Unless he changes, you'll be unhappy.' Reminiscent of Fellini's Guido in *8½*, Woody Allen's filmmaker in *Stardust Memories*, and Jean-Pierre Leaud's in Truffaut's *Day for Night*, the self-absorbed and preoccupied Sing is an apt caricature of certain Hong Kong directors.

Several directors are named in the film, and some appear in cameos. As an art-film director, Wong Kar-wai can be readily identified with Sing's aspirations. Watching the first rushes, which Sing has filmed with Wong's signature blurred-action style, producer Chung objects: 'There's too much movement, everything's blurred. You can't see Mango in the nude. This is a blue movie, you know? It doesn't have to be artistic like Wong Kar-wai but commercial like Wong Jing.' Later, Anthony Wong appears in a cameo as Wong Jing, the antithesis of Wong Kar-wai. One of the crew likes his movies, commenting on his 'definite block-buster with Stephen Chiau,' while Dicky, Sing's cinematographer, who had previously been fired by Wong, says they're 'awful'; Sing adds, 'Everyone knows he's an asshole.' Chung emphasizes that 'Wong Jing's film still holds the highest box office record in the past two years.... You'll understand better.... See how the audience enjoys it, swearing, laughing?' In this way, *Viva Erotica* sets the extremes of Hong Kong filmmaking, noting both its commercial intent and its artistic merit. That Sing injects his vision into the film he's making and gets his actors to 'convince me it's real' suggest the power of filmmaking; that Sing is making another skin flick at the end of this story, with cast and crew in the nude, implies business as usual. Similarly, what does one make of Mango, whose faked moaning is supplanted by passionate groans? Does she indeed register the 'persistent sense of dislocation between the unrealized female self and the projected female stereotypes'[13] or is she simply another bimbo body onscreen?

'Derek Yee' is the other director named in this meta-filmic movie, and Lau Ching-wan portrays him; he is someone Sing knows who appears at the screening of his art film *A Streetcar with No Wheels* on a bill with *Chinese Torture Chamber Story*, which Sing has attended with Chung. The former film makes only $7,000 in twenty-four theaters, three of them empty, while the latter makes $1 million at one midnight show. Yee's last words to a reporter are 'the audience has a right to choose.' Then he spontaneously runs past a group of actors with an aspiring and eager director shooting a student independent movie nearby, and jumps into the sea to his death, because of poor reviews. Sing has also encountered this untapped talent, and in one scene, as the unnamed director relates the words of advice Yee offered him, the audience sees the scene with Sing substituting for the young novice, deep in conversation with Yee. 'Never give up,' is the wisdom Yee offers; Sing asks, 'If you're such a smart thinker, why choose to die?' 'I'm human, I've weakness,' the director admits. 'Sometimes you will do stupid things. If given another chance, I'll not choose death.' It's an important moment, repeating the encouragement May has given her boyfriend, as well as opening Sing's eyes to himself: 'My life before was a joke, I never finished what I started. Halfway through the film. Halfway through my love life.' He tells cast and crew, 'Movies are similar to football. They need teamwork.' Together, in a collaborative effort, they complete the film, Sing pouring his emotions into his filmmaking and his girlfriend – the proverbial 'happy ending.' Most important for the Hong Kong film industry is the belief that films can be entertaining, successful, artistic, and have a message.

'Movies are illusions,' Chung reminds Sing in this fiction, suggesting the opposite. He continues, 'If you are on top, you can do anything you want. This is the rule of the game. You've been in this line for over ten years.' He asks the question that haunts Sing, 'Other than making movies, what else can you do?' For the time being, Sing is already one step ahead, fantasizing Chung as an office assistant delivering documents. Sing is making movies in his head, and the numerous fantasies in the film bear out the power of images. As Harvey observes, 'Cinema is, after all, the supreme maker and manipulator of images for commercial purposes,'[14] as is evidenced by the commercial emphasis that has always been a part of Hong Kong's film industry. Yet a large part of Sing's identity depends upon the image-making in his head. As May tells him when they are reunited, 'I love you because you are a filmmaker.' *Viva Erotica* critiques movies while loving them. As Gerima notes, 'The process of assembling and reassembling our creation in sight and sound is a constant and intense exploration for a higher societal aesthetic gratification.'[15]

Hong Kong's entertainment industry, film and television as well as the music business, has been spoofed many times. Chi Li's *Heaven Can't Wait* (1995), combines Hong Kong's fixation on media-fabricated images with its forebodings about the future by focusing upon the news media as its primary satirical target. Media presence pervades this film, from ubiquitous television screenplay to the behind-the-scenes and on-the-scene competition and deal-making between reporters, television show hosts, newscasters, and media moguls. A reporter (Karen Mok), dumped by her boyfriend/business partner, explains, 'he has changed channels,' thus equating their relationship to a television show. Superficially a parody of people's gullibility and captivation with new-age religions, the real aim is to critique the media's power to con the public and its potential to turn 1 July 1997 into 'spectacle.' The concept of a mode of information parallels Marx's mode of production in presupposing that social relations are historically constituted and transitory. If a mode of production designates the way that objects are made and exchanged, a mode of information indicates how symbols are used to communicate meanings and constitute subjects. As was witnessed globally via CNN and other media conglomerates, the handover did indeed become a spectacle of pomp, pageantry, parties, and fireworks.

Opening with the 1969 televised moon landing (believed by Hong Kongers to be 'staged') and closing with a representation of moon life (Anita Yuen as the Moon Goddess complaining about Americans), the narrative connects the media to global capital, where 'all things present will be history in a blink,' markets are open in 'Taiwan, Singapore, Malaysia, China, even North America,' 'Hong Kong is so lovely … strictly business,' and 'business is business … you'll find a new deal.' Fung, the cynical conman with heart (Tony Leung Chiu-wai) deals with the devil (a media mogul) to promote Chan Chun (Jordan Chan) as a reincarnated Buddhist monk called Da Da. A real-estate and stock market business partner joins the media mogul to form a conglomerate which 'can package Da Da properly. Help him to break the territorial boundaries to land upon the overseas market, including China, the largest market on earth. By that time, he will be the most valuable software we have.' Da Da, then, is to be exploited, used up and disposed of when he no longer suits vested interests. Their ability to deliver immediately and manipulate demand reflects the integration of a global network of flexible accumulation and specialized services, having merged television, telephones, computers, and satellites to advance the ability to process information and transact business.

After 'staging' several 'miracles' (fabricated by the media mogul), the masses envision Da Da as a savior from 'Judgment Night in Hong Kong.' As Poster states, 'the television set is a new speech context, one radically different from the past in that the speaker (understood as the entire apparatus of the broadcast) controls the context to a hitherto unimaginable extent.'[16] Capitalizing upon the ominous forebodings of the apocalypse, from ping-pong hailstorms and curious migrations of turtles, to lightning striking the Tsimshatsui clock tower (long a symbol of Hong Kong's prosperity), all is set to the powerful reverberations of Carl Orff's *Carmina Burana* as the staged 'Judgment Night' culminates in pure spectacle. A Da Da Christ carries his cross to Golgotha to be burned at the stake like Joan of Arc, a sacrificial lamb for his people, not unlike the colonized psychological space appropriated by media conglomerates in their presentation of the handover as a series of parties, ceremonies, and massive entertainments for all to experience virtually on the tube, overcoming the limitations imposed by geography and material history, (re)presenting phenomena in an almost uninterrrupted flow. The 'media bacchanalia' which gathers steam throughout the story incites the supplicants to demand a martyr. Who better than Chan Chun, who doesn't know what Hong Kongers need to know, how to count money.[17] Paradoxically, Da Da, 'signifying nothing,' is only a media-enhanced image on a flat screen; but, meaning everything, he embodies the fear of what will happen to profitable Hong Kong business practices post-June 1997. Accordingly, Fung and Chan Chun choose a Hawaiian paradise from which to plan their next business venture, and thereby escape the travails of Hong Kong.

Actor/auteur Stephen Chiau, Hong Kong's most popular comedian in recent years, is best known for his goofball characterizations, a mass of contradictions, in period parodies and urban comedies. Both arrogant and self-serving, smart-alecky and uncompassionate, his characters, when push comes to shove, make sacrifices, choose good over evil, and have some heart. His onscreen personae are always gifted with a special talent which sets them apart from others, to which Chiau adds a self-reflexive self-parodying, upping of the ante with each additional film as he has more with which to play. He is both annoying and lovable, and audiences either love or hate him.

Early on Chiau served as a representative for disaffected Hong Kong youth who had trouble looking ahead to a bright future; in contrast, their self-sacrificing and hard-working successful elders found him crude and impolite. More recently, however, Chiau has reached across generational lines to tap into a larger audience.

In addition to the slapstick and bodily funtions that are favored in his humor, Chiau also relies upon obscure puns and 'nonsense' language known as *mo-lay-tau* (literally nine follows eight, but nine doesn't have anything to do with eight), its definitions ranging from 'without a shred of meaning,' to 'at evens and odds.' In the period parody *Royal Tramp 2* (1992) his character Bond is told, 'Shut up, or I will cut your tongue out!,' to which he responds, 'I live on my tongue, how can you do that to me?' Critic Li Cheuk-to identifies the rise of *mo-lay-tau* in the early 1990s as one response to the Tiananmen Square massacre, 'when Hong Kong people needed some kind of therapy to overcome the shock and the trauma. So they ran away from reality and vented their frustration in senseless laughter.'[18] In another period parody, *Hail the Judge* (1994, directed by Wong Jing), Chiau's character's 'fighting words' are unheard on the soundtrack although the actor's mouth keeps moving and his body language is active. Issuing from his mouth are streams of hundreds of tiny shapes, including rainbow-colored stars, fish, circles, hearts, and fireballs, which defeat his enemies Wong Fei-hung style (they are created through postproduction special effects). The scene is set in a brothel, and on its wall is the plaque 'King of the Argument.' Nonsense rules the day! Or, perhaps an insane response in a insane world is sane after all.

In contrast to Li's tag of 'escapist,' Linda Chiu-han Lai sees Chiau's creations, which are heavily dependent upon an intense use of Cantonese slang, as empowering Hong Kong audiences, because only native practicing Cantonese speakers (or those living in Hong Kong and especially fluent) get the jokes. Chiau uses common Cantonese expressions, but reinvests them with new meanings, not always translatable into Chinese (for Mandarin speakers reading subtitles) or indeed into English. Several examples will illustrate the point. In an early scene of *God of Cookery* set on a skyscraper rooftop (with the distinctive Bank of China building seen in the background), Chiau's 'cooking god' is making a deal with nemesis Ng Man-tat, who proposes putting the cooking god's face on instant cup noodles. As Chiau offers him a glass of wine and they toast the partnership, he calls the Triad businessmen *shuey-guei*, literally meaning 'ghost.' What Chiau means is 'old friend'; the English subtitles read, 'Drink it, asshole.' Actually, Chiau is being set up by this 'old friend.' In *Royal Tramp 2*, Bond's sidekick Dor Lung (Chan Pak-cheung) dresses as a woman at an inn to get the lay of the land; he points out to the innkeeper that one of the patrons is a woman disguised as a man; impressed, the innkeeper says, 'My respect for you is like a flowing river' (continuous); he receives a smack from Dor Lung. *Yum-gane* literally means 'respect' or 'admire,' but it is used here as 'penis.' Later when Bond appears and explains to Dor Lung his plan to seduce the Single Hand Nun's student Ah Or (Michelle Reis), Dor Lung repeats the expression. Shortly thereafter the aphrodisiacs appear.[19] Thus, argues Lai,

> The intense use of Cantonese slang privileges a distinct viewing community comprising not just any Chinese person, nor even any Hong Kong citizen, but only those active residents who have partaken of everyday life and popular culture in the colony in recent years.[20]

Part of Chiau's overwhelming appeal, then, is that he is shaping contemporary Hong Kong identity.

During August 1997, in the aftermath of the return festivities, *Lawyer Lawyer* was released. Set near the end of the Qing dynasty, the story moves, as soldiers had done for the ceremony, from the Mainland to Hong Kong to follow the travails of its characters. Chiau plays Chan Mon-gut, a famous lawyer who is a 'cocky, wise and cunning brain-truster. He loved to play jokes on others and raise hob to make himself proud and happy. That's why he had numerous enemies.' So begins the characterization of a typical Chiau performance. Chan's wife Wu Man (Karen Mok) returns unexpectedly from Britain, where her husband has sent her to study law, although she has in fact studied fashion design. His faithful servant Foon (Eric Kot), after having one joke too many played upon him and seeking to gain the affections of Shui Lotus (Chingmy Yau), leaves for Hong Kong to better his fortunes. Unknown to Foon, he is the lost son of the wealthy Sir Ho Sai; Foon is framed for murder by Ho Sai's greedy son, a conniving lawyer named Ho Chun. Much of the story centers on Foon's false imprisonment and trial, and the Mainlander Chan's attempts to represent him in the British colony's courts. The scenario fits many Ah Can narratives, as the Mainlander-come-to-Hong Kong eventually outwits both Brits and locals. The overtly racist and classist judge tells Chan,

> This is the British court, not the poor court of you Chinese. I don't know what you are doing here. You don't know anything about law. Please go back to study more. Even if you don't think of your reputation, you'd think of the face of your fellow people.

There is a send-up of by-the-book interpretations of the law with no regard for justice, reason, or practicality. When Ho Sai, in British formal dress, recognizes Foon as his son in court and a frame-up is apparent, the gentleman's testimony is discounted because he failed to swear upon the Bible, having merely placed his hand upon it. And despite Ho Chun's inadvertent confession, Chan is held in contempt of court and Foon sentenced to hanging. When Ho Sai dies of a heart attack from shock at seeing the long lost son he thought was dead, his body is fittingly draped in the British flag. Of the judge, Chan notes to his wife, 'He always mentions the United Kingdom. It seems he's forgotten that Hong Kong was leased to the UK. They have to return it one day. Damn it! How dare he be that cocky in our territory?' Obviously, the movie is full of references to the handover and the 'face' of the powers involved. Tellingly, Ho Chun's alibi is that he was reading *A Tale of Two Cities* on the evening of the murder; Chan asks where he left off, 'the soldiers met Snow White, is that right?', to which the confused Chun responds positively before withdrawing.

In this fact and fantasy mixture, the thinking behind the Joint Declaration and the way it was produced (without the direct involvement of Hong Kongers) is questioned. Wu Man, in defense of her husband and Foon, challenges the court. She says, 'I am not well-educated, but I don't understand one thing. What is more important, legal procedure or life?' She tells the 'learned' judge, 'I think you have studied so many years of law that you have got nothing at all. Like my husband, I haven't studied law. But I dare to open my eyes to see what's right and wrong.' At his execution, Foon yells, 'You kill me, but many, many Ho Foons will appear,' suggesting a potential uprising. The enterprising Chan turns the tables on the courts, holding the judge to the 'letter of the law' (a law of course, made without the consent of the people, just like the legal document of 'one country, two systems'): 'You just ordered to hang him, but not to hang him to death.... Think before you speak, otherwise you will lose the face of the British government.' Humor aside, this film expresses deep concern for justice in the aftermath of the imposed Joint Declaration and what is to come.

Reprieved, one year later, Foon poses with the Chans for a photograph, all decked out in Western formal dress. Only Shui Lotus is absent, having been sent by her husband to Britain to study English literature, particularly Shakespeare. Chiau's film additionally identifies the mixture of contemporary Hong Kong identity as a hybrid. Pushing beyond Mainland boundaries into the heart of Hong Kong, Foon gets a job at the sophisticated, largely British-frequented Hong Kong Club, where he performs in the Lion Dance for tourist voyeurs; he and the photographer of the closing scene get mop-top early-Beatles-style haircuts at Number Nine Nathan Road. Forced to undergo baptism prior to the trial (become 'Anglicized'), Chan observes an Anglo woman's figure revealed in wet clothes (while all the men have nose bleeds – that is, are sexually aroused). Chan comments, 'I hate blondes,' as the minister tries to drown him. The cultural mix is noted.

Chiau's films, in common with other period-piece parodies, draw from and celebrate a Chinese history shared with the Mainland. They also distance themselves from Mainland culture, developing a local Hong Kong history. As Michael Ryan notes, 'Film representations are one subset of wider systems of social representation (images, narratives, beliefs, etc.) that determine how people live.'[21] While contemporary Hong Kong comedies reflect society at large, they in turn influence it by offering numerous alternatives to the direction in which the society will proceed. How Hong Kong is, and would like to see itself in the future, can be glimpsed on any Hong Kong movie screen.

ELEVEN

ALL'S WELL ENDS WELL, HAPPY TOGETHER?

Two filmic moments, distanced by a decade in time and by their proximity to July 1997, may help navigate the future of Hong Kong and its movies. Tsui Hark's *Peking Opera Blues* presents its three heroines sharing a drink. Sheung Hung, the revolutionary (Brigitte Lin), peers through a magnifying glass at the globe in her father's library. She says, 'The world is so big. Where can I go?' Tsao Wan, the out-of-work servant (Cherie Chung), asks, 'Are you planning to go somewhere?' 'Everyone is running away,' replies Sheung Hung, 'Running for life.' Pat Neil, the Peking Opera wannabe (Sally Yeh), interjects, 'But this is a nice place. Why do we have to run away?' Tsao Wan answers, 'We're running around, and finally we go back the same route.' This scene prophetically brings together the pervasiveness of transnational capital (the globe), Hong Kong culture ('a nice place'), and the filmmaker's vision (Lin's enlarged eye through the glass). Ten years later, in Alfred Cheung's Lunar New Year comedy *All's Well End's Well '97* a wealthy and socially pretentious Chinese couple, already British citizens, visit Chiau's home. They overlook nothing with their greedy eyes. Bearing a gift, the woman remarks that the British sausage is 'high in cholesterol and will help you commit suicide.' The couple insult Chiau's sister-in-law and his brother's Mainlander girlfriend ('Those guys from the Mainland all become robbers, those girls from the Mainland all become whores,' they say) but get their comeuppance from the others. When Chiau's father exposes the couple as Mainlanders, Hong Kong city boy Chiau traipses by, leading a country cow, as the family tells the couple to 'dye their hair blonde and get contact lenses, so they'll have fragrant farts' and criticizes them for 'becoming foreigners instead of Chinese.' Before being chased away with knives by Chiau and kicked to kingdom come, the wife worries about her pocketbook, while the husband uses her as a shield. It is a humorous scene certainly, but also a telling one, as the unappealing and acquisitive couple have lost their human kindness and cultural identity.

Since the early 1980s, Hong Kong cinema has addressed its unique identity, best expressed as doubleness. Past and present, early and late capital, Eastern and Western in orientation are wedded together by its history, economy, culture, and place. Influenced by its cultural roots and by Western film, and reinterpreting almost every genre, Hong Kong cinema has ignored overt politics; nevertheless, it has generously compensated for this by its inclusion of political subtexts in many genres. The potential effect of 1997 on the movie industry became a topic of concern, with views ranging from little, if any, to a great deal and attitudes running the gamut from optimistic to pessimistic. Some production companies and studios weighed offers from Singapore's government of handsome relocation tax breaks.[1] Canada's popularity as a destination for Hong Kongers leaving the colony suggested the potential of Toronto or Vancouver to emerge as a new enclave for Hong Kong filmmakers. On the one hand, Woody Tsung of the Territory's Motion Picture Industry Association maintained that, while 'it's natural to have some concerns,' China would not interfere because that would result in a mass exodus of talent and 'the collapse of the Hong Kong film industry.'[2] On the other hand, director Joe Cheung, invoking 'one country, two systems,' asserted that 'we must fight for freedom and creativity.'[3] Some, no doubt afraid of future ostracism or requital, were hesitant to criticize Chinese policies concerning, among other things, co-production arrangements, import quotas, and film content. Moreover, many actors and directors looked forward to exploring projects on the Mainland and in Mainland studios, working in new locations with expanded talent pools, and employing China for locations and as the source of narratives. Superstar actor Chow Yun-fat maintained that

> Once they open up the China market, a lot of the Chinese studios will get involved with Hong Kong production companies. A lot of independent production houses will produce stories which will be suitable for Hong Kong and Mainland China. Movies will be

shown in all of China. I'm very glad that China's government will take over the Hong Kong government and open up opportunities for Hong Kong filmmakers.[4]

According to Edward Wong, Chow insists that

> his eagerness to continue working in Hong Kong is also an expression of hope for his native city … he plans to scope out projects with directors in Hong Kong, Mainland China, and maybe Taiwan. He believes the handover will mean even more cross-border co-operation in filmmaking. And he already has two favorite directors in mind – the Mainland's much-lauded Chen Kaige and Zhang Yimou.[5]

One irony of the resumption of Chinese sovereignty over the territory is overwhelming pro-Beijing sentiment among Hong Kong's capitalist class. For their part, local film investors and theater owners viewed the Mainland's potentially vast market as ripe territory for expanding production, distribution and exhibition. Between 1988 and 1994, 113 feature films produced in China were co-productions with Hong Kong companies.[6] Those hoping that SAR movies would count as domestic productions and, therefore, not be subject to China's practice of restricting imported films to ten per year were disheartened on the eve of the handover by top-ranking PRC film official Duo Shoufang's indication that the Hong Kong industry would be accorded no special status. The upshot of this position is that Hong Kong filmmakers desiring to sidestep the import quota and the registration needed to have access to China's one-billion-plus audience would have to secure a Mainland partner and submit scripts for approval. Potential problems exist over such matters as the PRC's insistence on retaining domestic distribution rights. Meanwhile, on the screening front, Hong Kong's Golden Harvest opened its first Mainland multiplex, a four-screen theater, in Shanghai. Moreover, the company announced, only days before 1 July 1997, plans to build twelve-screen facilities in that city and in Guangzhou with an eye to eventually branching out to thirty locations.

Those looking to China for salvation were likely to be disappointed. Market behavior and audience tastes had shifted by the mid-1990s in several ways. First, video piracy was rampant. The crudest black marketeers would go to a matinee in a nearly empty theater, aim their camcorders at the screen, and shoot. They would then make multiple duplications of their 'master' tape. The sound and picture quality, according to Toh Hai Leong, was 'atrocious, with sometimes a cough here, a squelch there, or someone munching on biscuits, or somebody crossing the length of the front row with his or her head silhouetted against the screen.'[7] Pirate distributors and vendors possessed potentially lucrative 'bounty' due to widespread ownership of VCR machines among middle-class Hong Kongers whose fondness for watching films at home was growing. Second, home viewing led to home recording for family and friends; both costs and tapes could be shared among viewers, who could inexpensively build their own personal video libraries. Third, as the number of moviegoers declined, the expectations of those still going to theaters in the 1990s changed. Coinciding with a push by Hollywood to capture a larger share of the Asian market, the industry witnessed both a steep drop in local box office receipts from its 1989 peak (admissions shrank from 14.8 million in 1995 to 11.9 million in 1996 alone) and a sharp rise in theater screenings of movies by US majors (jumping from 10 per cent in 1992 to 49 per cent in 1997).[8] Director–producer Tsui Hark's comments in this regard are telling:

> In the past, people had a clear distinction between local films and Western films. People used to go to local films for what they couldn't find in Hollywood films. But now, the difference between the two is becoming less and less. Instead of having two standards like it used to be, people now choose what to see based on its production value. Naturally, people choose Hollywood production over Hong Kong's.

Apprehension about post-handover circumstances created what filmmaker Peter Chan calls a '1997 mentality … take the money and run.'[9] Or, as producer Terence Chang puts it, 'Greed had become a virtue. Integrity, sadly, had become a weakness, a crime.' To 'hit and run' was doubly attractive to some because many Hong Kong movies were, at one time, pre-production profit-makers. In buying distribution rights to finished products, Asian and overseas Chinese investors financed film projects that existed only on paper as signed contracts; Taiwanese distributors alone might put up two-thirds to three-quarters of the necessary funding.[10] In this frenzied climate, the prolific Wong Jing had thirty-two director, twenty-eight producer, and twenty-three writer credits between 1990 and 1996. The trend – a cinematic equivalent of the assembly-line 'speed up' that Tsui Hark calls 'cheap, fast, but no good' – partially explains the declining quality of Hong Kong pictures during this period. Films themselves were becoming formulaic. As Peter Chan maintains, 'we've actually been harvesting the fruit that our predecessors bred in

the 1980s, there's nothing new.' One consequence, the almost exclusive exporta-
tion of gangster/kung fu fare and poor sequels to earlier hits was followed by a
sharp drop in important Asian market revenues. That no Hong Kong imports
reached the top ten of the Korean box office between 1993 and 1997 is indicative
of their declining popularity.[11]

Hong Kong cinema's 'golden era' coincided with post-Joint Declaration anxiety,
as though filmmakers and film audiences were a synergistic tandem, each driving
the other to exceed their individual efforts. Of course, this same anxiety compelled growing numbers, including movie personnel, to consider a future away
from Hong Kong. As director Clara Law, who settled in Australia with her col-
laborator/partner Eddie Fong, indicated, 'to be honest and frank, I would not
like to be under the regime of the Communist government.'[12] Emigration became
a reference in pre-handover Hong Kong films as disparate as *An Autumn's Tale*, *All
About Ah Long*, *Chungking Express*, and *The Chinese Feast*. In Woo's *A Better Tomorrow 2*, shot in Hong Kong and New York, Lung (Dean Shek) flees Hong Kong
to New York. Ultimately the film advocates having it both ways. The conversation
between Lung and Ken, Mark's 'twin brother' (Chow Yun-fat) follows:

> Lung: 'This is, after all, not our own place.'
> Ken: 'Many try to leave home at all costs, many want to go home. Some cannot even
> find a temporary place to rest.'
> Lung: 'One's hope is always better.'

While the two return to Hong Kong to do battle with the evil Ko, the film
ends with New York scenes of Ken's rebuilt restaurant. Relocation overseas peaked
following the Tiananmen Square massacre in 1992, the year that John Woo's
frenzied *Hard Boiled* opened with Tequila (Chow Yun-fat) asking a fellow cop,
'have you ever considered emigrating?,' just before the mayhem of a teahouse
shootout begins. Few knew at the time of its release that the film would be Woo's
last Hong Kong picture, but by then audiences were beginning to stay away from
theaters, creative talent was drying up or looking elsewhere, and the industry was
entering the doldrums from which it has had such a difficult time recovering.

While allusions to leaving abounded in all genres, they generally avoided specific
mention of the handover. By not citing 'the return' as a reason for emigrating or
seeking third-country passports, filmmakers conceivably eluded controversy and

censorship. Terence Chang points out that few films dealt directly with 1997, 'although Tsui Hark's movies, from *Dangerous Encounters of the First Kind* to *A Better Tomorrow III* and the *Once Upon a Time in China* series, did touch upon it in various degrees.' State censorship – nothing new, given Britain's prohibition of anti-colonial messages from the industry's outset – was imposed more than twenty times between 1974 and 1988.[13] The system of censorship in Hong Kong continued to frown upon political films even as it became more liberal with respect to sex and violence. While Tsui's *Dangerous Encounters* was the most notable locally produced example to be subject to the censors' demand for changes and cuts, David King's *Home at Hongkong* (1983) was withheld from release until certain scenes, including a suicide in front of a television showing a picture of the Queen, were deleted. The 1988 code concerning potential harm to relations with other countries remains in effect. This clause, obviously intended to placate China, was also useful in mollifying Southeast Asian financiers and governments, upon whom the Hong Kong film industry depended for funding and market access. Both those who control investment and those who control ideas and images can determine product availability, thereby influencing scripts while simultaneously shaping audience tastes. Many, perhaps most, filmmakers develop what Michael Parenti calls 'anticipatory avoidance,' a form of self-censorship precluding the need for edict and heavy-handedness.[14] Yet Foucault asserts that power produces rather than merely negates and represses; he claims that wherever power exists, resistance does as well. Cinematic boat people, clock-watching, and face-offs, as well as Chinese diaspora, Japanese occupation, and Saigon-falling movies testify to the way that censorship can be a dialectical process whereby the dictates of state prohibitive power are circumvented.

Critic Tony Rayns asserts, however, that Hong Kong filmmakers engaged in a 'conspiracy of romanticisation and silence' with respect to 1997.[15] Citing Yim Ho's drama *Homecoming* (1984) as paradigmatic, Rayns reads the story of a beleaguered Hong Kong woman who 'finds herself' in rural China as quixotic and revealing of the cinema community's willingness to portray the People's Republic positively. Shot on location in China, the film was released in the year of the Sino–British Joint Declaration. An early 'return movie,' the film reflected, in part, the director's own personal background; raised in a pro-communist family, Yim participated in the 1967 anti-colonial rebellion in Hong Kong. Despite the picture having won a number of film awards, some in the colony compared *Homecoming* to 'United Front' communist propaganda.[16] Yet the film's idealization of the countryside is not rendered as an answer to the character Coral's (Josephine Koo) Hong Kong alienation; she is, after all, only on vacation. The rural setting itself, with a formally educated woman (Coral's childhood friend Pearl, played by Siqin Gaowa) running the local school, an enterprising and rebellious boy who desires city life, a man whose proudest moment is telling others about his son studying at UCLA, Coca-Cola cans, and talk of divorce destabilizes notions of a fixed provincialism. As Esther Yau points out, the PRC's 'intention to modernize informs the breakdown in the urban–rural dichotomy and, by implication, the differences between an industrial Hong Kong and a pre-industrial Chinese village.'[17] If Yim Ho looks for revelation on the Mainland, he does so nostalgically to counter a materialistic and soulless Hong Kong, in a manner Paul Willemen refers to as 'idyllic villages and communities peopled by 'authentic' (read folkloric) innocents in touch with "real values."'[18] Thus rural China is not a stand-in for the PRC *per se*, but an imaginary nation; the seemingly organic is an ideological and political construct, as Benedict Anderson tells us.

Johnny Mak's *Long Arm of the Law* (1984), produced in the same year, betrays fewer illusions. To begin with, the film treats Mainlanders with contempt. The story opens with thugs entering an unprotected Hong Kong by jumping a fence that separates the territories. Although things go wrong immediately when one of the gang is trapped by PRC attack dogs, the ease with which the former Red Guards 'invade' the colony reveals a specter haunting Hong Kong – 1967, when Mao's youthful Cultural Revolutionaries, positioned across the border and apparently poised to strike, inspired demonstrations and protests that turned into months of riots. In the movie, the desperate (read failed PRC socialism) Mainlanders' plan to carry out a jewel (read successful Hong Kong capitalism) heist goes awry after they murder a plainclothes police officer. Prior to this, they are depicted as base and carnal, indulging themselves with a series of prostitutes, on a spree that ends with one of the gang abusing one of the women for snubbing him. By forcing her at gunpoint to peform oral sex on him, the hood rapes the hooker while the Mainland violates Hong Kong.

Despite director Mak's negative characterization of the Mainlanders, he refuses a simple good guy/bad guy dichotomy. The Hong Kong police, a colonial force, are themselves revealed to be a crooked and greedy bunch. And the film does trade somewhat in the 'idealization of the "Third World" as a closely knit community.'[19] The Mainlanders are seen expressing loyalty to and concern for one another (one gang member cries at the loss of his comrade), in contrast to the officers' estrangement and piggishness. A gangster remembers the pleasure of riding a bicycle with his Mainland girlfriend during an interlude from the violence, although the innocence of the moment is intercut with the sounds of a brothel and pictures of nude women on the wall. Meanwhile, the character Ah Tai, moving between outlaw (the PRC) and informant (the British), suggests Hong Kong itself. In much the same way that the Sino–British negotiations determining the colony's fate did not include Hong Kongers, Ah Tai becomes expendable to the criminals, who use his body to protect their own during a getaway, as well as to the police, who coldly terminate him in 'gangland' fashion.

Shot largely vérité-style, *Long Arm of the Law* explodes into war in its final segments, when 'law enforcement,' as if responding to an insurrection, confronts the Mainlanders with machine-gun-equipped helicopters and anti-riot vehicles following their botched robbery attempt. Here Mak exposes the pretense of colonial justice; the rule of law is abandoned and the perpretrators must be caught no matter the cost so that order can be restored. Along the way, the police kill both the informant and an unlicensed doctor who offers medical treatment to a wounded gangster. Britain's much-ballyhooed 'hands-off' approach to Hong Kong notwithstanding, as Chandra Mohanty remarks, 'colonization almost invariably implies a structure of domination … and political suppression.'[20] The film ends inside Kowloon Walled City, a dungeon-like place housing the lumpen and the miscreant; not covered by nineteenth-century Sino–British treaties, the area was subject to neither Mainland nor colonial rule.[21] There the cops finish off the Mainlanders with multiple automatic-weapons rounds, leaving them to rot in an attic alongside a pack of dead rats.

Homecoming and *Long Arm of the Law* represent polarized approaches to the Hong Kong/China question: romantic melodrama/violent actioner, bucolic virtue/urban anomie, hopeful about the return/cynical about the handover. The meditation of the former conveys educated and efficacious middle-class humanism; the rant of the latter communicates underskilled and alienated working-class cynicism. If negotiations over 1997 were a wake-up call, particularly for many in the liberal intelligentsia and professional-managerial stratum, the 1989 Tiananmen Square incident was an alarm that could not be shut off. As director Mak Tai-kit, a Vietnamese transplant in Hong Kong, warned, 'I am afraid. I dislike and distrust the Communists. We fled Vietnam for the same reasons. Before [Tiananmen Square] ... we thought maybe things would be all right. But now we are not so sure.[22] Filmmaker Ringo Lam attributes the declining appeal of his films among Hong Kong audiences in the 1990s to a comment he made after the Tiananmen Square events, which saw a million Hong Kongers take to the streets in protest:

> After all the bloodshed in Beijing, everybody is crying, and showing so much emotion in the media. Almost every fifteen minutes the television repeats the same news. Everybody is so sad. OK. I feel sad, too. But the thing lasted too long. After two, three weeks, I said, 'Can we break for awhile? Let's have the Dragon Boat Festival.' All of a sudden, everybody came after me. I said, 'I'm sorry,' and I went to Singapore and stayed there for a month. There were threats sent to my company. After that, all my movies didn't get a good response.[23]

Ten years after *Homecoming*, Yim Ho offered audiences *The Day the Sun Turned Cold* (1994), a work that draws comparisons with the recent Fifth Generation mainland directors (e.g. Chen Kaige and Zhang Yimou) who sought renewed meaning in what Rey Chow calls a 'return to nature.' In her view, these 'directors explore rural life in ways that, far from consolidating 'Chineseness'' as some form of essence dwelling in China's center, in effect help to "other" "China" through images of unfamiliar histories, identities, and livelihoods that persist peripherally in space and time.'[24] Yet, despite its stunning visuals and methodical pacing, *The Day The Sun Turned Cold* undercuts mythic longing and loss, thereby avoiding the 'legitimised (but unacknowledged as such) voyeurism' that Trinh Min-ha, among others, correctly criticizes about similar films.[25] Variously described as murder mystery, psychological drama, and family tragedy, the film is also a political parable. Produced, as was the earlier picture, on the Mainland, the movie was shot five years after the director witnessed his mother's PRC sympathies die. Yim remarks, 'for me, the whole thing stopped with the Cultural Revolution. My mother was the last hold-out; she lasted until Tiananmen Square. She cried in front of the TV screen, and that was the end of pro-Communist.'[26]

Set in the frigid hinterlands of Northern China, the movie recounts the tale of Guan Jin (Tuo Zhang Hua), who alleges that his mother Pu Pengying (Siqin

COMING HOME   Tuo Zhang Hua and Siqin Gaowa in Yim Ho's *The Day the Sun Turned Cold*

Gaowa) long ago murdered his father (Ma Jingwu) by poisoning his food. When Jin, an auto worker in the city, returns to the rustic village of his childhood, the love–hate relationship between him and his mother becomes evident. Based on an actual incident, the story unfolds as a series of flashbacks in which the physical environment and the familial situation are counterparts; the geographical region is barren while the parents' marriage is loveless. In exposing his mother's affair with another man, Jin the boy conceivably pushes Pengying towards the act that Jin the grown-up accuses of her committing. Yim's China in this film is a harsh place marked by the mother's endless toil preparing and selling frozen bean curd, the brusque schoolteacher father's death at an early age, and the son's self-torment over initially betraying his mother, then claiming that she is the murderer, and finally grappling with Pengying's conviction. In the penultimate scene, Jin sees his mother one last time, in a jail cell where she awaits execution. As the film closes, he runs from the prison's darkness towards a ray of light outside. Clutching a sweater that his mother has knitted him, Jin bursts through the door only to find emptiness. Looking out over an expanse of white snow, he tosses the sweater into a passing cart of firewood. In this 'homecoming,' the mother and child reunion is anguished; their inability to reconcile expresses gloom about what Hong Kongers could expect after 1997.

The post-Tiananmen Square period also produced one of the weirdest products of Hong Kong cinema, or of any cinema, for that matter: Mak Tai-kit's *Wicked City* (1994), released in the same year as *The Day the Sun Turned Cold*. Mixing genres as well as incorporating dislocation and displacement strategies, the film is frenetic in terms of mood, where the other is somber. Aspects of sci-fi, horror, action, suspense, melodrama, and special effects combine to create this cinematic chow mein. Drawing on the acid rain nightscapes and mood of *Blade Runner* and its replicants and blade runner squad, the teeth and shells of horrific *Alien* movie creatures, the travelling slime of *Ghostbusters*, and the human-friendly aliens of *Alien Nation*, the film is based on an ultra-violent and sexually graphic Japanese anime by Hideyuki Kikuchi. Hong Kong 1997, a 'neon-illuminated den of iniquity where capitalism ruthlessly exploits a proletariat,'[27] has been invaded by raptors or shape-shifters, which the government's top secret anti-raptor bureau must eliminate. The powerful 150-year-old Daishu (Japanese actor Tatsuya Nakadai), CEO of Asia Finance, is a pacifist raptor-disguised-as-human, who has penetrated the human economic system, and wants to conduct business in peace. He is thwarted by his greedy son Shudo (Roy Cheung), who secretly distributes the raptor street drug 'Happiness' in the raptor world and wants 'to make Hong Kong the first raptor city' by putting Happiness on its streets and by stopping time and making history go backwards.

Shudo's insatiable lust for power is exhibited by his overactive libido (he even has sex with a raptor pinball machine). Daishu's board of directors' meeting is intercut with Shudo's sexual ravishment of a flirtatious British public-relations woman. He rhapsodizes over his arousal by 'human blood ... fresh blood ... female blood' and forces himself on a female raptor, divulging 'I want to eat you whole.' If we conflate cannibal with vampire, Shudo's actions and words attest to Marx's assertion that 'Capital posits the permanence of value by incarnating itself

courtesy of Colin Geddes; permission of Film Workshop and Toho Film, Hong Kong

ENRAPTORED   Roy Cheung and Jacky Cheung in Mak Tai-kit's *Wicked City*

in fleeting commodities and taking on their form … But capital obtains this ability only by constantly sucking in living labour as its soul, vampire-like.'[28] The anti-raptor bureau boss seems to concur; he admits to Daishu, 'We humans are slaves to money.… When influenced by money we become short-sighted.'

Numerous exploding heads, fluid-gushing decapitated bodies, arachnid and motorcycle women, killing clock mechanisms, slithering and smothering raptor goo later, the climactic scene includes a Boeing 747 and the Bank of China building, providing not-so-subtle political overtones, reinforced by the two protagonists and the opening and closing cityscapes. The lead characters both undergo identity crises. Taki (Leon Lai) is torn between his job and the raptor he loves, and gripped by the fear of what their offspring might be; Ken Kai (Jacky Cheung), such an offspring, is half-human, half-raptor – a hybrid. The raptors, seen as the Mainland Chinese, have chosen a 'prime time to invade' – the year is 1997, when Hong Kong is to be returned to China. The film opens on a setting sun over Japan's red Tokyo skyline, which immediately recedes into its neon night. Shortly, a jet crosses the screen and brings with it the floating film title across the deep blue night sky; it descends across Hong Kong's neon-lit towers, a breathtaking cartography of shrines to commerce. The film closes with Daishu's rapid ageing and death, his last words, "The city is so lonely … I hope they'll never need the raptor's happiness." Cut to a blood red sky and rising sun over Hong Kong – post-1 July.

If a film such as *The Day the Sun Turned Cold* was elegiac about post-handover prospects, one like *Wicked City* was a down and dirty warning to expect the worst. Screen pessimism reflected growing cautiousness within the film community, particularly regarding the censorship issue, in light of Cheung Yuen-ting's experience with *The Soong Sisters* (1997). Ng See-yuen, the latter film's producer, remarked that 'China sees films as propaganda. If the divorce rate is going up, word comes down to make fewer films with extramarital affairs.'[29] It took five months to obtain script approval for *The Soong Sisters* from the People's Republic film bureau. When the film was completed, the negative print was held for over a year until fifty cuts were made. *The Soong Sisters* is a historical drama that tells of China's struggle for unity and subsequent nationalist-communist conflict from the point of view of three sisters from a powerful family. One (Ai-ling) loved money and married wealthy banker H.H. Kung. The second (Ching-ling) loved the nation; she wed Sun Yat-sen. The third (Mei-ling) loved power; she became Madame Chiang Kai-shek. Cheung's interest in the women's story grew when she began drawing parallels between their lives and her own:

> Born and raised in the British Colony of Hong Kong, I had never set foot on China until 1989, only to discover a country and a people I did not understand. With the coming of 1997, I tried to re-establish a link with the past, to study the history of China as we stepped towards the unknown future, and to find out who I really am. During this

search, I discovered three women who lived at the turn of the century, the Soong sisters, whose situation bore striking resemblance to my predicament. Sent by their pioneering father to study abroad [in the United States] during their childhood, when most Chinese women still had their feet bound, they returned from the West as total strangers to a country they called home – a home they hardly recognized, and a home that hardly recognized them. But the Soong sisters thought that they were in a unique position to create a new China. With the knowledge they had acquired from the West and the power of the Soong family, they fought to change the fate of their country, of their people, and ultimately, of their own lives, only to discover a force far stronger than they thought.[30]

A story of epic proportions, *The Soong Sisters* is two hours and forty-four minutes in length, which is unusually long for the Hong Kong industry, where ninety-minute films are the norm. Costing around US$5 million to produce, *The Soong Sisters* was a big-budget film by Hong Kong standards. Cheung says that she

was able to assemble my dream cast from Hong Kong, China, and Taiwan [Maggie Cheung, Michelle Yeoh, and Vivian Wu as the three sisters, Jien Wan as the father, and Winston Chao as Sun Yat-sen]. For the crew I got the best I could find in Asia – Arthur Wong as cinematographer, Eddie Ma as art director, Emi Wada as costume desgner, and Kitaro for the music score.

With her collaborator/partner, filmmaker Alex Law, the director spent

over a year for research, travelling all around China and Taiwan interviewing people who had known the Soong sisters. I also went to the United States to visit libraries which might have documents forbidden in China. It was like a dream come true, until the day I had to face the Chinese censors. I never realized that politics could have so much influence on what people do and think. Up till now, each of my films presented its unique kind of problems; some had to do with money and others to do with people. It had never been easy. But censorship is the most heart-breaking of all the problems.

Soong Ching-ling (Maggie Cheung), Chinese revolutionary leader Sun's wife and the most prominent character in the movie, was unwavering in her opposition to Chiang Kai-shek's purge of communists from the Nationalist Party following her husband's death. She later served as vice-chair of the People's Republic. In contrast, Soong Mei-ling (Vivian Wu), the wife of Chiang, was the principal target of PRC censors. The majority of the eighteen minutes of cuts that the committee of officials and historians imposed upon the final edit involved the youngest sister's attempt to save her husband after he had been kidnapped in 1936. Her defense of the Nationalist leader before a communist cadre (including a young Zhou Enlai) would be illegal on the Mainland today. Mei-ling went to Taiwan with her husband following the 1949 Chinese Revolution and she moved to New York City after Chiang's death in 1975. She was still living, at 101 years of age, in 1998. Meanwhile, the eldest sister Ai-ling (Michelle Yeoh) moved, appropriately enough, with her husband and one-time Nationalist government finance minister, to Hong Kong, saying 'there people don't care about politics, just finance.'

Wong Kar-wai's *Happy Together* (literally *Spring Light Leaking*, 1997) earned him the director's prize at Cannes in the spring of that year. At the time he remarked, 'I am not sure that after July first it would be approved … the subject is very sensitive.'[31] Subtitled *A Story About Reunion*, the film depicts the aftermath of a gay couple's break-up; it also offers a reaction to Hong Kong's then imminent return to China. Starring well-known and popular male leads Leslie Cheung and Tony Leung Chiu-wai as the lovers, the movie transgressed mainstream Chinese standards, leading to its Category III rating in Hong Kong and its being banned in Malaysia and South Korea (although it was eventually released in the latter). Wong dismissed the labelling of *Happy Together* as a gay film, insisting that the couple could just as well have been male and female but that they just happened to be men; for him, the story was about relationships. The movie is Wong's most direct political statement to date – a challenge to the 'normalization' of Hong Kong–Mainland relations on the eve of the handover.

The movie's opening images are revealing. One sequence is a lively and suggestive simulated sex scene between the two lovers, which is to be their last, filmed in black and white and with the camera as 'discreet and evocative as a camera position can be.'[32] The scene runs for less than two minutes, but as the couple kiss, touch, laugh, lick, tussle, and engage in anal sex, their intimacy, intensity and ordinariness, as well as their possessiveness, anger and fear, are shown. While the scene may be challenging to the comfort of some viewers, it is the immediate opening and fleeting ten seconds of the film that are most shocking (and curiously overlooked in film commentary). What stronger statement can the director make than to have two screen-sized passport pages, with photos of the protagonists, flashed and stamped along with the opening credits, the latter colored in the red and white of the Hong Kong flag? The film was released in May 1997, and

TANGO LESSONS   Leslie Cheung and Tony Leung Chiu-wai in Wong Kar-wai's *Happy Together*

remained in the Hong Kong box office top ten for four weeks. Leaving Hong Kong was indelibly printed on viewers' minds.

The director and his favorite collaborators, cinematographer Chris Doyle and production designer William Chang, went to Buenos Aires to make the movie because they were inspired by the literature of Latin American novelists like Manuel Puig, Julio Cortazar, and Gabriel García Márquez. Certainly the often convoluted narrative experimentation of these writers has found filmic expression in Wong's work. This film began as a loose adaptation of Puig's *Heartbreak Tango*, yet the story of a son discovering his father's gay lover is barely recognizable in the completed picture. Wong and Doyle have both provided similar and provocative explanations for their pronounced change of setting with *Happy Together*. Wong told an interviewer, 'For the past two years, everybody has been asking me about the fate of Hong Kong, and if my next film would be about 1997. I didn't have an answer, so I thought we should just walk away and try something else.'[33] Doyle likewise explained their intentions in the diary he kept during the shoot, and he also points out that Argentina was not at all what they had expected it to be. 'We came to Argentina to "defamiliarize" ourselves by moving away from the spaces – and, we hope, the preoccupations – of the world we know so well. But we're out of our space and depth here. We don't even know the city well … We're stuck with our own concerns and perceptions.'[34] Other obstacles, as far-ranging as disputes with the Argentine crew, insufficient lighting and camera uncertainties, Tony Leung being upset by the sexual explicitness of what he was asked to do, Leslie Cheung developing stomach problems and Wong Kar-wai's severe toothache, led to a six-week shoot turning into four months.

As is his habitual practice, Wong shot without a script, writing while shooting, drawing inspiration from music, the setting, working conditions, and actors. The director's process-oriented working method is organic, operating on the value of pursuit 'as' happiness rather than pursuit 'of' happiness. This approach makes room for collaboration, improvisation, and chance to become feature elements in his movies, allowing him to play along as well as disregard and eliminate preconceptions of the story. His work process probably exacerbated the difficulties on the shoot, and whether cast and crew were 'happy together' seems doubtful; nevertheless, those working with Wong are accustomed to his practice and have willingly participated because his results are always unexpected, invigorating, and interesting. Even Wong himself admits that he doesn't truly learn what his movies are about until he edits them. He says, 'Most of the time, I think I don't exactly know where we are heading but I am very sure about what we *don't* want. So that whole process is trying to go away from things we don't want and go toward other possibilities. Later on, during editing, we know exactly what happened.'[35] With *Happy Together*, almost half the film found its way to the cutting room floor.

The film's English title invokes not only the Turtles' 1960s' hit song but also irony and impossibility. The couple can't be happy together, yet they are miserable apart. The movie begins where movies usually end, with the couple's breakup, when they get lost searching for the Iguazu Falls. Both then 'start over' apart from each other, strangers in a strange land, in a position not unlike the Hong Kong filmmakers at work in Argentina. Wong elaborates, 'When I got to Buenos Aires

courtesy/permission of Kino International

SOFT SHOULDER   Leslie Cheung and Tony Leung Chiu-wai in Wong Kar-wai's *Happy Together*

I realized it's totally different. Because it's not so South America to me – Buenos Aires is cold freezing, and people are not so "hot." It's more like a European country, so we had to start all over again.'[36]

The first words spoken onscreen are Ho Po-wing's to Lai Yiu-fai: 'We could start over.' The conditional tense suggests the tenuousness of his effort and the fragility of their relationship. Po-wing stares at the tacky tourist lamp of the Iguazu Falls that they've acquired, while Fai leans against the wall with his back to Po-wing, and stares into a discolored and aged mirror in which we see his reflection. Just prior to their lovemaking, Fai's voice-over comments, 'Ho Po-wing always says "Let's start over." And it gets to me every time. We have been together for a while and broken up often. But when he says "starting over" I find myself back

with him. We left Hong Kong to start over. We hit the road and reached Argentina.' It is the first of many 'starting overs' in the story; the meaningfulness of the
conceit also resonates in the filmmakers' journey – they have left Hong Kong to
try something new. Not coincidentally, the characters Ho Po-wing (Leslie Cheung)
and Lai Yiu-fai (Tony Leung Chiu-wai) are named, respectively, after the focus-
puller and gaffer brought on the shoot.[37]

Fai comments that for Po-wing, 'starting over has many meanings' and his
observation is astute concerning the multivalences of 'starting over' in relation to
this movie. Within the story, Po-wing's attempts to 'start over' are always expressed
conditionally and reflect the fits and starts of his actions – 'One day we might
start over,' 'We could start over.' Uncertain at best, feeble at worst, Po-wing is the
needy child who wants independence and freedom but can't let go. In contrast,
Fai recognizes his emotional vulnerability. 'I didn't want to start over but return
to Hong Kong,' he claims in voice-over. He is reluctant to trust his ability to
resist the charms of his lover, so he refuses to see Po-wing on several occasions.
'I know what he'll say if I see him.' With the emphasis on Fai's character, Wong
states, 'The story is about how a person quits his habits.'[38] Po-wing is Fai's 'bad
habit': where Fai is stable, Po-wing is volatile; whereas Fai desires monogamy,
Po-wing is promiscuous. There is little talk between them; when they do speak,
they bicker, and argument leads to fighting. Gradually, through a series of 'starting overs,' Fai learns to get over Po-wing and on with his life. He doesn't stop
loving Po-wing, just as he doesn't choose to love him to begin with, but he makes
a choice about how to love him, where they can be 'happy together' – at a
distance.

Fai's starts are strengthened through the relationship he shares with Chang
(Chang Cheh), a young Taiwanese restaurant co-worker who befriends him.
Younger than Fai, and good-humored, Chang brings warmth and wide-eyed
innocence into the movie, set against the cold of the Argentine summer and Fai's
painful experience. Both outsiders in Buenos Aires, the two have loneliness and
their Chineseness in common. And, despite his apparent zest for living, Chang
has tasted unhappiness as well. 'I wasn't happy, that's why I came,' he confides to
Fai. 'I need to think things over before I go back.' Chang's problems remain
unspecified. Perhaps he's dealing with his sexual identity; perhaps not. Maybe he
just wants some adventures before settling into the quotidian. Unlike the evasive-

ness of Po-wing and Fai, who escape to Argentina rather than deal directly with their problems, Chang is working through his and plans to return home eventually.

'Listen carefully,' says Chang to Fai over beers at the Three Amigos cantina. 'You know, I think ears are more important than eyes. You see better with your ears. You can pretend to be happy but your voice can't lie. You can "see" everything by listening.' Music comes close to overwhelming the images in this movie; it certainly substitutes for dialogue. The lengthiest conversations turn up late in the film between Fai and Chang, not Po-wing, and the lovers' only extended conversation (about former partners) is fragmented by the camera and editing. Instead, words are often abrupt and indistinct, their rhythms and intonations more significant than their meaning. Loud music, like that played in Three Amigos or Bar Sur, drowns out conversation. And in numerous scenes, music carries emotional power, matched to the poetic images envisioned. 'If only film was jazz, if only we could jam.... We get closer to this with each film; my camera becomes more and more of a musical instrument,' Doyle writes. 'On and off, different film speeds, frame changes in shot … these are my key and register shifts. I riff, you solo, we jam towards a free form that we believe a film can be.'[39]

The film is saturated with the *nuevo tango* of Argentine composer and bandoneon player Astor Piazzolla, repeating several of his songs throughout. 'My music is sad because tango is sad,' Piazzolla explains. 'Tango is sad, dramatic but not pessimistic. Pessimistic were the old, absurd tango lyrics.'[40] The origins of tango were in the multicultural working-class slums and docks of Buenos Aires along the La Plata river in the late nineteenth century. The history of the music and its dance conveys suffering, sadness, and displacement. Regarded as scandalous and too sexually suggestive by the respectable burghers of town, the dance likewise held a fascination for them, eventually being co-opted and practiced in the finest Argentine and European salons in the early part of the twentieth century. Popularized by Rudolph Valentino in *The Four Horsemen of the Apocalypse*, the tango became a stereotype for the 'Latin lover.' Measured in duple meter with a syncopated, melancholic melody, the music requires a couple to visualize it, dancing physically close but with an unhurried elegance. The tango is a dance of passion, conflict, and domination; it is a dance for lovers. In *Happy Together*, the tango is actually danced on four occasions: first, by the dancers performing for tourists at Bar Sur; second, when Po-wing teaches it to Fai in their room; third, when they dance and kiss in the kitchen; and lastly, when Po-wing dances with a trick in the tango bar and imagines he's dancing with Fai. Yet in addition the tango motif metaphorically controls the film in terms of its emotional temperature and camerawork. The film is a dance, a tango between music and image, a relationship similar to the one described by Doyle to explain his method of cinematography: 'Our kind of camerawork is "anticipation and response. I need to follow the actor/dancer as much as I need him/her to lead."'[41]

The intimacy of the tango is apparent in the film's visual style, particularly its 'timeless' interiors, oddly lit with unusual camera angles, film speeds, and lensing, which are partly explained by chosen shooting conditions – a ten- by twenty-foot room, where shots from above were impossible and there was only so much wall and detail to shoot. 'Tony and Leslie's world is outside time and space,' Doyle writes, and interestingly he conflates the actors with the characters.[42] Likewise, Wong explains,

> I knew I couldn't make a movie about Buenos Aires because I don't know enough about this place. I thought, I will concentrate on these two guys from Hong Kong and in effect the only world that matters to them is in their room. We tried to create Hong Kong in Buenos Aires.[43]

When Po-wing comes back into Fai's life and the character feels alive again, the images are drenched in color, spilling over into the exterior shots – a polluted Buenos Aires sunset glows with reds and oranges. Fai's change in feelings is registered by the repetition of a scene from the boring routine of his job as a doorman at Bar Sur. He photographs yet another Taiwanese tour group arriving by bus, but when they won't remain still, he returns the camera to the tour guide, annoyed, saying, 'Fuck it.' When the scene is replayed, transformed by color, Fai is happy and seems to be unaware of the tediousness of his work. The bold coloration suggests warmth, the heat of a Buenos Aires winter, in opposition to the black-and-white coldness of its summer, and the great emotional distance between Po-wing and Fai.

Like the character Yuddy he played in *Days of Being Wild*, Leslie Cheung's Po-wing is a damaged soul, in such emotional distress that he inflicts pain on those closest to him – in this case Fai. He loves Fai as much as he is able to love, and is more desperately in need of the relationship than Fai is, although on the surface the opposite seems to be the case. In his part of the dance, Po-wing refuses to let his partner, or the cameraman, inside. He tells Fai, 'I just want to be with you. I really do,' and he means it. But he also must keep his partner at a distance, and the long shots which dominate the film's exteriors suggest his motivations, as well as the isolation of the Chinese characters in Buenos Aires. One filmic image resonates with Po-wing's characterization. Seated in their room at the table, Po-wing is glimpsed in a medium shot. He looks outside the balcony doors as a breeze gently blows the translucent curtains. One moment he is there, the next he is gone, while the rest of the shot remains the same. He is a ghost of a character, registered by his absence, his inability to commit to a relationship, and his confusion and pain. Perhaps this characterization accounts for much of the audience reaction abroad to this film – beautiful to watch, but cold. Likewise, among some gay audiences, the film is perceived as a statement about gay relationships as dysfunctional, suggesting a general homophobia. This is far from being the case, as Wong has consistently claimed: 'It is not a gay film. It's a love story about being lonely with somebody else; being happy together could also mean being happy with yourself, with your past.'[44]

Fai's happiest time with Po-wing, he tells us, is during Po-wing's recovery from his beating by a trick from whom he's stolen an expensive watch to give to Fai so that he can return to Hong Kong. Po-wing unexpectedly knocks on Fai's door and collapses into his former lover's embrace. Similarly, after hospital, he leans upon Fai in the taxi ride home. Unable to use his hands, which are in casts, Po-wing is totally dependent upon Fai for his survival. As the lamplight of the Iguazu souvenir revolves around the room, casting shadows on walls and objects, Fai, leaning against the wall like a spent lover, watches over the sleeping Po-wing. Shot in black and white, the scene lasts for just half a minute, with Fai's accompanying voice-over, only revealed to the audience because he cannot tell Po-wing. 'Some things I never told Po-wing. I didn't want him to recover too fast. Those days were our happiest together.' With the economy of several quick cuts and changes in film speed, Fai goes over to Po-wing and caresses his eyebrow with a single finger. Po-wing turns in his sleep. Fai looks at himself in the bathroom mirror. Happiness is brief for Fai, and who he sees in the mirror is open to question.

Wittgenstein writes,

> When people say 'everything flows' we feel that we are prevented from grasping the actuality, the actual reality. The process on the screen escapes us, just because it is a process. But we certainly describe something; and is it a different process? But the description is obviously connected with the picture on the screen. Our sense of helplessness must rest upon a false picture. Because what we want to be able to describe is something that we are able to describe.[45]

So what does *Happy Together* describe? It expresses distance, both physical and emotional; audiences who experience it as cold or distant have been affected by its power. Whether distance shots of Buenos Aires by night, on its north–south grid featuring the city center obelisk, neon signs and frenzied stream of car lights, all pushing the film speed; or the deep shadows cast at La Boca, with its silhouetted bridges and buildings which dwarf the characters; or the long shots of vast pampas and road, the physical distances and emotional separations of characters are huge. Doors close to separate them, just as spaces open to keep them apart. The alley soccer game played by the restaurant workers is like a De Chirico painting. Notwithstanding the cameraderie of the game, the sunspots on the camera and the extended shadows of the players on the cobbled street evoke silences. Fai is foregrounded from the group, and eventually, through starting over, he is a player as well.

Iguazu Falls appears twice in the film. Following the couple's break-up 'across a grassy space dissected by approach roads to the Patagonian highway,'[46] a jump cut to an aerial shot of the falls reveals the natural wonder in all its majesty. Shot from a helicopter with Chris Doyle leaning out and the helicopter circling at a 35-degree tilt, the image is sheer poetry in motion. As the blackened pools of water cascade downward into powerful, raw forces, the mushrooming white mist bubbles upward. It is a splendor to behold. Notes Doyle, 'No video, no photo, no place I've ever been has prepared me for the Falls. The roar, the rush, the energy.'[47] For a minute and a half, the Falls fills the screen as Caetano Veloso's mellifluous voice sings 'Cucurrucucu Paloma' to full orchestration. The Falls features as an ideal and impossible imagined place where the couple can be 'happy together,' and it is only their recurrence towards the film's end, where each looks at the Falls, Po-wing at the lamp and Fai actually there, that the couple are happy together, again, at a distance. The second appearance of the Falls repeats the first but also places Fai in the *mise-en-scène* with his accompanying voice-over: 'I finally reach Iguazu. Suddenly I think of Ho Po-wing. I feel very sad. I believe there should be two of us standing here.' For a full two minutes, similar shots of the Falls, in all its primeval glory, shine, accompanied by Piazzolla's 'Tango Apasionado' (Finale); its doleful tune is overtaken by the roaring rush of the Falls, the only sound heard for a full half-minute.

This music, and then the silence, are of supreme significance. It is the same music to which Fai and Po-wing dance earlier in the film. Their intimacy is tangible set against the blue fluorescent lighting exaggerated by the white-tiled walls. They become all lovers, in a place where time and space no longer matter, an impossible and ideal place which we all know cannot last. The music records the sorrow of this knowledge. This is Wong's love song to Hong Kong. Here the filmmakers come closest to creating what Marcuse calls 'an "authentic language" – the language of negation as the Great Refusal to accept the rules of a game in which the dice are loaded. The absent must be made present because the greatest part of the truth is in that which is absent.'[48]

The lost Po-wing 'starts over' again in Buenos Aires, moving into the room Fai has left behind, curled in a fetal position, crying, his clock changing time from 23:59 to 00:00 (an oblique handover reference). 'It's loneliness, departure, loss incarnate,' comments Doyle on the visual theme.[49] Po-wing has danced the last tango, his partner the former male dancer of the team that performed for the tourists at Bar Sur, yet in his heart and mind's eye, he is with Fai. They, too, dance to the 'Tango Apasionata' (Finale). Fai, meantime, has started over, through a series of jobs which take him from a restaurant kitchen to an abattoir, even occasionally prostituting himself to earn the airfare home. Doing what he formerly criticized his lover for, he begins to understand Po-wing better, and manages to return Po-wing's passport to him without meeting face-to-face – a final letting go of his former lover. Chang assists him, taking with him a recording of Fai's sobs to the lighthouse at Ushuaia, at the end of the world. Fai remarks, 'They say people with emotional problems can dump all their troubles there,' and Fai's sobs from the heart are left behind. Doyle comments: 'We didn't really know what certain details or colors or actions meant at the time we filmed them. They anticipated where the film would take us. They were in a sense images from the future – from the time we've only just reached.'[50]

The scene is marvelously shot, brightly lit, by Doyle on a boat using a tele-photo lens, going down to 8–12 frames per second, swooping and tracking by

Chang on the rocks at the lighthouse. It looks like the edge of the world, with random pans of sky, sea, Chang, and the lighthouse. The scene is invigorating and life-affirming, matched only by Fai's final scenes. Having worked nights and double shifts in the abattoir, he's already back on Hong Kong time. As his voice-over relates, 'Watching TV I realize Hong Kong is on the opposite side of the world from Argentina. How does Hong Kong look upside down?' We see with his inner eye, as a montage of Hong Kong's urban landscape of highways, skyscrapers, and malls plays upside down, accompanied by the white noise of radio.

Having earlier tried phoning home to make amends with his father for having stolen money from his father's friend and the son's boss, Fai writes a letter. 'At home I didn't talk to him. Now I want to tell him many things. I don't know what he'd think after the letter. In the end I say I hope he'd give me a chance to start over.' On a stopover in Taipei, we glimpse a television report of Deng Xiaoping's death and see Fai open the sliding glass doors of his hotel room. Next he moves through the night market of Taipei, visiting the food stall of Chang's family. Followed by a hand-held camera, Fai is reassured by the warmth and liveliness of the marketplace. He takes a photo of Chang from the stall, explaining in voice-over, 'I can see why he can afford running around so freely. There's a place where he can always return. I don't know when I'll see him again, what I know is if I want to I know where I can find him.' He is acknowledging the home Chang has to return to, and is thinking about his own. In Wong's most positive ending to date, Fai takes the Taipei train with the action moving rapidly. Half turning, glancing at his watch, he remembers the past. A hint of a smile crosses his face as he looks ahead, and the camera shows us what he sees – the future before him – Hong Kong. To the tune of Danny Chung's upbeat cover of 'Happy Together,' the train pulls into the station. Doyle writes, 'It's our brightest film in all senses of the word and looks like having the happiest ending of any Wong Kar-wai film.'[51]

Happy Together offers several possible scenarios for the reunion of Hong Kong and China: escape, lament, embrace, acceptance, and choice. Rather than provide simple commentary, the movie maps out complications, contradictions, and conflicts, reflecting the preoccupations and concerns of Hong Kong people on the brink of the handover. As Ryan observes,

> Films can ... help create a new social discourse by offering representations of new values, institutions, and modes of behavior for collective identification and internalized

modeling. Film discourse and social discourse intertwine as a struggle not over how reality will be represented but over what that reality will be. Films play a role in the social construction of reality in that they influence collectively held representations or ideas of what society is and should be.[52]

This 'milonga' (tango party) for three, featuring Hong Kong, the Mainland and Taiwan, is still playing. Another Piazzolla song, 'Milonga for Three,' plays as Fai's and Po-wing's life together begins to unravel; Fai and Chang socialize at the Three Amigos cantina; Fai's 'happy together,' reconciling his past to his present and future, gives hope.

TWELVE

MEET THE NEW BOSS, SAME AS THE OLD BOSS

Advance units of the People's Liberation Army (PLA) began crossing the border into Hong Kong several months prior to the 1 July 1997 return. Arriving amidst little fanfare and almost unnoticed, Chinese personnel began to replace the British military garrison with upwards of ten thousand Mainland troops. It was a far cry from the situation thirty years earlier when, during the heady days of the Cultural Revolution, British soldiers were placed on full alert in expectation of a Red Guard assault on the colony that never came. Of course, the present 'invasion' would be marked by the pomp and pageantry of handover ceremonies, bringing old and new colonials together in their designer attire to sip Meursault and sup on Beijing duck in 'surroundings that looked like Ralph Lauren had done Shanghai, circa 1920.'[1] The handover itself was the embodiment of spectacle. Costing more than US$130 million, events ranged from gala balls held at various swank hotels for local and foreign elites, to street parades for the vast majority of Hong Kong residents to a fireworks and laser-light show over Victoria Harbor. As the handing over of the keys to the city by Britain's Prince Charles to Tung Chee-hwa made evident, simulacra permeated the entire proceedings. The ceremonies reflected the basic reality of the transference of political sovereignty over Hong Kong from Great Britain to the People's Republic of China, masked and perverted by the fact that attendance at the official handover was limited to an invitation-only list of about four thousand foreign dignitaries. They marked the absence of that reality by turning the formal transfer of power from Britain to China into a Buddhist ritual.

And they actually bore no relation to the reality of the transfer, by becoming a performance in front of international television cameras for viewers around the globe (including a US$30 million party with a sunset send-off to the British).[2]

Politically, the handover meant a change in Hong Kong's government: a Special Administrative Region (SAR) chief executive replaced the colonial governor, and a provisional legislature took over from the legislative council. Where the British had appointed governors, Beijing delegated selection of the chief executive to a hand-picked committee. Many Hong Kongers see this as a mere rubber stamp for whomever the PRC want to fill the position. And where the legislative council after 1995 was the most democratic and open assembly in the colony's history (a belated and cynical expansion of political rights by the outgoing power), Beijing opted for a scheme that granted hegemony to business interests, who hold more than 50 per cent of the alloted seats, while underrepresenting the grassroots. Not unexpectedly, the first chief executive has strong ties to the Mainland: conservative businessman Tung Chee-hwa's relationship dates from the Chinese government's bail-out of his shipping firm in the 1980s. Upon taking office Tung expressed concern that labor union growth would eat away at profits and dull Hong Kong's economic competitive edge. Disturbingly, suspension of newly won labor rights – including union membership without discrimination, collective bargaining, and the use of union funds for political purposes – was among the first actions of the Chinese-appointed legislature. In the weeks and months following the handover, the Provisional Legislature restricted the franchise in legislative elections, curtailed powers of future elected legislators, and abolished collective bargaining and worker protection against anti-union discrimination. Subsequent actions included tightening regulation of political groups and public assemblies, abrogating provisions in Hong Kong's Bill of Rights concerning matters between private individuals, and exempting agencies of the Chinese government from Hong Kong laws, including those on privacy and sex discrimination.[3] Apparently, 'the interests of the capitalist class in Hong Kong and the rulers in Beijing are the same: keeping the workers down and minimizing popular politics.'[4]

Elections to establish a permanent legislature were held in the spring of 1998 amidst charges that the process was undemocratic. Chastising the restrictive vote as 'birdcage democracy,' critics of the regime took a variety of positions – from calling for the boycott of the ballot box, to running for office under protest, to accepting electoral rules on the grounds that it was possible for 'liberal democrats' to compose a meaningful minority bloc in the post-election assembly.[5] Complicated procedures allowed approximately 140,000 people from the professional-managerial stratum to elect a 400-member committee, responsible in turn for selecting ten councilors and thirty functional constituency legislators, principally to represent corporate, financial, and real-estate interests. The remaining twenty seats, which almost three million Hong Kongers were eligible to participate in electing, would represent geographical constituencies. An unprecedented 53 per cent of this electorate turned out in a driving rainstorm to cast a vote in an election widely recognized to be flawed. Defying polls which had projected that fewer than one-third would exercise their right of franchise, citizens began laying to rest the 'apathy' label. In electing fifteen 'pro-democracy' candidates, voters expressed both their dissatisfaction with Tung Chee-hwa's government and their desire for change.

Hong Kong's new govermment had the misfortune to assume power on the cusp of the Asian 'economic meltdown' that turned former high-growth economies into 'paper tigers.'[6] While Hong Kong did not experience the devastation of Indonesia, Malaysia, or Thailand, its financial markets were hit in October 1997 and August 1998 by speculators driving down currencies and stock markets throughout the region. Perceptions of the soundness of the territory's economy, with its export orientation producing trade surpluses instead of deficits, were tested when the government refused to devalue the Hong Kong dollar relative to other Asian currencies. With the strength of that dollar making SAR exports less attractive when compared to competitors, Hong Kong experienced negative growth rates for the first time since 1961 and 5 per cent unemployment (twice the rate at the time of the handover) during 1998.[7] Meanwhile, the Hong Kong Monetary Authority spent HK$118 (US$14.3) thousand million of reserve funds in stock-market operations, attempting to push out speculators who were both dumping the SAR's dollar and shorting local stocks and futures.[8]

The SAR goverment grappled with numerous problems during its initial year of existence, mishandling situations and making enough mistakes to provide its critics with ammunition. Chief Executive Tung came under fire for his tardy and inept response to a 'bird flu' epidemic: the wholesale killing of the territory's chickens followed doctors' expression of concern that the virus could spread from poultry to humans. Moreover, the incident called attention to the absence of a local health policy to deal with matters ranging from unhygienic food preparation to growing air pollution. Public debate ensued over the government's decision requiring three-quarters of secondary schools to teach in Cantonese dialect and the remainder to teach in English. Although the policy was touted by government officials as an attempt to arrest the spread of 'Chinglish,' and promoted as a matter of pride, parents with children in the former schools nevertheless perceived themselves as the 'losers': English-language schools are widely viewed as more successful in preparing students for higher education and well-remunerated employment. As Hong Kong became the most expensive city in the world in which to live, with a typical flat of 700 square feet selling for US$630,000,[9] opponents of the regime charged the government with backing away from plans to expand housing stock under pressure from real-estate developers. The government's difficulties were compounded by the fiasco surrounding the troubled 1998 summer opening of Chep Lap Kok airport. Unfortunately for the SAR government, the new facility opened to glitches and complaints when computer systems malfunctioned, leaving passengers and cargo stranded.

Despite evidence of political unease and the worst economic conditions in a generation, Hong Kong's first year as a Special Administrative Region of China closed with the two peoples in coexistence. Public activism and protest were neither as low-key as some maintained nor as widespread as others expected; many of the thousand-plus demonstrations reported by March 1998 involved small numbers of people.[10] The first anniversary was marked officially by ceremonies presided over by Chinese president Jiang Zemin, and unofficially by a freedom rally and human rights march sponsored by thirty 'pro-democracy' groups.

Post-handover cinema generally moved in two directions. One group of films continued travelling the well-worn path of violence and destruction. These post-return stories are characterized by doubt and nihilistic mayhem. Another path represents the 'can't we just all get along' message – Chinese characters from Hong Kong and the Mainland discover shared cultural values despite their differences, through co-operative efforts at learning mutual respect. The early post-return films *Full Alert* and *Destination Ninth Heaven*, released in July 1997, set the coordinates representing the two extremes.

Ringo Lam's *Full Alert* opens *in medias res*, with cops arriving at a murder crime scene, intercut with opening credits and a stamped postmark 'Hong Kong 1997' appearing next to the title, announcing its preoccupation from the start. An easily solved murder serves simply as a plot device to introduce criminal Mak Kwan (Francis Ng), cop Pao (Lau Ching-wan), and the crime-waiting-to-happen, a vault robbery. For the remainder, Pao (as in Justice Pao) attempts to prevent Kwan (so named after the god of both Triads and cops, and a character name Ng has used in numerous movies) from carrying out his plans, as Hong Kong's geography is mapped out one last time – 'they're heading for Central… Gloucester Road… the High Court Building… toward Hennessey Road… Wanchai North… force them to Sheung Wan where it's less crowded.' Yet Kwan's psychological make-up won't allow him to lose, and he will take revenge on the Jockey Club. Pao's intervention cannot change what is already under way; it can only ensure that both lose something. Subtextually, the Mainland will follow through with the Joint Declaration Agreement, as any changes would appear as a loss of face, and Hong Kongers will be affected no matter what they do. The structure is tightly wound, with the tension intensifying as the story progresses. Lam includes streetcar chases, shoot-outs, and an insider's look at the personal lives of the cops and criminals; violence is abrupt, brutal, and hands-on, whether it be the bludgeoning to death of a criminal by the boss with a shovel or Pao beating Kwan's head against his vehicle, then kicking him while down. When the criminal succeeds in getting into the vault and Pao cannot, Kwan tells him, 'We are standing on two different sides. I have to get back what I lost.' It is easy to visualize Kwan as a stand-in for Mainland and Pao for Hong Kong Chinese. The cat-and-mouse game and the mirror-imaging of cop and criminal come full circle when Pao kills Kwan's girlfriend in self-defense, but overreacts, emptying his pistol's chamber into her already lifeless body. Both men are haunted by killing; with Kwan's suicide and the case's completion, we are left with an image rarely glimpsed in Hong Kong movies – a Chinese man in close-up crying, as a requiem for all Chinese plays on the soundtrack through closing credits.

At the other extreme, Wong Chun-man's *Destination Ninth Heaven* was one of the first post-return films to convey co-operation: Hong Kongers and Mainlanders not only coexist but learn to get along. The story is a behind-the-scenes look at the development of a rocket launch at Xichiang, to send the Hong Kong Satellite Star, a communications satellite, into space. Ttimed to take place on reunification day, the project is a co-operative effort between the PRC government research institute and Hong Kong business interests, represented by wealthy entrepreneur Chin Ching (Winston Chiao). Mainland scientist Chieng Shan (Tony Leung Ka-fai), the designer behind the project, describes rockets not as weaponry but as communication and weather forecasting devices to be used in solving China's food shortage problem. He is a noble and symbolic character rooted firmly in the past and yet looking to the future. Scenes from his childhood link him to the country schoolchildren eager to learn and participate in making their country's future; documentary footage of the PRC's first rocket launch and references to its forty subsequent successful missions locate him in a story of progress and patriotism. When Chin's daughter Mona (Gigi Lau), a Harvard physics graduate, decides to involve herself in the project, Chinese cultures clash; through her experience, Mona overcomes her prejudices against Mainlanders and rejects her Hong Kong rich-girl lifestyle.

Chin's belief in Mainland investment for the future is underscored by the commitment his former lover Joey Yick makes by establishing Yishi Electronics Corporation factories in Tianjin. 'I find this is a good beginning, a real good chance,' she says. Tientsin officials explain that three guarantees are offered to foreign investors – confidence, honesty, and laws – and that 'the biggest guarantee we can give you is laws,' implying the PRC's commitment to the Joint Declaration Agreement. Most telling is Mona's conversion. The Mainland countryside is an idyllic, simple place, where the 'air is clean and quiet'; 'people here are not educated. Their quality is low too. But they have much concern and conscience,' Lin Hoi Yuen, Chieng Shan's wife, tells Mona, and she observes as much. When Mona takes her country schoolchildren to the Great Wall, one of her students promises, 'We won't let Hong Kong people down. We'll become good Chinese. We'll repay by appreciation to those persons who have helped us.' For good measure, Chieng Shan dies of stomach cancer following the successful rocket launch. For Mainlanders, life is sacrifice, but with Hong Kongers' co-operation, the life of all Chinese will improve.

Some post-return movies maneuver between the extremes in their exploration of complex relationships. Among films that examine identity and desire are Jacob Cheung's appropriately English-titled *Intimates* (1997) and Stanley Kwan's *Hold You Tight* (1998). Cheung's film, a moving portrait of two women's love and friendship, juxtaposes past and present in telling the story of Wan (Carina Lau) and Foon

(Charlie Young). Separated during a World War II Japanese bombing raid, the pair do not see one another for more than half a century, when Foon, in her life's twilight, returns home to China from the United States. Anita Tong's screenplay cross-cuts the trip, in which the elderly woman is accompanied by her former employer's daughter, with flashbacks of Wan and Foon together in earlier days. The younger woman (Theresa Lee), distraught over her boyfriend's decision to break off their relationship, is annoyed by Foon (who the audience later learns is actually Wan) when she dismisses the guy with 'don't waste time on him.' Woven throughout *Intimates*' dialectic of 'then and now' are issues ranging from arranged marriage, female sexual celibacy, and self-abortion to generational difference, male sexual exploitation, and lesbian companionship. Wan's and Foon's emotional re-union at the end is testimony to the bond that exists between them, much like that existing between Hong Kong and China after all these years. But it also conveys that homosexuals have emotional needs and sexual desires equal to those felt by straight people. Tong's and Cheung's message is tolerance and acceptance of the right to live an openly sexual life, whether on the screen or in the street, without recrimination. Meanwhile, Kwan's *Hold You Tight*, his first feature since becoming the most prominent Hong Kong film person publicly to acknowledge his homosexuality, examines gay and straight relationships. This intricate picture examines how chance enters into the lives of four characters. Bored housewife Moon (Chingmy Yau) resorts to sex with a young lifeguard. Her husband Fung-wai (Sunny Chan) appears not to know what he has been missing in his marriage until Moon is killed in a plane crash. Real-estate agent Tong (Eric Tsang), cruises gay saunas at night and befriends the widower while trying to pick him up. Dou-jie (Ko Yu-lun), Moon's teenage suitor, begins following Fung-wai after her death, only to fall in love with him.

Donnie Yen's *Ballistic Kiss* (1998) revives Hong Kong action as mood piece. A low-budget production by Hong Kong standards, costing about US$475,000, this feature not only harkens back to the on-the-fly nuts-and-bolts approach of mid-1980s' moviemaking but draws from the stylishness of Wong Kar-wai's art cinema via Japanese auteur Kitano Takeshi. Yen makes camerawork a character, using stylish artificial lighting – primarily smoky blues but also lurid greens and reds – to establish and sustain tone. Experimenting with close-ups, slo-mo, flash-pans, and white-outs, Yen is searching for his own distinctive style of storytelling and filmmaking by adding dramatic tension and strong visual contrasts. When hardcore martial arts fans complained that the camerawork was too fast to see much of the action, they failed to appreciate the rhythm and feel of the film.

Ballistic Kiss includes six violent action sequences, mostly combining guns and martial arts. Two are grandly orchestrated: one set on Causeway Bay's Times Square mega-mall rooftop, the other in a darkened movie theater. Countless squibs squirt blood as bodies fly, guns reverberate, and bones crack. Like a fighter, the camera creates heady visuals as it roves, zooms in and out, and dizzily flash-pans across the action, re-creating the confusion, intensity, energy, and 'feel' of a fight. Yet all the scenes begin abruptly in the midst of slowly built dramatic tension; they are absorbed by the moody introspection of the main character, hired hit man Cat (Donnie Yen), whose presence prevades the film through blue lighting and Yukie Nishimura's beautiful melancholic music, featuring piano, strings, and woodwind, as he laments his state and that of Hong Kong. Cat reflects, 'It's all the same after a while. People's lives are actually pretty pathetic,' and comments that, 'there comes a time in your career when you wonder what it's all about.'

The literal translation of the movie's title, *Kill Some People, Dance a Little*, indicates the movie's rhythms; so does Cat's philosophy of life – 'Some days it rains, some days it shines … Rain, rain, it sucks. I hate the fucking rain … I wonder when will it stop?' For the viewer, there is much more mood than action; for Cat there is more rain than sun. This alienated loner dances with an imaginary partner and, dream-like, in a series of dissolves, on the rooftop with Carrie (Annie Wu), the 'angel' of his imaginings, a moment so fragile and transitory that it stops abruptly and disappears. Loving from afar, he has watched her on her balcony across from his apartment in Happy Valley. 'I have to look at you every night before I sleep and dream as if you were my angel,' he thinks, the camera cutting between Carrie, gazing across her balcony, and Cat, inside, peering through the slats of half-opened blinds. Carrie is part of a police unit put on special assignment to find an assassin – Cat. Little happiness is to be had here, and is apparent only for moments, as when they meet as if by chance while waiting for a bus, or when Cat slowly reaches out his hand to her, or when they passionately embrace.

Stylish cinematography (a collaboration between Yen, Wong Ka-fai, and three other cameramen) is as significant and striking in the fighting as in the extended sad and touching drama. White-outs are used to indicate flashbacks played out in

Cat's mind, including betrayal by his best friend and Cat's abuse in prison. Close-ups on the faces of Cat and Carrie, with cuts between them and voiced-over complementary thoughts, bring them together. Other close-ups of personal objects and slow-pans across their apartments are telling devices of characterization. Long shots from rooftops as the couple overlook Hong Kong identify a sense of place and their part in it. In one such scene, when Cat has told Carrie that 'there is no good or bad in this world, just weak and strong,' Carrie suggests that 'in life you find other things as well, good things.' Cat turns to look at her and the camera follows him, shooting in slo-mo as he approaches her. He reaches out his hand to her, a close-up of his open palm held for a few seconds, then a reverse two-shot from over Carrie's shoulder revealing Cat's tender expression. Before she can reach out to him, there is a brief fade to black and a cut to the couple dancing on the rooftop. This is one of those wonderful moments, full of emotion and the establishment of a tenuous goodness in the world of post-return Hong Kong. Yen says, 'I'm very demanding and specific when it comes down to my film; each frame of the work is my view of how I wanted to present on screen.... When you watch my films, you're feeling my heart.'[11]

Ironically, distances between people abound despite Hong Kong's compactness. From the radio call-in show with DJ Simon (Cat's regular confessional) to numerous flashbacks (Cat's days in New York), contacts, thoughts and feelings are kept at arm's length. The Hong Kong cops decide that the assassin they're hunting is probably a Mainlander, not a Hong Konger – he comes from a distance, not within. Carrie must endure a neighbor's loud lovemaking while talking 'long distance'; she tells her mother, 'you know how I am, I just haven't *found* the right one,' referring to her lack of a relationship. Rather than share intimacy with a partner, she sits in an empty movie theater running a porn movie and watches vicariously while bullets hammer away around her. Cat asks her, 'Have you ever tried talking to friends and realized afterwards that you didn't really say anything?' Indeed, words between them, though personal, are measured. The film opens with a disembodied voice over a black screen as Simon croons, 'We spend ten hours a day, everyday, at work with a mask on. We say and do things that we don't want to say and do. I'm tired. Aren't you? Tonight let's be ourselves. Give me a call. Let's share your secrets.' The camera reveals him in a blue-filtered light, surrounded not by companions, or even people, but by machinery of his trade,

courtesy/permission of Bullet Film Productions Ltd and Donnie Yen

SHOT IN THE HEART   Donnie Yen in Donnie Yen's *Ballistic Kiss*

futilely going around in circles, getting nowhere, as he twirls in his mechanical chair. Even the code shared by Cat and his former partner works by adding distance to their set meeting places. Distance, isolation, and miscommunications define lives.

Shared by Hong Kongers are work and its burden. 'I have to work nights,' Cat tells Simon. 'I just do my job when I have orders,' says Cat; the DJ recounts that many professions, including those of movie stars, prostitutes, mailmen, DJs and the governor, receive orders, adding, 'Basically, from the first day we are born, we take orders.' Such is life in the post-1997 world. Cat's former partner Wesley Wong (Jimmy Wong), currently working for a big-time criminal, can't believe he has been fired (and will be eliminated) because 'I always do a nice job for you'; now the double-crosser is double-crossed. In post-return Hong Kong, where the current perception is that the government is increasingly out of touch with the people, Hong Kongers turn on each other, whether cops against the criminals, criminals against each other, women against men, or vice-versa. Wong uses Carrie as a bodyshield against bullets just as others use his girlfriend. Wong's girlfriend betrays him but rationalizes that 'it's only business.' Wong slaps Carrie's roommate brutally and repeatedly across the face while his henchman punches her hard enough to knock her out. The cop special force unit doesn't notify its superiors when trailing Cat because they fear a bad report will be filed against them. Promoted in the police force, Carrie resentfully informs Cat that her job is to clean up the mess the killer leaves behind. The agent (Vincent Kok) employing Cat tells him, 'You're like a pizza man, you always deliver,' to which Cat retorts, 'I deliver when I get paid.' The agent then tempts him with another job. 'Easy money, how about it?' he asks. He proclaims that Cat is 'the best,' but tells the next gun-for-hire (sent to eliminate Cat) the same. People in this scenario work against each other, or 'take care of business' simply for financial gain. 'You know, Hong Kong! Materialistic!' says Cat. Responding to Asia's current economic crisis, these panicked Hong Kongers scapegoat each other.[12]

The movie is dark both visually and thematically; this is represented through the light-sensitive, and therefore generally darkened, glasses that Cat wears. His vision of Hong Kong is dark indeed. Twice in the film he describes what he sees, first in Cantonese looking over the flats of Happy Valley from a rooftop, and second in English voice-over, near the film's end as he lies dying, having been 'ballistically kissed.' He is surrounded by cops, who are running around him pointing guns as he painfully and ineffectually reaches for his glasses, a visual representation of Hong Kongers' confused struggle against their own. Carrie, hysterical, strains, held back by others, but breaks free to hold the dying Cat. Her roommate looks on, genuinely moved but puzzled, and we view the scene, shot in slo-mo, through her eyes. In voice-over, Cat narrates once more: 'It is so quiet and peaceful. But if you really look at each home, each window and look inside those ordinary lives, what do you see? Sons stealing from mothers, wives betraying husbands, the rape of children, women being beaten.… Anger, sickness and despair.' Carrie likewise shares a similar view. 'Are there any values in human life any more?' she asks her roommate. When she puts on Cat's glasses while visiting his grave at the film's end and the musical theme recurs, we know that his perspective has been passed on to her. A black-and-white sequence, with Cat moving through the streets, appears very early in the film and recurs with his death, following Carrie into the graveyard. This absence of color, this bleakness, reflects Hong Kong belongers' psyche amidst the return and the Asian economic crisis.

Much as sweeping Mainland repression of Hong Kong failed to materialize, draconian restrictions on the film industry were little in evidence. Actor Jordan Chan has witnessed no 'chilling effect'. Meanwhile, director Chueng Yuen-ting, in noting that the censorship system remains the same, says, 'nothing much happened and we are free to make films now as before.' Industry and public pressure spared the 1998 Hong Kong International Film Festival of political editing by forcing the government to overturn its decision to prohibit the screening of *History in the Making: Hong Kong 1997*, a series of short documentaries. Three Hollywood pictures believed to be too controversial for Beijing's liking opened in the SAR as well: *Seven Years in Tibet* and *Kundun*, which deal with Buddhist Tibet, considered sovereign territory by the Chinese government; and *Red Corner,* starring Dalai Lama devotee Richard Gere as a US businessman who is framed by corrupt PRC oficials.

A greater immediate threat to the cinema's well-being was the Asian financial meltdown; as Derek Elley wrote in early 1998, 'since Hong Kong's handover to China, there have been no signs of film production being either helped or hindered. The raising of finance rather than reds under the bed is the main problem for producers.'[13] Currency devaluations in Bankok, Jakarta, Kuala Lumpur, Manila, and Seoul exacerbated the trend of falling Asian box-office revenues as overseas distributors balked at paying the higher prices resulting from the relative strength of Hong Kong's dollar (which remained pegged to the US dollar). A few voices suggested abandoning overseas markets altogether, though autarky hardly seems a realistic option given the SAR's small audience base, one made even smaller by rising unemployment and wage reductions in the territory itself. One consequence of five years' falling local movie ticket sales has been a decrease in output: the approximately one hundred Hong Kong movies of 1997 (about half the number made in the early 1990s) dropped to around fifty in 1998. Disppearing profits even expedited the withdrawal of the Triads from the film business.

According to filmmaker Cheung Yuen-ting,

> the current Asian economic crisis is affecting the film industry in a profound way. The audience is very careful about the choice of which film to see. That's why they flock to see big Hollywood films which guarantee good value for money. Furthermore, some of our most popular stars have crossed over to Hollywood. Because of the shrinking economic situation, local films are made on shoestring budgets and very tight schedules. That makes it even harder for local films to compete with Hollywood films. Many of the big local film studios have been forced out of business or forced to reduce their yearly output. However, since there is no major trend now, it is easier for filmmakers like myself to find financing for non-mainstream types of films. Since everybody is at a loss as to what type of films can make money, film bosses are willing to bet on filmmakers who can provide a full script and a reasonable cast.

Golden Harvest's Raymond Chow suggests that much of what is wrong with Hong Kong movies is due to the paucity of good screenwriters. Historically, such writers have been poorly paid; companies typically pay about US$12,500 for a completed script, with authors generally waiving rights to residual and royalty payments. In the past, of course, many productions were shot without written stories or dialogue. However, the commercial, not to mention critical, success of films such as Peter Chan's script-driven *He's a Woman, She's a Man* and *Comrades, Almost a Love Story* in the declining 1990s' market did not go unnoticed. Meanwhile, superstar Jackie Chan has offered HK$1 million (about US$125,000) for a good screenplay, while the Milkyway Image company hired a Hollywood 'script doctor' to introduce 'American techniques to make Hong Kong films better,' according to creative development director Christina Lee.[14]

Other problems continue to dog Hong Kong cinema. First, unauthorized copy-
ing of video compact discs (VCDs) remains prevalent despite stepped-up efforts
– including barcodes stamped on legal discs, police raids, monetary rewards for
information leading to convictions, and stiffer criminal penalties – to combat
bootlegging. As film critic Paul Fonoroff notes, 'A movie can come out for the
12:30 show and by 5 o'clock you can buy VCDs for sale on the street.'[15] Pirated
discs are of poorer quality than theater screenings and studio-manufactured home-
viewing formats; nevertheless, they have captured about 40 per cent of the
industry's business. In light of the economic downturn, actor Jordan Chan's comment seems apropos: 'Because people's income is less, they naturally will have less
entertainment. Copied VCDs are more popular, people are less willing to go to
the theater, more people stay at home.' Hong Kongers can purchase five black-
market discs for the equivalent of US$13, less than one-third of the cost of going
five times to the cinema; and, as the proprietor of one store selling illegal disks
remarked, 'If you don't like the quality, you can bring them back and exchange
them for something else.'[16] Despite the industry's introduction of discounted ticket
prices in the summer of 1997, both movie attendance and box office receipts
declined for a fifth year while the number of theater closings grew.

Second, the Hong Kong box office continues to feel Hollywood's impact as the
showing of imported films climbed to a historic high of 69 per cent in late 1997.
Although the top ten for that year showed more local productions than foreign
movies, revenues from the latter far exceeded those from the former. For example,
income from *The Lost World: Jurassic Park* far exceeded perennial winner Jackie
Chan's entry *Mr Nice Guy* (1997) to finish number one.[17] The 1998 Lunar New
Year market, dominated in years past by the likes of Chan, Stephen Chiau, and the
Young and Dangerous series, went to *Titanic*; it not only beat Chan's *Who Am I?*,
Chiau's *The Lucky Guy*, and *Young and Dangerous 5*, but remained in the top ten for
five months, including ten weeks at number one, becoming the all-time leading
performer in Hong Kong film history. Theater runs of the Hollywood débuts of
local stars Michelle Yeoh and Chow Yun-fat, *Tomorrow Never Dies* (1997) and *The
Replacement Killers* (1998), did little to stop the *Titanic* juggernaut. As many as eight
foreign films could be found in the box office top ten at a given time in 1998.[18]
Yet even the opening of a third foreign-owned theater chain, committed to showing mostly Hollywood productions, cannot hide the fact that the growing presence

of imported motion pictures coincides with a steep decline in overall movie attendance.

As profits evaporated, motion picture production companies either went out of business or resorted to borrowing working capital from banks. Depression-level conditions reduced film industry employment from 6,000 in 1995 to 3,500 two years later. Hit hard by economic losses, two of Hong Kong's locally owned theater chains looked to reduce costs by merging their operations, a move some thought would narrow the range of films shown and reduce the quantity of movies screened, thereby driving out smaller businesses and creating even more unemployment. As Cheung Yuen-ting point outs, 'the problem of the crew and cast working on several films simultaneously is gone. But other problems arise, people try to finish films in nine days and the budget of some of the smaller productions is down to under a million Hong Kong dollars' (less than US$150,000). With trained film personnel either laid off or leaving the industry in search of job security elsewhere, the advent of cheaper labor led Tsui Hark to remark, 'sad to say, there are crews who actually have no idea what they are supposed to do on the set.' A self-fulfilling prophecy is at work here: the quality of Hong Kong films, which produce little revenue and fail to turn a profit, is criticized; investors reduce future financing, which results in smaller budgets and shorter production time; a downward spiral in quality of pictures ensues.

In certain instances, the making of more vicious movies may be another consequence. For example, one retrograde trend that has emerged from the financial crisis in Hong Kong is a series of what performer Karen Mok deplores as 'rape films requiring little budget and production.' In one sense, films such as *Raped By an Angel II* and *III* (both 1998; both reaching number two at the local box office), *Severely Rape* (1998), and *Rape Trap* (1998) correspond to the male-centered voyeurism associated with cinematic rape that Molly Haskell described some years ago. Thus they produce as well as mirror the ideological notion that men desire to, and in fact do, control women. Although such films were never absent from the screen in the past, recent Hong Kong rape films go beyond the mere assertion of male power and phallic domination and link voyeurism to sadism. In *Raped II*, an ostensible comedy, potential victims are murdered for refusing to submit to their assailant. As Laura Mulvey charges, 'Sadism needs a story';[19] the one told here, in effect, punishes women for Hong Kong's recent economic difficulties.

Producer/director Wong Jing, whose stock-in-trade is the recycled small-budget 'quickie,' issued a public appeal to established Hong Kong actors to reduce their salaries during troubled times. Pace-setters Jackie Chan and Stephen Chiau command, respectively, salaries of US$3 million and US$2.2 million per film. Unsurprisingly, the highest paid women make less – an indication, according to actor Karen Mok, 'that the male lead in a movie remains more important to audiences than the female lead.' Josephine Siao's US$700,000 and Maggie Cheung's US$380,000 topped the list in 1997.[20] Although comparatively small next to the asking prices of a Jim Carrey or a Demi Moore in Hollywood, these figures are indicative of the dilemma that faces Hong Hong filmmakers trying to cast popular performers in productions with an average budget of US$640,000. With film production down and faced with calls to take pay cuts, some performers turned to advertising, where they could command 'big bucks' for little time and effort. Stars Chow Yun-fat and Maggie Cheung have both appeared in Hong Kong commercials. Popular actors Leon Lai, Aaron Kwok, Michelle Reis, and Jacky Cheung were among those who earned more money from selling products than from movie roles in 1997. Singer Faye Wong even joined up again with Wong Kar-wai, who directed her in *Chungking Express*, to sell products for Motorola.

Wong Jing himself often uses low-paid young newcomers in his films, many of which are ridiculous comedies and sexploitation flicks. Reminiscent of the 'seven-day wonders' of an earlier era, these films allow him to flood an otherwise lean market, play hit-and-miss at the box office, score periodically, and in the process continue to attract financial investors. His willingness to maintain production has been praised by some; *Ming Pao Daily* columnist Kwok Hin-ching wrote, 'There are those who don't enjoy Wong Jing's films, but many film workers have to thank him. Without Wong Jing, two-thirds of the remaining people would have been unemployed. To them, the first step of saving the market is saving their own jobs.'[21] As the summer of 1998 ended, the persistent Wong had seven of the ten Hong Kong releases in local theaters and was moving ahead with plans to complete eight further pictures by the year's end.

The post-handover period proved a difficult one for Raymond Chow and Golden Harvest as the firm suffered from the events that originated with the Asian stock market crash. Experiencing declining profits and registering operating losses, the company sold the rights to more than fifty of its films to a Taiwanese satellite television station. In addition, the economic downturn led to the down-sizing of the film production department by almost 50 per cent. The company experienced a different kind of loss in early 1998 when one of its co-founders, Leonard Ho, died. Golden Harvest was then forced to leave its headquarters and studio location of almost thirty years after the SAR government refused to renew a land-lease contract, opting instead to turn the property into developable real estate.[22] The government also rejected the firm's bid for a site on which it proposed to build a US$77 million state-of-the-art movie studio, a decision that left the company contemplating Singapore officials' offer of free land to relocate its operations. Later, amidst rumors that prize asset Jackie Chan was considering putting an end to his two-decade relationship with the company, Golden Harvest took legal action against director Tsui Hark and his Film Workshop for alleged cost overruns in the production of eight films (including four in the *Once Upon a Time in China* series) in the 1990s; Tsui's attorneys in turn filed a counter-suit asking for back-payment on three of the *China* films.

Chow's Golden Village partnership with Australia's Village Roadshow, created in 1992 to build multiplex theaters throughout Asia, also turned sour. With the price of its stock shares dropping to historic low levels, Golden Harvest became subject to shareholder pressure and vulnerable to potential takeover. Village Roadshow, owner of 16 per cent of the company, won a Hong Kong court order blocking a June 1998 sale of shares to Rupert Murdoch and two Asian billionaires, Malaysian Robert Kuok and Hong Kong resident Lee Ka-shing.[23] The Australian firm simultaneously initiated a hostile buyout, which Chow initially fought off with an infusion of capital from Lee and wealthy fellow Hong Konger Kwok Hok-nin. When the dust settled some six weeks later, Village Roadshow, paying less per share than its original offer, had increased its interest in Golden Harvest to 25 per cent.[24] While both sides put their best face forward following the tiff, others raised questions about the Hong Kong firm's future. Critics charged that the privately owned Golden Harvest film production enterprise was dependent upon the success of Jackie Chan releases and the company's profitable public-stock distribution and exhibition network. Moviemaking may have become jeopardized by Village Roadshow's aggressiveness in pushing ahead with what managing director Graham Burke called 'our expansion across all markets with more multiplexes opening over the next five years.'[25]

Hong Kong's film industry shake-out was a classic example of what follows a period of overproduction, the condition Marx characterized as 'production without regard to the limits of the market.'[26] Periodic crises, inherent to the capitalist mode of production, stem from a constant striving for greater profits. Reflecting investor confidence, the two hundred-plus local movies produced yearly in the early 1990s left excessive expansion and inflated wage costs in their wake. Yet slumping box office returns and withering production existed alongside other structural changes. Hollywood 'discovered' the Asian market in the years prior to the financial meltdown. Commenting on a region that accounts for 30 per cent of the international motion picture trade, Thomas Elliot, managing director of United Artists International, said in 1996, 'The entire movie business is exploding in that part of the world.'[27] Cinematic 'eye candy' aggressively peddled as the latest big-budget blockbuster raises the financial and technological stakes needed to compete on a global scale. And as Ella Shohat and Robert Stam point out, 'Hollywood films often arrive ... "preadvertised," in that much of the media hype ... reaches the Third World through journalistic articles and TV even before these films are released locally.'[28] Even the economic crisis could not dissuade US distributors and exhibitors from proceeding with plans to expand: AMC International, for example, opened an eleven screen multiplex in Kowloon in the summer of 1998. Sizing up the future, Barr Potter, chairperson and CEO of Largo Entertainment, said: 'The Asia flu is here but it will get better, it will be cured.'[29]

By 1998, some were predicting the imminent demise of Hong Kong cinema; yet into the fray charged veterans such as Raymond Chow in an attempt to assuage such fears. For his part, Chow pointed out that observers had predicted a similar death some thirty years earlier when television was introduced into Hong Kong. At seventy years of age, the man whose company has led the industry for more than two decades asserted that he was confident about the future because of the cyclical character of moviemaking, adding that 'this is a business which, perhaps more than any other, thrives and succeeds on energy and enthusiasm ... it can not only survive but flourish in the most adverse of times.'[30] In this spirit perhaps, industry observers and principals were hopeful about developments on several fronts in 1998. Investors re-enter markets when economic indicators such as employment, prices, and wages have been on the wane; film companies duly began announcing plans to expand output. Charles

Heung's Wins organization unveiled a ten-film line-up for 1999. When the Brilliant Idea Group announced fifteen films, top executive Lee Kwok-hing sounded a nationalist note: 'I feel Hong Kong viewers worship the West ... we have to support our own. Everyone has to sacrifice a little, like actors have to reduce their film salary. Only then can we make it past this difficult time!'[31] Even Shaw Brothers indicated that it would return to film production, making six to eight films per year and releasing additional movies through a subsidiary, the Metropolitan Film Company.

A group of Hong Kong filmmakers known for both quality and socially relevant movies – including Gordon Chan, Jacob Cheung, Joe Cheung, Alex Law, John Sham, and Derek Yee – founded the non-profit-making Creative Alliance with initial seed money of about US$5 million to make five pictures. Actors and directors will have a direct stake in any film they work on, as a portion of all salaries are to be invested in production. Over-budget expenses will be paid out of the production team's share. In addition, six local companies – China Star, Century (Nin Doi) International, Jing Art, Media Asia, Mei Ah, and Shaw Brothers – formed Hong Kong Film City, a consortium designed to pool investment resources. With start-up financing in excess of US$25 million and the intention of producing twelve films in its first year of operations, and a long-range goal of twenty releases per year, Film City appeared to be an ambitious attempt to rebuild a portion of Hong Kong's decimated movie market. Of course, economic contraction functions to clear markets of weak competitors, leaving renewed production in fewer hands. Thus, this new combination may further strengthen Wong Jing's position in the industry, given that three of the firms involved have previously invested in his movies.

Hong Kong's government, which, Tsui Hark complains, 'long refused to help' the film industry, took a number of steps in 1998 to address the dire circumstances. Acting on a report issued by Tung Chee-hwa, SAR officials established a film services office and a film advisory committee (this fell short of the film development department wanted by movie personnel) and launched a small grant program for budding filmmakers. They also held discussions with their counterparts in Hollywood, expressed support for a sixty-acre movie theme park, and streamlined the application process for on-location shoots. Shooting without a license, long an industry practice, received increased attention following three

1997 incidents: shrapnel from a multi-car collision killed a crew member working on Teddy Chan's *Downtown Torpedoes*; residents of an apartment building called the fire department to an explosion that was traced to Ringo Lam's production of *Full Alert*; Alfred Cheung was arrested while making *The Group*.[32] In the latter instance, extras in Special Duty Unit (SDU) jackets brandishing firearms caused a public panic on the street. The government worked with the local movie industry in organizing the second annual Hong Kong Filmmart, an international trade show promoting Hong Kong pictures, and sponsored Hong Kong film festivals in Berlin, London, Milan, and Sydney. Plans to build a 95,000 square foot movie studio drew criticism from some filmmakers that financial subsidies and low-interest loans would be more useful, although opponents of direct funding, citing a similar program in Taiwan, countered that such assistance could degenerate into political cronyism and corruption. Finally, Chief Executive Tung's October 1998 Policy Address included an announcement that the government would allocate money (US$12.8 million) to a film technology fund. Industry reaction was reserved; as *Mingo Pao Daily* columnist Kwok Hin-ching asked, 'By spending HK$100 million on developing computer special effects, will dying Hong Kong film be saved?'[33]

Despite the enormity of ongoing difficulties in the post-handover era, some industry observers saw glimmers of hope. Critics praised Fruit Chan's ironically titled *Made in Hong Kong* (1997), a low-budget (US$80,000), decidedly non-commercial effort that won awards at twenty international film festivals. Shot using ends of film stock the director had collected and featuring young street punks instead of professional actors, the film is both a stark depiction of the hardships associated with poverty and an unglamorous portrayal of Triad life. Born on the Mainland, director Chan appears less concerned about the uncertain implications of Hong Kong becoming part of China again than he does about the idea that there are Hong Kongers with no future to look forward to at all. Meanwhile, box-office watchers applauded Andrew Lau Wai-keung's manga *The Storm Riders* (1998), a big-budget (by Hong Kong standards – US$6.4 million) high-tech affair that set a new all-time local opening day record for ticket receipts. This picture is a martial arts fantasy replete with myriad state-of-the-art special effects that push postproduction work in the Hong Kong industry to a higher standard. Providing Golden Harvest with something positive in a time marked by bad news,

courtesy/permission Golden Harvest Entertainment; © 1998 (China) Pictures Limited & Centro Digital Pictures Ltd.

TECHNO-POWER   Aaron Kwok in Andrew Lau's *The Storm Riders*

The Storm Riders' success in otherwise weak local and regional markets convinced the company to increase projected 1999 productions from seven films to ten.

Whichever factor one emphasizes in explaining Hong Kong film doldrums, be it Asian economic crisis, creative flight (i.e. John Woo, Chow Yun-fat, and Michelle Yeoh), Hollywood imports, low production values, poor scripts, unsophisticated special effects, or video piracy, China remains the salvation for many, if not most, in the industry. Beijing researcher Hu Ke states that 'Hong Kong cinema has entered the Mainland through various forms: imports of films, co-productions, video products, television broadcasts, and video piracy.'[34] Keynes's observation that we are all dead in the long run notwithstanding, many in Hong Kong are banking that capitalism will get the better of the PRC if film producers and distributors can gain access to the 100,000-plus movie screens and the thousand million potential moviegoers on the Mainland. In discussing the ostensible advantages of the Chinese working with Hong Kong studios made profitable by access to China's market, Golden Harvest executive Tom Grey cited higher wages, improved equipment, and better films. Grey went on to suggest that 'we may find a new cinema emerging. The Hong Kong commercial aspect with the artistic look of the Mainland.'[35] That business mien, however, worries Mainland filmmaker

Chen Kaige, who characterizes it as 'Make a film that can make money or otherwise you are not a good director.'[36]

Writing about the end of British rule in Hong Kong, prior to the handover, Ackbar Abbas mused,

> When sovereignty reverts to China, we may expect to find a situation that is quasi-colonial, but with an historic important twist: the colonized state, while politically subordinate, is in many other crucial aspects not in a dependent subaltern position but is in fact more advanced – in terms of education, technology, access to international networks, and so forth – than the colonizing state.[37]

This may, in large part, explain China's reticence about absorbing Hong Kong during the 1967 riots in the colony, a circumstance that foreshadows the Mainland's unwillingness to act contrary to its perceived economic interests following the handover. Deng Xiaoping's post-Mao era maxim 'To get rich is glorious' might well have been proclaimed by a Hong Kong real-estate mogul. The PRC's current market-oriented strategy has meant there are growing similarities between the respective economic systems. Expanding trade and investment between the two had resulted in extensive integration such that, in effect, Hong Kong already existed as part of China when the Union Jack was lowered for the final time. Today, the Special Administrative Region is a financial, transport, technology-transfer, and human resources center for the People's Republic while serving as a gateway to and from the Mainland.[38]

Generally forgotten in the run-up to 1997 was the fact that China has also become part of Hong Kong, Deng's 'neo-Open Door' policy in the 1980s having led to cultural reciprocity and travel as well as economic exchange. With Beijing's grip loosening, Hong Kong's influence on Mainland people, particularly young urbanites, flourished. From fashion and hairstyles to cuisine and design; from language and literature to movies and music; the territory's East–West hybrid imports began to define China's emergent popular culture.[39] The future success of Hong Kong movies on the Mainland will be determined by their ability to sustain this growing hegemony. The question may well be decided by the PRC's willingness, or not, to relax distribution rules for Hong Kong films – in other words, to treat them as domestic products not subject to strict foreign import quotas. To paraphrase Marx and Engels, a specter haunts Hong Kong cinema – the specter of

Hollywood. The popularity of Hong Kong film crested in China in the early 1990s and neither Hong Kong imports nor joint ventures with Chinese studios have done well at the box office since. As with Asia generally, Mainland audiences have begun to express a preference for US-produced pictures; hence Hollywood studios are poised to capitalize on further PRC market liberalization.

Capitalism's unique power is its ability to subordinate all social relationships and processes to an economic dynamic involving a ceaseless chase for profits. Moving forcefully through time and sweeping away all traditions, it creates the impression that people living in a 'society without guidance or control' can 'thrive, be safe and enjoy well-being.'[40] Yet the contradictions inherent to capitalist societies are magnified in Hong Kong. On the one hand, a global communication and transportation system allows an elite class of local businessmen and media stars to circulate internationally. If Alan (Tony Leung Chiu-wai) leaving on a boat in the final scene of *Hard-Boiled* signifies John Woo's Hong Kong swan-song, the moment also conveys the message that Woo and others can now work in Hollywood, the epicenter of the world film industry. On the other hand, the territory serves as a magnet for 'contract workers' from Indonesia and the Philippines, recruited to take on the 3-D jobs which the middle class is no longer willing to do and on which society depends. Much as Woo raised Hong Kong's profile in the US film industry, the territory's export-processing/free-trade zone, with its low wages and poor working conditions, has become a model for 'enterprise zones' in declining areas such as South Central Los Angeles, a short drive down from Tinseltown.

Hong Kong is in the vanguard of locations around the globe where a professional-managerial stratum that helps to make capital more mobile can be observed wearing, drinking, and driving the same international brands as they watch the same cosmopolitan movies and listen to the same popular music. Crucial to this development has been the proliferation of commodified imagery, a significant aspect of what Jameson calls 'the cultural logic of late capitalism.' Overcoming limitations imposed by geography and material history, electronic communications make possible the current emphasis on events and happenings. Immediate delivery, both real and perceived, is indicative of a shift in the way that capitalism works. Together with new and more vigorous efforts to manipulate demand, reduced turnaround time reflects the integration of a global network of flexible accumulation and specialized services.

Called the most 'international city in the world,'[41] contemporary Hong Kong collapses space and time in a spectacle of hyperreality and cultural vertigo. Described by director Ronny Yu as a place where people routinely say 'tell me about the latest gadget,' the city has been the beneficiary of merging systems of television, telephones, computers, and satellites designed to coordinate the interests, process the information, and transact the business of far-flung transnational concerns.[42] Hong Kong is the world's first major city to have a fully digitized telephone network. Hong Kong has Asia's busiest international telephone traffic, the highest rate of telephone penetration, and the highest connection of optical-fiber cables. It has the world's second highest rate of facsimile. Hong Kong is the world's fourth largest printing center.[43] Additionally, about 17 per cent of Hong Kong's population uses pagers, representing one of the highest market penetration rates in the world.[44] *Boston Globe* film critic Betsy Sherman remarks that in Hong Kong theaters, cellular phones ringing during a movie are not uncommon, nor is phone conversation unusual.

Rey Chow points out the 'founding of Hong Kong as a city converges with an epochal change in the world's value system – from the stability of landed culture to speeds and currencies of trade.'[45] As such, the former colony's legacy of commerce and materialism was the only option available. Unlike Huang Yaoshi in *Ashes of Time*, however, Hong Kong people have begun to struggle against the historical amnesia that accompanies mobility and transience. And contrary to Ouyang Feng in the same film, they have tried to remember without shame. But 'all that is solid melts into air'[46] in capitalist modernity, and many residents live in a perpetual present looking for maximum financial gain in a minimum of time. Progress is a Faustian bargain and as former Citicorp CEO John Reed, commenting on global consumerism, says, 'What works in New York also works in Brussels, Hong Kong, and Tokyo.'[47]

The flashy side of Hong Kong capitalism is found in the postmodern glass and steel structures that rise up in myriad shapes and form the cityscape that Mark (Chow Yun-fat) notices in *A Better Tomorrow* and Fung (Tony Leung Chiu-wai) observes in *Heaven Can't Wait*. If screen action and comedy allow film audiences to displace their anxieties, such diversion cannot hide the pollution that has turned the blue waters of the territory's deep harbor into brown sewage, the flotsam of industrial society. Neither can they eliminate the social inequities that the free market engenders, nor prevent the inevitable economic crises that *laissez faire* policies cannot effectively manage. Writing before the July 1997 handover, film scholar Tony Williams asserted that 'most Hong Kong films depict a survival myth to counter a gloomily envisaged historical and cultural apocalypse.'[48] In considering John Woo's work from *A Better Tomorrow* to *Hard Boiled*, Williams maintains that the director's work 'involves parallels between vanishing traditions confronting pressing realities of the modern world and a colony in danger of losing its very identity.'[49] Thus Hong Kong cinema has been 'crisis cinema,' at once paralleling, producing, and reflecting the identity, legitimacy, and sovereignty predicament of the people themselves.

Hong Kong cinema portrays a post-traditional people whose social structure is weakening and whose cultural values are being challenged. Fealty is giving way to what Macpherson termed 'possessive individualism,' as the young seek higher-income occupations and professions to place them outside of family control. Ironically, their parents' single-minded focus on 'making money' initiated this development. Hong Konger identity, which 'lives between and across various cultures, communities, and countries … [is] constantly reshaped by this kaleidoscopic experience.'[50] Or, as Jackie Chan asked in the title of his first Special Administrative Region film, *Who Am I?*, Colonial-Chinese syncretism is threatened by Americanization, code for the cultural-economic agenda sweeping the globe. Marlboro cigarettes have become the leading brand sold in Hong Kong; twenty years ago they accounted for less than 1 per cent of the market's share. Competitor Philip Morris introduced its Virginia Slims label by pitching 'women's liberation,' even though only 1 per cent of Hong Kong women under the age of forty smoke cigarettes.[51] The US Chamber of Commerce in the SAR is the largest outside the United States. By the late 1990s, more than one thousand US firms had Hong Kong operations; there are 147 McDonald's restaurants.[52] Add to this milieu the looming specter of Britain's handover of the colony to the People's Republic, and the result has been 'environmental turbulence.'[53] Is it any wonder that cinema using action, spectacle, and violence to resolve problems became so popular? Stephen Chiau's 1999 Lunar New Year release *King of Comedy* lampoons such movies, appropriating Woo's signature face-offs as Karen Mok and Chiau point guns at each other. With 1 July 1997's passing, the sovereignty question has apparently been answered. Nevertheless, the potential for a Habermasian 'legiti-

courtesy/permission of Karen Mok and Eleanor Morris

FACE TO FACE   Karen Mok and Stephen Chiau in Chiau's *King of Comedy*

mation crisis' exists if the Special Administrative Region government cannot maintain a general level of public support – a condition dependent, in no small measure, on continuing economic prosperity. Dire warnings about PRC authoritarianism, leading to political unrest and peoples' renewed exodus, have yet to be borne out, but as Rey Chow suggests, Hong Kong's uniqueness is an 'in-betweenness and an awareness of impure origins ... [that] distinguishes ... [it's] "Chinese" self-consciousness and differentiates it from other Chinese cities.'[54] Struggle for political democracy, civil liberties, and human rights was likely with or without the Joint Declaration; after all, the British denied Hong Kong people basic rights until 1992. Yet a focus on the liberal middle stratum's concerns should not ignore the role that social class dialectic can play. Labor militancy in the 1960s forced social

courtesy/permission of Milkyway Image (HK) Ltd.

HEADBANGING Simon Yam in Patrick Yau's *Expect the Unexpected*

policy concessions; more recently, the territory experienced nascent class politics during the year before the handover.

Much as Hong Kong politics has only periodically exhibited working-class features, the concept of class in much film criticism and theory is marked by the presence of its absence.[55] Something ideological is going on in both instances. With respect to the former, an economy characterized by small companies, the hegemony of cultural values alternately based on family and individual, and a free-market environment inhospitable to labor organizing mitigate against a class 'in itself' becoming a class 'for itself.' As for the latter, contemporary cultural studies has judged class analysis as reductionist; many film critics and scholars practice self-contained readings of film narratives; and the concept of class challenges the cultural production system, of which intellectual labor is part, of late capitalist society. Yet we live in a time when capital's 'global logic' of accumulation, commodification, and profit-maximization is approaching maturity. Recent portents of an 'accumulation crisis' means Hong Kong will remain a 'city on fire' in relation to its sense of self and place. Its cinematic representations will continue to encode world-views, value systems, and lifestyles complicit with market co-optation, planned obsolescence, and consumer taste. But cinematic meaning, found in the dialectic between production and consumption of film, results from decoding as well; audience experience cuts through socially and culturally constructed codes, fragments of knowledge and memory, and personal emotions. John Woo's *Better Tomorrow* films told an elder's story and Andrew Lau Wai-keung's *Young and Dangerous* series passed quickly into middle age. More recently, Patrick Yau's *Expect the Unexpected* (literally *Unusually Sudden*, May 1998) combined both stories as chaotic nihilism. Cops leading a crime unit against a dangerous robbery gang ignore bungling, desperate Mainlanders who are more vicious. In the unexpected ending, everyone dies except one woman, who survives to tell the tale, the latest scenario for Hong Kong's future. In a world where images play a central role in human understanding, films that address continuing questions and issues raised by crisis phenomena may help Hong Kongers build a firewall to help them get out of the twentieth century alive and, subsequently, step into the next millennium without getting burnt.

EPILOGUE

HONG KONG CALLING

Directors   Peter Chan, Cheung Yuen-ting, Johnnie To, Stanley Tong, Tsui Hark, John Woo, Donnie Yen, Ronny Yu

Producers   Terence Chang, André Morgan

Actors   Jordan Chan, Roy Cheung, Chow Yun-fat, Amy Kwok, Lau Ching-wan, Jon Kit Lee, Tony Leung Ka-fai, Karen Mok, Anthony Wong, Ruby Wong, Simon Yam, Michelle Yeoh

Cinematographer   Chris Doyle

Dialogue Coach   Karen Huie

Personal Assistant   Misha Skoric

TAKE ONE

Chang   'Hollywood did have a tradition of hiring foreign non-English speaking directors and converting them into one of their own.... But never before had an Asian director succeeded in making the transition.'

Yu   'When we were working in the 1980s, nobody in Hong Kong would dare to think, "I might work in Hollywood some day." Oh, come on! It's almost like going to the moon.'

Peter Chan   'It's always intrigued me how a foreign director can go to a country and make films not of his own culture and language.'

Leung   'When you talk about the widespread, increasing number of people going to Hollywood, I think it has to do with a market demand problem.'

Yeoh   'Hong Kong film sensibilities concern energy and realism. I think Hollywood has embraced these ideas. The choreography of fights and stunts has translated well to Hollywood movies such as John Woo's *Face/Off* and Kirk Wong's *Big Hit*. Hong Kong people adapt to practices over here and are practical enough not to let those impede their ability to do their jobs.'

Cheung Yuen-ting   'I have met executives from big Hollywood film companies who know Hong Kong films by heart.'

Woo   'It is ironic that Hollywood began to imitate Hong Kong movies in the late 1980s and 1990s because Hong Kong films (to a certain degree) are imitations of Hollywood films, so Hollywood is imitating Hollywood!'

Yen   'I'd like to work in the US because Hollywood films have had such a profound effect on my life and work. Hollywood really has the best of everything – actors, production values, special effects, music, and I'd like to have the chance to experience that level of filmmaking.'

Chow   'You have to grab the golden egg and hold it, if you have a chance.'

BEING WOOED

Chang   'My idea of coming to Hollywood started in mid-1990 when I received phone calls from people expressing their desire to work with John Woo. At that time we were very successful in Hong Kong. But John needed to grow as an artist. He needed to expand his scope... he needed more technical support. It was also his dream to make American films. I was just trying to help him fulfill his dream. The stumbling block was his ability to speak English. I hired an American tutor for John. For two hours per day and six days per week, John worked with him for six months.

I am happy that we did it. We left Hong Kong when its movie industry was at its height... And we ventured into something that is totally unknown. John moved his entire family to Los Angeles. For him, there was no turning back.'

Woo 'I wasn't used to the Hollywood system when I started shooting *Hard Target*. Never before in my career had an actor had final approval over the editing, the script, the casting. [He] hired his own editor and did his own cut which the producers completely rejected.'

Chang 'Despite the mediocre script, [*Hard Target*] is probably the best picture Van Damme has been in. Although it made money for Universal, Tom Pollack allegedly said John did not know how to make an American film. *Broken Arrow* is the perfect film to prove Pollack wrong, a straightforward action film with tons of special effects.'

Morgan 'So Stanley came, Peter came, John Woo was already here by then, Michelle got the part in the Bond picture, Ringo Lam came over, Samo Hung came, Jackie was back and forth… So it grows.'

HOLLYWORKING

Chang 'After *Hard Target*, Sam Raimi and Rob Tapert offered John a project called *Shadow War* at Universal. Then Fox offered John *Tears of the Sun*. For this one year and eight months when we were working on these two aborted projects, I did not get paid one cent. John had some development money, but he was in debt. Things began to pick up after the success of *Broken Arrow*.'

Woo '*Broken Arrow* was also an unpleasant experience. The studio executive tried to block any changes to the script, some of the people we had to work with were not good, and the line producer would control and change things behind my back. Luckily, the chairman of Fox let me make some of the final decisions. But all of the game playing really comes out in the final product: the style is incomplete.'

Chang 'All doubts in the industry regarding whether John could handle American actors was instantly gone [after *Broken Arrow*].'

Woo 'We changed it [*Face/Off*] to make it more thought-provoking for the audience and more spiritual. Audiences are sick of empty movies. The studio was a little worried because they're not used to an action film with strong drama, but once they saw some dailies they could see it would work. At last I was working with people who really knew how to appreciate each other.'

BEING WOOED   John Woo directing John Travolta and Nicolas Cage in *Face/Off*

Chow   'My character in the original script [for *The Replacement Killers*] was Caucasian. Since Columbia Pictures bought the script, they wanted to change the part into Asian so that I can play him. I met with the writer Ken Sanzel a couple of times. He wanted to see what I was like.'

Peter Chan   'Here we are [making *The Love Letter*]. It's an all-white cast and almost all the crew that we had from New York was white. And the guy that's heading the whole production is Chinese, not even born and raised here. Nobody ever questioned me when I was giving direction.'

Huie   'When we started working with Jackie [Chan, laying soundtrack for English-speaking release of *Supercop*], we asked him if there was any special food he'd like brought in for his sessions. "No, I'm a simple guy," he said. All he had on his podium were his cue sheets, a pencil and a binder clip to play with. He worked hard to get his lines right.'

Doyle   'Psychologically, yeah [I'm finding it difficult to work here]. I think the dynamics and the questions and the logistics are a little more complicated because [Hollywood's] such an unwieldy machine. We're more concerned with filmmaking, how to translate ideas. Here it's more concerned with career and the formula and unions which can close up the show.'

Tsui Hark   'A Hollywood production requires lots of planning. However, too much planning means little flexibility. For example, in *Double Team*, we found out on the set that it was just too dangerous to use a real knife for a particular shot. So, we asked the Props Master to make us a props knife. He said he needed two weeks to do that, but we didn't have two weeks to shoot one shot. So instead of waiting, we built one on the set and that got him upset. How ridiculous that is!'

Chow   'Every day I went to the set [*The Replacement Killers*], I was like a kid going to Disneyland.'

Tong   'The reason why I chose *Mr. Magoo* is because I have a daughter nine years old. Two years ago she said, "Dad, how come I couldn't see your movie?" I let her watch *Rumble in the Bronx*. When the bottles scene started, she was too scared to watch. She asked me, "When will I be able to see your movie?" I said, "Let daddy do a movie you can see, okay? I promise you." She was very happy to see *Mr. Magoo*.'

Yu   'For MGM, I did a kids' movie [*Warriors of Virtue*] about morals and values – and now I give you *Bride of Chucky*!'

Huie   'I was hired onto *The Corruptor* to be Cantonese dialogue coach to Mark Wahlberg, who co-stars with Chow Yun-fat. Gradually, more actors needed coaching. Chinese is a tonal language. Mispronouncing something can convey a whole different meaning. An actor I worked with was supposed to say three one-word syllables that meant "call the cops." When the director called cut and I burst out laughing (alone) he rushed up to me and asked what he said. By this time, everyone, including the director was surrounding me to know. Embarrassed, I blurted out: "Umm… you called for odiferous female orifice".'

courtesy/permission of Stanley Tong

DOWN BY LAW   Stanley Tong and Samo Hung on the set of *Martial Law*

Peter Chan   'There are certainly more politics because [there are] more people you have to meet with and fight with verbally. It's very tough for Hong Kong filmmakers because Chinese is not a verbal culture. We don't talk, we do it… I'm one of the more verbal Chinese, and I still find it very tough.'

Yu   We had nine puppeteers, up to twelve [for *Bride of Chucky*] every day to operate all the facial expressions and body movements of Chucky. It's difficult to just say, "Okay, Chucky's angry now," or "Chucky is mad," or "Chucky is feeling cynical now," or "Chucky is Chicky." I had to stand in front of them and act… so I had to become Chucky. I don't think I did a good job with Tiffany. I should be more feminine.'

Skoric 'It [*The Corruptor* shoot] was a family atmosphere and Jasmine [Chow] made it fun. An actor like Yun-fat, who is experienced enough to know what will be asked of him in advance, makes the day-to-day lives of the crew very easy.'

Chow 'I belong to the set [*The Corruptor*], I don't belong to the trailer.'

BORDER CROSSINGS

Chang 'It was certainly easier for other Hong Kong directors to work in Hollywood after the success of John Woo.'

Karen Mok '*Face/Off* has many John Woo touches in it, but at the same time it's very geared towards the American market. Other Hong Kong filmmakers can't just cross over and make films in Hollywood. Of course, it might be the trend right now to put in some kind of Asian or Hong Kong factor, but I don't think anyone is really looking at being the flavor of the month. That is not the main point. The main point is being able to have staying power.'

Kwok 'Hong Kong directors like Ringo Lam and John Woo will open the door for others. It depends upon their abilities. They need some luck.'

Peter Chan 'The way Hollywood works: there are agents and managers and they know who to show your tapes to and how to position you in the town. It's a lot of things that are not really about making movies. André Morgan was totally [instrumental].'

Morgan 'With Stanley Tong, I had seen *Supercop* and was blown away by the action and what he had done with Jackie Chan's character because it was so fresh compared to what Jackie had been doing. Stanley did *Rumble in the Bronx* and I was very impressed with the hydrofoil going through the streets. I sent word to Stanley I would like to work with him some day.'

Peter Chan When I wrapped *Comrades* I finally decided that's the time I wanted to leave. It's based on many, many reasons, partly 1997. I always wanted to take

courtesy/permission of Peter Chan

FATHERS AND SONS   Peter Chan directing Tony Leung Ka-fai and Tony Leung Chiu-wau in *He Ain't Heavy, He's My Father*

that as a breaking point to be able to stay farther away from it to kind of assess what the situation will be like.'

Jordan Chan   'I feel so happy about Mr. Chan Ho-sun [Peter Chan] who can make "literary" movies in Hollywood. That means Hollywood has confidence in other kinds of Hong Kong movies besides action films.'

Chang   'Actors have a lot harder time breaking through, since there is still a strong resistance to Asian faces on the screen. Jackie Chan and Chow Yun-fat are huge stars in Asia, which is still an increasingly huge market despite the recent economic crisis. Michelle Yeoh is an Asian *and* a woman, which makes it harder.

Despite the success of *Tomorrow Never Dies*, it is not easy for her. We have to create projects.'

Ruby Wong 'The most important thing for me to consider is the role in a movie. For the time being, I believe my company will arrange it. If the company thinks there is no problem, then I will go ahead and do it.'

Huie 'The facets to Asian stereotypes, reactions to them, what to do about them are complex. Stereotyping seems an American rite of passage. People I know, upon hearing and dealing with the controversy of Asian stereotypes, have decided to use another minority to avoid it completely. This hurts us in many ways too. We're not seen, we don't work and don't serve as reminders that we are a part of the American fabric.'

Tong 'Originally I said I needed someone younger to play Mr. Magoo, like Nathan Lane, but he was already attached to another movie. So I have Leslie Nielsen, he's a great actor but he's seventy-two years old, so I felt like my hands were tied. All our star can do is walk, stand, or sit to do the action, so when you see the sequence where he's riding the ironing board down [the slope], he's just standing, when he's going down the waterfall, he's just sitting, or when he's going on the paddlewheel boat, he's just walking.'

Chow 'My agents and my manager picked this project [*The Replacement Killers*] for me. As my first English language film, I do not think it is a difficult film for me to do.'

Tong 'If you want to do an action show, you really have an action star, like Samo Hung. To do *Martial Law*, I really have to have someone like Samo to execute the choreography, and then I can make it better.'

CALIFORNIA DREAMIN'

Woo 'I am glad for the successes of my friends and contemporaries. I think America rewards talent no matter what its race.'

To 'The opportunity of going to Hollywood is like the first time I entered the television network where I had to do what the producer wanted and I had to do my best for the studio. I hope I can learn more things from overseas, and I can do precisely what I do in Hong Kong under a different environment.'

Cheung Yuen-ting 'My dream is to be able to make films wherever in the world that I can find a story.'

Roy Cheung 'If the opportunity comes around, I would very much like to work in Hollywood because it would be a good learning opportunity for me. I would like to work with Martin Scorsese because he is brilliant in directing Mafia films. I would like to work with Robert De Niro because he is an intelligent actor who can interpret a wide range of characterizations.'

Leung 'Going to Hollywood is not my chief consideration. Rather, it is important for me to consider whether there is a good script.'

Anthony Wong 'From a commercial standpoint, I am very much interested. From a creative point of view, I am not interested at all.'

Lau 'I am very interested in acting in movies in Hollywood. I think if you want to achieve something, you have to pay the price, because when you receive a good script or a good role, you won't dispute what you will be paid.'

Yam 'Maybe there are some new directors who have new ideas so we can create new sparks. If I can go to Hollywood, I hope I can cooperate with the new directors.'

Jordan Chan 'I had the chance of acting in Jackie Chan's film *Rush Hour*, but at the last minute I had to cancel. If I can have another chance, I'm sure I will try again.'

John Kit Lee 'Hundreds upon hundreds of people showed up to see Yun-fat every day that we filmed [*The Corruptor*] in [New York's] Chinatown. It was really quite a scene.'

Chow 'I want the US audience to think, when they see me for the first time on the screen, "Here's a buddy, coming from the east."'

NOTES

CHAPTER ONE

1. Hong Kong Trade Development Council, 'Scoreboard for Economic Success of Hong Kong,' http://www.tdc.org.hk (15 July 1997).
2. The Chinese characters for Hong Kong mean Fragrant Harbor (pronounced Heung Gong, the 'eu' resembling the syllable in French; an apparent reference to the area's one natural blessing that long ago lost any pleasant aroma that might have given rise to the name). However, Nigel Cameron points out that this accounts neither for the voice inflections that differentiate one Cantonese word from another nor for how Cantonese was romanized. The word's origins may stem from characters that mean Heang-Keang (fragrant stream) or Hoong-Keang (red torrent). Both phrases refer to a waterfall that once supplied Hong Kong with fresh water. *Hong Kong: The Cultured Pearl*, Hong Kong 1978, p. x.
3. David Wen-wei Chang and Richard Y. Chuang, *The Politics of Hong Kong's Reversion to China*, New York 1998, p. 131. For a discussion of the British wars against China between 1839 and 1860 that focuses on the merchant-smugglers' criminal opium trade, the English industrialists' desire to expand their markets, and the imperialists' mistreatment of the Chinese, see the articles (originally published in the *New York Daily Tribune*) collected in Karl Marx and Frederick Engels, *On Colonialism*, Moscow 1959.
4. G.B. Endacott, *A History of Hong Kong*, 2nd edn, Hong Kong 1983, p. 194.
5. Bubonic plague, a disease of rats transmitted to human beings through flea bites, infected Hong Kong between 1894 and 1898, killing several thousand people and forcing thousands of others to flee to Macao. A 1907 investigation into sanitation efforts disclosed that property owners and building contractors paid program officials not to enforce rat-proofing and mosquito spraying laws. Cameron, *Hong Kong: The Cultured Pearl*, pp. 117–23, 142.
6. Ibid., p. 161; Roger Buckley, *Hong Kong: The Road to 1997*, Cambridge 1997, p. 9.
7. Cameron, *Hong Kong: The Cultured Pearl*, p. 98.
8. Frank Welsh quotes a Miss Bird as reporting that 'You cannot be two minutes in Hong Kong without seeing Europeans striking coolies with their canes or umbrellas.' *A Borrowed*

Place: The History of Hong Kong, New York 1993, p. 278.

9. John Flowerdew, *The Final Years of British Hong Kong: The Discourse of Colonial Withdrawal*, New York 1998, p. 18.

10. An early anti-British incident was a 1857 poison attack by breadmakers, who added arsenic to loaves baked for consumption in the European community. While none died, a number of Westerners were taken seriously ill. In addition to fifty-two employees of the bakery who were exiled, the aftermath witnessed mass arrests and deportations of Chinese. Cameron, *Hong Kong: The Cultured Pearl*, pp. 57–8; Engels, 'Persia and China,' in *On Colonialism*, p. 123. Another example was a strike by coolies protesting inspection of their housing quarters during the bubonic plague of 1894. The action was short-lived after the Governor took a hard line and banished several strike leaders from the colony. Cameron, *Hong Kong: The Cultured Pearl*, p. 123.

11. Chinese sailors were paid far less than their European counterparts. Their 1922 work stoppage encouraged domestic servants, engineers, and coolies with similar grievances to walk off their jobs as well. During the strike, colonial troops fired into a crowd of Chinese workers attempting to cross the border into Guangzhou, killing five. Meanwhile, the 1925–26 general strike, in which more than one million Chinese withdrew their labor at one point, resulted in the deaths of sixty-three Chinese at the hands of the British military. Flowerdew, *The Final Years*, pp. 19–20.

12. Melinda Parsons, ed., *Hong Kong 1984*, Hong Kong 1984, p. 246.

13. Political scientist Lucien Pye has asserted that, 'among the refugees in Hong Kong it is possible to find people who had sincerely wished to be accepted by the Communist regime but who were persistently rebuffed and discriminated against because of previous associations and were driven eventually, much against their wills, to change their allegiances.' *The Spirit of Chinese Politics: A Psychocultural Study of the Authority Crisis in Political Development*, Cambridge 1968, p. 183. Author Jacques Guillermaz, on the other hand, has argued that the communists encouraged frightened industrialists to return from Hong Kong and that 'care was taken to reassure heads of firms, treat them with caution, and safeguard their authority' until 1955. *The Chinese Communist Party in Power 1949–1976*, Boulder 1976, p. 30.

14. Hong Kong Trade Development Council, 'Scoreboard'.

15. Ibid.

16. World Bank, *Social Indicators of Development 1994*, Baltimore 1994, p. 212; Hong Kong Government Information Center, http://www.info.gov.hk (16 July 1997); Hong Kong Water Supplies Department, http://www.info.gov.hk (16 July 1997).

17. Cameron, *Hong Kong: The Cultured Pearl*, p. 117.

18. Hong Kong Census and Statistics Department, '1996 Population By Census Summary Results,' http://www.info.gov.hk, 15 July 1997.

19. World Bank, *World Development Report 1996*, New York 1996, pp. 185, 197. According to the World Bank figures, distribution of income in Hong Kong roughly parallels that of the United States. A 1994 report prepared by the Society for Community Organizations and the Hong Kong Human Rights Commission revealed greater inequality, with the poorest 20 per cent of households sharing only 4.3 per cent of income and the richest 20 per cent of households sharing 52.8 per cent of income in 1991. 'A Report to the United Nations

Committee on Economic, Social and Cultural Rights on Housing Rights Violations and Poverty Problem in Hong Kong,' http://www.scar.utoronto.ca (10 October 1998).

20. Ronald Skeldon, 'Labor Market Developments and Foreign Worker Policy in Hong Kong,' in *Migration and the Labor Market in Asia: Prospects to the Year 2000*, Paris 1996, p. 186.

21. The Hong Kong Census and Statistics Department neither collects nor maintains distribution-of-wealth information. 'Forbes Richest People in the World,' *Associated Press*, 13 July 1997. A society's wealth is generally more concentrated among its population than is income. For example, the richest 10 per cent of the US population claimed 68.4 per cent of the country's net worth in 1995 and the top 0.5 per cent owned 27.5 per cent of the nation's wealth. Doug Henwood, 'Measuring Privilege,' *Left Business Observer*, 17 July 1997, p. 3.

22. For a discussion of Hong Kong's housing problem focusing on the Tsamshuipo neighborhood, see Peter Engel, 'Brother Can You Spare an Inch? How to Survive in the World's Most Crowded Place,' *Left Curve*, no. 19, 1995, pp. 97–119.

23. Janie Van Oss, 'Hong Kong in Transition: The Culture,' http://www.glue.umd.edu, 8 July 1997.

24. Daniela Deane, 'The Dark Side of Prosperity in Hong Kong, An Epidemic of Child Suicides,' *Washington Post*, 6 January 1993, p. C3.

25. Karl Marx, *Capital* Volume 1, New York 1967, p. 760. Marx discusses the violent genesis of capitalism, by which simple commodity production turned into capitalist commodity production, in the chapter on 'primitive accumulation' in this volume. He later backed away from the assumption that his account of Western Europe could be transformed into a general theory of the historical course of all people. See Teodor Shanin, *Late Marx and the Russian Road*, London 1983, pp. 34–6.

26. David Dodwell, '"Smoke and Mirrors" Hide True Picture of Robust Economy,' *South China Morning Post*, 25 November 1996, http://www.hongkong97.com.hk (13 June 1998); Stephen W.K. Chiu, K.C. Ho, and Tai-lok Lui, *City-States in the Global Economy: Industrial Restructuring in Hong Kong and Singapore*, Boulder 1997, p. 71.

27. Ibid., p. 144. Union density in manufacturing is less than 10 per cent. Shop floor organizations are particularly weak and unions have little power to mobilize collective actions such as strikes.

28. For a discussion of the gendered racism to which imported Filipina domestics in Hong Kong are subjected, and the way in which capitalism and patriarchy work together in the 'global economy' to limit large populations of women to marginal, poorly paid jobs with no political and few legal and social rights, see Ludmilla Kwitko, 'Filipina Domestic Workers in Hong Kong and the New International Division of Labour,' in Jayant Lele and Wisdom Tettey, eds, *Asia: Who Pays for the Growth? – Women, Environment, and Popular Movements*, Aldershot 1996, 107–23. For an examination of Hong Kong industry that has chosen to adopt 'offshore relocation' to the Mainland as its principal restructuring strategy, see Lai Si Tsui-Auch, 'Regional Subcontracting and Labor: Information/Communication Technology in Hong Kong and Shenzhen,' in Gerald Sussman and John A. Lent, eds, *Global Productions: Labor in the Making of the Information Society*, Cresskill 1998, pp. 145–72.

29. Welsh, *A Borrowed Place*, p. 489. Kickbacks and payoffs were believed to be in the hundreds of millions of dollars and the scandal resulted in a prison term for, among others, then

Chief Police Superintendent and expatriate Peter Godber. The Hong Kong government was forced to create an Independent Commission Against Corruption (ICAC) in 1974 to investigate corruption. Ironically, the first ICAC director was a man named Jack Cater, who would eventually rise to the position of Hong Kong's General Secretary.

30. Ernest Mandel, *Late Capitalism*, London 1975, p. 574. Mandel distinguishes three epochs of capitalist expansion: market capitalism, characterized by the rise of industrialism; monopoly capitalism, identified with the age of imperialism; and multinational capitalism, marked by the spread of transnational corporations. Fredric Jameson draws heavily on Mandel in specifying postmodernism as the 'cultural logic of late capitalism.' *New Left Review* 146, 1984, pp. 53–92. The term 'late capitalism' has the unfortunate connotation that capitalism is approaching its death throes.

31. Robert Heilbroner, *The Nature and Logic of Capitalism*, New York 1985, p. 171.

32. Hong Kong Trade Development Council, 'Economic and Trade Information on Hong Kong (15 July 1997).

33. Hong Kong's old airport, Kai Tak, was bordered by tall downtown buildings, making landings and takeoffs precarious. Dorinda Elliott, 'Hong Kong's Field of Dreams,' *Newsweek*, 6 July 1998, pp. 32–3. Mee Kam Ng and Allison Cook argue that further large-scale harbor reclamation is unsustainable and they recommend that the government work together with its citizens on an integrated urban development strategy. 'Reclamation: An Urban Development Strategy Under Fire,' *Land Use Policy*, vol. 14, no. 1, 1997, pp. 5–23.

34. Such programs include *Videofashion News*, *Planet Fashion*, *Fashion Televison*, and *Sexy Mode*. Cheng Yew-meng, 'Culture and Lifestyles,' in Nyaw Mee-kau and Li Si-ming, eds, *The Other Hong Kong Report 1996*, Hong Kong 1996, p. 475.

35. Ronald Skeldon, 'Emigration and the Future of Hong Kong,' *Pacific Affairs* 63, Winter 1990–91, p. 507. Skeldon, in noting that Australians and Canadians commonly refer to Hong Kong émigrés as 'yacht people,' suggests that the popular image of the Hong Kong migrant as a brash millionaire who drives up real-estate prices by purchasing large quantities of property in Sydney, Toronto, and Vancouver, while not entirely inaccurate, is distorted and exaggerated.

36. Ian Scott, 'Political Transformation in Hong Kong: From Colony to Colony,' in I. Scott, ed., *The Hong Kong–Guangdong Link*, New York 1995, p. 195.

37. S.L. Wong, 'Prosperity and Anxiety in Hong Kong Reexamined,' in S.K. Lau et al., eds, *The Development of Social Indicators Research in Chinese Societies*, Hong Kong 1992, pp. 217–23.

38. Patricia Wen-Sei Tse, 'The Impact of 1997 on Political Apathy in Hong Kong,' *Political Quarterly*, April–June 1995, p. 214; Robert Chung Ting-Yiu, 'Survey on People's Reaction Towards the New Functional Constituency Elections in September 1995', and 'District Board Members First Survey Summary Report,' University of Hong Kong Public Opinion Program, http://www.ssrc.hku.hk (9 July 1997).

39. Many of the 12,500 Vietnamese who returned home in the last eight months of 1996 did so under a forced program intended to close the Hong Kong detention camps. 'Staying On?', *The Economist*, 11 January 1997, p. 36.

40. James North, 'Boom and Bust,' *In These Times*, 17 March 1997, p. 26.

CHAPTER TWO

1. Hong Kong's film industry employed six thousand workers (0.2 per cent of the workforce) and earned US$776 million in 1995 (0.16 per cent of GDP). 'Film Entertainment Services,' http://www. info.gov.hk (8 July 1997).

2. The flurry of activity in Canada by US film companies during the 1930s was a response to the 1927 British Film Act. That law, stemming from growing concern with Hollywood dominance of the movie industry in the UK, imposed a screen quota. However, US corporations found a loophole in the law: films produced in the dominions (such as Canada) were exempt from the quota. Financing by US companies later dried up when the British parliament closed the loophole. Manjunath Pendakar, 'Hollywood North: Film and TV Production in Canada,' in Gerald Sussman and John A. Lent, eds, *Global Productions: Labor in the Making of the Information Society*, Cresskill 1998, pp. 215–16.

3. Paul Fonoroff indicates that, of over five hundred Hong Kong feature films produced prior to World War II, only four still exist. He attributes this to three factors: (1) the Japanese military melted down films to extract their silver base during its war-era occupation of the British colony; (2) locals have thrown away prints; (3) Hong Kong's heat and humidity have taken their toll. Fonoroff goes on to state that nearly half of the four thousand Hong Kong movies produced between 1945 and 1970 are missing as well. *Silver Light: A Pictorial History of Hong Kong Cinema 1920–1970*, Hong Kong 1997, p. xi. Only in 1992 was an archive established to collect, catalogue, and preserve Hong Kong cinema artifacts. By 1998, the archive's planning office had acquired two thousand film titles (many from Beijing, where some movies were stored to avoid Hong Kong's humidity, and others from San Francisco's Chinatown World Theater which imported Hong Kong Cantonese films in the 1940s and 1950s) and over sixty thousand items of related materials. A multi-purpose center, providing for study and documentation as well as film programs and exhibitions, was to open in 2000 in Sai Wan Ho on Hong Kong Island. Katherine Stephan, 'Preserving Pix Past,' *Variety*, 22–28 June 1998, p. 37; 'Hong Kong Film Archive,' http://www. info.gov.hk (14 November 1998).

4. Some confusion exists as to the surname of this individual. We have identified him as Brodsky, as Fonoroff and Stephen Teo have recently done. Fonoroff, *Silver Light*, p. xii; S. Teo, *Hong Kong Cinema: The Extra Dimensions*, London 1997, p. 3. Roy Armes also names this individual Brodsky in his *Third World Film Making and the West*, Berkeley 1997, p. 137. John Lent, following I.C. Jarvie, identifies Brodsky as Polaski. *Asian Film Industry*, Austin 1990, p. 92. See I.C. Jarvie, *Window on Hong Kong: A Sociological Study of the Hong Kong Film Industry and Its Audience*, Hong Kong 1977, p. 5. Jay Leyda, too, had earlier called this individual Polaski in his *Dianying: An Account of Films and the Film Audience in China*, Cambridge 1972, p. 270. Finally, Lent notes that Law Kar refers to Brodsky as Brasky in his 1975 San Fransisco State University Master's degree thesis. Hong Kong's cinematic origins are examined in N.A. Tilden, ed., *Early Images of Hong Kong and China*, Hong Kong 1995. See in this collection especially Law Wai-ming, 'Hong Kong's Cinematic Beginnings 1896–1908,' pp. 23–6; Law Kar, 'Early Impressions of the Hong Kong Cinema: 1909–1915,' pp. 28–9; Stephen Teo, 'Tracing the Electric Shadow: A Brief History of the Early Hong Kong Cinema,' pp. 45–52. Our account of the history of Hong Kong's film industry from its origins through the 1960s relies on Teo's *Hong Kong Cinema*, and, unless otherwise noted, all film titles, firm

and personnel names, and years that pictures were produced in that period are from this source.

5. Three films starring Ruan Lingyu were *Spring Dream in the Old Capital* (1930), *Wild Grass* (1930), and *Love and Duty* (1931). Ruan, who some compared to Greta Garbo, committed suicide in 1935 after being subject to scorn and public humiliation for an alleged adulterous affair. William Rothman has likened Ruan to 'Marlene Dietrich without the theatricality.' See 'The Goddess: Reflections on Melodrama East and West,' in Wimal Dissanayke, ed., *Melodrama and Asian Cinema*, Cambridge 1993, pp. 59–73. In *Goddess* (1934), Ruan plays a woman who resorts to prostitution to support her born-out-of-wedlock son. After the boy is expelled from school because the authorities learn of her work, Ruan's character argues with her despised pimp, accidentally kills him, and is sentenced to prison. For an examination of the incident that led to Ruan's death as it related to the shifting status of women and the media in the political economy of urban China in the 1930s, see Kristine Harris, 'The *New Woman* Incident: Cinema, Scandal, and Spectacle in 1935 Shanghai,' in Sheldon Hsiao-peng Lu, ed., *Transnational Chinese Cinemas: Identity, Nationhood, Gender*, Honolulu 1997, pp. 277–301. Ruan is the subject of director Stanley Kwan's *Center Stage* (1991), a 'movie within a movie' with Maggie Cheung playing the tortured actress and also appearing on screen as herself preparing for the role.

6. Gere La Due has pointed out that 'talkies' arrived later in China and Hong Kong, in part because of a lack of technology, but also because filmmakers exploited the commonality of written Chinese to reach larger audiences. La Due writes that, 'there is a difference between Cantonese and Mandarin phrasing, frequency of character, etc., but one group reading the other would be more like American vs. British vocabulary, whereas spoken is more like French vs. Portuguese.' 'A Look at Some Western Misconceptions and Misunderstandings About Hong Kong Film,' *Cineraider 2*, June 1994, p. 43. Li Beihai (Li Minwei's brother), whose role in early Hong Kong cinema included co-founding China Sun, managing UPS, and establishing the China Sound and Silent Film Production Company, directed the colony's first all-talking motion picture, *A Fool's Marriage* (1934).

7. Lent, *Asian Film Industry*, p. 93.

8. Harris, 'The *New Woman* Incident,' p. 280. *Song of the Fisherman*, which set a Hong Kong box-office record with its 84-day run, won an award at the 1935 Lenin Film Festival in Moscow.

9. 'Other dialect' movies have been produced as well. For example, Amoy films are marketed almost exclusively to Hong Kong's Amoy minority population and to Amoy-speakers in Malaysia, the Philippines, Singapore, Taiwan, and Thailand. Stephen Teo, 'Hong Kong's Electric Shadow Show: From Survival to Discovery,' in Law Kar, ed., *Fifty Years of Electric Shadows*, Hong Kong 1997, p. 17. For a more complete consideration of post-World War II Hong Kong film genres running from the late 1940s through the late 1960s, see the first section of Teo's *Hong Kong Cinema*. Included are chapters on 'sing-song girl' and 'father and son' movies. For discussions of post-war Hong Kong Cantonese film, see the essays collected in *Cantonese Cinema Retrospective* (1960–1969), Hong Kong 1982; *Cantonese Melodrama (1950–1969)*, Hong Kong 1986; *Cantonese Stars of the Sixties*, Hong Kong 1996.

10. Paul Fonoroff, 'Orientation,' *Film Comment*, May–June 1988, p. 53.

11. Fonoroff, *Silver Light,* p. xviii; Teo, *Hong Kong Cinema*, pp. 40–41.

12. For an examination of Hong Kong's post-World War II cinematic 'culture wars' that laments the politicization of art, but that is, on the whole, more critical of the film left wing than it is of the film right wing, see Law Kar, 'The Shadow of Tradition and the Left–Right Struggle,' in Li Cheuk-to, ed., *The China Factor in Hong Kong Cinema*, Hong Kong 1990, pp. 15–20.

13. Notable left-wing Hong Kong films from the early 1950s include Wang Weiyi's Cantonese *Tears of the Pearl River* (1950), Li Pingqian's *The Awful Truth* (1950), Yue Feng's *Modern Red Chamber Dream* (1952), and Zhu Shilin's *Between Fire and Water* (1955). Right-wing releases included Tu Guangqi's *Half Way Down* (1955), focusing on refugeed middle-class intellectuals living in a Hong Kong resettlement camp who refused to accept the permanent loss of China to the communists, and Tang Huang's comedy, *Life with Grandma* (1955), about a family that fled the Mainland to escape communism; they reminded moviegoers to respect custom and practice decorum even as they acclimated themselves to modern life in the colony.

14. Teo, 'Hong Kong's Electric Shadow Show,' p. 20. Taiwan's policy of barring movies produced in the People's Republic and its practice of boycotting actors who made films on the Mainland continued through the 1980s. Actor Tony Leung Ka-fai, whose film career began in 1983, remarks that, 'I encountered problems when I was making movies on the Mainland … Taiwan rejected the movies that I was involved in; thus it affected my market value in the movie business at that time.' He notes, however, that 'this discrimination no longer exists. In fact, you can see some movies which are produced by China and Taiwan together.'

15. Lent, *Asian Film Industry*, pp. 98–9. The author notes that the 'self-contained unit kept 1500 actors/actresses under contract, as well as 2000 other staff, maintained its own drama school of 120 students; published periodicals that boosted Shaw stars, and used a wardrobe of 80,000 costumes of all dynasties.' Lent also indicates that the Shaw studio worked three eight-hour shifts daily.

16. Fonoroff, *Silver Light*, p. xx.

17. For a discussion that, in framing differences between Hong Kong and Taiwanese films in terms of escapism and realism repeats the common criticism that the former is marked only by commerce, entertainment, and fantasy, see Chiao Hsiung-Ping, 'The Distinctive Taiwanese and Hong Kong Cinemas,' in Chris Berry, ed., *Perspectives on Chinese Cinema*, London 1991, pp. 155–65.

18. For an analysis of Golden Harvest that, on the one hand, credits its success to an ability to adapt to changing market conditions while, on the other hand, raising questions about the company's future viability in light of economic globalization and Hong Kong's 1997 handover to China, see Steve Fore, 'Golden Harvest Films and the Hong Kong Movie Industry in the Realm of Globalization,' *The Velvet Light Trap*, no. 34, Fall 1994, pp. 40–58.

19. André Morgan, in recounting that ownership of guns and blank ammunition was outlawed in Hong Kong under the British, says that

> as the only Caucasian at Golden Harvest in the early 1970s, one of my jobs was to go to the police department and explain why we needed an import license to bring guns in. As a non-Chinese, I could go see the senior police officers, who were British. They said OK, figure out what security you can give these guns because we don't want them used in riots. I turned around and went to see the commanding officer of the local army depot, who was also British, and got the British army to become the guardian of imitation

guns that I imported from America. This allowed the Hong Kong film industry to start making movies with more realistic looking guns.

20. Lent, *Asian Film Industry*, p. 100.

21. Popular 1970s' Hui Brothers movies included *Games Gamblers Play* (1974), *The Last Message* (1975), and *The Contract* (1978).

22. La Due, 'A Look,' p. 43. Jarvie, writing on the cusp of the Cantonese-dialect resurgence, had doubted

> that there will be any sustained revival of the Cantonese movie [because they] stand pat towards the modern world; they use local culture and personalities, folk-stories, popular operas.... Mandarin movies, on the other hand, stem from the emerging national consciousness; tend to be produced in sophisticated urban surroundings ... by culturally cosmopolitan Chinese; and to treat stories and use the movie medium in a way that comes to some kind of terms with progress and the modern world.

Jarvie, *Window on Hong Kong*, p. 87. For a discussion positing the use of Cantonese subtitles and titles in Hong Kong cinema as politically subversive vis-à-vis both the Mainland and Taiwan, see Tan See Kam, 'The Hong Kong Cantonese Vernacular as Cultural Resistance,' *Cinemaya* 20, July–September 1993, pp. 12–15.

23. Lent, *Asian Film Industry*, p. 101.

24. For an examination of what Ackbar Abbas calls Hong Kong's 'culture of disappearance,' a concern for historical and cultural definition precipitated by the expectation of its extinction, see his *Hong Kong: Culture and the Politics of Disappearance*, Minneapolis 1997. For a discussion that frames the early work of the Hong Kong 'new wave' directors in terms of the 'abyss between tradition and modernity,' see Li Cheuk-to, 'The Return of the Father: Hong Kong New Wave and its Chinese Context in the 1980s,' in Nick Browne et al. eds, *New Chinese Cinemas: Forms, Identities, Politics*, Cambridge 1994, pp. 160–79.

25. Terence Chang, recalling his days running Tsui Hark's and his wife Nansun Shi's Film Workshop in the late 1980s, says,

> They came to me because they did not want to bring their conflicts at work into their home. The first year was really exciting. The company was new, vibrant, and a lot of great films came from that time. Tsui Hark was very idealistic. He wanted to round up the best directors in Hong Kong and put them under one roof. He wanted to create an environment where all the directors, under his leadership, could be given the opportunity and nourishment to make artistic, yet commercial pictures. Film Workshop at the time had also a group of exclusive contract actors, including Chow Yun-fat (whom it shared with Cinema City), Sally Yeh, Tony Leung Ka-fai, and Joey Wong.

26. Thea Klapwald, 'H.K. Helmers in H'wood,' *Variety*, 23–29 June 1997, p. 89; Keith Richburg, 'How Hong Kong's Film Industry Got Shanghaied,' *Washington Post Sunday*, 9 July 1995, p. G5. Tsui Hark's most expensive Hong Kong movie, *Once Upon a Time in China* (1991), cost US$8.4 million; his first 'Hollywood' production (actually filmed in Europe with multinational crews), *Double Team* (1997), cost US$40 million to make. Special Administrative Region (Hong Kong) Film Top Ten Box Office Page, http://www.geocities.com/Tokyo/Towers/2038, 30 April 1997 (12 June 1997).

27. La Due, 'A Look,' pp. 45–6. The author notes that 'English subs are usually translated from the Mandarin subs, which are in turn made from a Cantonese script, all independent of the film footage.'

28. John Woo began his career as an actor. He relates that

> it was hard to get a chance to work in films so I began ... on the stage. The reason I wanted to be an actor is that I was really shy. I never make a beautiful well-phrased sentence. As a kid, I had difficulty – I stuttered and spoke slowly. In acting you train to speak fluently and to express your emotions. That was my first purpose. I also overcame my fear of meeting people. I was very active on stage. I acted in and directed modern plays. I was a star in school. When I was on stage I was totally different. Girls liked me and my performance. I felt cool like James Dean in *Rebel Without a Cause*.

29. Discussing why he became a filmmaker, Tsui Hark says:

> I went to film school simply because I like to express my feelings on certain issues through film, which was a pretty popular medium during the 1960s. We spent a lot of time in movie theaters. At that time I was already thinking how to make Chinese cinema more interesting. I remember my older brother told me that such an idea could never be done simply because American TV drama was already better than our movies. But still, I decided to study film [at the University of Texas]. In my second summer, I was working on a term paper on experimental filmmakers in the 1960s. I went to New York and joined New York News Reel for a few months as my internship. My first exposure was shooting documentary.

30. Describing his entry into the film industry, Stanley Tong says,

> When Bruce Lee came out, I went crazy about martial arts. I began studying martial arts when I was twelve ... In 1980 I got a chance to go into Shaw Brothers Studio and got introduced to [director] Lau Kar-leung ... he asked me to show him some moves ... and asked me what I wanted to do. I said I wanted to be like Bruce Lee, an action star. He said if you want to do this you have to learn from a stunt man, so I started work as part-time stunt man. My parents hated the idea, especially my mom, who didn't want me to do any crazy work. I still did it, but she didn't know until I broke my shoulder and couldn't go home. I hid at my brother's ... five days later she found me and was crying that I was doing the job which kept her heartbroken. Then we sat down and had a very frank family meeting. I said I love the business, I want to be in the business. My dad told me that it's important to choose a job that you love and enjoy, then it's not working for the money. You will invest your time in doing it, even though you don't get paid for it ... He asked me what I wanted to do in the future. At that time I was saying I wanted to be a stunt coordinator. I didn't know I wanted to be a director yet ... I started to figure out it was important to choreograph with the camera. I started to work as a camera assistant to become a camera operator. I worked as a script supervisor ... I became a first A.D. In Hong Kong the first A.D. helps the director make the first cut, so I got to learn from the editor.... Then I got work postproduction ... in 1988 I directed my first film.

31. Michel Ciment, 'A Chat with Wong Kar-Wai,' http://www.xs4all.nl/~chinaman/chat.html #begin (6 July 1997).

32. Berenice Reynaud, 'High Noon in Hong Kong,' *Film Comment*, July–August 1997, p. 22. Dialogue coach Karen Huie recalls that 'Jet Li once mentioned that at screenings he sometimes doesn't recognize his own movies because they edit in segments from other films, changing the plot sometimes.'

33. Cheung Yuen-ting's first movie, *The Illegal Immigrant* (1983), began as her New York University Film School thesis. She notes,

> Luckily I got sponsorship from Shaw Studio of Hong Kong and I made it into a 35 mm film. The budget was US$180,000. I used my classmates as crew members. They were really happy to have the chance to work on a feature film and nobody cared about money or work-load. I had a cast of non-professionals – friends from New York Chinatown, Triad members, and illegal immigrants who played themselves. I used equipment and old film stocks from school. It was hard work, everyone in the crew had to do several jobs at the same time, but it was also a lot of fun.

34. Despite the less than ideal work conditions on the set of Hong Kong film productions, Roy Cheung believes that they are 'the best in Asia.' He notes, however, that 'when I joined the business, it took thirty days to make a film; now they can only afford ten shooting days.'

35. Beth Accomando, 'Eat My Bullet,' *Giant Robot*, no. 6, 1996, p. 48. Actor Simon Yam appeared in more than one hundred movies between 1989 and 1998. Yam, whose skin was burnt during the making of *Bullet in the Head*, says,

> Because many times we work on four to five movies at the time, I often feel tired. We cannot do our best under this situation. This is the disadvantage of producing movies in Hong Kong. As for the advantage, [the work process] can improve a person's ability to react. We prepare fast [because] we usually get the script just before we shoot the scene. If you give us a scene, we can interpret that scene in three minutes.

   On Chow Yun-fat and film work, Tony Leung Ka-fai says, 'Mr. Chow Yun-fat is a creative and professional actor. I can learn a lot of things through cooperation with him, not only about acting skills but also [about things] beneficial to my attitude about working.' As if to prove this point, he goes on to remark that, 'I don't think there [has been] a change in the working conditions, but I have changed the demands I have for my work.'

36. Karl Marx, *Capital* Volume 3, New York 1967, p. 86.

37. Stephen Teo, 'The Silken Screen,' *Cinemaya* 25–26, 1994–95, p. 48. Teo points out that increased labor-force participation among Hong Kong women corresponded to the importation of Filipina domestic workers.

38. Judith Mayne, *Women at the Keyhole: Feminism and Women's Cinema*, Bloomington 1990, p. 118.

39. Teo cites Tang Shuxuan as the first woman director to make an impact in Hong Kong. Tang directed two films, *The Arch* (1970) and *China Behind* (completed in 1974, banned from public release until 1987), considered precursors to Hong Kong's cinematic 'new wave' of the 1980s. Teo, 'The Silken Screen,' p. 47.

40. Bey Logan, *Hong Kong Action Cinema*, Woodstock 1995, p. 117.

41. Jeff Yang, et al., *Eastern Standard Time*, Boston 1997, p. 77; Toh Hai-leong, 'A Swan Song: Decline of the Hong Kong Cinema – Before 1997,' *Kinema*, Spring 1997, p. 53. Ryan Law, editor of the *Hong Kong Movie Database*, points out that, because a time lag occurs between production and release, peak production figures require close examination. Law, e-mail

correspondence, 13 July 1997.

42. Margaret Sullivan, 'Salon Aids Local Prod'n Handover,' *Variety*, 23–29 June 1997, p. 86.

43. Logan, *Hong Kong Action Cinema*, p. 117.

44. Terence Chang, letter to Tyler Stokes, 11 November 1996. D&B Films was started in 1984 by multimillionaire Dickson Poon, owner of a chain of upmarket jewelers and boutiques in Hong Kong, in partnership with martial artist actor/director Samo Hung.

45. Stanley Tong relates that

    > there were no roads in the mountain area of New Guinea where we were shooting. I had convinced my staff to sign a form saying that they were willing to work at their own risk. The authorities would not let us shoot a war [because of the different tribespeople] and I was about to close down production because this was a major scene. I'm asking myself why is this happening on my first film, there goes my career. So I asked the police if we could split the groups in half and let them 'fight' their own people and it worked. Then, halfway through production, I had to fly back to Hong Kong to raise additional money to be able to finish the movie.

46. Fredric Dannen and Barry Long, *Hong Kong Babylon: An Insider's Guide to the Hollywood of the East*, New York 1997, p. 110.

47. Cheung Pui Fong, 'Return Countdown Chow Yun-fat,' *Next*, http://www.geocities.com/ Athens/8907/nextv394.html, 9 May 1997 (1 March 1998). In the commercial-oriented system, adds actor Anthony Wong, 'what choices do actors have? NONE.'

48. Karl Marx, *Grundrisse*, New York 1973, pp. 328–9.

49. Marx, *Capital*, Volume 1, New York 1967, p. 714.

50. Logan, *Hong Kong Action Cinema*, pp. 122–3; Dannon and Long, *Hong Kong Babylon*, pp. 24–37; Karim Raslan, 'Dangerous Liaisons: Hong Kong Organised Crime and Film Industry,' *Singapore Business Times*, http://egreto.stanford.edu/hk/articles/Triad.html, 13 Feb 1993 (23 May 1997).

51. Andy Chan was depicted in Steven Lo Kit-sung's biopic *Tragic Fantasy: The Tiger of Wanchai* (1994), an example of so-called 'big timer' films dealing with real Triad leaders.

52. *Sing Tao Daily*, the offending newspaper, is known for sensational reporting. Following a series of actions by the actor's parents, the paper issued a small retraction a month later, noting that Mok's actual brother, a Cambridge Ph.D., was lecturing on international law in Britain at the time of the incident. Later, a Hong Kong court imposed a punitive sum of HK$20,000 (about US$2,500) on *Sing Tao* for false publication, which was paid to a charity of the actor's choice (Hong Kong Children's Cancer Foundation).

53. David Ansen, 'Chinese Takeout: U.S. Films with a Hong Kong Flavor,' *Newsweek*, 19 February 1996, p. 66. Doug Henwood notes, however, that while 'accountancy may have a reputation for dullness … it can be the scene of great creativity.' *Wall Street*, New York 1997, p. 100.

54. Accomando, 'Eat My Bullet,' pp. 47–8.

55. Paul S.N. Lee, 'The Absorption and Indigenization of Foreign Media Cultures: Hong Kong as a Cultural Meeting Point of East and West,' in Law Kar, ed., *Hong Kong Cinema in the '80s: A Comparative Study*, Hong Kong 1991, p. 83.

56. Homi Bhabha, 'The Commitment to Theory,' in Jim Pines and Paul Willemen, eds, *Questions of Third Cinema*, London 1989, p. 128.

57. Uma Magal, 'The Globalization of Cinema: A Reverse Angle,' *Asian Cinema*, Winter 1995,

pp. 125–30. Film scholar Tony Williams, in commenting on Hollywood copies of Hong Kong action techniques, says: 'There's a complexity and a particular finesse to the stylistic works of these directors in Hong Kong cinema. Most American directors who try to copy it really do not reproduce it very well. What they generally do is … reproduce the violence in a gratuitous way.' Peter Hum, 'Hong Kong Takes on Hollywood,' *Ottawa Citizen*, 26 October 1997, p. D9.

58. Teo, *Hong Kong Cinema*, p. 6.

59. John Woo, "About John Woo,' *Asian Cult Cinema*, no. 20, p. 55.

60. Howard Hampton, 'Once Upon a Time in Hong Kong,' *Film Comment*, no. 33, July–August 1997, p. 16. Much as his breakthrough *Zu* gave rise to a Hong Kong special effects industry, Tsui Hark's animation for *A Chinese Ghost Story* may spawn a Hong Kong animation industry. Costing US$5 million and taking four years to make, the production utilizes 3-D visuals, Dolby surround sound, and name stars for the voices of the characters. Special Administrative Region (Hong Kong) Film Top Ten Box Office Page, 9 May 1997 (20 May 1997).

61. For a discussion positing that Tsui Hark subversively incorporated his encounter with the Hong Kong Panel of Film Censors into alterations that he made to *Dangerous Encounters*, see Tam See Kam, 'Ban(g)! Ban(g)! *Dangerous Encounter* – 1st Kind: Writing With Censorship,' *Asian Cinema*, Spring 1996, pp. 83–108.

62. Ibid., pp. 91–2. Hong Kong censors are more likely to prohibit social and political material than they are to forbid films containing sex and violence. In fact, a 1988 film censorship ordinance allowed for more nudity and sex in films. Lent, *Asian Film Industry*, p. 118. One development has been the production of so-called Category III (for persons aged eighteen and above only) films such as *Sex and Zen* (1991) and *Naked Killer* (1993). In 1997, 39 per cent of films (662 out of 1,697) approved for public exhibition in Hong Kong received a Category III classification, 20 per cent (336) received a Category I (suitable for all ages) rating, 17 per cent (296) were classified as Category IIA (not suitable for children), and 24 per cent (403) were assigned a Category IIB (not suitable for young persons and children) classification. Categories I, IIA, and IIB are advisory, while Category III is enforced by law. 'Film Classification in Hong Kong,' http://www.info.gov.hk (9 November 1998). British censorship of Hong Kong cinema for political reasons was a long-standing practice. In 1928, the chief censor told the United States Consul-General that he was responsible for sustaining British eminence in 'a small settlement of white men on the fringe of a huge empire of Asiatics.' That same year, a United Artists agent in Hong Kong indicated that forbidden topics included 'armed conflict between Chinese and whites' and depictions of 'white women in indecorous garb or positions or situations which would tend to discredit our womenfolk with the Chinese.' Ella Shohat and Robert Stam, *Unthinking Eurocentrism: Multiculturalism and the Media*, London 1994, p. 112.

63. Michel Pêcheux, *Language, Semantics, and Ideology: Stating the Obvious,* London 1982, pp. 156–9.

64. Mas'ud Zavarzadeh, *Seeing Films Politically*, Albany 1991, p. 94.

65. Theodor Adorno and Max Horkheimer, *Dialectic of Enlightenment*, New York 1972.

CHAPTER THREE

1. Michael Beaud, *A History of Capitalism 1500–1980*, New York 1983, p. 18.

2. Woo also notes that the actor who plays Frank in this movie, the character with a 'bullet in

his head,' is played by Jacky Cheung, who 'reminds me of my younger brother. In both his performances and his personality he is so innocent and pure. This to me is the most important quality in an actor.'

3. Ted Elrick, 'The Woo Dynasty Comes to Hollywood,' http://dga.org/dga/dganews/v20–5/woo.html, (16 July 1996).

4. Woo further elaborates:

> At that time I never dreamed of working in movies. I wanted to be a minister. I was raised and educated in the church. I had seen so many people suffering I just wanted to help, like the church did. I wanted to send the message of God … I always found my dreams in movies whether it was a musical like *Singing in the Rain* or a western like *High Noon*, which was one of my favorite films. I was mostly influenced by the French New Wave (Truffaut) and French gangster films.… After high school, my family couldn't afford to continue my education and Hong Kong didn't have a film school. So I stole film theory books from the library. Theories on editing … on directing. Books on technique. Hitchcock. Orson Welles. Eisenstein. Art books. Philosophy books. That is how I learned film theory and film as a spiritual art. I also learned about filmmaking from watching many, many movies. At the time, Hong Kong distributed movies from all over the world. I got to see movies about different cultures from Europe, Japan, India, etc.… Then I joined a group of young people who were crazy about movies. We all made experimental films. At the time, Hong Kong movies were really bad. They were poor-quality copycat films. I wanted to make films that looked good. The second inspiration was the French New Wave. The idea of a director as an auteur. It was revolutionary. The crews were smaller, like twenty people, with a single camera and small budgets, and they made good movies. This encouraged me by showing that I didn't need a lot of money or a big crew to make a good movie. So I determined to be a film director. I was twenty.

5. Maitland McDonagh, 'Things I Felt Were Being Lost,' *Film Comment*, September–October 1993, p. 52.

6. Diane Carson, 'Van Damned: *Hard Target* Draws Fire For Its Violence,' *The Riverfront Times* (St. Louis), 25–31 August 1993, p. 31; quoted by Tony Williams, 'To Live and Die in Hong Kong,' *CineACTION*, vol. 36, 1995, pp. 42–52.

7. John Woo's description of Chow Yun-fat: 'His acting is so natural and so true, from his heart. Also, I like his personality, his real character. He likes to help people. He's a real shining knight to me.' *The Killer*, director John Woo, 1989, videodisc, Voyager Criterion Collection, 1993. Chow Yun-fat's description of Woo comes from a *Village Voice* interview (14 May 1991) by Berenice Reynaud, p. 60.

8. Sun Longji, 'The Deep Structure of Chinese Culture,' in Geremie Barme and John Minford, eds, *Seeds of Fire: Chinese Voices of Conscience*, New York 1988, pp. 30–35. Jenny Kwok Wah Loh uses Sun Longji's main theory of Chinese culture to discuss Chinese and Hong Kong popular cinema; see her 'A Cultural Interpretation of the Popular Cinema of China and Hong Kong,' in Chris Berry, ed., *Perspectives on Chinese Cinema*, London 1991, pp. 166–74.

9. Andy Webster, 'Duel Nature,' *Premiere*, July 1997, p. 64. Translators Erik Johnson and Juanita Huan Zhou correctly note the translation error in this article: *Jung* should read *zhong*, consistent with the other Mandarin terms.

10. Karl Marx, *Capital* Volume 1, New York 1967, p. 762.

11. Berenice Reynaud, 'The Killer,' *The Village Voice*, vol. 36, 14 May 1991, p. 60.

12. Elrick, 'The Woo Dynasty.'

13. Lori Sue Tilkin, 'The Journey of the Knight-Errant From Past to Present,' M.A. thesis, Washington University, St. Louis 1997, pp. 61, 4.

14. Woo, *The Killer*.

15. Ibid.

16. Tilkin, 'The Journey of the Knight-Errant,' p. 37.

17. Frankie Chan composed the music for the movie and pop star Roman Law sang the *Last Hurrah for Chivalry* theme song. The lyrics include: 'It was destiny that we met/ With our swords we devastated mutual foes…/ Praises and honors of yesterday have become causes for regrets…/ Though we now meet as old friends/ The swords we carry are of hatred/ I am unable to throw my sword away/ What can I do but lament in the wind and the rain?'

18. Woo, *The Killer*.

19. Marx, *Capital* Volume 1, p. 733.

20. Kenneth Li, '1001 Faces,' *A Magazine*, June/July 1996, p. 29. Woo says he first noticed Chow based on a newspaper article describing the actor's charitable activities with children's orphanages.

21. Woo, *The Killer*.

22. Woo believes that 'A good movie brings out your emotions and memories.' He cites Coppola's *The Godfather* and explains,

    Brando stands over his dead son, Sonny, with tears in his eyes and says, 'See how they mess with my son.' This scene affected me so much because it reminded me of the greatness of my own father and the sacrifices he made for me when I was a boy.

23. Marx, *Capital* Volume 1, p. 632.

24. The children sing: 'Who can leave behind their homeland and forget their childhood?/ Who dare look at yesterday's sorrow to take away our smiles?/ The youth don't understand the world that dirties their purity/ Let the teardrops roll down your face/ Sing out warmness/ Stretch out your arms/ And hold your dream and the real you/ Your tender smiles give me strength.' It is interesting to note that Woo refers to his films as his 'children.' He says, 'I can't really choose between my films because they are all like my children, each has a special place in my heart.' Filmmaking, then, suggests hope for the future.

25. Williams, 'To Live and Die in Hong Kong,' p. 52.

26. Woo himself calls the character 'Jeff,' a nod at Alain Delon's character in *Le Samourai*, although subtitled versions use 'John' because of the nickname and familiar 'Ah-John' used by both Sidney and Jenny (see *The Killer*). In the movie, 'the killer' never reveals his name to the cop.

27. Woo, *The Killer*.

28. Western critics have used such phrases as 'master blaster,' 'ultraviolent arias' and 'homo-erotic charge' to describe John Woo and his action films. Julian Stringer, while not rejecting knowingly playful and self-reflexive readings, suggests that they are matters of taste that 'restore textual power to white Western spectators at the very time when economic and social privilege is being lost by white people in Hong Kong.' 'Problems with the Treatment of Hong Kong Cinema as Camp,' *Asian Cinema*, Winter 1996/97, p. 58. Similarly, Mikel J. Koven, in suggesting that the films express 'traditional Chinese masculinity,' does not discount

gay appropriations, but he remarks that 'men in Western cultures do not touch or become physically intimate with one another outside of the romantic relationship.' 'My Brother, My Lover, My Self: Traditional Masculinity in the Hong Kong Action Cinema of John Woo,' *Canadian Folkore*, vol. 19, no. 1, 1997, p. 65. Tony Williams acknowledges that the films lend 'themselves to gay readings' but points out that 'the east does not always reproduce western conventions of masculinity and femininity.' 'To Live and Die in Hong Kong,' p. 48. Patrick Tan, for his part, asserts that 'homosexuality exists in Eastern society as in any other. However, it exists mostly as a non-issue rather than a topic to cogitate over.' 'East/West Politics,' *CineACTION*, no. 42, p. 49. Berenice Reynaud, Steve Rubio, and Jillian Sandel are among those who have noted 'homoeroticism' in Woo's movies. B. Reynaud, 'John Woo's Art Action Movie,' *Sight and Sound*, May 1993, p. 23; S. Rubio, 'The Meaning of Chow (It's in His Mouth),' and J. Sandel, 'A Better Tomorrow? American Masochism and Hong Kong Action Films,' *Bad Subjects*, 13 April 1994, http://eserver.org/bs/13/Rubio-Sandel.html, (25 August 1998). Sandel states that John Woo informed her that he enjoyed the aforementioned article and she maintains that, irrespective of his filmic intentions, he is not opposed to homoerotic interpretations of his work. 'Reinventing Masculinity: The Spectacle of Male Intimacy in the Films of John Woo,' *Film Quarterly*, vol. 49, no. 4, Summer 1996, p. 34. Publicly, Woo has indicated that viewers can construe his films in myriad ways.

29. The early introduction of the theme song, which links John, Jenny, and Li, sets the tone: 'Another quiet tear streaks down my face/ Another night of desolation and solitude/ Just accept me for what I am/ Don't make promises you can't keep/ Who needs dreams when we have each other?/ Who needs tomorrow when we have today?'

30. The tape John and Li play of Jenny singing includes these lyrics: 'No regrets, no remorse, let bygones be bygones/ No sighs of melancholy, no tears of self-pity/ I don't care about what's right or wrong/ I'm not sentimental about the past/ Just set me free from this reverie, for the pain lingers on/ It dwells deep in my heart and soul/ Only time will tell if we are meant for each other/ My tears and laughter are my own indulgences.'

31. Critic David Chute on *Hard-Boiled*, director John Woo, 1992, videodisc, Voyager Criterion Collection, 1994.

32. Marx, *Capital* Volume 1, p. 763.

33. Ibid., p. 757.

34. Woo, *Hard-Boiled*.

35. Berenice Reynaud, 'Woo in Interview,' *Sight and Sound*, May 1993, p. 27.

36. Woo, *Hard-Boiled*.

37. Ibid. Woo's opening remarks bear a striking similarity to the words of well-loved filmmaker Charlie Chaplin, whose oeuvre has been given numerous political and social readings. Chaplin stated, 'There are those who always attach social significance to my work. It has none.... To entertain is my first consideration ... I have no political aims whatsoever as an actor.' Roger Manvell, *Chaplin*, Boston 1974, pp. 141–2. Note that Chaplin attaches the qualifier 'as an actor.'

CHAPTER FOUR

1. Bey Logan, *Hong Kong Action Cinema*, Woodstock 1995, p. 126:

It was a British fanzine editor, Rick Baker, who first coined the term 'heroic bloodshed' in the magazine *Eastern Heroes*. What are the specifications of this genre? 'That it's a Hong Kong action film that features a lot of gunplay and gangsters rather than kung fu,' he says.... 'Lots of blood. Lots of action.'

2. Bey Logan, 'Ringo Lam: Director on Fire,' in Rick Baker and Toby Russell, *The Essential Guide to the Best of Eastern Heroes*, edited by Lisa Tilston, London 1995, p. 89.

3. The number of crimes reported in 1986 was 81,411, a 2.3 per cent increase from 1981, translating into 1,500 crimes reported per 100,000 population. Total reported crimes held steady through 1994. There were 17,232 reported violent crimes that year, at a rate of 284 per 100,000 population. Altogether, 49,784 persons were arrested – 899 per 100,000 population. 'UN Profile – Hong Kong,' http://www.ifs.univie.ac.at/~uncjin/profiles/hongkong. html, 4 August 1998; 'Hong Kong Reported Crimes Per 100,000 Population,' http://web3.asial.com.sg/timesnet/data/hk97/stats28.html (4 August 1998); 'Hong Kong in Figures: Law and Order,' http://info.gov. hk/hkfigs/laworder.html (4 August 1998).

4. Logan, 'Ringo Lam,' p. 90.

5. Rolanda Chu, 'On the Lam: An Interview with Ringo,' *Hong Kong Film Magazine*, vol. 4, 1995, p. 18

6. Logan, 'Ringo Lam,' p. 89.

7. Ibid., p. 87.

8. Chu, 'On the Lam,' p. 19.

9. 'UN Profile – Hong Kong.'

10. The lyrics describe the experiences and emotions of these two characters: 'The world changes, disappointing sometimes/ All my decisions are painful grumbles/ Been frustrated, experienced failure/ But people are still dissatisfied, never understand/ Unrewarding/ Should fight for happiness/ All my decisions seem meaningless.'

11. Chu, 'On the Lam,' p. 20.

12. 'Prison admissions' includes both convicted felons and those awaiting trial. In 1986, the year before the film's release, there were 10,662 prison admissions in Hong Kong, with 7,646 of those prisoners being convicted, 1,607 for robbery, 1,209 for drug possession, 246 for intentional homicide. By 1992, prison admissions numbered over 13,500, with an average daily population of 11,886. There were 2,487 incarcerations for violent crimes and 617 for property crimes. 'UN Profile – Hong Kong'; 'World Fact Book of Criminal Justice,' http://www.ojp.usdoj.gov/bjs/pub/ascii/wfbcjhon.txt (4 August 1998).

13. Law Kar, 'Hero on Fire: A Comparative Study of John Woo's "Hero" Series and Ringo Lam's "On Fire" Series,' in Law Kar, ed., *Fifty Years of Electric Shadows*, Hong Kong 1997, p. 69.

14. Logan, 'Ringo Lam,' p. 89.

15. Male and female voices alternate and join in unison to sing the song: 'Brother, if you've got help from your friends and treasure everybody/ The world would be a better place/ Brother, if you give your heart and work together at your best/ You would meet friends wherever you go.'

16. *School on Fire*'s excessive violence, from the first fight, which makes its way from school into the streets, to a Triad's rampage and destruction, the characters' frenzied emotions, and its depiction of youth as hopeless and victimized, makes it a difficult film to watch. The film was banned almost everywhere, according to Lam, who had forty cuts imposed by the

board of censors on one of his *On Fire* films (the version screened in Taiwan had an hour's running time).

17. 'World Fact Book of Criminal Justice.'

18. 'UN Profile – Hong Kong.'

19. 'World Fact Book of Criminal Justice.'

20. Hong Kong Cinema Database, 'Hong Kong Cinema,' http://egret0.stanford.edu/cgi-bin/hkquery (6 July 1997).

21. We first encountered the term 'Triad Boyz' on Shelley Kraicer's website, 'Shelley Kraicer's Chinese Cinema,' http://www.interlog.com/kraicer/young.html (30 June 1997). The term is now often used to describe youth gang movie clones of the *Young and Dangerous* series.

22. Ron Murillo, 'Young and Dangerous: An Overview,' *Cineraider*, vol. 6, January 1997, p. 27. The June 1998 release of the sixth installment, *Young and Dangerous: The Prequel*, resulted in disappointing box-office receipts, as reported by the *Sing Tao Daily* of 8 June 1998. The Special Administrative Region (Hong Kong) Film Top Ten Box Office Page, http://www.geocities.com/Tokyo/Towers/2038, 3 June 1998 (14 June 1998).

23. Roger Buckley, *Hong Kong: The Road to 1997*, Cambridge 1997, p. 61.

24. Karl Marx, *Capital* Volume 2, New York 1967, p. 319.

25. Karl Marx, *The Eighteenth Brumaire of Louis Bonaparte*, New York 1963, p. 1.

26. Marx, *Capital* Volume 1, p. 695.

CHAPTER FIVE

1. For analyses of the martial arts genre that range from the historical and philosophical to the poetic and semiotic, see the essays in Lau Shing-hon, ed., *A Study of the Hong Kong Martial Arts Film*, Hong Kong 1980, and those in *A Study of the Hong Kong Swordplay Film (1945–1980)*, Hong Kong 1981. The majority of the essays in Li Cheuk-to, ed., *A Study of Hong Kong Cinema in the Seventies (1970–1979)*, Hong Kong 1984, examine this genre as well.

2. Lori Sue Tilkin, 'The Journey of the Knight-Errant From Past to Present,' M.A. thesis, Washington University, St. Louis 1997, p. 2.

3. Yu Wo-man, 'Swords, Chivalry, and Palm Power: A Brief Survey of the Cantonese Martial Arts Cinema, 1938–1970,' in Lau Shing-hon, ed., *A Study of the Hong Kong Swordplay Film*, p. 99.

4. Tilkin, 'The Journey of the Knight-Errant,' p. 52. For a detailed discussion of the production methods and aesthetic principles of Peking Opera, see A.C. Scott, 'The Performance of Classical Theater,' in Colin Mackerras, ed., *Chinese Theater: From Its Origins to the Present Day*, Honolulu 1983, pp. 118–44.

5. Yu Wo-man, 'Swords, Chivalry, and Palm Power,' p. 102. Ren Pengnian is also believed to have made the first feature-length film in China, *Yan Ruisheng* (1921).

6. Tony Rayns, 'Director: King Hu,' *Sight and Sound*, vol. 45 #1, Winter 1975/76, p. 11.

7. Lin Nien-tung, 'The Martial Arts Hero,' in Lau Shing-hon, ed., *A Study of the Hong Kong Swordplay Film*, p. 13.

8. Rayns, 'Director: King Hu,' p. 10. King Hu's use of Peking Opera to make a political point conveys why Chinese governments have attempted to control opera in the interests of public order and conformity. As Barbara E. Ward indicates, 'The fact that the drama was a major vehicle for the inculcation of values did not at all guarantee that the values so inculcated

were necessarily orthodox or politically innocuous.' 'Regional Operas and Their Audiences: Evidence from Hong Kong,' in David Johnson et al., eds, *Popular Culture in Late Imperial China*, Berkeley 1985, p. 186.

9. Sek Kei, 'The War Between the Cantonese and Mandarin Cinemas in the Sixties or How the Beautiful Women Lost to the Action Men,' in Law Kar, ed., *The Restless Breed: Cantonese Stars of the Sixties*, Hong Kong 1996, p. 31.

10. Frederick Engels, *The Condition of the Working Class in England*, Chicago 1984, p. 108.

11. Bruce Lee also made *The Way of the Dragon* (1972), which was not released in the USA until after the success of *Enter the Dragon*. The martial artist died during production of *Game of Death* (1973; released 1978), only appearing onscreen in the final moments, fighting basketball star Kareem Abdul-Jabbar. Lee's death has been the subject of much speculation over the years. Doctors attributed it to an aneurysm caused by cerebral edema (swelling of the brain), the result of an allergic reaction to headache pills. But some in his legion of fans believe that he was poisoned, by rival kung fu masters or by jealous film industry personnel. Others relate stories of Lee's involvement with gangsters and drug pushers, or claim that males in his family are subject to an old Chinese curse. Strangely, Lee's son Brandon was killed some twenty years later during the filming of *The Crow* (1994). See Richard Meyers, Amy Harlib, Bill and Karen Palmer, *From Bruce Lee to the Ninjas: Martial Arts Movies*, New York 1991, pp. 13–44; and Bey Logan, *Hong Kong Action Cinema*, Woodstock 1995, pp. 22–43.

12. Stephen Teo, *Hong Kong Cinema: The Extra Dimensions*, London 1997, p. 111.

13. Morgan also reminds us that while 'Bruce Lee was a product of the Hong Kong environment and the Hong Kong film industry, he was also part of Hollywood. He was the first crossover, making "face" accessible to non-Asian audiences. Bruce's goal was to make a movie in Hollywood for American audiences and then return to Hong Kong to make a film for Chinese audiences.'

14. For a list of Hong Kong martial arts films made between 1969 and 1982, which includes thumbnail descriptions and reviews, see Thomas Weisser, *Asian Cult Cinema*, New York 1997, pp. 221–60.

15. Logan, *Hong Kong Action Cinema*, p. 63.

16. Ng Ho, 'A Preliminary Plot Analysis of Cantonese Comedy,' in *The Traditions of Hong Kong Comedy*, Hong Kong 1985, p. 24.

17. Li Cheuk-to, 'Postscript,' in *A Study of Hong Kong Cinema in the Seventies*, p. 130.

18. Kwan came back from retirement (1970) to portray Wong Fei-hung in four further films: *The Skyhawk* (1973), *The Magnificent Butcher* (1979), *The Magnificent Kick* (1980), and *Dreadnaught* (1981). Tony Williams suggests that these movies are a bridge between older and younger martial arts heroes and values. 'Kwan Tak-hing and the New Generation,' *Asian Cinema*, vol. 10, no. 1, Fall 1998, pp. 71–7.

19. Beth Accomando, 'Battle of Harkness,' *Giant Robot* 8, 1997, p. 28.

20. Howard Hampton, 'Once Upon a Time in Hong Kong,' *Film Comment* 33, July–August 1997, p. 16.

21. Teo, *Hong Kong Cinema*, p. 170.

22. Ange Hwang, 'The Irresistible Hong Kong Movie *Once Upon a Time in China* Series – An Extensive Interview with Producer/Director Tsui Hark,' *Asian Cinema*, Fall 1998, p. 12.

23. The real Wong Fei-hung apparently had four wives during his lifetime, none of whom was

his aunt. The first three died at a young age. The fourth was a sixteen-year-old named Mok Gwai-lan, whom Wong met at a martial arts demonstration in 1903 at the age of fifty-six. A skilled martial artist and teacher, she was a rarity, a woman who taught classes for men. 'Wong Fei-hung: The Movie Portrayals/The True Story,' http://www.geocities.com/Tokyo/Ginza/5990/wong/html (25 November 1998).

24. Cheng Yu, 'Anatomy of a Legend,' in Li Cheuk-to, ed., *A Study of Hong Kong Cinema in the Seventies*, p. 25.

25. Robert Ray, *A Certain Tendency of the Hollywood Cinema, 1930–1980*, Princeton 1985, p. 152.

26. Martial artists rate Li's *wushu* superb, although purists think the series relies too much on special effects and wire tricks. Ron W. Lim's 'The Martial Artist's Guide to Hong Kong Films' website reviews and rates films for their martial arts quality. http://www.ronlim.com/martial.html (2 December 1998). Chinese martial arts have become known in the western world by the name kung fu, which, more literally, means physical skill. The word *wushu*, derived as it is from *wu* (martial) and *shu* (art), more accurately identifies the practice. Antonio Flores, 'The Name Wushu,' *Wushu: Chinese Culture, Recreation, & Sports*, http://www.wushu-exchange.com (9 December 1998).

27. Hwang, 'The Irresistible,' p. 17.

28. David Chou, 'Once Upon a Time in China and America,' *SMR Home Theatre*, http://www.smr-home-theatre.org/dvd (25 November 1998). Tsui Hark's penchant for screwball comedy was established in his 1981 parody of gangster flicks, *All the Wrong Clues*.

29. Paul Chun-ming Ng, 'The Image of Overseas Chinese in American Cinema,' in Law Kar, ed., *Overseas Chinese Figures in Cinema*, Hong Kong 1992, p. 94.

30. Alan Wilde, *Horizons of Assent: Modernism, Postmodernism, and the Ironic Imagination*, Baltimore 1981, p. 45.

31. Parker Tyler, *Magic and Myth of the Movies*, New York 1970, p. xviii.

32. Teshome Gabriel, 'Towards a Critical Theory,' in Jim Pines and Paul Willemen, eds, *Questions of Third Cinema*, London 1989, p. 48.

33. Rey Chow, 'Between Colonizers: Hong Kong's Postcolonial Self-Writing in the 1990s,' *Diaspora*, vol. 2, no. 2, 1992, p. 55.

34. Ricky Lau's five *Mr. Vampire* movies (1985–92) also appeared during this period. Premissed upon the custom of 'corpse driving,' whereby a Taoist priest transports the dead to safe burial sites, the initial success of these horror-comedy flicks spawned multiple copycat productions. Qing-era literature includes stories of cadavers becoming vampires when they take in the breath of a living person. Chinese vampires are said to move by hopping on two legs, and, in contradistinction to their Western counterparts, they do not suck blood, having instead long sharp nails that they use to rip apart people's flesh. While Hong Kong filmmakers apparently lifted the practice of bloodsucking from Hollywood Dracula films, Marx's use of vampirism to describe Capital (a metaphor that we cite more than once in this book) remains apt in that at least one earlier novel compares the living dead to the avaricious. For a discussion of both cinematic and literary Chinese vampires, see Ng Ho, 'Abracadaver,' in Li Cheuk-to, ed., *Phantoms of the Hong Kong Cinema*, Hong Kong 1989, pp. 29–35.

35. For a discussion of devils, gods, legends, myths, and the supernatural in Chinese literature that includes excerpted poetry and prose, see Lu Hsun, *A Brief History of Chinese Fiction*, trans. Yang Hsien-yi and Gladys Yang, Beijing 1964. For an examination of the Chinese supernatural that draws on a variety of disciplines and methodologies, including history,

anthropology and literary studies, see Meir Shahar and Robert P. Weller, eds, *Unruly Gods: Divinity and Society in China*, Honolulu 1996.

36. Tanaka Issei, 'The Social and Historical Context of Ming-Ching Local Drama,' in Johnson et al., eds, *Popular Culture in Late Imperial China*, p. 149.

37. Colin Mackerras, *The Rise of the Peking Opera 1770–1870*, Oxford 1972, p. 218.

38. Colin Mackerras, 'Theater and the Masses,' in *Chinese Theater*, p. 167. For a collection of Mao's writings on the arts, see *On Literature and Art*, Peking 1967.

39. Charles O. Hucker, *China's Imperial Past: An Introduction to Chinese History and Culture*, Stanford 1975, p. 71.

40. P'u Sung-ling, *Strange Stories from a Chinese Studio*, trans. Herbert A. Giles, New York 1969. Bewitched by ghosts and other esoterica, P'u apparently spent his life collecting and writing tales about them. His stories appeared only in manuscript form during his lifetime; publishers rejected his literary style and his poverty prevented self-publication. The *Strange Stories* collection was eventually published after his death by a grandson. Known to the Chinese as the *Liao Chai Chih I*, or simply as the *Liao Chai*, it was also the source of Li Hanxiang's *The Enchanting Shadow* (1960).

41. Tsui Hark's reputation for imposing his own vision on other directors' films has led some, such as Stephen Teo, to refer to him as the auteur of *Chinese Ghost Story* and its sequels, rather than Ching Siu-tung. Teo, *Hong Kong Cinema*, p. 227. Howard Hampton, in asserting that this attribution is erroneous, writes that while 'Tsui may have applied structure to Ching's dazzling flights of fancy, the serenely lunatic vision is entirely Ching's.' Comparing *Chinese Ghost Story* to Tsui's *Once Upon a Time in China*, Hampton's view is that

> [while] both succumb to the lure of formula and ritualized familiarity, Ching's tone is much surer throughout. Tsui offers phoney-endearing characters … and many crassly genteel bits of business, but Ching goes for flow in spite of characterization – his particularity there is in the dream not the insipid dreamers.

H. Hampton, 'Once Upon a Time in Hong Kong,' *Film Comment*, no. 33, 1997, pp. 24–6.

42. Peter Smith, 'A Chinese Ghost Film-Maker,' in Rick Baker and Toby Russell, *The Essential Guide to the Best of Eastern Heroes*, edited by Lisa Tilson, London 1995, p. 135.

43. Michael Ryan and Douglas Kellner, *Camera Politica: The Politics and Ideology of Hollywood Film*, Bloomington 1988, p. 182.

44. Smith, 'A Chinese Ghost Film-Maker,' p. 137.

45. Philip Green, *Cracks in the Pedestal: Ideology and Gender in Hollywood*, Amherst 1998, p. 79.

46. Janice Radway, *Reading the Romance*, London 1987, p. 217.

47. Tim Greenwood, 'Have Sword Will Travel,' in Baker and Russell, eds, *The Essential Guide to the Best of Eastern Heroes*, p. 83.

48. We have adopted Howard Hampton's delicious phrase, although our use is somewhat different from his in the article 'Once Upon a Time in Hong Kong.'

49. A eunuch first appeared as a character in King Hu's *Dragon Gate Inn*, a film dealing with the *tung ch'ang*, a secret service established by Ming Court eunuchs that operated outside the bounds of accountability. Eunuchs were prominent figures in many of China's historical dynasties; as emperors' personal servants, they often had unmatched opportunities to ingratiate themselves to rulers and become their political confidants. Some became so powerful that they were *de facto* governors themselves, controlling administrative appointments and

staffing official positions with toadies and trucklers. Sek Kei, 'Hong Kong Cinema from June 4 to 1997,' in Law Kar, ed., *Fifty Years of Electric Shadows*, p. 123; Rayns, 'King Hu,' p. 10.

50. The phrase is used by David Bordwell to describe a willful transgression of Western norms of moderation and credibility – 'to surpass that appeal to realism which makes the typical Western comparatively diffuse in its stylistic organization and emotional appeal.' 'Aesthetics in Action: Kung Fu, Gunplay, and Cinematic Expressivity,' in Law Kar, ed., *Fifty Years of Electric Shadows*, p. 86.

51. Smith, 'A Chinese Ghost Film-Maker,' p. 137.

52. Teo, *Hong Kong Cinema*, p. 200.

53. Sek Kei, *The Restless Breed*, p. 31.

54. Sam Ho, 'Licensed to Kick Men: The Jane Bond Films, in Sek Kei, ed., *The Restless Breed*, p. 40.

55. 'The Hong Kong Handover,' *BBC World Service*, http://www.bbc.co.uk/worldservice/hongkong/hkide.htm, 16 May 1997 (5 June 1998).

56. Hong Kongers sought residency in countries such as Gambia, Jamaica, and Tonga – over forty countries in all. Curaçao, Guam, Paraguay, and South Africa were among the nations that sent agents offering to exchange domicile for money. The small Central American country of Belize even offered a passport with no residency requirement for US$23,800. The Panamanian consulate, a relative of Manuel Noriega, reportedly sold over three thousand bogus passports to desperate Hong Kongers. Mark Roberti, *The Fall of Hong Kong: China's Trimuph and Britain's Betrayal*, New York 1996, pp. 265–6.

57. 'Model' operas retained a few features of traditional operas, including acrobatics and swordfighting, but the subjects, dress, representations, and sets were rendered revolutionary and modern. Mackerras, *Chinese Theater*, p. 167.

58. Kwitko, 'Filipina Domestic Workers,' in Jayant Lele and Wisdom Tettey, eds, *Asia: Who Pays for the Growth? – Women, Environment, and Popular Movements*, Aldershot 1996, p. 111; 'Hong Kong,' Asian Demographics Ltd, http://www.asiandemographics.com, 22 August 1998 (1 October 1998).

59. Michelle Yeoh was known as Michelle Khan in the years prior to her 'retirement' and four-year (1988–92) marriage to Dickson Poon, former owner of defunct D&B Films. Speaking of her career as a woman in a male-dominated industry, Yeoh says, 'I've been lucky in my career as my male peers have always regarded me as an equal. I hope that I have earned that respect due to an uncompromising dedication to acting and performing my own stunts. Therefore, my view may not be common for the rest of the women working in Hong Kong film. I have played strong female characters in my movies and I think that partly reflects my own personality.'

60. Alison Jaggar, *Feminist Politics and Human Nature*, Brighton 1983, p. 132.

61. Ann D. Jordan and Carole Peterson, 'Hostage to Tradition: Equality for Hong Kong Women,' *China Rights Forum*, Fall 1995, http://www.hrichina.org (8 September 1998).

62. Barbara Creed, *The Monstrous Feminine: Film, Feminism, Psychoanalysis*, London 1993, pp. 154–5; 'Dark Desires: Male Masochism in the Horror Film,' in S. Cohan and I.R. Hark, eds, *Screening the Male: Exploring Masculinities in Hollywood Cinema*, London 1993, p. 132; 'From Here to Modernity – Feminism and Postmodernism,' *Screen*, vol. 28, no. 2, 1987, p. 60.

63. According to Ronny Yu, he felt obliged to show courtesy to Liang by informing him of changes that he wished to make in the story. Yu says, 'as I was leaving, he said "kid, don't fuck up my book."' Liang later refused Yu's offer of a videotape copy of the film.

64. Ronny Yu, who suffered from polio as a child, says 'when I was a kid, I had nobody to play with, no buddies to roll around and get dirty with, I had to create my own world, my own fantasies. I lived in my own little stories.' He also went to the movies a lot. The director, pointing out that he had no formal film training, says that 'everything I do is from the gut. I didn't plan to be a director, but I've always challenged myself. I jump from genre to genre because I challenge myself. That's why my work is so different.'

65. Mas'ud Zavarzadeh, *Seeing Films Politically*, Albany 1991, p. 208.

66. Howard Hampton, 'Venus, Armed: Brigitte Lin's Shanghai Gesture,' *Film Comment*, September–October 1996, p. 42.

67. Guido Henkel and Lieu Pham, 'The Bride With White Hair,' *DVD Review*, http://www.dvdreview.com/html/dvdreview/the_bride_with_white_hair, (23 December 1998).

68. Stephen Connor, *Postmodern Culture: An Introduction to Theories of the Contemporary*, Oxford 1989, p.173.

69. Walter Benjamin, 'The Work of Art in the Age of Mechanical Reproduction,' in John G. Hanhandt, ed., *Video Culture: A Critical Investigation*, Layton 1986, pp. 27–52.

70. British cabinet member Alastair Goodland used the phrase 'through train' to describe Britain's handover of Hong Kong to China. Roger Buckley, *Hong Kong: The Road to 1997*, Cambridge 1997, pp. 124–5.

71. Nancy Fraser, *Unruly Practices: Power, Discourse, and Gender in Contemporary Social Theory*, Minneapolis 1989, p. 176.

72. Rey Chow, 'King Kong in Hong Kong: Watching the "Handover" From the USA,' *Social Text* 55, vol. 16, no. 2, Summer 1998, p. 100.

CHAPTER SIX

1. For a comprehensive and detailed account, see Chan's autobiography (written with Jeff Yang), *I Am Jackie Chan: My Life in Action*, New York 1998. Chan is also the subject of Clyde Gentry III's *Jackie Chan: Inside the Dragon*, Dallas 1997; and Jeff Rovin and Kathy Tracy's *The Essential Jackie Chan Sourcebook*, New York 1997. Based on interviews with the actor and those he has worked with, Gentry's book focuses on Jackie Chan's martial arts and filmmaking techniques. The Rovin and Tracy book is part biography, part annotated filmography, all fanzine. Jackie Chan considers Alex Law's *Painted Faces* (1988), based on his and the Seven Little Fortunes' experience at Yu Jim-yuen's China Drama Academy, to be less accurate than Chen Kaige's depiction of an opera school in his 1993 *Farewell My Concubine* (for which Chan turned down the leading role that eventually went to Leslie Cheung), saying that the latter better conveys the severity of both the training regimen and Master Yu. *Jackie Chan: Inside the Dragon*, p. 7; and Bey Logan, *Hong Kong Action Cinema*, Woodstock 1995, p. 8. Chan discusses the ten years he spent at opera school at length in his autobiography.

2. Chan, *I Am Jackie Chan*, p. 219.

3. Logan, *Hong Kong Action Cinema*, p. 63.

4. Gentry, *Jackie Chan: Inside the Dragon*, p. 20.

5. Ibid., p. 21.

6. Rovin and Tracy, *The Essential Jackie Chan Sourcebook*, p. 135.

7. Gentry, *Jackie Chan: Inside the Dragon*, p. 25.

8. Chan, *I Am Jackie Chan*, p. 21.

9. Bernard F. Dick, *Anatomy of Film*, 2nd edn, New York 1990, p. 227.

10. Robert Sklar, *Movie-Made America*, New York 1975, p. 119.

11. Jackie Chan's first Hollywood career consisted of two supporting roles and two starring roles – in Burt Reynolds' *Cannonball Run* (1981 and 1984) pictures and in the critical and commercial bombs, *The Big Brawl* (1980) and *The Protector* (1985), respectively.

12. Samo Hung's *Eastern Condors* was the first of several brutally graphic Vietnam War-era Hong Kong films released in the late 1980s and early 1990s; these included Tsui Hark's *A Better Tomorrow 3: Love and Death in Saigon* (1989) and John Woo's *Bullet in the Head* (1990). Although *Eastern Condors* did poorly at the box office (as did Tsui's and Woo's pictures), many consider Hung's movie to be the best synthesis of kung fu and guns. Recalling the *Dirty Dozen,* the United States military sends a commando team of Asian-American and immigrant Asian convicts into Vietnam to destroy a munitions silo left behind during its 1973 withdrawal from the country before the North Vietnamese discover it. Promised a pardon and US$200,000 each for a successful mission, the squad is left to fend for itself after the government aborts the mission. The cast includes Samo Hung's future wife, Joyce Godenzi, as an anti-communist Cambodian guerrilla fighter; Yuen Wah as a laughing maniacal North Vietnamese general; as well as Yuen Biao, Yuen Woo-ping, and Haing S. Ngor in the follow-up to his Oscar-winning role in *The Killing Fields*. *Eastern Condors* is critical of both the North Vietnamese and the United States and raises the issue of extant tension among Asian nationalities.

13. Yuen Biao's filmography includes appearances in *Zu: Warriors of the Magic Mountain* (1983), *Eastern Condors* (1986), *The Iceman Cometh* (1989), *Once Upon a Time in China* (1990), and *Shogun and Little Kitchen* (1992). He also produced and directed *A Kid from Tibet* (1991).

14. Roger Buckley, *Hong Kong: The Road to 1997*, Cambridge 1997, p. 5.

15. Leo Ou-fan Lee, 'Two Films From Hong Kong: Parody and Allegory,' in Nick Browne et al. eds, *New Chinese Cinemas: Forms, Identities, Politics*, Cambridge 1994, p. 204.

16. Ramie Tateishi, 'Jackie Chan and the Re-invention of Tradition,' *Asian Cinema*, vol. 10, no. 1, Fall 1998, p. 80.

17. Ibid., p. 81.

18. Chan, *I Am Jackie Chan*, p. 283.

19. Ibid., p. 182.

20. Ibid., p. 283. Jackie Chan writes that he began placing stunt outtakes at the end of his movies to communicate to audiences the actual danger that he and his stunt team face in their work. He confesses that he is scared each time he places his life in jeopardy and reminds readers that he has been injured numerous times while shooting film stunts.

21. Aaron Anderson, 'Action in Motion: Kinesthesia in Martial Arts Films,' *Jump Cut* 42, December 1998, p. 3.

22. Gentry, *Jackie Chan: Inside the Dragon*, p. 164. Jackie Chan produced Stanley Kwan's art-house films *Rouge* and *Actress* during this period as well. Ibid., pp. 78–84.

23. Jackie Chan's mega-stardom allows him the luxury of time. He took seven days to work up the courage to do the clocktower fall in *Project A*. *I Am Jackie Chan*, pp. 284–5. Gentry notes that *Project A 2*'s hide-and-seek scene in Maggie Cheung's apartment took ten days to prepare, and he quotes Chan saying that it took one month to shoot. Gentry, *Jackie Chan: Inside the Dragon*, p. 152. The making of *Operation Condor* took almost a year from preproduction to release. *The Essential Jackie Chan Sourcebook*, p. 187.

24. As their references to 'Battling Asian Babes' and 'Deadly China Dolls' attests, Rick Baker and Toby Russell of the *Eastern Heroes* fanzine lust after more than Hong Kong's 'heroic bloodshed' action flicks. To sample their predilections, see *The Essential Guide to Deadly China Dolls*, London 1996, which comes with a 'not suitable for minors' warning.

25. Chan, *I Am Jackie Chan*, p. 320.

26. Of *Rumble in the Bronx*'s finale, Stanley Tong says,

> I dreamed of doing it for two years before making [the movie]. After *Supercop* in 1992, I was on Australia's Gold Coast (Queensland) representing Golden Harvest on a location search. I was on the beach waiting for a helicopter when I saw a small hovercraft pick up some tourists to go out sightseeing. The hovercraft comes in and [Tong laughs] blows sand all over me. I had a feeling so strong watching it land and take off that if I could get something of a bigger size, I could run it on the freeway through downtown. That would be something no one has ever done before. So I had the sequence in my mind for two years.

27. Stanley Tong would later borrow from himself in the making of *Mr. Magoo* (1996), his first Hollywood directorial effort. Mr. Magoo (Leslie Nielsen), mistaking an ironing board for a snowboard due to his poor eyesight, rides the device down a mountain slope and through a ski competition while chased by numerous foes; the scene alludes to Jackie Chan's snow chase in *First Strike* and required split-second timing and coordination. Where Jackie jumps from the mountain and grabs on to a helicopter mid-air, Mr. Magoo falls head-first into the snow.

28. Chiao Hsiung-ping, 'The Distinctive Taiwanese and Hong Kong Cinemas,' in Chris Berry, ed., *Perspectives on Chinese Cinema*, London 1991, p. 162.

29. Martial arts purists have made special note of Michelle Yeoh's kick boxing, an ability that likely stems from her background in ballet and sports. Originally from Malaysia, she says that 'I was always very athletic and represented [my country] in squash and swimming, but dancing was my passion. I attended the Royal Ballet School in England and had every intention of becoming a prima ballerina. Unfortunately, an injury meant that my back could not take the strain and pressures of a professional dance career.' Tong incorporated a humorous bit with Chan and Eric Tsang, who showed up for a day's work. Identically dressed with large fake breasts (one using water balloons, the other a child's toy that keeps making a noise), the actors do double-takes upon seeing each other: mirror images, one a cop, the other a criminal. The setting, a Tak Hing Street jewelry store, alludes to the original plot of *Supercop* dismissed by Tong; Chan had intended the story to be about a Hong Kong jewelry store heist. Then, while in the store to foil a would-be robbery, Chan's cop speaks on his cell phone with 'Uncle Bill' (Bill Tung, a favorite to play Chan's uncle or immediate cop superior). 'What? You are sending me to America?', he asks, a reference, of course, to Chan's (and Tong's) coming to 'America' for *Rumble in the Bronx*.

30. Stanley Tong says that 'I couldn't sleep for two weeks before shooting the tunnel scene because I didn't know how to do it and I couldn't afford special effects. I learned by reading books from Industrial Light and Magic (George Lucas's company). We built a miniature tunnel going uphill to sustain the flow of water. I had two trucks pour water so that when it reached the bottom a current was created that pushed the water through the tunnel.'

31. Although Johnnie To directed his first movie in 1978, he spent most of the 1970s and 1980s

working in television. Of his initial film experience, he says 'I discovered that my ability was limited because I did not have enough knowledge. Therefore I went back to television. About seven years later, I started my movie business but did not get fully involved until 1990. I wanted to be a director from the beginning, but I needed time to develop my skills. Actor Anthony Wong, who trained and worked in television, credits To with 'leading me to the movie industry. He is my coach.'

32. Betsy Sherman, 'Hong Kong "Trio" Hits Brattle,' *Boston Globe*, 6 January 1998, p. E4.

33. Mee Kam Ng and Allison Cook, 'Reclamation: An Urban Development Strategy Under Fire,' *Land Use Policy*, vol. 14, no. 1, 1997, p. 15.

34. James T.H. Tang, 'Hong Kong's Transition to Chinese Rule: The Fate of the Joint Declaration,' in Judith M. Brown and Rosemary Foot, eds, *Hong Kong's Transitions, 1842–1997*, New York 1997, pp. 157–60.

35. Despite his two years of study in Beijing, Yen admits he was still reckless during his first years in Hong Kong. During the shooting of a *Drunken Tai Chi* scene involving fireworks, he says that 'I got too close on one shot and suffered a major burn to my arm. I have a scar from it to this day.'

36. Logan, *Hong Kong Action Cinema*, p. 173. Donnie Yen received hands-on action choreography experience on other films in which he appeared. Calling *Satan Returns* (1997) a 'kind of crazy Hong Kong version of *Seven*,' Yen says: 'I liked the fact that I had such a different "look" for the film, kind of *Blade Runner* with Elvis Costello.' He also choreographed 'the jousting match between Michelle [Yeoh] and Flying Monkey in *Wing Chun*, a scene that was difficult to shoot because of all the elements involved, including the camera cranes, the horses, the fire, the actors, their various doubles (riding doubles, fire doubles, fighting doubles).' Says Yen,

> the fire equipment in China, where we were filming, wasn't as sophisticated as it is in Hong Kong, so we were burning more of the set for longer than we needed to. We were actually shooting in three places for that one scene, over a nine-day period. I'm quite proud of that scene.

37. Mas'ud Zavarzadeh, *Seeing Films Politically*, Albany 1991, p. 193.

38. Sek Kei, 'The War Between the Cantonese and Mandarin Cinemas,' in Sek Kei, ed., *The Restless Breed: Cantonese Stars of the Sixties*, Hong Kong 1996, p. 31.

39. Ibid., p. 33.

40. 'Wolf Symbolism,' http://www.wolves-on-web.com, 27 October 1998 (9 January 1999).

41. Louis Althusser, *For Marx*, London 1969, p. 100.

42. Po Kam-hung, 'Legend of the Wolf,' Hong Kong Film Critics Society, http://filmcritics.org.hk (1 October 1998).

43. Dana Polan, 'Postmodernism and Cultural Analysis Today,' in. E. Ann Kaplan, ed., *Postmodernism and Its Discontents*, London 1988, p. 52.

44. Yuen Wah is, perhaps, best known for his bad-guy roles in *Eastern Condors*, *Dragons Forever* and *Iceman Cometh*. Like Yuen Biao, against whom he has been paired in a number of movies, Yuen Wah is a small lean man with great quickness, much litheness, and formidable gymnastic skills.

45. Fredric Jameson, 'Postmodernism and Consumer Society,' in Kaplan, ed., *Postmodernism and Its Discontents*, p. 19.

CHAPTER SEVEN

1. David Faure, 'Reflections on Being Chinese in Hong Kong,' in Judith M. Brown and Rosemary Foot, eds, *Hong Kong's Transitions, 1842–1997*, New York 1997, p. 111.
2. Karrie Jacobs, 'Hong Kong Chaos Theory,' *Guggenheim Magazine*, Spring 1997, p. 37.
3. Ackbar Abbas, *Hong Kong Culture and the Politics of Disappearance*, Minneapolis 1997, p. 81.
4. Ibid., p. 1.
5. David L. Eng uses the phrase for his study of *Rouge*, drawing from one of a series of Abbas lectures at the University of California, Berkeley in 1992. See D.L. Eng, 'Love at Last Site: Waiting for Oedipus in Stanley Kwan's *Rouge*,' *Camera Obscura*, vol. 32, September–January 1993–4, p. 97. Abbas used the phrase in 'The New Hong Kong Cinema and the *Deja Disparu*,' *Discourse*, vol. 16, Spring 1994, p. 66.
6. See Li Cheuk-to, 'The Return of the Father: Hong Kong New Wave and Its Chinese Context in the 1980s,' in Nick Browne et al., eds, *New Chinese Cinemas: Forms, Identities, Politics*, Cambridge 1994, p. 167 for the first view; and for the latter, see Stephen Teo, *Hong Kong Cinema: The Extra Dimensions*, London 1997, p. 150.
7. Teresa de Lauretis, 'Rethinking Women's Cinema: Aesthetics and Feminist Theory,' in D. Carson, L. Dittmar, and J.R. Welsch, eds, *Multiple Voices in Feminist Film Criticism*, Minneapolis 1994, pp. 140–61. We are indebted to Denise Tse Shang-tang for her insights into Hui's films, in a paper entitled 'Coming into Gender Consciousness,' delivered at the Asian Cinema Studies Society Conference, Trent University, Peterborough, Ontario, August 1997.
8. Guillermo Gómez-Peña, *New World Border*, San Francisco 1997, p. 82.
9. Sheila Rowbotham, *Woman's Consciousness, Man's World*, Harmondsworth 1973, p. 57.
10. Gómez-Peña continues: 'At times it is an abyss, a wall, or a spiderweb. Other times it is an infected wound, or a membrane. Some days it's more like a hole, even a tunnel; and suddenly, it becomes a mirror, a bear hug, or a sudden flash.' 'Border Culture and Deterritorialization,' *La Linea Quebrada/The Broken Line*, no. 2, n.p., 1978; cited in Lucy Lippard, *Mixed Blessings: New Art in a Multicultural America*, New York 1990, p. 223.
11. Cheung Yuen-ting says

    An Autumn's Tale was my second feature and the first time I worked with professional actors.… The budget [just US$500,000] was still very low for a new director. But by then I had already got some basic crew members in New York who would work for me for a very low price. I was very lucky to have Chow Yun-fat as the male lead. When I asked to him to act in my film, *A Better Tomorrow* hadn't come out and he hadn't become a mega-star yet. Otherwise, as a new director, I would never have the nerve or the money to hire him.… I don't think the West has realized his potential. Apart from being a very good actor, he is also a very good person.

12. Gayle Rubin, 'The Traffic in Women: Notes on the Political Economy of Sex,' in Rayna R. Reiter, ed., *Toward an Anthropology of Women*, New York 1975, p. 158. Rubin's passage takes off from Marx: 'A Negro is a Negro. Only under certain conditions does he become a slave. A cotton-spinning machine is a machine for spinning cotton. Only under certain conditions does it become capital.' See Karl Marx, *Wage, Labor and Capital*, New York 1933, p. 28.
13. Karl Marx, 'Economic and Philosophic Manuscripts,' in *Karl Marx: Early Writings*, edited by T.B. Bottomore, New York 1963, pp. 177–8.

14. Alison M. Jaggar, *Feminist Politics and Human Nature*, Totowa 1983, p. 308.

15. The lyrics of 'Thinking Of' are as follows: 'Thinking of when my ancestors decided to leave China/ They never knew what it was like there/ Full of worries they thought/ The foreign land must be very different…/ Thinking of how each day passes and I sow/ For the sake of my children/ That they might be given the best education/ To live freely and grow up a complete person/ Thinking of who would want to leave one's homeland/ I only want to return sooner/ Time, please wait awhile/ Chinese people are born with patience unbounded.'

16. The lyrics of the song are as follows: 'I think of you every time I close my eyes/ You're like an alluring slogan that won't leave/ In a world of deceit and betrayal/ We all have to learn to protect ourselves/ My beloved comrades, let me believe in your loyalty/ Perhaps I am not a perfect example of love…/ It's an unbroken force which compels us/ To lose our way to find ourselves/ Comrade, my love, let me embrace you/ Hand in hand/ Joy and sorrow, parting and reunion – the story always ends the same… / The same hand, the same blood/ Surviving under the same glorious sun/ If you open your eyes/ And give me a promise from the heart.' The final passage is sung towards the film's end, and, unlike the driving rock beat of the rest of the song, is delivered lyrically and in ballad style.

17. Mark Poster, *The Mode of Information: Poststructuralism and Social Context*, Chicago 1990, p. 5.

18. Karl Marx, *Capital* Volume 1, New York 1967, p. 265.

19. Abbas, 'The New Hong Kong Cinema,' p. 75.

20. Rey Chow, *Primitive Passions: Visuality, Sexuality, Ethnography, and Contemporary Chinese Cinema*, New York 1995, p. 24.

21. Ibid.

22. *Comrades* director Peter Chan, describing the movie he would like to make, articulates issues of Hong Kong Chinese identity and the diaspora:

   The movie I want to make eventually is about a bunch of kids growing up in the 1940s and the early 1950s in Thailand, and how they dream about China as home and … live in this very romantic Thai world that was really beautiful and what happens when they finally get to go back to China…. I have all these stories from friends of my parents' generation and how that one love for your home country destroyed people's lives forever…. It's out there. It's about my heritage … [about] the rootlessness of Chinese, which is a sense shared by a lot of Chinese.

23. Karl Marx, *The German Ideology*, edited by C.J. Arthur, New York 1970, p. 85.

24. Actor Roy Cheung explains,

   Rose was a turning point in my career. It was very daring of the director to cast me, a typecast villain, for that role. I don't know whether I am satisfied or not with being typecast as a villain. All I can say is that my appearance is that of a villain and it has helped me a great deal in my acting. I would very much like to tackle other kinds of roles. There really aren't a lot of choices for actors in the local system and environment; the only choice is do it or quit.

   Cheung played similar Triad members with heart in *Mongkok Story* (see Chapter 4) and *Beast Cops* (see Chapter 12), both of whom die violently, as does the character in *Rose*. Most recently Cheung has played a hero monk in *Storm Riders* (see Chapter 12); not only is he a 'good guy,' but he also survives.

25. Marx, *Capital* Volume 1, p. 265.

26. Director Johnnie To says that '*All About Ah-long* was the first time I was able to have the freedom to produce the movie I wanted to make … Eighty percent of the movies I'd made had made money, so he [the producer] gave me that chance … I rather love *All About Ah-long* … [which] was the drama I wanted to shoot, and I had great authority over what I wanted to do.'

27. Karl Marx, 'The Holy Family,' in *Selected Writings*, edited by David McLellan, New York 1997, p. 134.

CHAPTER EIGHT

1. Geoffrey O'Brien, 'Blazing Passions,' *New York Review*, 24 September 1992, p. 41.

2. Ibid., pp. 41–2.

3. Betsy Sherman, 'Woo Gets Into the US Action,' *Boston Globe*, 20 August 1993, p. 48.

4. Fredric Dannen and Barry Long mistakenly attribute Raymond Wong, Yu's other mentor, as offering the director this advice. See *Hong Kong Babylon: An Insider's Guide to the Hollywood of the East*, New York 1997, p. 166. Yu explains that Hui told him early on,

    Ronny, you don't know what you're getting yourself into … It's a tough life. You have to go away, leave your family behind. You have to think movies twenty-four hours a day. If you can tell me you can do that, I'll say, good luck kid, continue. If you feel the fire inside you, all this devotion and commitment.… If you feel like one day you walk onto the set, you want to go home, you want to go to the restaurant, then stop. Your fire has slowly, slowly disappeared and when that part disappears, no matter what you say, your work will reflect that, the audience will pick it up.

5. Homi Bhabha, 'Postcolonial Authority and Postmodern Guilt,' in Lawrence Grossberg et al., eds, *Cultural Studies*, New York 1992, pp. 57–8.

6. Cheung quoted in *City Entertainment Biweekly*, no. 328; cited in *The 16th Hong Kong International Film Festival* (catalogue), Hong Kong 1992, p. 113.

7. A typical cage home is at 24 Fuk Tsuen Street at Taikoktsui, where around one hundred lodgers live in a flat of one thousand square feet. Normally, each flat will have one or two toilets and a kitchen shared by all the inhabitants. Not only are such flats severely overcrowded; they are often also fire traps. 'On the Margins of a Booming City: Housing for the Poor in Hong Kong,' *China Rights Forum*, Summer 1996, http://www.icg.org (8 September 1998).

8. Marx's description:

    The cellar dwelling of the poor man is a hostile dwelling … He cannot regard it as his home, as a place where he might at last say, 'here I am at home.' Instead, he finds himself in another person's house, the house of a stranger who lies in wait for him every day and evicts him if he does not pay the rent. He is also aware of the contrast between his own dwelling and a human dwelling such as exists in that other world, the heaven of wealth.

    Karl Marx, 'Economic and Philosophic Manuscripts,' in *Karl Marx: Early Writings*, edited by T.B. Bottomore, New York 1963, p. 177.

9. Cheung, *The 16th Hong Kong International Film Festival*, p. 113. Cageman accurately details the deplorable living conditions of 'singletons' like 69-year-old Lo Chek, who lives amidst noise, overcrowdedness, filth, and tedium. Having worked as a 'coolie' for more than forty years, Lo rents a bedspace in a thirty-year-old building in Taikoktsui, along with one hundred other tenants. 'On the Margins of a Booming City.'

10. Frederick Engels, *The Condition of the Working Class in England*, Chicago 1984, p. 60.

11. Frederick Engels, *On the Housing Question*, Moscow 1975, p. 23.

12. Engels's description of urban life captures the efect:

> The hundreds of thousands of all classes and ranks … crowd by one another as though they had nothing in common, nothing to do with one another, and their only agreement is the tacit one, that each keep to their own side of the pavement, so as not to delay the opposing streams of the crowd, while it occurs to no man to honour another with so much as a glance. The brutal indifference, the unfeeling isolation of each in his private interest becomes the more repellant and offensive, the more these individuals are crowded together, within a limited space.

> Engels, *The Condition of the Working Class*, pp. 57–8.

13. Mikhail Bakhtin, *Rabelais and His World*, trans. Helene Iswolsky, Bloomington 1984.

14. Ibid., p. 9.

15. Terry Eagleton, 'Wittgenstein's Friends,' *New Left Review*, no. 135, 1982, p. 90.

16. Cheung, *The 16th Hong Kong International Film Festival*, p. 113.

17. Ibid.

18. Sek Kei, 'Hong Kong Cinema from June 4 to 1997,' in Law Kar, ed., *Fifty Years of Electric Shadows*, Hong Kong 1997, p. 124.

19. Ronny Yu explains that Raymond Wong remembered seeing a horror movie called *Midnight Charm* (1937, directed by Ma Shui Wei Pan) as a child, and he proposed a remake of the film. The original was regarded as a masterpiece of suspense. The plot concerns a 1930s' singer with an avant-garde style whose politics offended the local elders. Having fallen in love with a powerful warlord's daughter, as an actor he is looked down upon, having the status lower than a beggar. The warlord burns his theater and the singer's face is disfigured. With the Chinese under Japanese occupation, he dons a mask and becomes a freedom fighter. Yu explains that he wanted to make a story about 'unconditional love,' and that his wife advised him not to do a story with anti-Japanese sentiment. So instead the film draws upon 'class differences and prejudice.' Yu indicates that it took some convincing on Wong's part for him to direct the movie, because 'it's a love story, it's songs, a death sentence. It's very close to 1997. Who has the time and mental state to watch a period romantic movie with songs? … I went in with the writer and changed the story around.' Yu, it seems, lived up to the challenge. The film was number fifteen in terms of gross takings for 1995 in Hong Kong, earning HK$13,288,873 (about US$1.7 million). Hong Kong, Kowloon, and New Territories Motion Picture Association Ltd., *Hong Kong Film 1994–1995*, Hong Kong 1996, p. 170.

20. Arjun Appadurai, 'Disjuncture and Difference in the Global Cultural Economy,' in Patrick Williams and Laura Chrisman, eds, *Colonial Discourse and Postcolonial Theory: A Reader*, New York 1994, p. 327.

21. *Phantom Lover* was shot at the Beijing Film Studio on the Mainland, and Yu says he was

looking for some 'new faces' for the roles of the younger lovers. He found actors Wong Lui and Lau Lam (who plays Landie) at the Beijing Film School. Shot in five weeks, seven days a week, the film cost approximately US$4 million. Synch sound was used and Yu went to Vancouver to incorporate Digital Theatre System sound (DTS), making *Phantom Lover* the first Hong Kong film to use DTS.

22. Marx, 'Economic and Philosophic Manuscripts,' p. 191.

23. Antonio Gramsci, 'Anfisa by Andreyev at the Carignano,' in *Selections from Cultural Writings*, edited by David Forgacs and Geoffrey Nowell Smith, Cambridge 1985, p. 75.

24. Cheung had several hit songs from the movie. He also served as co-executive producer on the film, although, according to Yu, he wanted no credit for the staging of the theater set pieces, for which he was responsible, including the famous Romeo and Juliet balcony scene. Cheung also wrote the songs for the movie, including 'I Lost You in My Lifetime,' 'Tightly Hold Each Other with Love,' and the theme song, which repeats the wistful lines, 'One day will come when our desire is fulfilled and I'll carry you towards eternity.' As Yu relates, 'He [Leslie Cheung] and I see something in the story that's really close to heart … close to him and close to me … So close to home that you want to tell the story.'

25. Hui's statements appeared in the press book for the movie, distributed and supplied by Kino International, and provided to us by Bill Thompson of Columbia University. By 1975, South Vietnam was disintegrating. US military personnel numbered only in the few thousands, United States B-52 bombing missions had abated, and the South Vietnamese military was proving incapable of fighting an effective war on its own. The North Vietnamese began a final offensive in the South in the New Year and by March South Vietnamese troops were pulling back from the countryside in a desperate attempt to protect Saigon and other cities. Hundreds of thousands of civilians in the Central Highlands fled as well, many of them to die in the crossfire. In April, as Saigon fell, television cameras broadcast pictures of South Vietnamese frantically clamoring to get aboard helicopters airlifting people from the roof of the US embassy. More than 70,000 South Vietnamese fled to US naval ships positioned in the South China Sea as columns of North Vietnamese tanks were entering the city.

26. The movie's script is credited to Dai Foo Ho, phonetically similar in meaning to 'Big Spenders' or 'Big Billionaires' and the Chinese name of a huge hostess club called Volvo. Actually, the story was written by a Film Workshop writing team, which included 'Tsui as the brain behind [the] team,' according to Terence Chang.

27. Marx, *Capital* Volume 1, New York 1967, p. 645.

28. Tsui also communicated the horrors of the Vietnam War for its people in this movie in personal terms through the nearly mute character Pat, an orphan separated from his parents in Hue during the New Years' offensive, and taken in by Mun's father. Despite the language barrier, Pat rather than Mun understands how meaningful the twenty-year-old signboard for the uncle's shop is for the old man when he is leaving Vietnam and much of his life behind. And, unlike the Chinese expatriates, Pat, who has become a soldier, chooses to remain in his homeland to search for his family when he has the opportunity to flee with Mun and Mark on one of the last helicopters out of Vietnam.

29. Woo's Tiananmen reference is taken from Berenice Reynaud, 'Woo in Interview,' *Sight and Sound*, May 1993, p. 27. Woo elaborated for us on the autobiographical aspects of the movie:

> Our family was so poor we lived in slums and had to go to the back of restaurants for leftovers to keep from starving. The place I lived had no trees, no blue skies, no sunshine. There were buildings everywhere. It always rained.
>
> Every day when I woke up I saw unfortunate people. I'm not ashamed of being poor, but I hated to see some of the things that went on around me. Slums everywhere. No privacy. People too close together. Hundreds of thousands of families lived together. There was so much noise. When I stepped out the front door into the alley, the junkies would be injecting themselves with heroin. The neighbors would be yelling at them or beating them with mops to try to get rid of them.
>
> When you turned around there would be people gambling. Fighting. Beating each other up for ten cents. The playground was filled with wiseguys chasing each other and cutting each other with butcher's knives. Every time I walked through an alley I assumed I was going to get beaten up. I tried to prepare myself by carrying rocks. Growing up in this environment I saw only a cruel and depressed world.
>
> I was in hell too long. I tried to work out the ugliness of that world in *Bullet*. Why do people hate? How one man can betray another for money? It was a very intense experience, but it was so rewarding to me.

All of the details Woo describes here can be found in the film.

30. Karl Marx, *Towards a Critique of Political Economy*, New York 1970, p. 213.
31. Tony Williams, 'To Live and Die,' *CineACTION*, vol. 36, 1995, p. 51.
32. Woo goes on to describe the reaction to the film, and the personal betrayals that followed:

> The premiere of *Bullet in the Head* was a catastrophe; people were walking in and out. I heard some people saying, 'Why do companies give money for shitty films?' The movie did very badly and all my movie industry friends turned their backs on me.… Only three people stood by me while the film dearest to my heart flopped. My friend and producer Terence Chang said, 'It's a good film.' My boss, one of the studio heads, said, 'We're going to lose money, but it's the best film you've ever made.' And my good friend Chow Yun-fat. Still, I lost many friends after that, which is another reason I left Hong Kong. Now *Bullet* is highly regarded internationally by critics and fans.

33. In 1931 Japanese troops entered Manchuria following the bombing of a Japanese-owned railway train in the territory. Shortly thereafter, in early 1932, riots erupted in Shanghai in protest over Japan's occupation of Manchuria; the city was under siege for more than a month. Full-scale war between the two countries ensued in 1937, and Shanghai fell to the Japanese military. Public services such as gas, electricity, transit, and telephones, all British- or US-owned in Shanghai, were taken under Japanese control. Banking, trading, and industrial production in the city were either taken over by the Japanese or shut down. Japan occupied Shanghai until the end of World War II in 1945. Japan's military occupation of Hong Kong in December 1941 was swift and decisive, as Britain's colonial government was not adequately prepared to defend the territory. Much as would be the case with the Joint Declaration more than forty years later, Hong Kong residents were forced to the sidelines as others decided their fate. In the three-and-a-half years of Japanese control that followed the Christmas Day surrender, more than one million people left the colony, the population falling to less than 600,000.

34. Although *Shanghai Blues* is generally comedic, this beautiful song serves to indicate the spontaneous and direct bittersweet feelings that seep through the movie: 'The evening breeze is carrying your dreams and mine/ Can we borrow some time to hold each other?/ The dream we're holding is like the breeze/ Carrying our tender love./ Is the love in my heart the dream in your heart?/ Could we borrow a bridge to let the two meet?' It is a good example of how Hong Kong filmmakers mix genre elements. Tsui says, 'I think we filmmakers often find ourselves trying to fill up the missing something of the audience's emotions and psychological needs.' Similarly, he told Craig Reid, 'People live in small places within themselves, and they need a place to escape.' See Craig D. Reid, 'Interview with Tsui Hark,' *Film Quarterly* 48, Spring 1995, p. 39.

35. With us, as well as in other interviews, Doyle consistently explained the artistry of the work by comparing his method of working to the intimacy of sex. Speaking of his work with actors, for example, he says: 'It's really about sex, … your sense of sharing.… I sense something for us to share [with the actors] and to share with other people.… [They] have something to give and it comes through.'

36. Edward Gargan, 'Hong Kong's Master of Internal Pyrotechnics,' *New York Times*, 12 October 1997, Section 2, p. 13.

37. See Jean-Paul Sartre, *Being and Nothingness*, trans. Hazel E. Barnes, New York 1956.

38. Tony Rayns, Review of *Days of Being Wild*, *Sight and Sound*, no. 12, 1994, p. 42. Rayns calls Wong Kar-wai a 'poet of time': 'No other director since the (distant) heyday of Alain Resnais has been so attuned to the effects of time on memory, sensation and emotion. Few other directors have ever imbued their movies with such a metaphysical sense of time at work: dilating, stretching, lurching, dragging, speeding by.' See Rayns, 'Poet of Time,' *Sight and Sound*, September 1995, p. 12.

39. Wim Wenders, *Emotion Pictures: Writings on the Cinema*, London 1986, p. viii.

40. According to Christopher Doyle, 'Everyone has one or two things to say in life. You're refining and even learning what you want to say. You're this close and you have to move on to try to say it another way.'

41. Haile Gerima, 'Triangular Cinema, Breaking Toys, and Dinkesh v Lucy,' in Jim Pines and Paul Willemen, eds, *Questions of Third Cinema*, London 1989, p. 78.

42. Juanita Huan Zhou, '*Ashes of Time*: The Tragedy and Salvation of the Chinese Intelligentsia,' *Asian Cinema* 10, Fall 1998, p. 62.

43. See Trinh Minh-ha, 'Outside In Inside Out,' in Pines and Willemen, eds, *Questions of Third Cinema*, p. 144. Wong's blurring of characters and actions illustrates Trinh's point. The blind swordsman's wife loves Huang Yaoshi and waits for him, not her husband; the woman loved by Ouyang Feng and Huang Yaoshi loves and waits for Ouyang Feng, not her husband. The shoeless swordsman's wife waits for him. The egg woman is told, 'Remember, there's always someone waiting for you.' Murong Yin loves Huang Yaoshi and waits for him but sleeps with Ouyang Feng, thinking of Huang Yaoshi; Ouyang Feng sleeps with Murong Yin, thinking of his brother's wife. Murong Yang hires Ouyang Feng's services to kill Huang Yaoshi; Murong Yin hires him to kill Murong Yang.

44. Curtis Tsui, 'Subjective Culture and History: The Ethnographic Cinema of Wong Kar-wai,' *Asian Cinema Studies*, Winter 1995, p. 110.

45. As cinematographer Christopher Doyle relates,

> It's light. Water is a very easy medium to work with as long as you have the right light.... We happened to have seen it and we went with it.... Those kinds of things you could plan, but in the production system of the rest of the world ... it's like *Days of Heaven*.... What happens in our way of working is you see it and you go for it and then you work out where it works later. In the American system you may see that, if you spend enough research and time on location, and you may say, this is the perfect time to shoot such a thing, but then they say where are we going to put the trailers.

46. Curtis Tsui, 'Dissecting the Visual Artistry of Wong Kar-wai Part IV: *Ashes of Time*,' http://www.xs4all. nl/~chinaman/fconnection4.html#begin (6 July 1997).
47. Karl Marx, *The Eighteenth Brumaire of Louis Bonaparte*, New York 1963, p. 15.
48. Marx, 'Economic and Philosophical Manuscripts,' p. 139.
49. Lawrence Van Gelder, 'Pain of an Aging Warrior,' *New York Times*, 17 May 1996, p. C7.
50. Says Doyle, 'Repetition is a theme in life. People get divorced and remarried, you know. It's the same thing.'
51. Rey Chow, 'Souvenir of Love,' *Modern Chinese Literature*, vol. 7, 1993, p. 64.
52. Gayatri Chakravorty Spivak, 'Can the Subaltern Speak?', in Patrick Williams and Laura Chrisman, eds, *Colonial Discourse and Postcolonial Theory: A Reader*, New York 1994, p. 87.
53. Michael Ryan, 'The Politics of Film: Discourse, Psychoanalysis, Ideology,' in Cary Nelson and Lawrence Grossberg, eds, *Marxism and the Interpretation of Culture*, Chicago 1988, p. 478.
54. Michel Ciment, 'A Chat with Wong Kar-wai,' *Positif*, no. 410, April 1995, http://www.xs4all.nl/~chinaman/chat.html#begin (6 July 1997).
55. Various critics and commentators have discussed Wong's influences. See Tony Rayns, Review of *Chungking Express*, *Sight and Sound*, no. 9, 1994, pp. 19–20; J. Hoberman, 'Another New Cult Hero from HK,' *Premiere*, March 1995, pp. 50–51; Chuck Stephens, 'Time Pieces: Wong Kar-wai and the Persistence of Memory,' *Film Comment*, January 1996, pp. 12–18; and Tsui, 'Subjective Culture and History.'
56. Ackbar Abbas, 'The New Hong Kong Cinema and the *Deja Disparu*,' *Discourse*, vol. 16, no. 3, Spring 1994, p. 66.
57. Tony Rayns, 'It's All About Trust,' *Cinema Papers*, August 1996, reprinted in Hong Kong Cinema Database, http://egret0.stanford.edu/hk/articles/doyle.html (1 October 1998). Doyle explained to us the different rhythms of steadicam and hand-held shots:

> All steadicam operators should study *Temptress Moon*.... I don't think you'll see any difference between the two. It's 40 per cent steadicam and 45 per cent hand-held and the rest is bits and pieces. A steadicam is more in the American tradition of 'there shouldn't be any bumps in the road.' The camera should be a fluid, mellifluous, and unobtrusive oberserver or revealer of the content of the film.... Whereas our hand-held camera is much more in the face, much more dynamic, much more reportage, much more about energy and the sweat on people's faces; as steadicam has this fluidity which is sometimes not energizing. For example, a steadicam cannot pan as fast as a crane, or even a tripod, and especially a hand-held camera.... I think hand-held is jazz and steadicam is more four-four time ... it has to go through something to get to the next stage, whereas the hand-held camera can disregard the intermediate steps and go ... much more quickly, with much more drama and much more energy.... You are open and much more responsive to the actors than a steadicam can be.

58. Stuart Cohn, 'Fast Track,' *Los Angeles View*, 1–7 March 1996, p. 15.
59. Henri Lefebvre, *Everyday Life in the Modern World*, New York 1971, pp. 68–109.
60. Marx, 'Economic and Philosophical Manuscripts,' p. 192.
61. Sheila Rowbotham, *Woman's Consciousness, Man's World*, Harmondsworth 1973, p. 109.
62. Not coincidentally Wong has used a handful of Hong Kong pop stars to populate his films. From Andy Lau (*As Tears Go By*, *Days of Being Wild*) to Jacky Cheung and Leslie Cheung (*Days of Being Wild*, *Ashes of Time*), from Karen Mok, Takeshi Kaneshiro and Leon Lai (*Fallen Angels*) to Faye Wong and Takeshi Kaneshiro (*Chungking Express*), the singers/actors fit comfortably into their bodies and use them effectively onstage and onscreen. In *Chungking Express*, Faye Wong's freestyle dancing to 'California Dreamin',' as she juggles condiment containers and lip-synchs to the lyrics expresses a free spirit in tune with the advice of Haruki Murakami's Sheep Man:

    'Dance,' said the Sheep Man. 'Yougottadance. Aslongasthemusicplays. Yougottadance. Don'teventhinkwhy. Starttothink,yourfeetstop. Yourfeetstop,wegetstuck. Wegetstuck, you'restuck. Sodon'tpayanymind,nomatterhowdumb. Yougottakeepthestep. Yougotta limberup. Yougottaloosenwhatyoubolteddown. Yougottauseallyougot. Weknowyou'retired, tiredandscared. Happenstoeveryone,okay? Justdon'tletyourfeetstop…. Dancingiseverything,' continued the Sheep Man. 'Danceintip-topform. Dancesoitallkeepsspinning.'

    Haruki Murakami, *Dance Dance Dance*, New York 1995, p. 86.
63. Rowbotham, *Woman's Consciousness, Man's World*, p. 112.
64. Ciment, 'A Chat with Wong Kar-wai.'
65. Marx explains the mysteriousness 'because the relation of the producers to the sum total of their own labour is presented to them as a social relation, existing not between themselves, but between the products of their labor.' Marx, *Capital* Volume 1, p. 72.
66. Ibid.
67. Marx, *Towards a Critique of Political Economy*, p. 152.
68. Tsui, 'Subjective Culture and History,' p. 119.

CHAPTER NINE

1. Li Cheuk-to, 'Introduction,' in Li Cheuk-to, ed., *The Traditions of Hong Kong Comedy*, Hong Kong, 1985, p. 9.
2. During this period comedies accounted for around 22 of an average 123 films per year, or 17 per cent. Ryan Law, e-mail correspondence, 17 and 25 August 1998.
3. Law Kar, 'A Comparative Analysis of Cantonese and Mandarin Comedies,' in *The Traditions of Hong Kong Comedy*, p. 13.
4. Bey Logan, *Hong Kong Action Cinema*, Woodstock 1995, pp. 142–3.
5. According to Jenny Kwok Wah-lau, 'Hui's classic story is of the everyday person who is caught in the reality of a fast-paced society, moving more and more toward Westernization and metropolitanization. In some films his characters are unaware of the change and hence get caught in impossible situations. In others, they try to fight against the encroaching reality of progress, while others try to compromise without actually grasping what is taking place around them.' 'Besides Fists and Blood: Hong Kong Comedy and Its Master of the

Eighties,' *Cinema Journal*, 37, Winter 1998, p. 26.

6. Logan, *Hong Kong Action Cinema*, pp. 142–3.

7. Stephen Teo, *Hong Kong Cinema: Extra Dimensions*, London 1997, p. 141. Ronny Yu relates Hui's 'Hong Kong Everyman' to the looming shadow of the return. He says that in the colony,

> Everybody is trying to do something, either making money or making a name, before the deadline [1997] comes.... That's why the Hong Kong film pace is so frenetic.... The audience is like that. Their daily life is like that. They communicate like that.... Tell me the bottom line. What do you want from me? ... We want to make money. Fine, that's it ... any artistic value ... no, no. Anything goes.... If you look at Michael Hui's characters, man, they are an exact copy of what Hong Kong people are like. All they see is money. They are mean, they have no cultural sensitivies. Don't tell me to go to the library, don't tell me to go to museums, right? I don't care. But tell me, what's the latest gadget now? Cell phone? Pager? Just purely like going in the fast lane.

8. Li Cheuk-to, 'Tsui Hark and Western Interest in Hong Kong Cinema,' *Cinemaya*, 21, 1993, p. 51.

9. Teo, *Hong Kong Cinema*, p. 120.

10. Henri Lefebvre, 'Toward a Leftist Cultural Politics: Remarks Occasioned by the Centenary of Marx's Death,' in Cary Nelson and Lawrence Grossberg, eds, *Marxism and the Interpretation of Culture*, Chicago 1988, p. 80.

11. Georg Lukács, *Marxism and Human Liberation*, New York 1973, p. 252.

12. Michael Parenti, *Make-Believe Media: The Politics of Entertainment*, New York 1992, pp. 106–7.

13. Director Johnnie To in fact felt constrained by the Lunar New Year format. He says, 'I've changed a lot since I made ... *Eighth Happiness*. This movie was just like talking about an event, like a group of people making a show ... I did not like *Eighth Happiness*.' To, who wanted more drama in his comedies, notes however that 'making movies is teamwork, [they are] not [made] by only one person ... in the 1980s, many people participated and made changes in the film world.'

14. Paul Willemen, 'The Third Cinema Question: Notes and Reflections,' in Jim Pines and Paul Willemen, eds, *Questions of Third Cinema*, London 1989, p. 18.

15. Karl Marx, *Towards a Critique of Political Economy*, New York 1970, p. 211.

16. Norman Denzin, *Images of Postmodern Society: Social Theory and Contemporary Cinema*, London 1991, p. 9.

17. Mark Poster, *The Mode of Information: Poststructuralism and Social Context*, Chicago 1990, p. 59.

18. Karl Marx, *Capital* Volume 1, p. 270.

19. Lukács, *Marxism and Human Liberation*, pp. 252–3.

20. Ibid.

21. Ashish Rajadhyaksh, 'Debating the Third Cinema,' in Pines and Willemen, eds, *Questions of Third Cinema*, p. 173.

22. Betsy Sherman, personal interview with Peter Chan, 22 September 1998.

23. Saski Sassen, *The Global City: New York, London, Tokyo*, Princeton 1991, p. 13.

24. Karl Marx, 'The Holy Family,' in *Selected Writings*, ed. D. McLellan, New York 1997, p. 134.

25. David Harvey, 'The Urban Process Under Capitalism,' *International Journal of Urban and Regional Research* 2, 1978, p. 124.

26. Sei Kei, 'The City and the Village,' in *The Traditions of Hong Kong Comedy*, p. 32.

27. Susan Strange, *Casino Capitalism*, Oxford 1986, p. 1.
28. Trinh Minh-ha, 'Outside In Inside Out,' in Pines and Willemen, eds, *Questions of Third Cinema*, p. 134.
29. As with *Eighth Happiness*, director Johnnie To similarly complained about *The Fun, the Luck and the Tycoon*, 'because it showed during the New Year period … I had to compromise with my boss … I had hoped to put some drama in the comedy … I wanted to produce a film which had some funny scenes in the drama. This movie was trying [for me] because people pretty much appreciated movies like … *Eighth Happiness* at that time.'
30. Cheng Yu, 'Uninvited Guests,' in Li Cheuk-to, ed., *The China Factor in Hong Kong Cinema*, Hong Kong 1990, p. 98.
31. Marx, 'The Holy Family,' p. 141.
32. Sek Kei has written about the city–village trope in earlier comedies. See his 'The City and the Village,' in *The Traditions of Hong Kong Comedy*, pp. 32–5.
33. *Now You See Love, Now You Don't* was Alex Law's first directorial attempt at comedy. The film grossed over HK$36 million (about US$4.6 million), the filmmaker's best box office performer.
34. Alex Law points out that 'Chow Yun-fat, who grew up in a fishing village in the New Territories himself, [is] one of the very few Hong Kong actors who can actually speak native Hong Kongese.'

CHAPTER TEN

1. Gayle Rubin, 'The Traffic in Women: Notes on the Political Economy of Sex,' in Rayna R. Reiter, ed., *Toward an Anthropology of Women*, New York 1975, p. 179.
2. See MPIA (Hong Kong, Kowloon and New Territories Motion Picture Industry Association Limited), *Hong Kong Films 1994–1995*, Hong Kong, 1996, p. 170.
3. Chan elaborates,

   It's a very Asian thing because Asian men and women have less physical differences than Caucasians. We don't have hair on our chests. A lot of us don't even grow beards, we need to shave a little bit, a moustache, there's nothing. We're not really hairy people. Our physical builds, our heights are not that different. Our skin is very soft. A lot of Asian men's skin is as soft as a woman's. It's sometimes very intimidating. For example, I have long hair. People walk behind me, they think I'm a girl … Then, when a bigger man taps you on the shoulder like a buddy, and all of a sudden it's almost like a guy tapping on a woman's shoulder … people think you're something, you're somebody else. Those are the kinds of fears Asian men have and I'm just trying to build it into the scene.… A lot of my friends share those views. We just don't talk about it.

4. Jean Bethke Elshtain, *Public Man Private Woman*, Princeton, 1981.
5. Bertell Ollman, *Alienation: Marx's Conception of Man in Capitalist Society*, Cambridge 1976, p. 135.
6. Misha Skoric, personal assistant to Chow Yun-fat on the Toronto production of *The Corruptor*, offers evidence that Hong Kong film people have brought their fondness for food (and the camaraderie that accompanies it) with them to North America. According to Skoric, Chow was 'known to carry a food tray around serving people [on the set].' In addition, the actor and his wife, Jasmine, 'hosted a dinner for the cast and crew in Toronto and another one for the crew that travelled to New York.' Actor Jon Kit Lee (Jack in *The Corruptor*)

corroborates: 'I treasure every moment I spent with that man [Chow]. The work we did together, meals we had, the chats in between takes, if that sounds a tad sappy, well it is.'

7. Cheung Yew-meng, 'Culture and Lifestyles,' in Nyaw Mee-kau and Li Si-ming, eds, *The Other Hong Kong Report* 1996, Hong Kong 1996, pp. 474–5.

8. Bo relates:

> There are 108 dishes in Qing Han. It's held three whole days, six banquets. Ingredients and cooking methods around the whole of China are adopted. It's the essence of Chinese cookery. When the Manchurians conquered China, Han Chinese could only hold lower-ranking posts. Qing and Han struggled for power. Kangxi Emperor wanted to solve the dispute between Qing and Han, so he held a birthday banquet when he was sixty. Han dishes and Qing dishes were combined. Qing and Han officials attended the banquet together, so it's called 'Qing Han Imperial Feast.' After the Wuchang Uprising, common people learned the royal cuisines. The 'Beijing Imitation Restaurant' was established. But their offspring had an argument. They were divided into Nui Faction and other factions. They had their own way.

9. Lyrics from the song include: 'In our days life isn't really so hard/ You come with me/ I ain't afraid of bad days/ We can drink and watch the moon/ We can't stop the turning of life/ It's still great even if there are ups and downs/ In our days life is hard/ For love/ Nothing to worry/ I'm afraid I'll be lonely/ Chasing after you.'

10. As Engels notes,

> As with clothing, so with food. The workers get what is too bad for the property-holding class. In the great towns … everything may be had of the best, but it costs money.… The habitual food of the individual working-man varies naturally according to his wages. The better paid workers, especially those in whose families every member is able to earn something, have good food as long as this state of things lasts … this presupposes that the workman has work. When he has none, he is wholly at the mercy of accident and eats what is given him, what he can beg or steal … The quantity of the food varies, of course, like its quality, according to the rate of wages.

See F. Engels, *The Condition of the Working Class in England*, Chicago 1984, pp. 100, 105.

11. Karen Mok (Karen Morris) is a Canto-pop star in her own right, but as Sister Turkey, she belts out her anthem, professing her love for the 'God of Cookery' too: 'Righteousness and honesty is valuable/ I dare go to hell to fight/ I'm willing to sacrifice for buddies/ I'm willing to die for girls/ My blood is bleeding for love/ I'm prepared to die/ Who dare challenge me?'

12. Haike Gerima, 'Triangular Cinema,' in Jim Pines and Paul Willemen, eds, *Questions of Third Cinema*, London 1989, p. 81.

13. Sheila Rowbotham, *Woman's Consciousness, Man's World*, Harmondsworth 1973, p. 109.

14. David Harvey, *The Condition of Postmodernity*, Oxford 1989, p. 323.

15. Gerima, 'Triangular Cinema,' p. 78.

16. Mark Poster, *The Mode of Information: Poststructuralism and Social Context*, Chicago 1990, p. 45.

17. We are indebted to the artist Masami Teraoka for his visual inspiration regarding media and society. See his four-panel watercolor *Media Bacchanalia* in James T. Ulak et al., *Paintings By Masami Teraoka*, New York 1996, pp. 104–5.

18. Li Chek-to, 'The Melodrama Strikes Back: Hong Kong Cinema 93–94,' in *The 18th Hong Kong International Film Festival* (catalogue), Hong Kong 1994, p. 99.

19. Hong Kong belonger Jo Jo Ka-yi Wong provided these and other examples for us. In *Forbidden City Cop* (1996), Chiau's Ling Ling Fat gives his wife (Carina Lau) some Chinese perfume, and she notices it is not the scent he had upon him earlier (from another woman). He tells her it is *yeah-hearn*, literally the 'smell of the night.' What he means is it 'stinks.' Gum So (Carmen Lee), the other woman, shows up at his wife's birthday celebration, disrupting the family gathering, in order to buy *chirreta*, which means 'homecoming,' wishing, as she says, for the man she loves to return – she hasn't seen him in days. His wife suggests she buy *tu-wo* instead, which means 'living alone'; when the wife recognizes the woman's scent as the one she smelled on her husband, a fight breaks out between them. The wife is poised to throw a Tang Dynasty ceramic horse at her; Ling Ling Fat orders her to put down the horse, and calls her *gearn*, literally 'ginger,' but he means 'brave'. Actually, he is setting up Gum So and still loves his wife. However, to bait the trap, he leaves with Gum So. Noticing the moon up in the middle of the sky, he tells her that is exactly the time they can 'make love'; he says *gour-yeah*, which literally means to 'do or create something.' When conflicts and problems present themselves, Chiau's characters respond with 'have some tea and eat some dumplings,' and he will pantomine the action of so doing. *Cha* and *bau*, literally 'tea' and 'dumplings,' is slang for 'take it easy, sit and think about it.' Customarily, Hong Kongers enjoy Sunday afternoon tea and dumplings, during which time they talk and discuss ideas.

20. Linda Chiu-han Lai, 'Nostalgia and Nonsense: Two Instances of Commemorative Practices in Hong Kong Cinema in the Early 1990s,' in Law Kar, ed., *Fifty Years of Electric Shadows*, Hong Kong 1997, p. 95.

21. Michael Ryan, 'The Politics of Film: Discourse, Psychoanalysis, Ideology,' in Cary Nelson and Lawrence Grossberg, eds, *Marxism and the Interpretation of Culture*, Chicago 1988, p. 479.

CHAPTER ELEVEN

1. Barbara Scharres, 'The Road to Hard Target,' *American Cinematographer*, September 1993, p. 64.

2. Maureen Sullivan, 'Handcuffs After Handover?', *Variety*, 30 June–13 July 1997, p. 30.

3. Maureen Sullivan, 'Hong Kong Filmmakers Mull a New World Order,' *Variety*, 21–27 April 1997, p. 25.

4. 'Hong Kong's Better Tomorrow,' http://www. channela.com/hk97/style/chow_yun_bt.html (12 July 1997). Now defunct, *Channel A* was a 'virtual community' that attempted to introduce Asian-American commerce and culture to the Internet.

5. Ibid.

6. 'Feature Films Produced in China,' *Variety*, 21–27 August 1995, p. 63.

7. Toh Hai Leong, 'A Swan Song: Decline of the Hongkong Cinema – Before 1997,' *Kinema*, Spring 1997, p. 55.

8. Thea Klapwald, 'Pic Biz Awaits China Syndrome,' *Variety*, 9–15 June 1997, p. 92; Don Groves, 'Mixed Messages Mark CineAsia,' *Variety*, 8–14 December 1997, p. 123.

9. Klapwald, 'Pic Biz Awaits China Syndrome,' p. 92.

10. Tony Rayns, 'The Well Dries Up,' *Index on Censorship*, http://www.oneworld.org/indexoc/

issue197/tonyrayn.html, January 1997 (16 September 1998).

11. Daiwon Hyun, 'Hong Kong Cinema in Korea: Its Prosperity and Decay,' *Asian Cinema*, Spring 1998, pp. 38–45.

12. Fredric Dannen and Barry Long, *Hong Kong Babylon: An Insider's Guide to the Hollywood of the East*, New York 1997, p. 108.

13. In 1928, the Hong Kong censor remarked to the local American General Consul that his responsibility was to sustain British eminence in a 'small settlement of white men on the fringe of a huge empire of Asiatics.' That same year, a United Artists representative in Hong Kong indicated that proscribed topics included 'armed conflict between Chinese and whites,' and depictions of 'white women in indecorous garb or positions or situations which would tend to discredit our womenfolk with the Chinese.' Ella Shohat and Robert Stam, *Unthinking Eurocentrism: Multiculturalism and the Media*, London 1994, p. 112. Forbidden films in the 1970s and 1980s included three from Vietnam, two from China, seven from Taiwan, and Akira Kurosawa's Soviet-produced *Dersu Uzala* (1975), which was considered anti-Chinese. *The Coldest Day in Winter* (1981), a Taiwanese movie critical of the Cultural Revolution, was pulled from the theater one day after its release, ostensibly under pressure from the Xinhua News Agency (the PRC's *de facto* consulate in Hong Kong at the time). Another Taiwanese production, *If I Were Real* (1981), about corruption among Chinese commmunist leaders, eventually had its ban lifted, apparently after the Mainland government's attitude towards the film changed. Li Cheuk-to, 'Political Censorship: The Fatal Blow,' *Cinemaya*, Summer 1989, no. 4, pp. 44–5. Li notes that Hong Kong's official film censorship was introduced in 1953.

14. Michael Parenti, *Inventing Reality: The Politics of the Mass Media*, New York 1986, p. 36; *Make-Believe Media: The Politics of Entertainment*, New York 1992, p. 191.

15. Rayns, 'The Well Dries Up.' An exception to the 'kid gloves' treatment, as the author terms it, is Shu Kei's *Sunless Days* (1990), a post-Tiananmen Square documentary about the filmmaker's, his family's, and his friends' future.

16. Li Cheuk-to, 'The Return of the Father: Hong Kong New Wave and Its Chinese Context in the 1980s,' in Nick Browne et al., eds, *New Chinese Cinemas: Forms, Identities, Politics*, Cambridge 1994, p. 169.

17. Esther Yau, 'Border Crossing: Mainland China's Presence in Hong Kong Cinema,' in Brown et al., eds, *New Chinese Cinemas*, p. 196.

18. Willemen, 'The Third Cinema Question: Notes and Reflections,' in Jim Pines and Paul Willemen, eds, *Questions of Third Cinema*, London 1989, p. 18.

19. Yau, 'Border Crossing,' p. 188.

20. Chandra Talpade Mohanty, 'Under Western Eyes: Feminist Scholarship and Colonial Discourses,' in Patrick Williams and Laura Chrisman, eds, *Colonial Discourse and Post Colonial Theory: A Reader*, New York 1994, p. 196.

21. Walled City was a place where one could purchase illicit drugs and unsanctioned medical procedures; the inhabitants made do with makeshift utilities because electric and water services were unavailable. The area was razed in 1992 and turned into a public park. Yau, 'Border Crossing,' p. 189.

22. Craig D. Reid, 'Bloodthirsty, Shapeshifting Aliens Run Amuck Through the Latest Entry in the Cinematic Asian Invasion,' *Fangoria*, no. 132, May 1994, p. 52.

23. Dannen and Long, *Hong Kong Babylon*, pp. 101–2.
24. See the discussion of this phenomenon in Rey Chow, *Primitive Passions*, New York 1995, pp. 35–43.
25. Trinh Minh-ha, 'Outside In Inside Out,' in Pines and Willemen, eds, *Questions of Third Cinema*, pp. 133–4.
26. Dannen and Long, *Hong Kong Babylon*, p. 162.
27. Roy Holfeinz and Kent E. Calder, *The Eastasia Edge*, New York 1982, p. 102.
28. Karl Marx, *Grundrisse*, New York 1973, p. 646.
29. Sullivan, 'Hong Kong Filmmakers Mull a New World Order,' p. 25.
30. Cheung Yuen-ting also points out that

    > the Chinese censors claimed they could not find the negatives of a scene which was censored from the film. It is the scene of Soong Mei-ling in a conference room in Xian with a group of rebellious generals. The generals had kidnapped her husband and Soong Mei-ling was trying to convince them that releasing Chiang Kai-shek was the only way out for China and for the revolution.

31. Lokman Tsui, 'What's this Wong Kar-Wai,' http://www.xs4all.nl/~chinaman (6 July 1997). With few exceptions, portrayal of gays in Hong Kong cinema has served as comic relief or as a vehicle for 'normalizing' heterosexual identity. Thoughtful exceptions include Wong Yak-sun's *The Twin Bracelets* (1991), a scathing look at the oppression experienced by two women desiring to express their love for one another in a culture of arranged marriages, and Shu Kei's *A Queer Story* (literally *Gay Man at Forty*, 1996), which examines the life of a closeted middle-aged man torn between his boyfriend who loves the night life and his girlfriend who is pressuring him to marry her.
32. Christopher Doyle, 'Don't Try for Me, Argentina,' in *Projections 8: Filmmakers on Filmmaking*, ed. John Boorman and Walter Donohue, Boston 1998, p. 163.
33. Joan Dupont, 'Remaking Hong Kong – In Buenos Aires,' *International Herald Tribune*, 17 May 1997, p. 20.
34. Doyle, 'Don't Try for Me, Argentina,' p. 163.
35. Jason Anderson, 'Beginning of the End,' *Toronto Eye*, 4 December 1997, p. 30.
36. Ibid.
37. Doyle, 'Don't Try for Me, Argentina,' p. 163.
38. Anderson, 'Beginning of the End,' p. 30. Christopher Doyle was enamoured of the line 'Starting over means heading for one more break-up.' See 'Don't Try for Me, Argentina,' p. 181. For both director and cinematographer, starting implies ending.
39. Doyle, 'Don't Try for Me, Argentina,' p. 164.
40. 'Piazzolla.Org The Center for Astor Piazzolla on the Internet,' http//www.piazolla.org/interv/index.html#english (20 October 1998). Wong Kar-wai explains,

    > To me, Frank Zappa [whose music is also used on the soundtrack] and Astor Piazzolla are counterparts in their own cultures: Bad Boys enriching the music with a new sense of life.... I met with the late, great Piazzolla's son, Daniel, to discuss the rights to the music.... 'I believe my work would not be complete without your father's music,' I told him.

    Director's Statement, *Happy Together*, Original Motion Picture Soundtrack, Rock (HK) Records, 1997.

41. Doyle, 'Don't Try for Me, Argentina,' pp. 165–6. Describing the tango, Wong adds,

    > Tango turned out to be a very different thing from what I had imagined. The music, the technique, the atmosphere.... Someone once described tango as 'the vertical expression of a horizontal desire.' During my little affair with tango, I came to see that person knew what she was talking about. (Director's Statement)

42. Doyle, 'Don't Try for Me, Argentina,' p. 182.
43. Anderson, 'Beginning of the End,' p. 30.
44. Dupont, 'Remaking Hong Kong,' p. 20. For a discussion that takes seriously the various criticisms of Wong Kar-wai – that political and social issues are not a priority for him, that he has no sense of obligation to be fair to the gay community of which he is not a part, that his heterosexual male privilege allows him to sidestep issues important to queer Asian communities – while concluding that *Happy Together*'s importance lies in having brought explicitly gay Asian sexuality to the screen, see Denise Tang, 'Popular Dialogues of a "Discreet" Nature,' *Asian Cinema*, vol. 10, no. 1, Fall 1998, pp. 198–207.
45. Ludwig Wittgenstein, 'The Nature of Philosophy,' in Anthony Kenny, ed., *The Wittgenstein Reader*, Oxford 1994, p. 275.
46. Doyle, 'Don't Try for Me, Argentina,' p. 171.
47. Ibid., p. 178.
48. Herbert Marcuse, *Reason and Revolution*, Boston 1960, p. x.
49. Doyle, 'Don't Try for Me, Argentina,' p. 159.
50. Ibid., p. 182.
51. Ibid., p. 181.
52. Michael Ryan, 'The Politics of Film: Discourse, Psychoanalysis, Ideology,' in Cary Nelson and Lawrence Grossberg, eds, *Marxism and the Interpretation of Culture*, Chicago 1988, p. 483.

CHAPTER TWELVE

1. Maynard Parker, 'The City on a Hill,' *Newsweek*, 14 July 1997, p. 46.
2. Blacky Ko, director of *Days of Being Dumb* and an actor in *A Better Tomorrow*, *Young and Dangerous 2* and *3*, and *Mahjongg Dragon*, marked the return by jumping the bridge that connects Hong Kong and the Mainland on a motorcycle.
3. The Adaptation of Laws Bill was a response to controversies surrounding the refusal of China's official new agency, Xinhua News, to release files requested by pro-democracy activist and former legislator Emily Lau and to the refusal of the SAR Secretary of Justice Elise Leung to prosecute *Hong Kong Standard* (an English-language newspaper) owner Sally Aw, a personal friend of Chief Executive Tung, for defrauding advertisers by inflating circulation figures. 'Law Puts Hong Kong Government Above Law,' International Freedom of Expression Exchange Clearing House, 14 April 1998, http://www.democracy.org.hk (1 September 1998).
4. Dave Lindorff, *The Nation*, 7 April 1997, p. 26.
5. Anthony Lee, 'Bird Cage Democracy,' Hong Kong Voice of Democracy, http://www.democracy.org.hk, 29 March 1998 (1 September 1998); Emily Lau, 'Hong Kong to Hold Undemocratic Election,' ibid., 26 April 1998 (1 September 1998). Public opinion took a noticeably negative turn on some, but by no means all, social, political, and economic issues

between the July 1997 handover and the May 1998 legislative elections. The majority expressing satisfaction with Hong Kong life declined from 86 per cent to 71 per cent, while those indicating satisfaction with the general performance of the Hong Kong government fell from 66 per cent to 48 per cent. In addition, disapproval of Chief Executive Tung's performance rose from 29 per cent to 36 per cent. Moreover, those worried about their personal standard of living rose from 16 per cent to 30 per cent, and those worried about Hong Kong's economic prospects increased from 18 per cent to 42 per cent. On the other hand, those who felt concern about corruption and personal freedom in the SAR dropped from 49 per cent to 28 per cent and from 20 per cent to 15 per cent, respectively. There was slightly less worry about political stability (70 per cent to 66 per cent) and only slightly more concern about government efficiency (25 per cent to 29 per cent). Interestingly, the figure for those expressing satisfaction with the PRC in dealing with Hong Kong affairs leaped from 45 per cent to 67 per cent while those indicating satisfaction with the SAR government in dealing with China rose from 44 per cent to 56 per cent. 'Preparing to Go to the Polls for the First SAR Election,' Hong Kong Transition Project, May 1998, http://www.hkbu.edu.hk (5 September 1998).

6. Numerous articles discuss the crisis and explain its causes. Brief primers include Doug Henwood, 'Asia Melts,' *Left Business Observer*, 21 January 1998, pp. 1, 4–5, 7; Chalmers Johnson, 'Cold War Economics Melt Asia,' *The Nation*, 23 February 1998, pp. 16–19; Martin Hart-Landsberg, 'Inside the Asian Crisis,' *Against the Current*, March/April 1998, pp. 26–9; Robert Kuttner, 'What Sank Asia,' *Businessweek*, 27 July 1998, p. 16.

7. Official 1998 data revealed that 700,000 of Hong Kong's three million working people were earning less than half the median income (US$16,152) while another 130,000 were earning between half and two-thirds of that amount. Hardest hit have been women over the age of thirty. Meanwhile, the SAR government budget focuses on the financial and property sectors. The number of Hong Kong billionaires in the *Forbes* magazine list of the world's two hundred wealthiest individuals grew from seven to nine between 1997 and 1998, although the SAR's richest person, Lee Shau-lee, was a 'victim' of the 35 per cent decline in Hong Kong property values associated with the Asian economic crisis. Lee fell from number four overall (US$14.7 thousand million) to number nine (US$12.7 thousand million). The plummeting financial situation also 'hit' real-estate magnates the Kwok (Walter, Thomas, and Raymond) Brothers, who fell from number eight (US$12.3 thousand million) in 1997 to number twenty-five (US$7.4 thousand million) in 1998. Mark Graham, 'Jobs Swept Away as Recession Rips into Hong Kong Economy,' *Sunday Times Internet Edition*, http://www.profound.co.uk (23 August 1998); Mark Landler, 'It's a Dark and Stormy Night… and Here's Hong Kong Trying to Line the Clouds With Silver,' *New York Times*, 29 August 1998, p. D1; 'Trade Unionist Queries Official Unemployment Figures,' Hong Kong Voice of Democracy, 20 October 1998 (30 October 1998); '700,000 HK People Below Poverty Line,' Hong Kong Voice of Democracy, 31 October 1998 (1 November 1998); Katherine Bruce, 'The Billionaires: Asia,' *Forbes*, 6 July 1998, pp. 196–8.

8. '$118B Spent on 33 Blue Chips,' *Hong Kong Standard*, 27 October 1998, http://www.hkstandard.com (2 November 1998). Under a linked exchange system, in place since 1983, the Hong Kong dollar is pegged to the United States dollar at a rate of HK$7.80 to US$1. Contrary to common assumption, Hong Kong does not have a 'currency board' whereby notes are issued either by said board or by a unit of the central bank. In Hong Kong, bank

notes are issued by authorized note-issuing banks (NIBs) outside the government. This indirect note-issuance and withdrawal mechanism (NIWM) differs from a currency board operating under a central bank clearing and reserves system. Tsang Shu-ki, 'A Study of the Linked Exchange Rate System and Policy Options for Hong Kong,' Hong Kong Policy Research Institute, October 1996, http://www.hkpri.org.hk (5 September 1998).

9. 'Hong Kong tops Tokyo as Most Expensive City,' *Orlando Sentinel*, 29 June 1998, p. A6; Yi-zheng Lan, 'An Economic Roundup of Post-Handover Hong Kong,' *Asia Society*, May 1998, http://www.asiasociety.org (5 September 1998).

10. Daniel C. Turack, 'Hong Kong After July 1, 1997: Are Human Rights Preserved?', paper delivered to the sixteenth annual Association of Third World Studies meeting, Durham, North Carolina, 8–10 October 1998. Hong Kong police played Beethoven over public loud-speakers to drown out an opposition event on the evening of the 1997 handover. A number of individuals were convicted of various activities ranging from picketing outside a World Bank Summit and defiling the Chinese national flag to disrupting the provisional legislature and assaulting law-enforcement officers. Demonstrators appeared at the polling station where Chief Executive Tung Chee-hwa voted on the day of the Legco election; 40,000 braved a rainstorm to march and commemorate the Tiananmen Square massacre; and protests accompanied US President Bill Clinton during his 1998 visit to Hong Kong.

11. Yen explains why drama and action are similar:

> Many had asked me how to distinguish shooting action and drama. Well, I don't. Martial art is a form of expression; an expression from the inner self to your hands and legs; we humans can not fly. Like all forms of life in our universe, a gesture, a smile or just walking down the street is an expression. For example, I would not choreograph a person raising a right fist then the left leg in a particular order, it's the rhythm as a whole, from raising an eyebrow to the entire whole movie. For me, shooting, editing, and scoring rely on rhythm. It must be part of you. The essence of art is flow, the flow of images, the flow of music, the flow of communication between an artist and the audience.… Music has a lot to do with my martial arts and filmmaking concept. In fact, I think each film is like a piece of music composition like everything else in life; there is the rhythm; whether making a film or composing music, the goal is to stir the emotion in the heart of the audience.

12. The economic crisis affected the making of the movie. As Yen told interviewer Tom Mes,

> I was very ambitious and very positive and optimistic about how *Ballistic Kiss* could come out. Then problems started to come … because of the whole crisis of the stock market in Asia, all of the cashflow that I relied on stopped coming. So I had a lot of financial problems in the process, many of my crew I had to pay lower fees. I was trying to make a good movie to start off with and in the end it just became trying to finish a movie.… When *Ballistic Kiss* ran into financial problems half-way through I returned the downpayment.

Tom Mes, 'Donnie Yen Rebel Genius,' at http://www.projecta.net/donnie2.html (13 January 1999).

13. Derek Elley, 'Strong Chinese Fest Lineup,' *Variety*, 9–15 February 1998, p. 59. In style-conscious Hong Kong, actor Lau Ching-wan's comment that one consequence of declining

film finances is that '[now] if we want to shoot a scene, we will use a Japanese car instead of a BMW' is not as trivial as it sounds. The statement indicates a dual effect: there has been both a decline in Hong Kong's social and cultural status, and a simultaneous drop in the position of the film industry.

14. Richard James Havis, 'Once Thriving Film Biz Battles the Blues,' *Variety*, 22–28 June 1998, p. 34.

15. 'Pirated Movies are Big Business. But the HK Film Industry is Fighting Back,' *Cable News Network*, 8 September 1997.

16. Neil Strauss, 'Hong Kong Film: Exit the Dragon?', *The New York Times on the Web*, http://www.nytimes.com, 2 August 1998 (2 August 1998).

17. '*The Lost World: Jurassic Park* is the Highest Grossing Film in Hong Kong in 97,' Special Administrative Region (Hong Kong) Film Top 10 Box Office, http://www.geocities.com/Tokyo/Towers/2038, 31 December 1997 (4 November 1998). Steven Spielberg's film earned US$7.5 million to Chan's US$5.8 million in Hong Kong.

18. Included among 1998 top ten imports was Hong Kong-born Wayne Wang's *Chinese Box*, a film that frames the 1997 handover in the context of a terminally ill British journalist (Jeremy Irons), a rehabilitated Mainland call-girl (Gong Li), and a physically scarred Hong Kong street hawker (Maggie Cheung).

19. Laura Mulvey, *Visual and Other Pleasures*, London 1989, p. 22. Arjun Appadurai notes that

> fantasies of gendered violence [that] dominate the B-grade film … both reflect and refine gendered violence at home and in the streets, as young men (in particular) come to be torn between the macho politics of self-assertion in contexts where they are frequently denied real agency, and women are forced to enter the labor force in new ways on the one hand, and continue the maintenance of familial heritage on the other.

Arjun Appaduri, 'Disjuncture and Difference in the Global Cultural Economy,' in Patrick Williams and Laura Chrisman, eds, *Colonial Discourse and Postcolonial Theory: A Reader*, New York 1994, p. 336.

20. Jet Li's US$3.5 million and Michelle Yeoh's US$1 million salaries – unprecedented film incomes for individual Hong Kong performers for their time – were earned for their first Hollywood performances, *Lethal Weapon 4* (1998) and *Tomorrow Never Dies* (1997), respectively. 'Jet Li Tops the Hong Kong Film Star Salary Chart,' Special Administrative Region (Hong Kong) Film Top Ten Box Office Page, 25 February 1998 (11 November 1998); 'Michelle Khan (Yeung Chi King) Becomes the Highest Paid Hong Kong Actress,' Special Administrative Region (Hong Kong) Film Top Ten Box Office Page, 23 July 1997 (30 October 1998). Other top-paid Hong Kong actors include Andy Lau US$1,000,000, Leslie Cheung US$770,000, Tong Leung Chiu-wai US$500,000, Tony Leung Ka-fai US$325,000, Anita Mui US$325,000, and Anita Yuen US$190,000.

21. Kwok Hin-ching, 'Can the HK$100 Million Fund Save Hong Kong Film?', Special Administrative Region (Hong Kong) Film Top Ten Box Office Page, 9 October 1998 (21 October 1998).

22. Mee Kam Ng, Professor of Urban Planning at the University of Hong Kong, relates that a land-lease is a contract between the government and the land-leasee. Standard land-leases are for seventy-five years; while usually renewable, they may be subject to further conditions imposed by the government. Upon expiration of a contract, leasees enter into renewal

negotiations with the government. The incentive for the latter to place property on the auction block is to generate important revenue for Hong Kong's government. Mee Kam Ng, e-mail correspondence, 10 November 1998.

23. Maureen Sullivan, 'Chow Spreads Words of Optimism on Biz,' *Variety*, 29 June–12 July 1998, p. 10.

24. Don Groves, 'Village Reaps Golden Harvest with Accord,' *Variety*, 10–16 August 1998, p. 14.

25. Ibid.

26. Karl Marx, 'Theories of Surplus Value,' *Marx and Engels on Economics, Politics, and Society*, edited by John Elliott, Santa Monica 1981, pp. 245–6.

27. Don Groves, 'Asia's Exhibition Boom,' *Variety*, 29 January–4 February 1996, p. 39.

28. Ella Shohat and Robert Stam, *Unthinking Eurocentrism: Multiculturalism and the Media*, London 1994, p. 185.

29. Maureen Sullivan, 'Temporary Crisis,' *Variety*, 29 June–12 July 1998, p. 10.

30. Ibid.

31. 'Ng Jing and Wong Jing Will Create What Kind of Reaction,' Special Administrative Region (Hong Kong) Film Top Ten Box Office Page, 10 September 1998 (21 October 1998).

32. 'This Year's Unauthorized Film Making Cases,' Special Administrative Region (Hong Kong) Film Top Ten Box Office Page, 8 October 1997 (30 October 1998).

33. Kwok Hin-ching, 'Can the HK$100 Million Fund Save Hong Kong Film?'

34. Hu Ke, 'The Influence of Hong Kong Cinema on Mainland China,' in Law Kar, ed., *Fifty Years of Electric Shadows*, Hong Kong 1997, p. 171.

35. Beth Accomondo, 'Hong Kong Film Industry,' *National Public Radio: Morning Edition*, 24 June 1997.

36. Ibid.

37. Ackbar Abbas, *Hong Kong: Culture and the Politics of Disappearance*, Minneapolis 1997, pp. 5–6.

38. For a discussion of Hong Kong's economic role in China, see Chanqi Wu, 'Hong Kong and Greater China: An Economic Perspective,' in Warren I. Cohen and Li Zhao, eds, *Hong Kong Under Chinese Rule: The Economic and Political Implications of Reversion*, Cambridge 1997, pp. 122-6.

39. For discussions of how Hong Kong has been shaping China's popular culture, see Geremie R. Barme, 'Hong Kong the Floating City,' *Index on Censorship*, January 1997, http://www.oneworld.org (8 November 1998); Tim Brace and Paul Friedlander, 'The New Long March: Popular Music, Cultural Identity, and Political Opposition in the People's Republic of China,' in Reebee Garofolo, ed., *Rocking the Boat: Mass Music and Mass Movements*, Boston 1992, pp. 116–18.

40. Douglas Dowd, *The Waste of Nations*, Boulder 1991, p. 20.

41. Gerald Segal, *The Fate of Hong Kong*, New York 1993, p. 29.

42. Richard Lee, son of Lee Ka-shing (Asia's most prominent tycoon), in joint venture with US-based Intel, plans to construct the world's biggest broadband pipeline across Asia by turning hundreds of millions of televisions into fully functioning network computers. See Douglas C. McGill, 'Empire of the Son,' *Wired*, May 1999, pp. 161–3, 184–8.

43. Hong Kong Trade Development Council, 'Scoreboard for Economic Success of Hong Kong,' http://www.tdc.org.hk (15 July 1997).

44. Hong Kong Trade Development Council, 'Economic and Trade Information on Hong Kong,' http://www.tdc.org.hk (15 July 1997).

45. Rey Chow, 'Things, Common/Places, Passages of the Port City: On Hong Kong and Hong Kong Author Leung Ping-kwan,' *Differences: A Journal of Feminist Cultural Studies*, vol. 5, no. 3, 1993, p. 196.

46. Karl Marx and Frederick Engels, *The Communist Manifesto*, Harmondsworth 1967, p. 83.

47. Richard Barnet and John Cavanagh, *Global Dreams: Imperial Corporations and the New World Order*, New York 1994, p. 297. The career of actor/pop star Leslie Cheung parallels the contemporary ebb and flow of capital in a global marketplace. Successful as a pop icon and popular primarily with adolescent female fans, Cheung retired from singing in 1990, moved to Vancouver, and became a Canadian citizen. After the failure of the bank which housed the bulk of his assets, he came out of retirement and began making recordings and touring once again. Cheung achieved film success as well, turning in a fine performance in Mainland director Chen Kaige's *Farewell My Concubine* (1993), as well as in numerous Hong Kong pictures (including *The Phantom Lover* and *He's a Woman, She's a Man*). The performer completed a 1997 world concert tour, and was invited to sing in Beijing to commemorate the handover. Although the tour was judged a triumph, the film *Temptress Moon* (1996), which found Cheung working a second time with director Chen Kaige, was neither a commercial nor a critical success. In the meantime he has invested heavily in Hong Kong real estate and a themed coffee shop. John Woo says that he would like to bring Cheung, among other Hong Kong actors, to Hollywood; however, as Cheung explains, 'I'm quite important in the Asian market.… Why bother doing something in Hollywood unless it's a very nice script?', Betsy Sherman, 'Hong Kong Star Cultivates US Audience,' *Boston Globe*, 18 June 1997, p. B1.

48. 'Space, Place, and Spectacle: The Crisis Cinema of John Woo,' *Cinema Journal* 36, Winter 1997, p. 71. For other discussions of the concept of crisis cinema, see Michael Ryan and Douglas Kellner, *Camera Politica: The Politics and Ideology of Contemporary Hollywood Film*, Bloomington 1988; and the collection of essays in Christopher Sharrett, ed., *Crisis Cinema: The Apocalyptic Idea in Postmodern Narrative Film*, Washington DC, 1993.

49. Williams, 'Space, Place, and Spectacle,' p. 73.

50. Guillermo Gómez-Peña, *The New World Border: Prophecies, Poems & Loqueras for the End of the Century*, San Francisco 1996, p. 7.

51. Barnet and Cavanagh, *Global Dreams*, pp. 142, 193–4; Stephen Rosskamm Shalom, *Imperial Alibis: Rationalizing U.S. Intervention after the Cold War*, Boston 1993, p. 169.

52. Mark Landler, 'In Hong Kong, McDonald's Is in the Doghouse,' Special Administrative Region (Hong Kong) Film Top Ten Box Office Page, 7 October 1998 (12 November 1998).

53. We have adopted Miron Mushkat's term for use in this context. See his 'Environment Turbulence and the Prospects of Hong Kong: A Need for Caution,' *East Asia: International Review of Economic, Political, and Social Development*, 1989, p. 161.

54. Rey Chow, 'Between Colonizers: Hong Kong's Postcolonial Self-Writing in the 1990s,' *Diaspora*, vol. 2, no. 2, 1992, p. 57.

55. A collection of essays that use class analysis in film studies is David E. James and Rick Berg, eds, *The Hidden Foundation: Cinema and the Question of Class*, Minneapolis 1996. The collection takes its title from Marx, quoted in its frontispiece: 'It is always the direct relationship of the owners of the conditions of production to the direct producers … which reveals the innermost secret, the hidden basis of the entire social structure.' *Capital* Volume 3, New York 1967, p. 791.

INDEX

Page numbers in bold type refer to illustrations.